This Is Our
CHURCH

This Is Our
CHURCH

A HISTORY OF CATHOLICISM

MICHAEL PENNOCK

Ave Maria Press AVE Notre Dame, Indiana

The Subcommittee on the Catechism, United States Conference of Catholic Bishops, has found that this catechetical high school text, copyright 2013, is in conformity with the *Catechism of the Catholic Church* and that is fulfills the requirements of Elective Course B of the *Doctrinal Elements of a Curriculum Framework for the Development of Catechetical Materials for Young People of High School Age*.

The Ad Hoc Committee to Oversee the Use of the Catechism, United States Conference of Catholic Bishops, has found this catechetical text, copyright 2007, to be in conformity with the *Catechism of the Catholic Church*.

Nihil Obstat: The Reverend Michael Heintz
               Censor Librorum

Imprimatur: The Most Reverend John M. D'Arcy
               Bishop of the Diocese of Fort Wayne-South Bend

Given at Fort Wayne, IN on 20 June 2007.

Founded in 1865, Ave Maria Press is a ministry of the United States Province of Holy Cross.

www.avemariapress.com

Trade edition: ISBN-10 1-59471-075-9   ISBN-13 978-1-59471-075-9

High school edition: ISBN-10 1-59471-169-0   ISBN-13 978-1-59471-169-5

Cover and text design by Andy Wagoner.

Printed and bound in the United States of America.

Dedication

To a new generation of God's People exemplified in the lives of five special persons, my grandchildren:

Natalie Louise Anhold

Nathan Thomas Pannell

Lily Morgan Pennock

Allison Marie Anhold

Noah Michael Pannell

Engaging Minds, Hearts, and Hands for Faith

An education that is complete is the one in which the hands and heart are engaged as much as the mind. We want to let our students try their learning in the world and so make prayers of their education.

Fr. Basile Moreau,
Founder of the Congregation of the Holy Cross

This text encourages you to study the history of the Church in a holistic manner, that is, incorporating the dimensions of mind, heart, and hands. This task is encouraged through

- discerning truth through thorough questioning, further research, and in-depth study. Many names and events will be introduced. When your interest is piqued, use the inspiration to investigate more about the topic or person of interest.

- prayerfully recognizing the divine element of the Church. Though the Church is in historical time, it also transcends history. Only in faith can we see the Church as the bearer of divine life with its place in history.

- actively participating in the mission of the Church to love as Jesus did, especially in love and in service of the poor and those with special needs.

Table of CONTENTS

Acknowledgments

I wish to thank my son, Christopher Joseph Pennock, M.A. in Classical Languages, for the expert care he gave reading this manuscript and making many helpful suggestions. His scholarly pursuit of learning is a source of great pride to me.

Thanks, too, to my editor, Mike Amodei, of Ave Maria Press. His support and encouragement over the years have helped me incalculably. He is a Christian gentleman par excellence.

Fr. Ted Ross, S.J., a leading Church historian and incomparable teacher, gave me a love of history when I had the good fortune of having him in high school. Another Jesuit and long-time colleague, Fr. Larry Ober, S.J., a history instructor at St. Ignatius High School, Cleveland, Ohio, exemplifies for me the very meaning of teacher. I will always cherish the friendship and example of these two outstanding men.

Finally, I would also like to acknowledge Dr. Walter Gray, emeritus professor in the department of history at Loyola University of Chicago, who taught and advised me as an undergraduate. He is an outstanding and brilliant scholar who makes history come alive.

All of these superb men deserve my admiration and gratitude.

1

The Mystery of the Church
IN SALVATION HISTORY

But you are "a chosen race, a royal priesthood, a holy nation, a people of his own, so that you may announce the praises" of him who called you out of darkness into his wonderful light. Once you were "no people" but now you are God's people; you "had not received mercy" but now you have received mercy.
—1 PETER 2:9–10

Firm FOUNDATION

Alegend about the bloodthirsty Roman emperor Julian tells us that after Constantine had legalized Christianity throughout the Empire, Julian tried to set back the clock. He systematically began to hunt down and kill Christians and re-establish the old pagan religions and gods. In June of 363, in a battle against the Persians, Julian was wounded in the side with an arrow, perhaps inflicted by one of his own disgruntled soldiers. The wound proved mortal. The story that comes down to us reports that as Julian lay dying that night, he took some of his own blood into his hands and flung it at the sun (which he worshiped as a god), crying out to Jesus: "Galilean, you won!"

Historically, there have been many attempts before and in the years since Julian to stamp out belief in Jesus and the Church herself. But Christianity has endured the assaults of the centuries that have tried to prohibit its membership and practice. Witness the attempts of the Communist regime in the Soviet Union in the twentieth century and its continued aftereffects in places like Cuba and China. In point of fact, the Catholic Church has survived and is the oldest institution in Western civilization.

Today, Christianity is the world's largest religion with more than two billion people (about a third of the world's population). Catholics are the largest group of Christians, numbering more than one billion, around 17 percent of the world's population, about 53 percent of the Christian population. Catholics outnumber Jews, Hindus, and Buddhists. Only Muslims have more members than Catholics, though there are many more Christians overall than Muslims.

The word *catholic* means "universal." Today, the Catholic Church can be found throughout the world, appealing to all people in all places at all times. Catholics, along with other Christians, believe that God became man in the person of Jesus Christ and that Christ was raised from the dead. Also, because Jesus himself established the Catholic Church that possesses the fullness of truth and all the means necessary for salvation, this means that Catholics:

- believe in the "one, holy, catholic, and apostolic Church" and all that she teaches through the Pope and bishops who are the successors to Peter and the Apostles;

- accept all Seven Sacraments of the Catholic Church;

- submit to the teaching authority of the Magisterium (the Pope and bishops who are in union with him) in matters of faith and morals.

✸ RECENT CHURCH NUMBERS

- There are nearly 1.12 billion Catholics worldwide, 17 percent of the world's population.

- About half (49.8 percent) of the world's Catholics live in the Americas.

- Worldwide, there are approximately 400,000 priests.

- Catholics make up about 23 percent of the population of the United States (around 69 million people).

- The Catholic Church runs the largest network of private schools in the United States. More than 2.35 million students are enrolled in 6,386 elementary schools and 1,203 high schools.

- Approximately 763,000 students attend 231 Catholic colleges and universities in the United States.[1]

MAJOR WORLD RELIGIONS

Christian	**2,133,806,000**
Roman Catholics	1,118,991,000
Independents	425,170,000
Protestants	375,815,000
Orthodox	219,501,000
Anglicans	79,718,000
Muslims	**1,308,941,000**
Hindus	**860,133,000**
Chinese Universists	**404,921,000**
Buddhists	**378,808,000**
Sikhs	**25,377,000**
Jews	**15,073,000**[2]

Why have the Church and Christianity endured? A sociologist might respond that the Church has lasted because it is a well-organized institution with clear lines of authority. The truth is that the Church persists because Jesus Christ established and sustains her. Christ established the Church and promised to be with her until the end of time. After Peter confessed Jesus to be the Messiah and the Son of God, Jesus said to him: "You are Peter, and upon this rock I will build my church, and the gates of the netherworld shall not prevail against it" (Mt 16:18). Despite the many persecutions of Christians, the Church is enduring and permanent. The Lord revealed why when he commissioned his Apostles before his Ascension into Heaven:

> Go, therefore, and make disciples of all nations, baptizing them in the name of the Father, and of the Son, and of the Holy Spirit, teaching them to observe all that I have commanded you. And behold, I am with you always, until the end of the age. (Mt 28:19–20)

This farewell address of the Risen Lord outlined the mission of the Church: to preach the Gospel, to baptize in the name of the Blessed Trinity, and to lead others to obey the commands of the Lord that bring eternal life. Note also that Jesus promised to be with the Church to the end of time. Christ's ongoing presence is the reason why Julian the Apostate, and every other worldly power, cannot prevail against the Church.

Why Study Church History?

This book traces the history of the Catholic Church, and in doing so helps to define her meaning. It begins with the premise of these previous paragraphs, namely that the story of the Church is the story of how God continues his work of salvation through her members, both individually and collectively, over two millenniums.

In the wake of several publicized scandals in recent years, some people today, influenced by hostile media frenzy, have judged that the Church is a dying institution, an abomination whose day has passed. Perhaps for some it is because they have imaged the Church as an art gallery meant only for perfect saints. But what a study of Church history reveals is that past ages have experienced their own crises, some much worse than today's. Rather than imagining the Church as some perfect group, we might better picture the Church as a hospital that ministers to sick sinners. And the truth is, all humans are sinners, even those who speak for Christ and try to put his teachings into practice.

Faithful Catholics can view the Church as a family with both human faults and shortcomings. Despite the imperfection we find in our families, it is in our families that we experience love and acceptance, even with our own personal foibles and sins. Our imperfect families remain a source of pride for us. Most of us do want to know the story of our people—the eccentric aunts, the brilliant grandparent, the brave immigrant ancestors, the crazy great uncle. Not to know our family story is to go through life ignorant of our heritage, and this is a real loss.

In a similar way, the study of the Church can result in a greater appreciation, love, and understanding of this Church that Jesus himself founded. The Church story is *our* story, too. Like our own family, the Catholic Church—in whom Jesus can be found—loves, accepts, nurtures, and sustains us through life's journey. We are the children of a vast family of believers who weathered the storms of the ages to bring Christ to us in this family of faith. It is worth our while to learn from our ancestors in the faith because, as the great Catholic apologist G. K. Chesterton once wrote, "The most dangerous people are those who have been cut off from their cultural roots."[3]

To know our roots is to appreciate where we have been so that we can continue to take Christ and his message to the people of the twenty-first century who are so desperately eager to hear his voice amidst the din of the age. And, once again, what strengthens the hope in the future for the Church is the promise of Jesus Christ himself that he will remain with us "until the end of the age."

Beginning in Chapter 2, this book is organized around a chronological retelling of the history of the Catholic Church. This chapter introduces a study of the meaning of Church—ecclesiology—considering the following topics and more:

- the meaning of the word *Church*
- the Church as *Mystery*
- some predominant images of the Church
- the traditional four marks or signs of the Church.

As the story of the Catholic Church proceeds, these and other meanings of Church will be re-examined as they apply to various historical periods.

The Meaning OF CHURCH
(*CCC*, 751–757; 777–778)

The word *church* brings to mind many mental images. One person may imagine the magnificent St. Peter's in Rome or their local parish *building*; others may think of nuns, priests, bishops, and the Holy Father all wearing traditional religious garb. Some may be reminded of their local parish as it worships at Sunday Eucharist or participates in other functions like parish missions, festivals, and food and clothing collection drives for the needy. Contemporary Church doctrines dealing with controversial topics like abortion, stem cell research, or capital punishment may be called to the forefront for others. Those who have studied theology in some depth may associate traditional and scriptural images like "Body of Christ" or

> *St. Peter's Basilica in Rome, Italy*

"God's People" for Church. All of these, and many more, are related to what the Church is.

Etymologically, the English word *church* (related to the German word, *Kirche*) is derived from the Greek *kyriake*, which means "belonging to the Lord (*Kyrios*)." In the Romance languages, church translates the Greek *ekklesia* or the Hebrew word *q_h_l*, both of which mean "those called out," a convocation, or assembly. In the Old Testament, *q_h_l* described the Chosen People. Yahweh assembled them on Mount Sinai to give them the Law and to form them as his holy people. The early Christians adopted this term to refer to themselves as God's new Chosen People, called out to preach that Jesus Christ is the Lord. The word also aptly described them as an assembly of believers whom Christ calls together to live a sacramental life and to live a life of fellowship and service for the sake of God's kingdom.

Today, Church refers especially to three rich and meaningful realities: (1) Catholics who come together at the liturgy; (2) the local parish community, a fellowship of believers in Christ; and (3) the universal community of believers throughout the world. According to the *Catechism of the Catholic Church*:

> "The Church" is the People that God gathers in the whole world. She exists in local communities and is made real as a liturgical, above all a Eucharistic, assembly. She draws her life from the word and the Body of Christ and so herself becomes Christ's Body. (*CCC*, 752)

Theological and biblical images further describe the Church, including some highlighted at the most recent **ecumenical** or worldwide council, the Second Vatican Council (1962–1965), mystery, Sacrament of Jesus Christ, People of God, Body of Christ, and Temple of the Holy Spirit. In addition, the New Testament mentions many vivid images of the Church that help us understand her mission and nature. These include:

- Our Mother or Holy Mother Church
- pilgrim
- the Bride of Christ
- Christ's flock
- cultivated field
- building of God
- Christ's vineyard.

Each of these images sheds light on Christ's love for his Church and his intimate union with her. For example, the Bride of Christ image underscores Jesus' profound love for his Church and his willingness to give up his life for each of her members. The flock image evokes the image of the self-sacrificing Good Shepherd whose voice we must listen to and follow to avoid getting lost or even destroyed on our journey.

Church as Mystery
(CCC, 767–768; 770–776; 779–780; 849–854)

In a famous speech to the bishops assembled at the opening of the second session of the Second Vatican Council, Pope Paul VI said of the Church: "The Church is a mystery. It is a reality imbued with the hidden presence of God."

The term *mystery* has rich biblical roots. For example, to describe God's hidden plan for human beings, the Bible speaks of the "mystery of Christ" or the "mystery of the Kingdom of God." Scripture is the record of salvation history. It recounts how our almighty God, who is beyond human comprehension, revealed his loving nature to us by communicating in word and in deed the eternal destiny he has in store for humanity. The climax of this history is Jesus Christ, God-made-flesh, who is the mystery of God's hidden plan made visible. St. Augustine, one of the Church's greatest theologians, added to the definition of mystery, naming it as "a visible sign of invisible grace."

To refer then to the Church as a mystery is to highlight the continuing work of Jesus Christ in human history. In the Church, the invisible, almighty God continues to work through the Catholic Church, which is a visible institution established by Christ to continue his saving work. In and through the Church, Christ fulfills and reveals his own mission "to unite all things in him" (Eph 1:10). The Church is intimately united to God's mystery of salvation through Jesus Christ. In writing to the Ephesians, St. Paul explains how the mystery of God's hidden plan is now being unfolded in the Church.

So then you are no longer strangers and sojourners, but you are fellow citizens with the holy ones and members of the household of God, built upon the foundation of the Apostles and prophets, with Christ Jesus himself as the capstone. Through him the whole structure is held together and grows into a temple sacred in the Lord; in him you also are being built together into a dwelling place of God in the Spirit. (Eph 2:19–22)

In the Church, the human and divine come together. The Church is a "communion of saints" that refers to the unity among three groups of people:

- the *pilgrim Church* (those who are living on earth today; also known as the "Church militant");
- the *Church suffering* (those undergoing purification in purgatory); and
- the *Church triumphant* (the blessed in heaven).

The Church is structured in a hierarchical way, yet she is Christ's Mystical Body; she is a visible society, yet a spiritual community; she is an earthly Church, but possesses the riches of Heaven.

Church as Sacrament

The Latin translation for the Greek word *mysterion* (*mystery*) is related to the term *sacramentum*, translated further as "sacrament." This term has rich meaning, including the concept of the outward or visible sign of the hidden reality of salvation. In brief, a sacrament is a special kind of sign or symbol. To symbolize the abstract, ordinary signs and symbols use concrete realities like shape and color to convey particular meaning. For example, a wedding ring symbolizes eternal love. A stop sign conveys the idea of needing to brake one's car at an intersection. Signs or symbols point to a reality; however, they do not cause it. Just because a person wears a wedding ring does not mean he or she will be faithful to his or her marriage vows. And the posting of a stop sign does not automatically mean a driver will use the vehicle's brakes.

A sacrament, on the other hand, is a special kind of symbol, an *efficacious* (effective) sign of grace instituted by Christ and entrusted to the Church. This means that Christ himself works through the sacraments. Their power comes from God in the Holy Spirit. A sacrament is a concrete, outward, visible sign that is, at the same time, what it represents. This is why it is right to call Jesus himself the mystery or Sacrament of Salvation. His saving work is the Sacrament of Salvation. He is the Sacrament of God's love for us. He not only points to God; he is God. He not only symbolizes God's love; he is God's love. He is what he represents—the mystery of God's love and salvation for humanity.

Jesus is known as the Prime Sacrament. As Jesus declares in John's Gospel, "Whoever has seen me has seen the Father" (Jn 14:9).

The Church, too, united to Christ can be called a Sacrament. The Second Vatican Council teaches:

> By her intimate relationship with Christ, the Church is a kind of Sacrament or sign of intimate union with God, and of the unity of all mankind. She is also the instrument of such unity. (*Lumen Gentium*, 1)

This means that the Church is a concrete, visible sign of Christ's presence to everyone. By embracing all people, and by welcoming them into the family of faith, the Church is the sign or Sacrament of the inner unity of all humans with God and a true sign or Sacrament of the unity of the human race.

Because the Church is united to him, Christ uses the Church as an instrument, a "universal Sacrament of salvation." One of the things this means is that "all salvation comes from Christ the Head through the Church which is his Body" (see *CCC*, 846). As an instrument in the Lord's hand, the Church reaches out in love to all people to unite them as one People of God, to form one Body of Christ, and to build up one Temple of the Holy Spirit. As an active instrument

➤ *Jesus Christ*

doing Christ's work, the Church must fulfill her *mission* as one who is sent. The Church continues the mission of the Son and the Holy Spirit who invites and enables us to share in the divine life. By power of the Holy Spirit, the Lord commissions his Church to share his love so each human can be saved and come to know the truth. This mission involves a fourfold task:

- *Share the Message.* Jesus commissioned his followers to preach the Gospel: "As the Father has sent me, so I send you" (Jn 20:21). The heart of the message is found in the *kerygma* ("proclamation"), the core preaching about Jesus as Savior. People of all ages need to know that Jesus is the Lord, the way, the truth, and the life. They must be invited to repent of their sins, accept Jesus Christ in faith, and be baptized with water in the Holy Spirit. The Church preaches this timeless message of good news in every age to help lead people to the Lord Jesus.

- *Live in Community.* There is an old saying that no one gives what he or she does not have. The Church must proclaim *and* live the Gospel it proclaims. Jesus said, "This is how all will know that you are my disciples, if you have love for one another" (Jn 13:35). To be a visible sign of love, and credible to nonbelievers, Christians must build up *koinonia*, that is, fellowship. Christ attracted people to him because of his love. Christians must be light to others by demonstrating through their faith, hope, and love that Christ is active in their midst.

- *Serve Others.* Christ came to serve, not to be served. At the Last Supper, the King of Kings washed the feet of his disciples to demonstrate that greatness in his Father's kingdom requires serving others. *Diakonia,* or service, is an essential task for the Church. Christ commissioned his Church to translate words of love into concrete acts of service for all people, especially the poor, the lonely, the imprisoned, the sick and suffering. The message of God's love for people must be made real through concrete acts of service. This means that the Church must imitate the Lord by following the path of poverty, obedience, sacrificial love, and service.

- *Worship the Lord.* The Church must be a worshiping community that acknowledges God as the source of life and all good gifts and is thus worthy of adoration, praise, and thanksgiving. The Church does so through *leitourgia,* that is, the liturgy (originally, "work of the public"). The liturgy is the work of the Blessed Trinity: the Father is the source of liturgy, Christ pours out the blessings of the Redemption he won for us on the cross through the sacraments, and the Holy Spirit enlightens our faith and encourages our response. The Church provides the rhythms of regular prayer and invites the faithful to participate in experiences like morning and evening prayers, grace before and after meals, the Liturgy of the Hours, and the Eucharist on Sundays and liturgical feasts throughout the years. Essential to the worship of the Church are the Seven Sacraments, life-giving signs of Christ's love that help Christians grow in holiness. Through the liturgy, and especially the Eucharist, which celebrates and creates Christian unity, the work of salvation is exercised. The **Paschal Mystery**—Christ's work of Redemption accomplished by his Passion, Death, Resurrection and Ascension—is celebrated and made present in the liturgy of the Church, especially the Eucharist. By uniting believers in love to the Lord and each other, the liturgy helps transform Christians into other Christs, visible signs of God's presence to others.

❂ *LUMEN GENTIUM* ON THE CHURCH

The Second Vatican Council issued sixteen documents, including a most important one on the nature of the Church, *Lumen Gentium.* This document is noted for its rich biblical, historical, and dynamic treatment of the Church. Here are some important passages from the document:

Founder of the Church

The Lord Jesus inaugurated her [the Church] by preaching the good news, that is, the coming of God's Kingdom. . . . In Christ's word, in His works, and in His presence this kingdom reveals itself to men (5).

Church as the "Mystical Body of Christ"

In the human nature which He united to Himself, the Son of God redeemed man and transformed him into a new creation (cf. Gal 6:15; 2 Cor 5:17) by overcoming death through his own death and resurrection. By communicating His Spirit to his brothers, called together from all peoples, Christ made them mystically into His own body.

In that body, the life of Christ is poured into the believers who, through the sacraments, are united in a hidden and real way to Christ who suffered and was glorified (7).

The Church and Christ

Just as the assumed nature inseparably united to the divine Word serves Him as a living instrument of salvation, so, in a similar way, does the communal structure of the Church serve Christ's Spirit, who vivifies it by way of building up the body (cf. Eph 4:16).

Christ was sent by the Father "to bring good news to the poor, to heal the contrite of heart" (Lk 4:18), "to seek and save what was lost" (Lk 19:10). Similarly, the Church encompasses with love all those who are afflicted with human weakness. Indeed, she recognizes in the poor and suffering the likeness of her poor and suffering Founder. She does all she can to relieve their need and in them she strives to serve Christ (8).

Scripture in the Church's long historical Tradition is filled with many images that speak to the "inexhaustible mystery of the Church" (*CCC*, 753). In the Old Testament the images are from the theme of the People of God. The New Testament builds on these images with Christ being at the center of his people.

People of God

(*CCC*, 781–786; 804)

The image of the Church as People of God has its roots in the pre-Christian era of God's covenant with Israel. The Old Testament period of salvation history not only prepared for the coming of the Messiah but also for the Church. From the beginning, we see how God intended to form a people. The book of Genesis tells how God created everything out of nothing, including human beings in God's own image. Humans were meant to be in a loving union with

God, but Adam and Eve sinned and evil and death entered human history. But God did not abandon Adam and Eve nor their descendants. In a covenant with Noah, God promised to never again destroy the world.

Approximately 2000 BC, God formed a special people through Abraham. When Yahweh asked the patriarch to leave his country and travel to a land we now know as Israel, God made a covenant, a binding contract, with Abraham. God promised Abraham that if he believed in, obeyed, and worshiped the one true God, he would be blessed with a land and many descendants. Abraham became the father in faith of a great nation when he trusted God's word, even though Sarah, his wife, was beyond childbearing age. And when she did give birth to Isaac, Abraham was willing to obey God's further tests, even the request to sacrifice his son. This action was never carried out, and because of his faith, Abraham was blessed with many descendants—the Israelites—who took their name from his grandson, Israel. The Israelites were later called Hebrews or Jews.

The Old Testament reveals how God was faithful to the Chosen People throughout their history, even when they were disobedient to God. A most notable demonstration of God's compassion (called *hesed* in Hebrew) was his deliverance of the Hebrews from slavery in Egypt (the Exodus) and his renewal of the covenant with Moses on Mount Sinai (ca. 1300 BC). There, God gave the Ten Commandments to Israel and promised them a land. He also revealed his sacred name as *Yahweh*, meaning "I Am Who Am." In return for God's blessings, the Chosen People were to obey the Law as a demonstration of their love and gratitude for God's care, protection, and the gift of a land.

By means of his covenant with an entire people, God showed that he wished to sanctify and save not only individuals, but this chosen nation. However, the remaining books of the Old Testament report the stormy relations between God and the Israelites, who time and again fell into sin and refused to observe the covenant. Despite their many lapses, God did not abandon them. He sent military leaders called judges and later prophets to remind them of their covenant promises. Yahweh allowed the Israelites to establish a monarchy. Israel's greatest king, David, prefigured Jesus, God's Chosen One who would establish God's kingdom and set up his Church to continue his work until the end of time.

Prior to Jesus, many of David's successors turned to idolatry and failed to worship Yahweh or act justly toward the poor. The kingdom was divided into north and south. Great prophets like Jeremiah were sent to

➤ *King David*

call people back to true worship and obedience to God, but their warnings often went unheeded. As would be expected, the northern kingdom of Israel fell to the Assyrians (722 BC) and subsequently the southern kingdom of Judah fell to the Babylonians (587 BC). Many Israelites were taken to captivity. But even at their lowest point, Yahweh did not abandon his people. Through prophets like the author of Second Isaiah, he promised that they would return to the Holy Land. Isaiah 53 reveals how Yahweh would send a Messiah to save the people.

When Persia captured Babylon, the Jews in exile were allowed to return to Israel where they once again worshiped Yahweh in Jerusalem's Temple. Prophets Ezra and Nehemiah led a reorganized Jewish religion and continually reminded the people of God's original covenant. These reminders were needed because foreign powers like the Persians, Greeks, Seleucids, and finally the Romans continued to dominate them. However, in God's good time, he sent his only Son, Jesus Christ, to fulfill the divine promises and to establish a new law of love, a covenant that extends not only to the Chosen People but to all people.

A message of the Old Testament is that God taught, preserved, and cherished his people. Christians share their ancestry and many things in common with the Jews: worship of the same God; the Ten Commandments; a rich tradition of prayer; shared beliefs about creation, human destiny, and so forth. From the Jewish people, a Messiah was born and a new covenant established in the blood Christ that makes it possible for anyone—no matter their race—to become members of God's family through faith in Christ and Baptism. Membership in the Church bestows on her members incalculable dignity as God's sons and daughters and enables the Holy Spirit to dwell in their hearts. This Spirit of love empowers the baptized to live Christ's law of love and to share in his priestly, prophetic, and royal ministries; to be salt of the earth and light of the world; and to become a sign of unity, hope, and salvation for the whole human race.

Church as Body of Christ
(CCC, 787–796; 805–808)

Closely related to the People of God image is the Church as the Body of Christ. The origins of this image are rooted in Jesus himself who taught that what we do to others we do to him (Mt 25:40) and that he is in union with his followers the way a vine is to its branches (Jn 15:5).

St. Paul highlighted the body imagery when he wrote, "Now you are Christ's body, and individually parts of it" (1 Cor 12:27). Christ is the head of this body. Each Christian is a member incorporated into Christ's body and united into one body by the Holy Spirit. The Holy Spirit overcomes all natural divisions of race, color, nationality, and sex and unifies the Risen Lord with his disciples. Additionally, the reception of the Holy Eucharist mystically enables Christ to live in them and the disciples to live in him.

> *"This is My Body."*

Being a member of Christ's body gives each person great dignity, as well as responsibility to play a specific role to build up the Church. The Risen Lord Jesus uses members of his body to reach out to others in love, compassion, and service by using their unique talents to continue his own work of salvation.

It is important to point out, however, that although the Church is mystically united with Christ, there is a distinction between Christ and his disciples. This distinction can be expressed in the image of bridegroom and bride. As the loving Bridegroom, Jesus Christ offered his life for his bride (the Church), purifying her by his blood and making her the fruitful mother of God's children.

> For in one Spirit we were all baptized into one body, whether Jews or Greeks, slaves or free persons, and we were all given to drink of one Spirit. (1 Cor 12:13)

Church as Temple of the Holy Spirit
(CCC, 747; 797–801; 809–810)

In writing to the Corinthians, St. Paul asked, "Do you not know that you are the temple of God, and that the Spirit of God dwells in you? . . . The temple of God, which you are, is holy" (1 Cor 3:16–17). Paul's image, borrowed from the Jewish belief that God dwelt in a special way in the Jewish Temple, stresses the unique presence of the Holy Spirit in the Church. As the human spirit gives life to the human body, the Holy Spirit's presence in the Church animates Christ's body. As St. Augustine so aptly put it, the Holy Spirit is the soul of the Church, making it his dwelling place, his Temple.

The Spirit's presence builds up the Church by uniting believers to the Risen Lord Jesus. The Holy Spirit also sanctifies ("makes holy") her members through the Scriptures, the Sacraments, various graces, and virtues that help members live an upright life. The Spirit also gives gifts (or *charisms*) to various disciples under the direction of the **Magisterium** to work for the common good and to accomplish the works of salvation, including gifts like prophecy, healing, and administration. Though not every member of Christ's body is blessed with every charism or a particular charism like those described above, all are blessed with the gift of love, the one gift St. Paul asserts surpasses all of the gifts. Love is the life of the Triune God, the gift that—if lived faithfully and courageously—draws people to Christ (see 1 Corinthians 13) and to his Church.

The three images of the Church highlighted at the Second Vatican Council as People of God, the Body of Christ, and the Temple of the Holy Spirit point to the Blessed Trinity's intimate involvement in the formation of the Church. The *Catechism of the Catholic Church* teaches that the Church is "the sacrament of the Holy Trinity's communion" with all people (*CCC*, 747). The Church is "a people brought into unity from the unity of the Father, the Son, and the Holy Spirit" (cf. *CCC*, 810).

More Images of the Church

Besides the three images that reflect the work of the Trinity in the Church, several other images of Church do well to describe her purpose and mission.

As noted, one of the four tasks of the Church is to preach the Gospel. This makes the Church a *herald*, an announcer of the good news, in imitation of Jesus who preached the coming of God's kingdom in his earthly ministry. This image highlights the Word of God. Jesus commanded his followers to preach the good news of salvation and call people to faith and repentance. In word and in deed, all members of the Church have a duty to communicate Christ's message according to their ability and station in life. Chapter 2 points out how the early Church took this obligation seri-

➤ *Symbol of the Trinity*

ously as Christianity spread throughout the Roman Empire. Today, the Church is faced with the same task—to make Christ and his Gospel known to the four corners of the world.

Service is also one of the important ministries of the Church and each Catholic. The love that will attract others to Christ is made visible in a *servant* Church. Service is not optional for followers of Christ. In imitation of the Lord, the Church must heal and reconcile, feed the hungry, give drink to the thirsty, welcome the stranger, clothe the naked, comfort the sick, visit the imprisoned. There has never been a time in her history when the Church has not been dedicated to the lowly, the suffering, and the poor. In its earliest days, Christians were noted for the way their love was blind in serving others, whether friend or foe. Today, the Church continues to undertake numerous tasks to serve, seeing her role as following in the footsteps of Jesus Christ: "The Son of Man did not come to be served but to serve and to give his life as a ransom for many" (Mt 20:28).

To carry on the many works of Christ, the Church must be organized. Therefore, it is also correct to understand the Church as an *institution* (see CCC, 874–896), a formal structure that enables the members of Christ's Body to continue his work in a systematic way. For example, the Church needs a tremendous amount of organization to serve people through hospitals, orphanages, schools, homes for the aged, hospices for the sick, and so forth.

Like any group that comes together to accomplish a task, the Church also needs an authority structure, roles for members, and rules of operation. Though the Church developed many of her institutional structures over the centuries, Jesus himself intended for an orderly and structured Church when he established the Church with Peter and the Apostles. The Apostles and their successors (bishops) derived their authority from Jesus himself. Clearly appointed leaders and administrators ensure that the Gospel is preached authentically and that Christ's work of salvation is continued down through the ages.

The bishop of Rome is the successor of St. Peter. Along with the other bishops, he is a pastor (shepherd) of souls entrusted with the task of teaching authentically Christ's Gospel. The Magisterium is a vital element that guides the Church in times of confusion, change, and false teaching. The other tasks of the hierarchy (the authority structure of Pope, bishops, priests, and deacons) include sanctifying God's People through the Sacraments and sacramentals and governing them through service and by inspiring them to use their gifts in their daily life to lead others to Christ.

The Church is also a *pilgrim* people (CCC, 901, 905, 909). A pilgrim lives life as a journey with a destination. Jesus was on a pilgrimage as he traveled around Palestine, but his vision and message were fixed steadily on the reign of God. The Church is also called to remain faithful to the Lord, the steady captain of a ship that sometimes finds herself in the midst of uncertain and even dangerous waters.

To be a disciple of Jesus takes courage. Christ said that to follow him involves picking up a cross, of suffering for the sake of his Gospel. Promoting Jesus' vision of peace and justice, especially fair treatment for everyone, including the most vulnerable is risky and often filled with pain and suffering to the point of death. Over the centuries, men and women have suffered martyrdom for their staying with their Lord and witnessing to him and his work. Even today, being a Christian often means stepping out of the mainstream, venturing forth to proclaim the Gospel truth. Ridicule, rejection, and even physical suffering sometimes result for being a faithful companion of Jesus.

Christian pilgrims, knowing that this life is not forever, keep their eyes fixed on the Lord who leads his disciples through the Holy Spirit. Regardless of the age, the Church is a community of hope that announces to people desperate for the truth that an eternal destiny awaits us at the end of the human journey. The Church confidently proclaims that if we live loving lives, we need not fear death because the Savior has in store for us "what eye has not seen, and ear has not heard, and what has not entered the human heart, what God has prepared for those who love him" (1 Cor 2:9).

Marks of the CHURCH

In the Nicene Creed, Catholics recite, "We believe in one holy catholic and apostolic Church." The four descriptive words of this statement help identify the true nature and mission of the Church. Traditionally known as the four "marks of the Church," *one, holy, catholic,* and *apostolic* help strengthen the faith of Catholics; at the same time, they are signs that can attract the attention of nonbelievers.

The marks of the Church are qualities that exist in the Church because of Christ and the Holy Spirit working in the Church. In some ways, they are a paradox, both realizations and challenges. The divine element exists in the Church, yet the Church is made of human beings who fall short of their Christian vocation. The history of the Church gives examples of when sinful believers—through their actions or failures to act—betrayed the very marks that should point to the presence of Christ in the Church. A few of these failures will be indicated below and more fully elaborated on as the story of the Church unfolds in subsequent chapters.

One

The source of unity in the Church is the Holy Trinity. The Church is one because she was established by Christ and given life by the Holy Spirit. The Catholic doctrine of the communion of saints is an extension of the belief that the Church is a communion of faith united by the Holy Spirit at Eucharist. The risen Lord is present in his word proclaimed at Mass and in the liturgy of the Eucharist under the forms of bread and wine. By the power of the Holy Spirit, the risen Lord binds and sanctifies the Church into a communion of the faithful. In addition, the Lord continues his prayer for unity in the Church:

> I pray not only for them, but also for those who will believe in me through their word, so that they may all be one, as you, Father, are in me and I in you, that they also may be in us, that the world may believe that you sent me. (Jn 17:21)

The virtue of charity (love) binds the Church into one people. Other bonds of communion include the profession of one faith (for example, in the Nicene Creed), the common celebration of worship (for example, in the sacraments), and the succession of bishops from the Apostles through the Sacrament of Holy Orders.

The true Church Christ founded *subsists* in the Catholic Church because in it can be found the *fullness* of the means of sanctification and an apostolic succession traceable to St. Peter. The Holy Father is both the symbol and servant of unity. Christ willed a unified community, but there exists in the Church a wounded unity. One example is the Eastern Schism, where a rift in unity between the Western and Eastern Churches culminated in their separation in 1054. Another major rupture in the unity that Christ willed for his Church took place in the sixteenth century during the Protestant Reformation. Today, there exist thousands of Christian communities that have separated from the Catholic Church. This certainly was not the intention of the founder. *Heresy* (denial of essential truths), *apostasy* (abandonment of faith), and *schism* (a rift in unity) harm the unity of Christ's Church and result from human pride and sin. Especially since the time of the Second Vatican Council (1962–1965), *ecumenism* (the movement to restore the unity of Christ's Church) has been a top priority for the Church.

Holy

Jesus Christ is the model of holiness in the Church. Jesus remains present in the Church and makes her holy. The Holy Spirit, the gift of the Father and the Son to the Church, also dwells in the Church and sanctifies her members. The Blessed Trinity, therefore, is the ultimate source of holiness in the Church.

The Church is also holy because she possesses the means for people to achieve holiness, for example, by participating in the Sacraments, reading the holy Scriptures, praying, reflecting on spiritual writings of the great saints and theologians, and so on. Also to be found in the Church are models of holiness like the saints, the preeminent one of whom is Mary. She is the Mother of God and our spiritual Mother as well. In this new age, Mary is the new Eve, the "mother of the living" and the Mother of the Church. "In her, the Church is already 'all-holy'" (CCC, 829).

Holiness in the Church remains a paradox because the Church consists of members who are sinful. Its proof is when words are translated into deeds and lives are given in love and service to others. But, Catholics throughout the ages have succumbed to sinfulness. Both individually and from the hierarchical leadership to the Pope, the Church has apologized for past sins that have caused harm to Christ's Body and calls all Christians to a renewal of their Christian commitment.

Catholic

The word *catholic* means "general" or "universal." It is believed that the martyr St. Ignatius of Antioch (ca. 50–107) was the first to apply this adjective to the Church.

The Church is catholic because of Christ's presence in the Body as her head, endowing the Church with everything humans need for their salvation: the fullness of divine revelation; a complete and correct confession of faith; the teaching authority of the Magisterium that is traceable to the Apostles; and a full sacramental life, especially the gift of the Eucharist.

The Church is also catholic because of her universal outreach throughout the centuries to all people in all places. Everyone is welcome in the Catholic Church; no one is excluded. The varied personal gifts of each member enrich the Body of Christ. In every generation, the Church must and does preach the good news to all people, inviting them to accept Jesus Christ as their Lord and Savior, to turn from a life of sin, and to be baptized into the community of believers, a community of faith, hope, and love.

A third way the Church is catholic is that she continues to teach all that Christ taught. The same essential faith has been professed, and worship practiced, since the time of the Apostles and shared by many diverse peoples separated culturally, linguistically, and geographically down through the ages.

The Church is also universal in the sense that each particular Christian community in a local diocese under its bishop is united to the Church of Rome. This catholicity manifests itself in various cultures, liturgical rites, and spiritual traditions and disciplines.

Christ's presence ensures that the Church will remain catholic and welcoming of everyone for all time. But, again, this mark of the Church is paradoxical. There have been times when some of the Church's members were intolerant of people, even engendering prejudicial attitudes against certain groups. The Church must always strive to preach the authentic Gospel lovingly to people everywhere, work to restore Christian unity, and respect all people who are struggling with belief but may not yet be open to hearing Christ's Gospel.

Apostolic

The Catholic Church traces her leadership directly back to St. Peter and the Apostles. This succession of leadership is one way that the Church is apostolic.

Also, the Church is apostolic because she professes the same creed and Christian way of life taught by the Apostles. A threat to apostolic successions occurred with the Western Schism of 1378–1417, when up to three men claimed to be the Pope. But with the guidance of the Holy Spirit, the Church's leadership survived this crisis and continued to preserve Jesus' message through the ages. Founded on the faith of Apostles, the Church continues to profess and live the faith today, led by the prophetic, priestly, and kingly ministries of the Pope and bishops, assisted by priests and deacons.

The word *Apostle* means "one who is sent." Every Christian is called to be a missionary, to share in Christ's mission of proclaiming in word and in deed the good news of God's bounteous love manifested in his Son, Jesus Christ. However, the success of fulfilling the apostolic mission depends on how well Christians remain in union with Christ, especially in their participation in the Eucharist, and in using the gifts of the Holy Spirit given to Christians to further Christ's kingdom.

MEMBERS OF THE CHURCH

St. Ignatius OF ANTIOCH

St. Ignatius of Antioch was a heroic martyr of the early Church. Little is known of his early life. He lived at the same time of the Apostles, most notably, John the Evangelist. One tradition claims that John converted him. Soon after his baptism, when he assumed the additional name of Theophorus ("God-borne" or "God-bearer"), Ignatius became the third bishop of Antioch (AD 69), an important center of Christian activity in the early Church. His distinguished ministry revealed how important the office of bishop was in the early Church.

Under the regime of the Emperor Trajan, Antioch's magistrates condemned Ignatius to the lion pit in Rome. They dispatched him to Rome under a guard of ten soldiers. On the way to Rome, Ignatius's escorts stopped in several cities where Christians met and befriended Ignatius. Later in the trip, he wrote seven letters to his newfound friends to encourage them to remain strong in their faith. These letters exhort the readers to remain loyal and obedient to their bishops. Ignatius saw bishops as the symbols of unity and right teaching in the Church. They were the only correct guides to dispel false teachings that had crept into the Church. In one of these letters, Ignatius was the first person to refer to the Church as the "Catholic Church."

Ignatius made it to Rome where lions devoured him in the Flavian amphitheater. The traditional date for his martyrdom is 107. His friends preserved his bones and received permission to take them back to Antioch. Today, his relics rest in Rome.

A Martyr for Christ

The following passage from Ignatius's "Letter to the Romans" anticipates his cruel martyrdom. It has inspired generations of Christians to remain faithful to Jesus in the face of persecution and death.

Pray leave me to be a meal for the beasts, for it is they who can provide my way to God. I am his wheat, ground fine by the lions' teeth to be made purest bread for Christ.

All the ends of the earth, all of the kingdoms of the world would be of no profit to me; so far as I am concerned, to die in Jesus Christ is better than to be monarch of earth's widest bounds. He who died for us is all I seek; he who rose again for us is my whole desire.[4]

The "Catholic" Church

In his "Letter to the Smyrnaeans," Ignatius refers to Christ's presence in the *Catholic* Church. It also underscores the important office of the bishop as the symbol of unity in the Church:

You must all follow the lead of the bishop, as Jesus Christ followed that of the Father; follow the presbytery as you would the Apostles; reverence the deacons as you would God's Commandment. Let no one do anything touching the Church, apart from the bishop. Let that celebration of the Eucharist be considered valid which is held under the bishop or anyone to whom he has committed it. Where the bishop appears, there let the people be, just as where Jesus Christ is, there is the Catholic Church. It is not permitted without authorization from the bishop either to baptize or to hold an agape; but whatever he approves is also pleasing to God. Thus everything you do will be proof against danger and valid.[5]

Summary

- The Catholic Church can be found throughout the world. The Church possesses the fullness of truth and all the means necessary for salvation.

- Two important meanings for the word *church* are "belonging to the Lord" and "those called out." The term applies to the local worshiping community as well as the universal community of believers.

- The Church is a mystery of God's love for humanity. A mystery is a reality filled with God's hidden presence. The Church is also Sacrament, or efficacious sign of grace instituted by Christ and entrusted to the Church. In the Church is a divine element (the presence of Christ and the Holy Spirit), as well as a human dimension. In describing the Church, the Second Vatican Council highlighted in a special way three images of the Church: People of God, Body of Christ, and Temple of the Holy Spirit. Other helpful images of the Church include herald, servant, institution, and pilgrim.

- Christ entrusts his Church with the fourfold mission of preaching the message of the Gospel (*kerygma*), modeling fellowship (*koinonia*), serving others in imitation of Jesus (*diakonia*), and worshiping God in community (*leitourgia*).

- The four marks of the Church—*one, holy, catholic,* and *apostolic*—identify the true nature of the Church and her mission. They help strengthen faith and attract the notice of nonbelievers. However, because the Church is made up of humans who sin, they are paradoxes that challenge Christ's followers in each age to live up to their Christian vocation.

Prayer REFLECTION

The Apostles' Creed is firmly rooted in an early baptismal creed used in Rome in the second century. It is a significant profession of faith because Peter, the Christ-appointed leader of the Church, established the Church in Rome. Thus, this authoritative prayer has its origins in the theological formulas that arose during the time of Peter and the Apostles.

This Apostles' Creed is logically ordered and prayerful. It highlights the essential Christian doctrine of the Blessed Trinity. In praying it, Christians proclaim their belief in:

- the first divine Person (the almighty and eternal God) and the wonderful work of creation;

- the second divine Person (Jesus Christ, God-made-man) and his marvelous work of Redemption;

- and the third divine Person (the Holy Spirit), who is the origin and source of sanctification that comes to us through Christ's one, holy, catholic, and apostolic Church (CCC, 190).

The Apostles' Creed
I believe in God,
the Father almighty,
creator of heaven and earth.

I believe in Jesus Christ, his only Son, our Lord.
He was conceived by the power of the Holy Spirit,
and born of the Virgin Mary.
He suffered under Pontius Pilate,
was crucified, died, and was buried.
He descended to the dead.
On the third day he rose again.
He ascended into heaven,
and is seated at the right hand of the Father.
He will come again to judge the living and the dead.

I believe in the Holy Spirit,
the holy Catholic Church,
the communion of saints,
the forgiveness of sins,
the resurrection of the body,
and life everlasting. Amen.

Scripture CONNECTIONS

Exodus 2:23–25; 3–12; 15–20; 24
These passages tell part of the story of God's creation of the Chosen People.

1 Corinthians 13
This chapter includes St. Paul's great reflection on the meaning of love.

Review and DISCUSSION QUESTIONS

1. What value is there in studying Church history?

2. To what would you attribute the long life of the Catholic Church?

3. How is the Church a "convocation"?

4. Which of the following images of the Church—Sacrament, People of God, Body of Christ, Temple of the Holy Spirit, Herald, Servant, Institution, Pilgrim—is most meaningful for you? Why?

5. How can you personally put into practice the fourfold mission of the Church of message, community, service, and worship?

6. In what way does today's Church embody each of the four marks of the Church? In your judgment, what else needs to be done to help each of the marks to become even more real in today's world?

7. Identify the following terms:

apostasy	church
diakonia	Ecumenical Council
ecumenism	efficacious symbol
heresy	hierarchy
kerygma	*koinonia*
leitourgia	*Lumen Gentium*
Magisterium	marks of the Church
mystery	sacrament
schism	

Learn BY DOING

1. Read the first two chapters of *Lumen Gentium*, the Second Vatican Council's *Dogmatic Constitution on the Church*. Note ten important statements about the Church from your reading. You can find this document online at:

   • the Vatican website: www.vatican.va

   • RCNet: www.rc.net/rcchurch/vatican2/lumen.gen

2. Work on your own or with a partner to complete the following:

- Create a piece of artwork that captures one of the images of the Church described in this chapter.

- Compose a one-sentence definition of the Church related to your image.

- List a specific action that you can do within the next few years to help the Church further her mission:

  - to more effectively spread her message,

  - to build up Christian community,

  - to serve the needy in our midst.

- Make one set of recommendations for the Church in this country and another for the universal Church.

- If you were a member of your parish's liturgy and worship committee, what would you commend about your parish's liturgical celebrations? What could you recommend for more active participation by the congregation?

2
Christianity TAKES ROOT

They devoted themselves to the teaching of the Apostles and to the communal life, to the breaking of the bread and to the prayers. Awe came upon everyone, and many wonders and signs were done through the Apostles. All who believed were together and had all things in common; they would sell their property and possessions and divide them among all according to each one's need. Every day they devoted themselves to meeting together in the temple area and to breaking bread in their homes. They ate their meals with exultation and sincerity of heart, praising God and enjoying favor with all the people. And every day the Lord added to their number those who were being saved.

—ACTS 2:42–47

The "SEED OF THE CHURCH"

One of the important Church leaders of the second century was Bishop Polycarp of Smyrna (69–155). Smyrna was located in present-day Izmir, Turkey. Polycarp, along with his friend St. Ignatius of Antioch, became a staunch defender of orthodox faith, opposing various heresies that had surfaced in Asia Minor. One of his writings survives—a letter written to the Philippians. In it he quotes from the Gospels of Matthew and Luke and cites various other New Testament texts, thus demonstrating the wide dispersal of New Testament writings at a relatively early age.

In 155, the aged Bishop Polycarp was arrested by a Roman official and told to renounce his "atheistic" beliefs of refusing to worship the emperor and other Roman gods. Polycarp knew the consequences if he did not do as they said: a painful death either by being torn to death by wild animals or being burned alive on a pyre. Three times he was asked to renounce his belief in Jesus Christ. But the aged man replied, "Eighty-six years have I served him, and he has done me no wrong: How can I blaspheme my King who saved me?"

An account of Polycarp's martyrdom, probably written by an eyewitness, recounted how the flames that burned around Polycarp did not kill him. This prompted one of his executioners to plunge his sword into his heart, out of which the martyr's blood flowed, extinguishing the fire. His persecutors then ignited the fire once again to burn the saint's corpse. His followers gathered their beloved bishop's bones and buried them in a site which they visited annually to celebrate the Holy Eucharist. (This is the earliest evidence of honoring saints on their feast days.)

Early Church theologian Tertullian wrote, "The blood of martyrs is the seed of the Church." The blood of the martyr Polycarp, and that of a host of other faithful early followers of Jesus, helps to explain the early growth of Christianity. Their dramatic witness and willingness to face suffering and death led others to wonder about their reasons for doing so and eventually to Jesus Christ himself. This chapter will look at martyrdom and some other "seeds" that produced the fruit of the expanding Church in the earliest centuries.

The Person OF CHRIST

We begin with a study of Jesus Christ in a book about the Catholic Church because the Church is the institution he founded. St. Joan of Arc would later say, "About Jesus Christ and the Church, I simply know they're one thing and we shouldn't complicate the matter." Jesus Christ is the Son of God made flesh, the Savior and Redeemer of humanity, and the Lord of history. People become members of the Church through faith in Christ and Baptism in his name. As members of the Church, they try to live in accord with Christ's teachings and make him known to the entire world.

Known as Jesus of Nazareth, Scripture records that Jesus was born sometime before the death of King Herod the Great (4 BC), perhaps in the year 6 BC. He was born in Bethlehem in Judea, on the outskirts of the powerful Roman Empire then ruled by Caesar Augustus. He was born during the relatively stable time known as *Pax Romana* ("Roman Peace"). His birth went unnoticed by the Romans. It took many decades before a Jewish historian (Josephus) or Roman writer (for example, Tacitus, Pliny the Younger, or Suetonius) mentioned him, and then typically only to complain about his followers—the Christians. The record of Jesus by these unbelievers is further evidence that he was a real person of history.

However it is the Gospels of Mark, Matthew, Luke, and John (written between AD 65–100) that are the primary sources of information about the Jesus of history. Their main concern is not biographical detail but to testify to faith

4–6 BC
Birth of Jesus of Nazareth

in the risen Lord Jesus Christ, to sustain and inspire Christian believers, and to convert nonbelievers.

The Gospels reveal that Jesus led a hidden life as a wood worker in the Galilean town of Nazareth until around AD 28, when he was baptized in the Jordan River by the prophet John the Baptist, a distant relative of his. After the arrest of John, Jesus began his own ministry by preaching "This is the time of fulfillment. The Kingdom of God is at hand. Repent, and believe in the Gospel" (Mk 1:14–15).

Jesus the Teacher

The Gospels time and again present Jesus as a wandering preacher who often used vivid and memorable stories known as parables to teach a powerful message. The principal theme of his preaching was the advent of God's kingdom, that is, that God's universal will for peace, justice, love, and salvation were being realized in the present. Key points of Jesus' teaching included:

- Although the kingdom appears small, its growth is inevitable, by God's own design. Jesus' initial gathering of followers and his foundation of the Church is the seed and beginning of the kingdom.

- God's kingdom is a gift, open to all people. God's love knows no bounds. God is like the merciful father in the parable of the prodigal son (Lk 15:11–32) who joyfully and unconditionally welcomes back his wayward children. God wants all people to accept his freely given love and to forgive others as we have been forgiven.

- This good news of God's love demands a whole-hearted response. To persist in a life of sin is no longer acceptable. We must repent, ask for God's forgiveness, and develop an intimate relationship with *Abba*, the endearing name Jesus used to call on God the Father.

- Following Jesus and living in his Father's kingdom requires that we love everyone, even our enemies. Jesus taught his followers to follow the law of love of God that requires loving our neighbor as our self.

Love especially manifests itself in concrete action to the least in our midst: feeding the hungry, giving drink to the thirsty, welcoming the stranger, clothing the naked, and visiting the sick and the imprisoned (Mt 25:35–36).

- Jesus predicts on more than one occasion that he will go to Jerusalem, "suffer many things . . . and be killed, and on the third day be raised" (Mt 16:21).

- Being a Christian requires service and commitment, picking up a cross in imitation of him. Following Jesus brings fulfillment in this life and incredible happiness in the next.

Jesus the Wonder Worker

Jesus' message was manifested in concrete deeds. All the Gospels tell us that Jesus performed miracles to demonstrate that God's power had broken into human history. These mighty deeds also authenticated Jesus' claim that he could teach in God's name and that the Father was present in him, his unique Son, accomplishing his will of salvation. The disciples of Jesus, as well as the crowds, witnessed these powerful signs, proclaiming boldly that "the blind regain their sight, the lame walk, lepers are cleansed, the deaf hear, the dead are raised, the poor have the good news proclaimed to them" (Lk 7:22–23).

Jesus the Pray-er

The Gospels also point out that Jesus prayed at significant and decisive moments in his life: for example, before God the Father addresses him at his Baptism and Transfiguration, and in the garden prior to the fulfillment of his Father's plan of love that culminated in Jesus' Passion, Death, and Resurrection.

Jesus' own model of prayer also inspired his disciples to learn to pray. One of his disciples said to him, "Lord, teach us to pray" (Lk 11:1) and he taught them the quintessential Christian prayer, the Our Father. The example of Jesus at prayer encouraged his followers to be people of prayer. Jesus' prayer on the Cross—"Father, into your hands I commit my spirit!" (Lk 23:46)—is his prayer that teaches that he and his followers are to always entrust every trial into the loving hands of God. Our prayer only has access to the Father if we pray "in the name" of Jesus.

28
Public ministry of Jesus begins

Reaction to Jesus

Although Jesus attracted followers who believed in him, he was rejected by some of the leading and influential Jewish groups of his day, including the Sadducees, the aristocratic Jewish leaders who controlled Temple worship. As collaborators with the Roman authorities, the Sadducees perceived Jesus as a threat to their power over the Jewish people. They also feared that they would be blamed by the Romans for any political disturbances attributed to Jesus. Some of the Sadducee leaders, including the high priest Joseph Caiaphas, cooperated in handing Jesus over to the Roman prefect, Pontius Pilate. The Gospel of John reports Caiaphas declaring, "It is better for you that one man should die instead of the people, so that the whole nation may not perish" (Jn 11:50).

Another Jewish sect that was opposed to Jesus was the Pharisees with whom he had much in common, including belief in resurrection, the need for virtuous living, and the importance of the Law. However, some Pharisees disapproved of Jesus' interpretations of the Law, for example, concerning healing on the Sabbath, the necessity of ritual washings, and association with public sinners. Jesus was accused of blasphemy for claiming to forgive sin, something only God could do. In addition, Jesus courted no favor when he challenged religious leaders to practice what they preached. Jesus despised religious hypocrisy, especially when it masqueraded as religious superiority.

Eventually, Jesus was arrested. At his trial before the religious authorities, he admitted to being the Christ, the Messiah, "the Son of the Blessed One" (Mk 14:61–62). His contemporaries thought of the Messiah in political and military terms, as one who would throw off the yoke of the Romans, perhaps through military means, and reestablish the Jewish nation. Jesus saw the role of the Messiah differently, as a Suffering Servant who would sacrifice his life for the salvation of all people.

John's Gospel reveals that Jesus' public ministry was short, lasting from one year to perhaps two or three years. The final week of Jesus' life was the perfect summation of a life lived for others. The details of that week include a celebration of the Last Supper set around a Passover meal with his Apostles, his arrest in the Garden of Gethsemane, trials before both the Jewish and Roman authorities, sentencing by Pontius Pilate, a brutal scourging, crucifixion, Death, and burial.

The sharing of the Last Supper was especially meaningful for Jesus and his Apostles. During his ministry, Jesus often ate meals with sinners to demonstrate God's acceptance and forgiveness of everyone. Jesus also described

Heaven as a banquet where people would enjoy fellowship in the presence of his loving Father. The Jewish feast of Passover celebrated the passing over of the angel of death on the Hebrew children and Yahweh's deliverance of the Chosen People from the Pharaoh. It also commemorated the birth of the Jewish

nation. Jesus, however, transformed the meaning of the meal. He became the New Passover, the Paschal Lamb slaughtered for the salvation of all. This special meal was to be the sign of a new covenant God was making with everyone, a covenant sealed in Jesus' blood. At the Last Supper Jesus gave thanks, broke bread, and said to his disciples, "This is my body that is for you." He then offered a cup and said, "This cup is the new covenant in my blood. Do this, as often as you drink it, in remembrance of me" (1 Cor 11:23–26). Under the consecrated species of bread and wine, Jesus is present in a "true, real, and substantial manner" (CCC, 1413).

Jesus ultimately was put to death on the charge of sedition, a crime under Roman law punishable by death. Jesus admitted to being a king, but he said to Pilate: "My kingdom does not belong to this world" (Jn 18:36). Pilate may have believed that Jesus was innocent of a crime, but he was afraid of being reported to the emperor for allowing a possible revolutionary to go free. So he ordered Jesus crucified.

Jesus' death most likely took place in the middle of the afternoon (3 p.m.) on the fourteenth day of the Jewish month of Nisan (April 7 on the solar calendar) in the year AD 30. This should have ended the story even before it began had Jesus of Nazareth been an ordinary victim of a miscarriage of justice. However, on the Sunday after his crucifixion, Jesus rose from the dead. The Apostles were startled by discovering him alive, risen to a new life. The Resurrection of Jesus became for them the definitive proof of his divine origin. It validated his teaching. It became the central fact of the preaching the Apostles were compelled to announce to their fellow Jews and to the rest of the world. Thus begins the story of Christianity and the story of the Church—the new People of God—to whom all are invited to join through faith and Baptism.

34
Martyrdom of Stephen; conversion of Paul

> ## WHAT THE CHURCH BELIEVES ABOUT . . .
> ### Our Communion in the Mysteries of Jesus
>
> Jesus' whole life is a mystery of Redemption, especially through the blood of his cross, but also at work throughout his entire life: in his Incarnation, in his hidden life, in his word, in his healings and exorcisms, and in his Resurrection. The mysteries of Jesus are for everyone. Their purpose is for us to share in all the mysteries of his Redemption.
> See *Catechism of the Catholic Church*, 514–518.

The Church's BEGINNING

The Acts of the Apostles, written by the author of the Gospel of Luke, serves as a historical record for the early days of the Catholic Church. The first chapter of Acts recounts Jesus' promise to send the Holy Spirit, his Ascension into Heaven, and the selection of Matthias as a replacement for the Apostle Judas. Some of the important events of the Acts of the Apostles are summarized in the sections that follow.

Pentecost

Acts 2 details the coming of the Holy Spirit. In an upper room in Jerusalem, the Holy Spirit descended in the form of fiery tongues on the Apostles; Mary, Jesus' Mother; and some other disciples gathered there in prayer and waiting. This divine event took place on the Jewish harvest feast of thanksgiving known as Pentecost ("fiftieth day" from the Passover). The coming of the Holy Spirit on Pentecost is sometimes known as the "birthday of the Church." The descent of the Holy Spirit empowered the Apostles and especially Peter to preach a sermon to the Jews gathered in Jerusalem for the festival. In a powerful address, Peter recounted what happened to Jesus and how his life related to the prophecies of the Old Testament. The Holy Spirit also formed the Church in the life of prayer.

With great enthusiasm Peter witnessed to the life and teaching of Jesus. He boldly proclaimed that the Death and Resurrection of Jesus, and the signs they were witnessing before their very eyes did, in fact, fulfill the prophecies about the Messiah. One of the signs occurring at that very moment was that Peter was speaking in tongues, that is, all the people gathered could understand him in spite of speaking different native languages. He called for faith

CA. 40
The word *Christian* first used to describe believers in Antioch

in Jesus Christ: "Repent and be baptized, every one of you, in the name of Jesus Christ for the forgiveness of your sins; and you will receive the gift of the holy Spirit" (Acts 2:38). As a result of Peter's powerful sermon, three thousand people were baptized that day.

Early Growth of the Church

In the early years, the Church grew because of the example of new Christians who shared possessions in common, prayed and worshiped together, and engaged in charitable works. It also grew because of vigorous preaching and the wonders and signs performed by the Apostles. A good example of the latter was Peter's curing a crippled beggar and preaching that this marvelous event was due to the power of the living Lord Jesus. Those who witnessed the cripple jumping and praising God were astonished. Five thousand of them converted on that day (Acts 4:4).

The earliest converts to Jesus Christ were Jerusalem Jews or those in Jerusalem for Pentecost. They considered themselves to be pious Jews who still worshiped in the Temple and recited their Jewish prayers. Early on, the Sanhedrin, the Jewish ruling body, and the high priest heard about the miracles and preaching of the Apostles and tried to silence any talk about Jesus. But Peter and John said they could not be quiet about what God had accomplished in Jesus. When the authorities threatened death, a Pharisee and respected member of the Sanhedrin, Gamaliel, wisely cautioned his fellow leaders:

> So now I tell you, have nothing to do with these men, and let them go. For if this endeavor or this activity is of human origin, it will destroy itself. But if it comes from God, you will not be able to destroy them; you may even find yourselves fighting against God. (Acts 5:38–39)

The Gentile Issue and Other Growing Pains

Growth in any organization brings problems. The first crisis in the Christian community involved Greek-speaking converts who came from cities around the Roman Empire. They complained that their widows were not getting their fair share when food was distributed to the poor. To solve this problem, the Apostles laid hands (a sign of ordination) on seven men of good reputation to take care of this and other tasks for the ordering of communal life. These men, known as *deacons*, enabled the Apostles more freedom to preach and lead others in prayer.

44
Execution of James, the son of Zebedee

Stephen was a well-known deacon whose forceful and courageous preaching showed that the Gospel went beyond mere observance of the Law and Temple worship. Jesus' salvation is meant for everyone; faith in Jesus is enough to gain salvation. This message infuriated the Jewish leaders who saw it as a threat to the very foundations of Jewish belief. Along with a young man named Saul, they drove Stephen from the city and stoned him to death. Thus, St. Stephen became the first *martyr* or "witness" for the Church.

Soon after, another persecution broke out against Christians, causing many of them to flee Jerusalem to other cities where they continued to preach the Gospel. Some reached Antioch in Syria, one of the leading cities of the ancient world. There the Gospel was preached to God-fearing Gentiles besides to the Jews in the synagogues. It was in Antioch that the followers of Jesus were called "Christian" for the first time. Antioch also became a missionary center for Gentile Christianity and the home base for the journeys of St. Paul, the converted Saul, the prime missionary to the Gentiles.

After Stephen's death, the deacon Philip began a successful preaching ministry to the Samaritans. Peter also had a central role in the welcoming of Gentiles. At the town of Jaffa, Peter had a vision that convinced him that the Gospel was meant not just for Jews but for all people. He baptized Cornelius, a Gentile centurion, and his entire household, as was the custom. Peter concluded, "In truth, I see that God shows no partiality. Rather, in every nation whoever fears him and acts uprightly is acceptable to him" (Acts 10:34–35).

The strict Jewish Christians in Jerusalem were upset that Peter mingled with "unclean" Gentiles because they did not observe Jewish dietary laws or were not circumcised, thus not members of the Chosen People. Peter quelled their negativity by reminding them that Jesus himself associated with outcasts and that he ordered the Apostles to preach the Gospel to the ends of the world. His argument calmed dissension for a time, but the issue of what to do with Gentile converts would fester for years to come among Jewish Christians in Jerusalem.

In the city of Jerusalem itself, persecution of the Christians was stepped up under the reign of Herod Aggrippa (AD 42–44). Herod harassed and arrested Peter. He put to death James, the brother of John and leader of the Church in Jerusalem. Another James, "the brother of the Lord," assumed leadership of the Jerusalem Church until he, too, was martyred in AD 62.

45–58
Three missionary journeys of Paul; writing of his epistles

WHAT THE CHURCH BELIEVES ABOUT . . .
Infant Baptism

From apostolic times when whole "households" received Baptism, infants may also have been baptized. Infants are baptized under the belief that Baptism removes the stain of Original Sin. Children, too, have the need of new birth in Baptism to escape the power of darkness and brought into a life of freedom as children of God. The Church and parents offer children the priceless gift of becoming a child of God soon after their birth by allowing infant Baptism.

See *Catechism of the Catholic Church*, 1250–1252.

MEMBERS OF THE CHURCH

Paul of Tarsus: APOSTLE TO THE GENTILES

 St. Paul is a towering figure in early Christian history. Approximately 60 percent of the Acts of the Apostles recounts his life's work, and roughly half of the New Testament books overall were written by or attributed to him. He was a vigorous missionary, courageous defender of the faith, brilliant theologian, builder and sustainer of Christian communities, and a brave martyr.

Saul (Paul's Jewish name) was born between AD 5 and 15 into a strict Jewish family in Tarsus in modern-day Turkey. As a citizen of Tarsus, he enjoyed the benefits of Roman citizenship and the advantage of an excellent education. Fluent in Greek, Aramaic, and Hebrew, he traveled to Jerusalem to study the Torah under the famous Rabbi Gamaliel (see above).

He may have been in the city at the same time as Jesus; however, there is no evidence that they ever met.

As a strict Pharisee, Paul rigidly applied the letter of the Law, for example, in helping to lead persecutions against Christians. Present at the stoning of Stephen, Paul thought it was blasphemous to call Jesus, a mere carpenter, the Messiah, Son of the Living God. Because of his zeal, the Sanhedrin sent him to Damascus to root out Christians who were evangelizing in the synagogues there.

CA. 49
Council of Jerusalem determines Gentiles need not be circumcised

Paul's Conversion

On his way to Damascus, Paul had a blinding vision in which the Lord asked him, "Saul, Saul, why are you persecuting me?" (Acts 9:9). This revelation convinced Paul that Jesus was alive and that he was indeed the Christ who lived spiritually in his followers.

Paul proceeded to Damascus and was baptized there by Ananias. He began to preach the Gospel, but his sudden shift in loyalties enraged his Jewish brethren who tried to kill him. After a stay in Arabia, Paul eventually made his way to Jerusalem. There he befriended Barnabas who introduced him to Peter and the other Apostles. Peter accepted Paul and saw his potential to proclaim the Gospel. Unfortunately, Paul was forced to flee the Jewish leaders once again, this time back to his hometown.

For ten years, Paul remained in Tarsus. He may have worked at his chosen trade of tent making, an occupation he used to support himself even when he became a full-time missionary. He also probably spent a good deal of time in prayer, developing a fervent relationship with the Lord that served him well for his later missionary activity. Eventually, Barnabas called Paul to Antioch to minister with him to the local Church there. Antioch supported the strongest Christian community outside of Jerusalem and served as headquarters for Paul's three remarkable missionary journeys around the Mediterranean basin.

First Missionary Journey: 45–49

Paul's first journey took him to Perga, Antioch of Pisidia, and the cities in Lycaonia. This journey established his practice of first proclaiming the Gospel to his fellow Jews in the synagogues. When the Jews did not listen to Paul, he turned to the Gentiles. He stressed the universal message of Christianity, that Jesus had come to save not only the Chosen People, but all people.

Paul saw the Holy Spirit as the source of unity for believers, not adherence to the precepts of the Jewish Law. Salvation is a gift from God. Therefore, Paul did not require his Gentile converts to follow Jewish customs such as circumcision or the dietary laws. Baptism into the Christian faith did not require a convert to become a Jew.

64
Nero blames burning of Rome on Christians;
persecution of Christians and death of Peter

WHAT THE CHURCH BELIEVES ABOUT . . .
Catholicity

The Church is catholic in two ways. First, the Church is catholic because Jesus is present in the Church, the fullness of his body, with the fullness of the means of salvation, the fullness of faith, and ordained ministry by apostolic succession. The Church is also catholic, or universal, because of her mission to the whole human race.
See *Catechism of the Catholic Church* 830–835.

The Council of Jerusalem

When Paul returned to Antioch, he met resistance from some Jewish Christians from Jerusalem. They opposed Paul's practice of freeing Gentile converts from the Mosaic Law. Even Peter, who had baptized Gentiles without requiring them to become Jews first, had caved into his Jerusalem friends and stopped eating with Gentile Christians who did not follow Jewish dietary customs. On this point, Paul firmly corrected Peter for compromising his beliefs.

The Council of Jerusalem (ca. 49) resolved the conflict, which had grown to threaten Church unity. Paul and Barnabas argued for freedom for the Gentiles while James supported imposing Jewish Law on all converts. Peter upheld Paul and admitted that it is the grace of the Lord Jesus Christ that saves a person, not imposing Jewish Law on all converts. Thus, the Council of Jerusalem decided that Gentile converts were not subject to Jewish regulations, except to avoid illicit marriages and to abstain from food offered to idols. The Apostles sent a letter to churches at Antioch, Syria, and Cilicia with the following requirements:

> It is the decision of the holy Spirit and of us not to place on you any burden beyond these necessities, namely, to abstain from meat sacrificed from idols, from blood, from meats of strangled animals, and from unlawful marriage. If you keep free of these, you will be doing what is right. (Acts 15:28–29)

This decision was critical for the future of the Church. Belief in Jesus Christ, not following Jewish Law, was the means for becoming a Christian. Christianity was no longer tied to Judaism. This solution to this crisis highlighted one of the marks of the Church—its *catholicity*, a universal religion

---

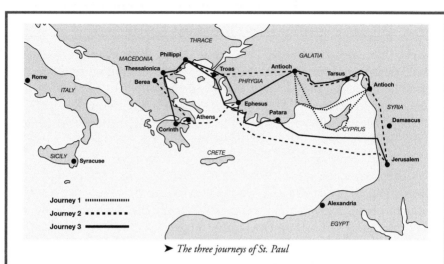

> ➤ *The three journeys of St. Paul*

open to all peoples in all places at all times. The groundwork for the rapid spread of Christianity was in place throughout the Roman Empire. Paul's message of universality opened the Gospel to all:

> There is neither Jew nor Greek, there is neither slave nor free person, there is neither male nor female; for you are all one in Christ Jesus. (Gal 3:28)

Paul's Second Journey: 49–52

Paul's second journey took him to Asia Minor where he dreamt about a man from Macedonia who begged him to come to his land to preach the Gospel. Paul heeded the dream and thus the good news came to Europe. He founded churches in Philippi, where the Jews had him arrested; Thessalonica; and Berea. He eventually made it to Athens where he tried to appeal to the philosophical minds of the Athenians. At first amused by Paul, Athenians scorned the teaching about the Resurrection. And most of them rejected his novel teaching about Jesus.

Paul had much more success in Corinth, a city known for its loose morals —gambling, prostitution, drinking. He lived there for eighteen months, working as a tentmaker during the week and preaching the Gospel on the Sabbath. He lived at the home of Aquila and Priscilla who also joined Paul on later missions. Corinth became one of Paul's most important churches, but some serious problems arose after he left there.

CA. 100–150
Writings of Apostolic Fathers

Paul's Third Journey: 53–58

After a short rest in Antioch, Paul spent almost three years in Ephesus, the capital of the Roman province of Asia Minor. Paul's preaching on monotheism raised the ire of the town's silversmiths who made idols for the worship of Artemis (Diana), the goddess of fertility. Paul was bad for business. His preaching turned people away from buying the little shrines made by the silversmiths. The silversmiths, along with some of Paul's Jewish opponents, eventually drove him out of the city.

After leaving Ephesus, Paul again went through Macedonia and Greece, eventually making his way to Jerusalem with a collection for the Church there. On this lengthy journey, Paul kept in contact with many of the churches he had founded by writing letters. For example, he wrote letters to the Ephesians and the Romans. While he was in Ephesus, he also wrote two letters to the Corinthians and one to the Galatians.

These epistles form an important part of the New Testament and typically instructed the new Christians on points of doctrine, answered their questions, and gave much practical advice on Christian living. For example, the Corinthians had developed many bad habits while he was gone— some of them were not sharing food with the poor who were assembled for the supper that accompanied the celebration of the Eucharist; others got drunk at those times. Paul had to reprimand them that they were committing sacrilege by their behavior at the Eucharist (see 1 Cor 11:17–34).

Paul's Death

When Paul was in Jerusalem, his enemies tried to execute him, but Roman troops placed him under house arrest in Caesarea for a two-year period. As a Roman citizen, Paul had the right to have a trial before the emperor in Rome. After a long, harrowing trip that included a shipwreck on Malta, Paul eventually made it to Rome. There he lived in rented, but guarded quarters where he continued his work of meeting fellow Christians and spreading the Gospel.

Acts ends without telling us anything more about Paul. Clement I, Bishop of Rome (ca. 92–101), reports in a letter that Paul was acquitted and freed. Tradition says that Paul may have left Rome on still another missionary journey, perhaps to Spain, but that he came back to Rome during

CA. 110
Martyrdom of Ignatius of Antioch in Rome under Trajan's persecution

the reign of terror of the emperor Nero. According to that view, he was decapitated in AD 67.

At the time of Paul's death, Christianity had been established throughout the Roman Empire. Roman efforts to eradicate Christianity had begun, but the fruits of Paul's labors could not be undone.

❁ THEMES IN PAULINE THEOLOGY

B esides being the early Church's greatest missionary, St. Paul was also her greatest theologian. He has influenced Christian thinking about Jesus Christ more than any other theologian in history. In the Pauline letters, we find these central theological themes:

- There is only one God, the Father of our Lord Jesus Christ.
- Salvation takes place through Jesus Christ.
- The Death and Resurrection of Jesus are the heart of the Gospel.
- We will all share in Christ's Resurrection.
- Salvation is a gift from God. We cannot earn it. It requires faith.
- Christians are one body, the Church, of which Jesus is the head.
- We become sons and daughters of God in union with Jesus through the power of the Holy Spirit.
- The Holy Spirit is the soul of the Church who enables us to call God Abba, Father.
- We are brothers and sisters of Jesus and each other. We have dignity and thus should love one another.
- To be a disciple of Jesus means we must suffer for him gladly.

Growth Amidst PERSECUTIONS

Tertullian once remarked that "the blood of martyrs is the seed of the Church." Recall that the word martyr means "witness." It was costly to believe in and witness to Jesus in the first centuries of the Church. A believer might have to pay with his or her life. Some of these early persecutions are detailed below.

140
Justin Martyr writes his *Apology*

Split from Judaism

Many Jews did not accept Christianity, but they tolerated Jewish Christians as long as they kept the precepts of the Torah. Most of the early Christians were Jewish. Those who lived in Jerusalem continued to practice the Jewish religion. As Acts reports, however, Christian preaching was unevenly accepted by Jews outside the Holy Land. At times, the missionaries were forcefully ejected from synagogues and civil disturbances took place. Thus, the Gospel was preached to the Gentiles, who were not required to submit to the Jewish Law as a requirement for Baptism.

As noted previous, in Jerusalem Jewish authorities did not quite know what to do with the Christians. Men like Gamaliel cautioned prudence, but this did not stop the execution of Stephen, the beheading of James the Apostle, and the periodic arrest of leaders like Peter and Paul. The decade of the 60s brought an especially fierce outbreak of persecution. In 62, the Sanhedrin accused James, the leader of the Jerusalem Church, of blasphemy. He was thrown from the roof of the Temple and then stoned to death. Thus began a period of persecution against the Christians.

In 66, the Zealots, a radical Jewish sect that hated Roman rule, were successful in starting a revolution against Rome. This Jewish Revolt of 66–70 was a stunning act of defiance against Rome but ultimately failed miserably and led to the destruction of the Jerusalem Temple in 70. The Jews who survived the revolt felt betrayed by the Jewish Christians, who did not help fight due to their belief in Jesus, the Prince of Peace. As a result, Jewish Christians were not welcome in synagogues.

When some rabbis met to reorganize their faith and settle the Jewish canon of Sacred Scriptures, Christians were definitively excluded from worshiping with Jews. The Church shifted to major cities like Rome, Antioch, and Alexandria. By the end of the first century, Gentile Christians had assumed a major role in Church affairs. The Church's catholicity, present from the day of Pentecost, was of focus again as the Church expanded beyond her Jewish roots.

Roman Reaction to Christians

Rome, in general, was tolerant of new religions. Initially the Roman government did not distinguish between Christians and Jews, tolerating the new faith as another Jewish sect. Thus, Christians were afforded the same privileges granted Jews throughout the Empire, for example, exemption from serving in the armed forces.

CA. 185
St. Irenaeus writes *Against Heresies*

But as Christians grew more numerous and visible, and Christian preaching became more prominent, Rome began to change its view. The Jewish historian Josephus, and Roman writers like Tacitus, Suetonius, and Pliny the Younger accused Christians of being subversive, superstitious, atheistic, and immoral. For example, because Christians refused to worship the emperor—something Rome required to foster unity in the Empire—Christians were branded as both atheistic and subversive, a threat to civic harmony and, as atheists, responsible for the gods punishing citizens with plagues, invasions, and earthquakes. Christians were ridiculed for their beliefs in the Incarnation and Resurrection. They were also accused of cannibalism for their practice of the Eucharist. Non-believers often misinterpreted the fraternal love practiced by Christians, accusing them of engaging in unspeakable sexual perversions.

Most persecutions of the first two centuries were brief and limited to a certain area. For example, the historian Tacitus tells us about the emperor Nero's persecution of the Christians in 64. Although Tacitus held the common prejudices toward Christians, he did report that Nero falsely accused Christians of the burning of Rome in order to deflect blame from himself for starting the fire. Nero tortured and crucified Christians, igniting their bodies as a spectacle for the bloodthirsty crowds. According to Christian tradition, Peter died by crucifixion in the first wave of Nero's persecution in 64; Paul in the second wave of terror in 67.

> Mockery of every sort was added to their deaths. Covered with the skins of beasts, they were torn by dogs and perished, or were nailed to crosses, or were doomed to the flames. These served to illuminate the night when daylight failed. Nero had thrown open the gardens for the spectacle, and was exhibiting a show in the circus, while he mingled with the people in the dress of a charioteer or drove about in a chariot. Hence, even for criminals who deserved extreme and exemplary punishment there arose a feeling of compassion; for it was not, as it seemed, for the public good, but [to] glut one man's cruelty, that they were being punished. (Tacitus, *Annals*, 15.44)[1]

The most severe persecution of the first century took place under the emperor Domitian (81–96) who required his subjects to worship him as a god. The Christians who refused to do so were executed. The book of Revelation reports how authorities hunted Christians in the seven churches in Asia

Minor. Pope Clement I, Bishop of Rome, wrote of persecutions in Rome in the 90s.

Pliny the Younger, the governor of Bithynia, wrote a letter to the emperor Trajan (98–117). In a famous letter that he wrote to the emperor, he revealed Christianity was a crime punishable by death, although his personal policy was not to ferret out Christians for special punishment. If he discovered that someone was a Christian, he gave the person the opportunity to renounce the faith. If the person refused, execution followed. Trajan replied this way:

> My Pliny,
> You have taken the method which you ought in examining the causes of those that had been accused as Christians, for indeed no certain and general form of judging can be ordained in this case. These people are not to be sought for; but if they be accused and convicted, they are to be punished; but with this caution, that he who denies himself to be a Christian, and makes it plain that he is not so by supplicating to our gods, although he had been so formerly, may be allowed pardon, upon his repentance. As for libels sent without an author, they ought to have no place in any accusation whatsoever, for that would be a thing of very ill example, and not agreeable to my reign.[2]

Under the emperor Hadrian (117–138) the persecutions ceased for the most part. But they became fierce again under emperor Marcus Aurelius (161–180).

Septimius Severus (193–211) decreed capital punishment for anyone who would convert to a religion like Judaism or Christianity. Sts. Perpetua and Felicity were martyred during his reign.

Decius (249–251) required all citizens to have a certificate proving that they offered sacrifice to the pagan gods of the Empire. Decius put to death anyone found without this proof. At this time, many Christians committed apostasy, the sin of denying one's faith, to avoid being killed. When the general persecution subsided, Christian leaders had to determine how to welcome back, if at all, "lapsed" Christians who abandoned Jesus to save their lives.

Emperor Diocletian

The last and perhaps worst of all the Roman persecutions took place under Diocletian (284–305). His aim was to uproot Christianity from the Empire. He tried to do it by confiscating the property of Christians, destroying their churches and sacred books, banishing them to hard labor, subjecting them to a host of tortures, and inflicting

231
Origen founds school at Caesarea (Palestine)

the death penalty. As was true of every persecution throughout the Empire, though, the degree of enforcement of the decrees against the Christians varied from province to province.

❀ APOLOGISTS

Apologists wrote primarily to convince Gentiles—especially the emperors, Roman officials, and Roman citizens in general—of the truth and high morals of Christians. *The First Apology* was written by the most famous Christian apologist of the second century, St. Justin Martyr (ca. 110–165). Justin was a convert from paganism, a philosopher, and a prolific writer. Only a few of his writings were preserved. Justin addressed his *First Apology* to the emperor Antoninus Pius (138–161), generally regarded as a highly principled ruler whose reign was mostly peaceful.

From Justin Martyr's *First Apology*, 113, 118:

> So we are called atheists. Well, we do indeed proclaim ourselves atheists in respect to those whom you call gods, but not in regard to the Most True God, the Father of righteousness and temperance and the other virtues, who is without admixture of evil. On the contrary, we reverence and worship Him and the Son who came forth from Him and taught us these things. . . .

> We who formerly delighted in fornication now cleave only to chastity. We who exercised the magic arts now consecrate ourselves to the good and unbegotten God. We who valued above all else the acquisition of wealth and property now direct all that we have to a common fund, which is shared with every needy person. We who hated and killed one another, and who, because of differing customs, would not share a fireside with those of another race, now, after the appearance of Christ, live together with them. We pray for our enemies, and try to persuade those who unjustly hate us that, if they live according to the excellent precepts of Christ, they will have a good hope of receiving the same reward as ourselves, from the God who governs all.[3]

250
Persecution under Decius;
question of what to do with lapsed Christians

To the Ends of the Empire

The Acts of the Apostles concludes with Paul in Rome. This was Luke's way of saying that the new religion had moved way beyond Jewish roots in Jerusalem. It had made its way to the political, social, and cultural heart of the Roman Empire. Along the way, Christian churches had sprung up throughout the Empire. In spite of persecutions, the Church's enemies could not stamp out this new faith. Christianity continued to grow steadily in numbers and influence. Retracing the reasons for this astounding growth focuses on the following:

- *Jewish communities were established in the Diaspora.* The Diaspora is the name for the dispersion of Jews outside of Jerusalem. When Jewish Christians like Paul set out to preach the Gospel, they were able to use the synagogues as a home base. When the Jews rejected the Gospel, the missionaries turned to local Gentiles who were more receptive.

- *Ease of communication and travel.* People in the empire spoke a common language—Greek at first, then Latin. There was a good system of roads and shipping. There was a common culture. These systems helped the missionaries preach everywhere and eased their travels around the Empire.

- *Pax Romana.* Peace of Rome was a propitious time in human history that had experienced relative peace for twenty-five years at the time of Jesus' birth. This stability lasted for another two centuries during the time of the first Christian missionaries.

- *Words supported by action.* People of the day were searching for spiritual meaning. The new mystery religions and the philosophy of Stoicism helped some. But they could not rival the appeal of Christianity with its call to repentance and its inspiring moral code. Searching people experienced the truth in the doctrines of a loving God, forgiveness, and Christian care and concern for one another. Christians backed up their words with action. Christian love proved to be an irresistible magnet to pagans who were seeking more to life than Roman games, orgies, and meaningless idol worship. The care for the poor, widows, and orphans, plus the willingness to die for faith in Jesus, greatly appealed to pagans. "See how they love one another" gave hope to slaves, women, and the poor. The good news also appealed to the educated who sensed that life had to mean something more than worshiping corrupt and immoral emperors as god.

303–305
Great persecution of Christians under Emperor Diocletian

Early Church WRITINGS

Written records of Church history, doctrine, and faith began to take form short-ly after Jesus founded the Church. Following a period of oral history, the Scrip-tures and other writings emerged and served as catechetical manuals, witness statements, and liturgical guides.

Holy Scripture

Pre-eminent among the early Church writings are the books of the New Testa-ment, composed from around AD 50 (1 Thessalonians) to perhaps as late as AD 130 (2 Peter). The four Gospels recount the life and teachings of Jesus Christ. The Acts of the Apostles tells the story of the early Church, focusing on the min-istries of Peter and Paul. The thirteen epistles either written by or ascribed to St. Paul, the letter to the Hebrews, and the seven "catholic" epistles of 1–2 Peter, 1–3 John, James, and Jude are filled with theological reflection on Christ and in-structions on how to live a Christian life. The book of Revelation is a prophetic book with profound symbolism meant to bolster Christians to remain steadfast during persecution. These twenty-seven books are inspired, foundational, and normative writings for the Church.

The books of the New Testament helped combat heresy, that is, false belief or teaching about a major doctrine. One important reason the biblical books were gathered together into an official list of approved works (canon) was to combat the heretic Marcion (excommunicated in 144), who denied that a good God could have created the material world. Marcion held that the God of the Old Testament could not be the Father of Jesus, but was inferior to Jesus be-cause he was vengeful and cruel. Therefore, he rejected the Old Testament. He claimed that it was not worthy of Christian belief and held that it belonged to a lesser demigod. He drew up his own list of Christian books that he claimed were inspired by the true God.

To meet Marcion's and other heretical challenges, the early Church re-lied on the ordained bishops who traced their power and leadership directly to the Apostles. By the early decades of the second century, with a few ex-ceptions, Church leaders agreed on the official canon of the New Testament, recognizing that all the approved books taught correct doctrine (that is, were *orthodox*) and were somehow associated with an Apostle.

WHAT THE CHURCH BELIEVES ABOUT . . .
The Canon of Scripture

The complete list of books in the Bible is called the canon of Scripture. It includes forty-six books for the Old Testament (forty-five if Jeremiah and Lamentations are counted as one) and twenty-seven books for the New Testament. The Old Testament remains an indispensable part of the Bible. Its books too are divinely inspired and retain value.
See *Catechism of the Catholic Church*, 120–130.

Writings of the Apostolic Fathers

The apostolic fathers of the Church were those men who personally knew the Apostles or their disciples. Prominent among these was St. Clement, the fourth Pope (92–101), who might have known both Peter and Paul. His *Letter to the Corinthians* helped settle a dispute there and made a strong case for apostolic succession. Clement's letter became very popular in the early Church and was later used to help support Catholic belief in the primacy of the Pope. Another apostolic father, St. Ignatius of Antioch, sent letters to seven churches that stressed the role of the bishop.

The Didache

The *Didache* (the "Teaching") is a catechetical document that may have been written as early as AD 60 but most probably around AD 100. Its author is unknown. The *Didache* mentions Christian doctrines like the Trinity, moral teachings, and explains the rites of Baptism and Eucharist. On Baptism, the *Didache* provides these instructions:

> The procedure for baptizing is as follows: After rehearsing all the preliminaries, immerse in running water "In the Name of the Father, and of the Son, and of the Holy Ghost." If no running water is available, immerse in ordinary water. This should be cold if possible; otherwise warm. If neither is practicable, then sprinkle water three times on the head "In the Name of the Father, and of the Son, and of the Holy Ghost." Both baptizer and baptized ought to fast before baptism, as well as any others who can do so; but the candidate himself should be told to keep a fast of a day or two beforehand.[4]

Apologetic Writing

The apologists were second-century writers who defended and explained Christianity to nonbelievers. Some apologetic works, like St. Justin Martyr's *Dialogue with Trypho*, tried to explain to Jews that Jesus fulfilled Old Testament prophecies about the Messiah, that the Church was the New Israel, and that Christian teaching fulfilled the Torah. But most apologists defended Christianity against pagan charges that Christians were disloyal Roman citizens or morally corrupt. St. Justin Martyr (ca. 100–165) was a notable apologist who tried to convince pagan intellectuals that Christianity is the truest and most intellectually satisfying philosophy.

Tertullian (ca. 160–220) was the first major apologist to write in Latin. His *Apology* defended Christianity against charges of immorality, subversion, and economic bankruptcy. As a theologian, he constructed doctrinal formulas like "one substance, three Persons" for the Blessed Trinity and "one Person, two substances" for Jesus Christ. Unfortunately, in his later years, Tertullian embraced a heresy known as Montanism that preached the imminent coming of Christ and taught a rigorous form of asceticism—including the renunciation of marriage.

Writings of the Church Fathers

The Church Fathers is a traditional title given to theologians of the first eight centuries. The Church Fathers helped to write and form Church doctrine which has remained in great authority through the ages. The Church Fathers were found in both the East and the West and are esteemed for their correctness of doctrine (*orthodoxy*—right teaching), their holiness (*orthopraxis*—right living), their universal acceptance throughout the Church, and for the essential contributions they made to Christian doctrine in these formative centuries of the Catholic Church story. A list of the Church Fathers is found on pages 84–86.

Among the prominent writings of the Church Fathers, St. Irenaeus of Lyons (ca. 130–202) effectively argued against Gnosticism in his *Against Heresies*. He also highlighted the importance of Church Tradition for arriving at religious truth. He wrote that the source of right teaching and belief resides with the Roman Church (with the bishop of Rome, the Pope, as the head) because the Church was founded by Jesus and entrusted to St. Peter. Clement of Alexandria (ca. 150–215) stressed the divine nature of Christ, especially against the fifth-century heresy of Nestorianism, which argued that there are two persons in Christ. Clement's theology applied Platonic philosophy to explain Christian teaching, and he adeptly used the allegorical method to study the meaning of the Bible. Among the more than eight hundred works of Origen (ca. 185–254) was *Hexapla*, which provided the then critical edition of the Septuagint translation of the Old Testament. Origen taught three ways of interpreting Scripture: the literal, the moral, and the allegorical. Controversial in his lifetime, though many of his works were influential up to the Middle Ages and are esteemed even today, Origen also held some controversial theological positions that were later condemned. For example, influenced by Neoplatonic philosophy, he wrote that the Logos (Son) is subordinate to the Father in dignity and power. He also denied the existence of hell, preaching in its place the universal salvation of all.

WHAT THE CHURCH BELIEVES ABOUT . . .
Interpreting Sacred Scripture

The Second Vatican Council taught that there were three basic norms for reading and interpreting the Scriptures in light of their being inspired by God. First, the reader must pay attention to the total content and unity of the Bible, not isolated passages. Second, the Bible must be read in light of the Church's entire Tradition. Third, attention must be made to the "analogy of faith." This means the coherence of the truths of faith among themselves within God's entire plan for Revelation.
See *Catechism of the Catholic Church*, 112–114.

Early CHRISTIAN LIFESTYLE

Christianity had become distinct from Judaism and other religions in the Roman Empire. Through persecutions and other challenges, the early Christians increasingly developed into a recognizable Church. This community of faith crossed ethnic and racial lines to embrace all people. Common practices and beliefs of local Christian Churches throughout the Roman Empire included preaching the Gospel, public prayer, a ministry of care for each member, initiation rites, Eucharistic fellowship, and a common view of life and human destiny. Some specific Christian practices and beliefs of the early Church are discussed below.

Sacraments

The sacraments of the Church are rooted in the words and actions of Christ. The practice of the sacraments developed from the beginning of the Church. In the early Church, Christian initiation, like today, included the Sacraments of Baptism, Confirmation, and Eucharist. The period of preparation known

as the catechumenate could take three years. During this time, the candidate for Baptism, usually an adult, would learn Christian teaching and the requirements for moral living. Becoming a Christian was serious business, so the candidate often had a sponsor who testified to the candidate's good behavior and renunciation of pagan ways. Initiation typically took place on Holy Saturday. The bishop would lay hands on the candidates, absolve their sins, breathe on them, and sign the cross on their foreheads, ears, and nostrils. Later followed another anointing, the Baptism itself, and reception of first Holy Communion.

For the celebration of the Eucharist, Christians gathered in each other's homes on Sunday. Later, Christians met in donated houses or in enclosed places in a garden or cemetery. However, by the middle of the third century, Christians began to build their own churches to worship in. An *agape* (literally "love-feast") often accompanied the Eucharist to celebrate Christian fellowship and unity. This practice was eventually abandoned, probably because of abuses that crept in. Celebrants delivered homilies that showed the continuity between Jesus' teachings and the Old Testament.

The bishop was the chief celebrant of the Eucharist. Christians received the Body of Christ and often took the Blessed Sacrament home to consume during the week. Early Christians strongly believed in the healing effect of the Lord's presence in the Blessed Sacrament.

The history of the Sacrament of Penance is complex. As Baptism wiped away all sin, including mortal sin, early Christians believed that the baptized would never reject God's love. Human nature proved otherwise and Christians did commit mortal sin. The belief and practice developed that only the bishop could offer absolution from grave sins like murder, adultery, divorce, and apostasy. This could be done only once and only after the penitent performed long, arduous penances. Being separated from God's people was a serious matter.

A major question that arose in the third century concerned what to do with the *lapsi*, lapsed Christians, especially those who renounced the faith during times of persecution. In the third century, Novatian taught that no bishop could absolve a person who rejected Jesus Christ (apostasy), murdered, or committed adultery. His desire for a Church of perfect Christians led him to **schism**.

In contrast to Novatian's rigorist approach, Pope St. Cornelius (251–253) declared that mortal sins could be forgiven if sinners repented and performed the proper penances. (Pope St. Callistus had earlier decreed that mortal sin could be forgiven if a person was truly sorry.) Later, the Council of Nicaea (325) taught that dying people could and should be reconciled to the Church.

Ordained Leadership

Jesus established the basic organizational structure of the Church when he singled out Peter as the rock of the Church. Though it took several centuries for Church ministries to develop into the forms we recognize today, even from ancient times Church ministers have been called bishops, priests, and deacons. The ministerial priesthood is different from the common priesthood of the baptized in that it confers a sacred power for the service of the faithful.

Peter, along with the Apostles, including Matthias who replaced Judas, were the eyewitnesses to Jesus' public life. Early missionaries like Paul and Barnabas also took on the name *apostle* (meaning "one sent forth"). Their chief tasks—carried on today by their successors—the bishops and Pope—were to evangelize (preach the Gospel) and to witness to its truth. Their privileged role gave the Apostles the supreme authority in the many churches they founded both within and outside Palestine.

From the earliest days, *deacons* or assistants helped the Apostles in their work, for example, by taking up collections for the poor, visiting the sick, and distributing Communion. Widows—women of prayer and service—often helped, including assisting women into and out of the baptismal pools of water.

The first century also had prophets who explained God's word and encouraged their fellow Christians and teachers who instructed converts (1 Cor 12:28–30). The office of *episkopoi* (bishops) or overseers became more and more important. The bishops' main responsibilities were to preside at the Eucharist, preach, baptize, and forgive sin. Because the Eucharist was the central act of Christian worship and a vital sign of Christian unity, it was natural for Christians to look to their bishops for inspiration, leadership, and direction on questions that might cause a rift in Christian unity.

At first there was little difference between bishops and elders known as presbyters (priests). Some New Testament writings refer to them interchangeably. In the Jerusalem Church, for example, a council of elders served as a kind of senate. This council would meet with the Apostles to settle disputes. As the

Church grew, though, the office of overseer (the bishop) dominated that of the priest (elder).

By the mid-second century, the present-day order of the hierarchy (sacred leadership) took shape. First was the bishop who served as the focus of unity in the local church. He also represented his church at regional meetings and wrote letters to other communities. Next were the priests who presided over the Eucharist in place of the bishop who could not attend all the liturgies around his growing diocese. Last were the deacons who served the various needs of the local church. Both priests and deacons were subordinate to the bishop.

The Bishop of Rome, the man we call Pope today, also held an increasingly important position among the bishops. He was the successor to Peter, the first Bishop of Rome, and resided in the imperial city, the place of Peter and Paul's martyrdom. Christians presumed that the Bishop of Rome's teaching would be in line with apostolic teaching. Rome, as the center of the Empire, was the ideal place for Christian leaders to defend the Church when she was under attack. Other bishops increasingly looked to the Bishop of Rome for leadership when disputes arose. And many of them made sure that their own teaching was in line with his.

WHAT THE CHURCH BELIEVES ABOUT . . .
Bishops as Successors of the Apostles

Bishops trace their lineage, by divine institution, to the twelve Apostles whom Christ ordained at the Last Supper and also commissioned to ordain successors until the end of time. Like the original Twelve who were united under the leadership of Peter, the bishops since have been united under the Pope.

See *Catechism of the Catholic Church*, 861–862.

Summary

- Christianity is founded on Jesus Christ who lived from 6 BC to AD 30.

- The Acts of the Apostles details the early history of the Church, especially the preaching ministries of the Apostle Peter and the convert Paul, the Apostle to the Gentiles.

- The Council of Jerusalem (ca. 49) was significant because it decreed that Gentiles were not subject to the Jewish Law. This decision helped the rapid spread of Christianity throughout the Roman Empire.

- Christianity definitively split from Judaism after the Jewish Revolt of 66–70. At first Rome tolerated Christianity as another Jewish sect. However, eventually Rome saw Christianity as a threat because faithful Christians refused to worship the emperor, a practice required by authorities to promote unity.

- *Pax Romana*, the prevalence of Jewish communities throughout the Empire, a spiritual hunger for the Christian message, the witness of martyrs, and loving, committed Christians helped Christianity grow in numbers in the first few centuries.

- The formation of the canon of the Bible helped combat early heresies as did the writings of the Apostolic Fathers, apologists like Tertullian who defended Christianity against the charges of non-believers, and early theologians like Origen and St. Irenaeus of Lyons.

  – The Sacraments of Baptism and the Eucharist were celebrated from the first days of the Church.

  – Jesus established the basic organizational structure of the Church when he commissioned the Apostles to shepherd, sanctify, and teach and singled out Peter as the rock of the Church. Bishops exercised their ministry in communion with bishop of Rome, the successor of St. Peter. Bishops were assisted by deacons and priests.

  – The Bishop of Rome (Pope) had an important position of leadership among the bishops because he was the successor of Peter upon whom Jesus founded his Church.

Prayer REFLECTION

St. Paul's letter to the Ephesians, if authored by Paul, was written while he was in prison, perhaps between 61–63 in Rome. Some scholars, however, hold that because of the letter's style, word use, theology of Church, and other points of doctrine, a disciple of Paul may have composed it, perhaps between 80–100.

The letter to the Ephesians teaches how the Church is rooted in God's saving love, revealed in Jesus Christ. It contains many beautiful passages that praise and bless God in both hymns and prayers. Pray this prayer from Ephesians 3:14–21:

> For this reason I kneel before the Father, from whom every family in heaven and on earth is named, that he may grant you in accord with the riches of his glory to be strengthened with power through his Spirit in the inner self, and that Christ may dwell in your hearts through faith; that you, rooted and grounded in love, may have strength to comprehend with all the holy ones what is the breadth and length and height and depth, and to know the love of Christ that surpasses knowledge, so that you may be filled with all the fullness of God.

> Now to him who is able to accomplish far more than all we ask or imagine, by the power at work within us, to him be glory in the Church and in Christ Jesus to all generations, forever and ever. Amen.

Scripture CONNECTIONS

St. Peter was a towering personality in Christianity's growth from its humble beginnings. These passages help construct a chronological profile of Peter's life, on whom Christ founded his Church. Make a chart noting the events described.

Luke 5:1–11	Matthew 14:22–33	Matthew 16:13–20
Mark 9:2–8	Luke 22:54–62	Luke 24:1–12
John 21:15–19	Acts 2:1–42	Acts 3:1–4:31
Acts 9:32–10:48	Acts 11:1–18	Acts 15:7–11

Review and DISCUSSION QUESTIONS

1. Summarize the essential Gospel message preached by Jesus Christ.

2. Describe the opposition that led to Jesus' Death.

3. Why is Pentecost sometimes known as the "birthday of the Church"?

4. How did Judaism react to Christianity? What brought about the definitive break between Judaism and Christianity?

5. Explain the significance of the following to the spread of Christianity:

- the baptism of Cornelius by Peter;
- the ministry of Paul to the Gentiles,
- and the Council of Jerusalem for the spread of Christianity.

6. Discuss at least two themes in Pauline theology.

7. Describe the details of at least two Roman persecutions of Christians.

8. Discuss the major factors for the growth of Christianity from AD 30–305.

9. Discuss some ways the early Church confronted heresy.

10. How did the Apostolic Fathers and apologists contribute to the growth of the Church?

11. Describe how the Sacraments of Baptism, Eucharist, and Penance were celebrated in the early Church.

12. How did the leadership structure in the early Church develop?

13. Identify the following:

Events

Council of Jerusalem	Jewish Revolt (66–70)

People

Diocletian	Domitian
Gamaliel	Josephus
Marcion	Nero
Novatian	Origen
Pope St. Cornelius	St. Irenaeus of Lyons
St. Justin Martyr	St. Paul
St. Peter	St. Polycarp of Smyrna
St. Stephen	Tacitus
Tertullian	Trajan

Terms

Apologist	Apostle

Apostolic Father	canon (of the Bible)
Didache	*episkopoi*
Gnosticism	heresy
hierarchy	martyr
orthodoxy	*Pax Romana*
Pharisee	Sadducee
schism	Zealot

Learn BY DOING

1. Learn about St. Paul's life and missionary journeys by reading and reporting on the following chapters of Acts of Apostles:

   - Acts 9:1–31 (Saul's conversion; see also Gal 1:11–17 and Acts 22:6–8)

   - Acts 13:4–14:28 (First Missionary Journey)

   - Acts 15 (Council of Jerusalem)

   - Acts 16:1–18:22 (Second Missionary Journey)

   - Acts 18:23–21:14 (Third Missionary Journey)

   - Acts 21:15–28:31 (Paul's arrest, trials, and arrival in Rome)

2. Report on some aspect of "The Christian Catacombs of Rome" at this website: www.catacombe.roma.it.

3. Visit "Into His Own," an excellent website that gives perspective on Jesus and early Christianity: http://virtualreligion.net/iho. Report on some primary texts you read.

4. Read and report on a section from a writing of one of the Apostolic Fathers or apologists mentioned in this chapter. Check the following:

   - New Advent: www.newadvent.org/fathers

5. Report on the martyrdom of Sisters Perpetua and Felicity. You can find their biographies at one of these websites:

   - Catholic Online Saints: www.catholic.org/saints/saint.php?saint_id=48

   - Catholic Information Network: www.cin.org/saints/petandfel.html

3
The Spread OF CHRISTIANITY

So, following the saintly fathers, we all with one voice teach the confession of one and the same Son, our Lord Jesus Christ: the same perfect in divinity and perfect in humanity, the same truly God and truly man, of a rational soul and a body; consubstantial with the Father as regards his divinity, and the same consubstantial with us as regards his humanity; like us in all respects except for sin. . . .

—DOGMA DEFINITION
OF THE COUNCIL OF CHALCEDON (451)[1]

The Love OF A MOTHER

The American writer Washington Irving once said, "A mother is the truest friend we have." A mother's love for her child is incalculable. A mother's love has also been essential in the story of the Church. For example, without the persistent, dogged determination and faith of St. Monica, the core of Christian theology and the Church herself, would have evolved in an entirely different way. The intellectual heritage of Western Civilization would be greatly diminished had this woman of strength given up on her son.

Born a Christian in 332 in Tagaste, Algeria, Monica was given in marriage to a violent-tempered civic official named Patricius, a pagan, who was guilty of adultery throughout his marriage. Caught in an unhappy marriage, which included dealing with a difficult mother-in-law, Monica was not deterred from living a Christian life of prayer and almsgiving. Monica had three children with her husband, two sons and a daughter. Much to her regret, Patricius did not give her permission to have them baptized into the Christian faith. Her intellectually gifted older son was sent to school in Carthage to develop his academic talents. However, he caused her great concern because he was a carousing youth, lazy and attracted to a heretical sect at odds with Catholicism.

Monica was consoled at the conversion of her mother-in-law and husband the year before his death. Monica did not remarry. Her younger son was an exemplary child, and her daughter entered religious life. But Monica was heartsick that her wayward eldest son had not yet converted. Shedding many a motherly tear over him, she prayed, fasted, and badgered the local clergy and bishop to pray for his conversion. At one point, her bishop assured her, "It is not possible that the son of so many tears should perish."

Monica prayed even more and pursued him relentlessly. She followed him, his mistress, and young son to Rome. But he had left for Milan by the time she arrived. This did not deter her, and she followed him there.

In Milan she met bishop St. Ambrose, who was also a great preacher. Ambrose's words finally penetrated the heart of Monica's son. She was able to see the fruits of her faith and relentless prayer. After seventeen years of resistance, her son Augustine finally relented and was baptized.

On her way home to Africa in 387, Monica died in Ostia, near Rome. Shortly before her death, she told Augustine:

> Son, nothing in this world now affords me delight. I do not know what there is now left for me to do or why I am still here, all my hopes in this world being now fulfilled. All I wished to live for was that I might see you a Catholic and a child of Heaven. God has granted me more than this in making you despise earthly treasures and consecrate yourself to his service.

Augustine subsequently wrote, in one of Western literature's finest masterpieces—*The Confessions*—about his mother's life and death, asking the readers of his work to pray for his parents.

Monica's enduring love for her son brings to mind the observation of the famous American author Ralph Waldo Emerson, who said, "Men are what their mothers made them." St. Monica and St. Augustine share consecutive feast days of August 27 and August 28.

Their lives correspond with how Christianity became the official religion of the Roman Empire as it endured the assaults of the barbarians, the emerging Muslim faith, and internal threats of heresy. Nevertheless, the Church established deep roots in the West during the fourth through ninth centuries, the subject of this chapter. The topics treated are:

- Christianity as an official religion of Roman society

- Achieving doctrinal orthodoxy

- Barbarians, the fall of Rome, and the rise of the papacy

- Monasticism

- Fathers of the Church

313
Constantine issues Edict of Milan resulting in legalization of Christianity

- Muslim invasions
- Charlemagne and the Church.

Roman Politics AND CHRISTIANITY

A central figure in Church history was the Emperor Constantine, born around 280 to a sub-emperor of Rome and a Christian mother, St. Helena. Helena was later responsible for building many churches and basilicas, especially in Bethlehem and Jerusalem. Constantine commanded a large army in the Western Empire and found himself and his troops engaged in a crucial battle at the Milvian Bridge in 312 outside Rome. In his *Life of Constantine*, the Church historian Eusebius reported that the future emperor had a dream before the battle. The dream revealed that he would emerge victorious if he would place the Chi-Rho (☧ —the first two letters of Christ's name in Greek) on the shields and banners of his men. Constantine did so, won the battle decisively, and was named emperor of the Western Roman Empire.

The Edict of Milan

Once in power, Constantine and his Eastern counterpart, Licinius, issued the Edict of Milan in 313, which tolerated Christianity throughout the Empire. Although the Edict allowed *all* religions freedom of worship, special favors were granted to the Church. For example, clerics were exempt from taxation and confiscated property was returned to Christians. Most importantly, the hunting, torture, and execution of Christians came to a halt.

In 324, Constantine defeated Licinius and became the sole emperor, an absolute monarch who united the divided Empire. He moved the seat of government to Byzantium, which he renamed Constantinople, in modern-day Istanbul in Turkey. Now ruling from the Eastern part of the Empire, where some theological rifts (especially the Arian heresy) were threatening the unity of the Church, Constantine became personally active in Church affairs. Most notably, he dealt with Arianism, a heresy that challenged Christ's divinity, by convoking the first Ecumenical Council at Nicea in 325. (More information on Arianism is found on pages 72–73.)

Constantine's motives for embracing Christianity were most likely mixed. He favored Christianity because he saw it as a strong unifying force in the Empire, a force for the good. But he was also superstitious as evidenced by his dream and his reluctance to be baptized until shortly before his death so that

325
First Ecumenical Council at Nicea;
condemns Arian heresy while formulating the Nicene Creed

he could continue his aggressive ways. Christianity's monotheism, its lofty ethical code that embraced all people, and its hierarchical system of Church governing were strong points of unity for the widely diverse peoples of the Empire. This unity helped the Empire maintain order and stability, much needed at this time when the barbarians stepped up their push against the margins of the Empire's borders.

At his death, Constantine's sons assumed power. Constantius ruled in the East (337–361) and was sole emperor from 350–361. He favored Arianism, al-

lowing it to prosper. On the other hand, Constans—who ruled in the West from 337–350, promoted the orthodox Church teachings from the Council of Nicea. Julian the Apostate (361–363) ruled next. He unsuccessfully tried to stamp out Christianity and revive paganism. However, Christianity was so firmly established that it flourished; even emperors who favored Arianism did not want a return to paganism. By 350, there may have been thirty to forty million Christians, roughly 57 percent of the population in the Roman Empire.[2] Christianity's further triumph came in 380, when Emperor Theodosius I pro-mulgated an edict that ordered everyone in the Empire

➤ *Emperor Theodosius I*

to become a Christian. Christianity became the official religion of the Empire.

Consequences of Legalized Christianity

The legalization of Christianity radically affected the Church's future. On the plus side, the work of **evangelization** (preaching the Gospel) to non-believers and barbarians became easier. The emperors helped the Church convoke Ecu-menical Councils to help settle disputes and divisive heresies. Eight councils were held between the fourth and ninth centuries. All the councils took place in the East with the greatest participation by the Eastern bishops, although the decrees of the councils had to be confirmed by the canons and decrees of the Popes.

The rapidly growing Church adopted Roman styles of administration. For example, parishes and dioceses modeled themselves on Roman political divi-sions. Church provinces imitated their civic counterparts. Bishops in provin-cial capitals acquired more prestige and authority than other civic colleagues in the province. Rome, Constantinople, Alexandria, Antioch, and Jerusalem emerged as the five great patriarchates, with Rome preeminent because Peter

➤ **328–373**
Athanasius, Bishop of Alexandria

had been the first bishop there and died there. Popes like Damasus, Leo the Great, and Gelasius asserted their primacy, especially in the power vacuum that resulted after the Empire's capital moved to Constantinople.

The Church adopted the Emperor Justinian's Code of Law and applied it to her own government. In addition, the Church found suitable ways to adapt many features of pagan religions into her own practice. For example, the Church began to use candles and incense in liturgies. During this period, the Church also promoted the veneration of saints which gave the faithful heroes to look up to and imitate. The cult of saints helped keep many new converts from their worship of pagan gods.

In spite of all the benefits of legalized Christianity, the Church faced new challenges. Forceful emperors saw themselves as defenders of the Church, but their interference in Church affairs also led to abuses, the most severe of which was known as **caesaropapism**, the combining of the power of the secular government with the authority of the Church. The Eastern churches were especially subject to the whims of the political rulers. The Western Church was more independent due to the authority and proximity of the Pope, the relative weakness of the Western emperors, and the distance from the Eastern capital.

Another negative element of Christianity was that many people became Christians simply to keep their citizenship. Their commitment to the Gospel was lukewarm. Many superstitions lingered, for example, people invested relics with magical powers. Before Constantine's conversion, Christians witnessed to peace. However, by the fifth century, a soldier with Roman citizenship had to be baptized a Christian. Many churchmen became powerful secular rulers. They gathered wealth, waged war, and often put the affairs of the civic order before spiritual matters.

Facing Theological CHALLENGES

Articles of faith like the Blessed Trinity, the person of Jesus Christ, and the question of grace were each addressed in the fourth and fifth centuries. These were fertile years for bringing clarity to orthodox Christian faith at a time when new heretical teachings had arisen that threatened the unity of the Church.

Most of the theological debates of this era took place in the Eastern Church which was more populated with Christians. Two leading theological schools grew in prominence in the East, the first at Alexandria in Egypt, the second at Antioch in Syria. Leading Church Fathers from these schools fiercely debated the core faith issues with those claiming heretical views. The emperors based

330
Constantinople becomes the new capital of the Roman Empire

in Constantinople had a central involvement by convoking Ecumenical Councils to which the Pope sent legates.

Arianism

Arianism, in contrast with Gnosticism which denied Jesus' humanity, denied Jesus' divinity. Arius (ca. 250–336) was a priest from Alexandria who was greatly influenced by Greek philosophy and its exalted belief in God. A human God was incomprehensible to Arius under this view. Borrowing from Plato's idea of a *demiurge* (the creator of the material universe who was not identical with the supreme God), Arius held that Christ was God's greatest creature who was made before time, but a creature nonetheless. His teaching that Christ was an adopted son and not divine had grave consequences for Christian teaching on salvation. Only God can effect Redemption. If Arius was right and the incarnate Word of God was not God, then humans would not really be redeemed. Even a meeting with the leaders of the Alexandrian church, and the Egyptian bishops that condemned him, could not swing Arius's teaching or the heresy that spread like wildfire throughout the Empire.

The Church Responds to Arianism

Constantine convoked the First Ecumenical Council of Nicea (325) to confront Arianism, hoping to preserve the unity of the Church and peace in the empire. Three hundred bishops, mostly from the East, came to Nicea, a small town near Constantinople. They quickly condemned Arius's teaching and offered a creed that spelled out clearly that Jesus is "consubstantial" with the Father, that is, Christ possesses the same nature as God the Father. Catholics recite this creed at Mass today, proclaiming Jesus' divinity and equality to the Father:

> We believe in one Lord, Jesus Christ
> the only Son of God,
> eternally begotten of the Father,
> God from God, Light from Light,
> true God from true God,
> begotten, not made, one in Being with the Father.

Arianism was slow to die out after the Council, but Arians led by Eusebius, the bishop of Nicomedia, and other Arians supported by Constantine's successors continued to teach the heresy, especially in the East and to invading barbarians.

•··

381
First Council of Constantinople condemns
Macedonianism and finalizes the Nicene Creed

St. Athanasius (ca. 297–373), the bishop of Alexandria, defended the Church, and reiterated Nicene teaching on Christ's divinity. He firmly taught that Christ "was made man that we may be made divine." He correctly held that if Christ were not God then he could not be our Savior. Only God could restore people to communion with him. Three Eastern Church Fathers—St. Basil of Caesarea (ca. 330–379), his younger brother St. Gregory of Nyssa (ca. 330–395), and St. Gregory of Nazianzus (329–389)—supported Athanasius and continued to appeal to moderate Arians, who held that the Son was "like to" the Father or "substantially like" the Father.

St. Ambrose (ca. 340–397), the bishop of Milan and a Father of the Church, helped combat Arianism in the West. He clashed with the Empress Justina when she tried to establish an Arian church in Milan. Under Ambrose's advice, the emperor Theodosius issued a series of edicts outlawing Arianism and paganism.

The teachings of the Council of Nicaea were confirmed at the Council of Constantinople in 381. The Council also corrected another heresy— **Macedonianism**—which held that the Son *created* the Holy Spirit who was in turn *subordinate* to the Father and the Son. The Council firmly taught the divinity of the Holy Spirit, but did not address the relationship between the Son and the Holy Spirit. (This unaddressed issue would later be a major factor in the schism between the Church in the East and the Church in the West.)

When Pope Damasus accepted the Creed that came from Constantinople at a synod in 382, the Arian threat to the Catholic faith within the Empire was, by and large, over, though it continued to survive in some barbarian tribes.

Christological Debates

After the Council of Constantinople, theological debate focused on how Christ was both divine and human. The Alexandrian school maintained that Christ's perfect divinity so penetrates his human nature that an internal unity results, like a blending or mixture of his human and divine natures. Antioch theologians stressed Christ's perfect humanity as if his divinity indwelled in the man Jesus as a person might live in a tent.

Nestorius, the patriarch of Constantinople, heightened the debate when he refused to acknowledge that Mary could be the Mother of God. He held that there were two *persons* in Christ—one divine, the other only human and that Mary was only *Christotokos*, mother of the human Jesus. St. Cyril of Alexandria (376–444) defended the title *Theotokos* for Mary, that is, "God-bearer" or

382
St. Jerome begins his translation of the Bible into Latin (the Vulgate)

Mother of God. He also taught that Jesus was one divine person, the Second Person of the Trinity. The Council of Ephesus (431) endorsed the position of St. Cyril and condemned Nestorianism.

WHAT THE CHURCH BELIEVES ABOUT . . .
Mary

Of all her titles, Mary's most exulted is "Mother of God." Jesus never ceased to be God either in the womb or after he was born. And his mother was Mary. As Cyril of Alexandria wrote,

> When (the Word) took his most chase body, animated by an intelligent soul, from the Holy Virgin, and came forth a Man, he did not cease to be God nor did He reject the dignity of his own preeminence; for in this, as I said, no change is known. (*Against the Emperor Julian*, 8)

The Church confesses that Mary is *Theotokos*, Mother of God.

The Council of Ephesus did not end all the Christological debates raging during the fifth century. After the death of St. Cyril, the chief abbot of the monks at Constantinople and other Alexandrian theologians voiced disagreement with the Ephesus formula and preached that Christ's human nature was absorbed into his divine nature "like a drop of honey into the water of the sea." This teaching became known as **Monophysitism**, which held that Christ possessed only one nature—a divine nature. In effect, Monophysitism denied that Christ was really a human being.

At the subsequent Council of Chalcedon (451), the doctrine of the hypostatic union was taught by Pope Leo I and endorsed by the council. This doctrine taught that in Jesus Christ, one divine person subsists in two natures, the divine and the human. Leo wrote:

> Accordingly while the distinctness of both natures and substances was preserved, and both met in one Person, lowliness was assumed by majesty, weakness by power, mortality by eternity.[3]

The council fathers proclaimed that "Peter has spoken through the mouth of Leo." They affirmed the teachings of the councils of Nicea, Constantinople, and Ephesus.

Monophysitism took root in Egypt, especially among the Copts, and various emperors tried to tone down the definition of Chalcedon to secure the loyalty of the dissidents in the Empire. The Third Council of Constantinople

385
Bishop Ambrose defies the Empress

(681) was convened to restate prior teachings: Jesus Christ is one divine person with two distinct natures—one human, the other divine. The Third Council of Constantinople also declared that because Jesus has two natures, he has two wills—one divine, the other human.

Through most of the Christological debates, the West was beset with one major theological question, the interaction of divine grace and human freedom resulting from whether or not people can save themselves due to their own good efforts, and one major concern, that all people accept Christ as their Savior. Pelagius, a popular monk-teacher from Britain who taught in Rome, reacted to the moral laziness in Roman society that absolved humans from personal responsibility in pursuit of the good. In contrast, Pelagius wanted to emphasize human freedom and the need to strive for personal holiness. Eventually, however, he held an exalted view of human nature, denying that the Original Sin of Adam and Eve had been transmitted to humans. Consequently, he argued that humans do not need divine assistance, or grace, as a help to achieve personal holiness or salvation. In effect, Pelagianism held that humans could save themselves without God's supernatural help.

St. Augustine of Hippo (354–420) was Pelagius's major opponent. His brilliant explanations demonstrated that humans are born with fallen natures tainted by Original Sin and its effects. He taught that God's grace is absolutely necessary for personal salvation. Pelagianism was officially condemned at the Council of Ephesus (431).

Although Pelagianism died out by the sixth century, the Protestant Reformation of the seventeenth century would once again take up issues like the relationship between good works, grace, and salvation. And commentators have observed that remnants of Pelagian self-reliance, with its denial of the need for God's grace and help, appear in many twenty-first century Europeans and Americans. So many self-sufficient contemporaries seem to rely on human ingenuity and the discoveries of science, technology, and medicine as the sources of their personal safety and salvation.

WHAT THE CHURCH BELIEVES ABOUT . . .
Freedom and Grace

God made us in his own image and likeness. Like God, we have a mind and a free will. God wants us to choose eternal life as intelligent and free human beings. This means that his freedom in giving us his grace must be met by our intelligent freedom in responding to his grace. See *Catechism of the Catholic Church*, 2002.

391–392
Emperor Theodosius makes Christianity the official religion of the Roman Empire

The Fall of Rome AND ITS AFTERMATH

Rome was attacked by the Visigoths in 410. To make sense of the sea of change taking place, St. Augustine wrote his brilliant *City of God*. The year 476 traditionally marks the definitive collapse of the Roman Empire in the West. Its existence can be traced to 27 BC. The collapse was a cataclysmic event for pagans and Christians alike. Pagans blamed Christians and their God for the collapse of Rome. Christians questioned how God could permit the deaths of innocents and the destruction of the center of civilization. More accurately, the division of the Empire between East and West deeply affected the West when the barbarian invasions of the fifth century overwhelmed Rome. For the Church, the fall of Rome was also an opportunity for out of it the Pope emerged as a strong leader, the Church found a champion in Clovis of the Franks, and the Church engaged in missionary activity to convert the barbarians.

Barbarian Invasions

Even decades before the birth of Christ, the "migration of nations" from the East to the West had begun. For several centuries, the Roman Empire had its hands full trying to keep the various barbarian migrations from overwhelming Europe. In the fourth century, the Asiatic Huns migrated West to benefit from its fertile lands and economic opportunities, and to gain protection from other warring tribes. Members of Germanic tribes had engaged in trade with Romans for centuries and had served as mercenaries in Roman armies.

After the middle of the fourth century, increases in population, the declining strength of the Roman armies, and further pressure from the Huns heightened the invasions into the Western Empire, now too weak to protect itself. With the death of the emperor Theodosius in 395, the way was open for the beginning of the end of the Empire in the West, an Empire that had grown weak through decaying morals and softness of life, an overextension of boundaries, and an inability to sustain its economy. The Visigoths besieged Gaul and Spain, the Vandals stormed North Africa, and the Ostrogoths and Lombards assaulted Italy. With the imperial forces now centered in Constantinople, Italy and Rome were especially vulnerable to attack. In 410, Rome fell to the Visigoth leader Alaric. The Vandals were on the doorstep of Hippo in Africa in 430, the year of St. Augustine's death. The city of Rome fell in 455, and the barbarian leader Odoacer deposed the last Rome emperor (Romulus Augustulus) in 476.

397–401
St. Augustine of Hippo writes *Confessions*

410
Visigoths sack Rome

Byzantine Empire

The Empire continued to exist in the East as the Byzantine Empire. The Byzantine emperor Justinian, who ruled from 527–565, married a popular actress, Theodora, who as empress had a strong influence on her husband. Justinian's general, Belisarius, defeated the Vandals in North Africa, the Goths in Italy, and the Visigoths in Spain. These victories gave Justinian control of Rome. But he was often at odds with the Popes, even imprisoning some of them because of Theodora's sympathies toward the heretical Monophysites. The aftermath of his ineffective leadership was local schisms in Italy and ill-fated military campaigns. Positively, Justinian supervised the rebuilding of the magnificent church Hagia Sophia (Holy Wisdom) in Constantinople that still stands today as a museum. He also instituted a major reform of civil law to reflect Christian values known as the Justinian Code. It is a collection of laws written in Latin that became the basis of European law. Its Christian orientation gave women and children more protection. But it still reflected the customs of its times, like bodily mutilation for some crimes and repressive measures against non-Christians, including the Jews.

Justinian's successors were weak. They tried to play the patriarch of Constantinople against the Pope. Both of these Byzantine emperors and the patriarchs of Constantinople were reluctant to take direction from the Pope in Rome. This helped contribute to the tragic schism between Eastern and Western Christianity in 1054. But Eastern Christianity had many positive contributions: a vibrant liturgical life, exquisite art and music, and a spiritual depth that resulted in hundreds of monasteries. The Eastern Empire survived, though greatly weakened until its ultimate demise in 1453 under the Ottoman Turks. The Ottomans were Muslim, followers of the Islamic faith. Islam would eventually shake the very foundations of Eastern Christianity.

The Rise of the Papacy

The fall of Rome brought with it a leadership vacuum which the Church, the only organized institution left, was able to fill for the benefit of the people. The Pope, the Bishop of Rome, became a leading figure in the Western world.

Pope Leo the Great (440–461) was Bishop of Rome in the Empire's last days. Pope Leo brought some order to a chaotic situation. He managed the affairs in Rome, fed the poor and, in 451, bravely convinced the feared Attila the Hun to spare Rome. Leo's most significant contribution was his ability to use biblical, historical, and legal arguments to assert the primacy of the Pope

431
Council of Ephesus affirms that Mary is the Mother of God and condemns Nestorius

among all bishops, taking the title *Pontifex Maximus* ("Highest Bridge Builder"), used formerly by the emperor to describe his role as high priest in the Roman religion. While the primacy of the bishop of Rome as head of the Church had been recognized from her earliest days, from Leo's time on, other bishops also looked to the Pope as supreme teacher, ruler, and judge in the Church, though the Patriarch in Constantinople would challenge this claim over the centuries.

Another outstanding Pope of the next century was Gregory the Great (590–604). He was the first to assume the title "Servant of the Servants of God." Through his many sermons, letters, books, commentaries, and reform of the liturgy (where he introduced a type of singing called "Gregorian chant"), Gregory secured the authority of the Pope and stabilized the Church throughout Europe and he promoted missionary activity.

Conversion of Clovis

In the secular arena, the Church gained strength in the West by allying itself with powerful allies, including the Franks. A fierce people, the Franks conquered other tribes in northern Gaul in the second half of the fifth century and established a kingdom there. Clovis, the king of the Franks, was baptized into the Catholic faith in 496, following the lead of his Christian wife, Clotilda. Clovis turned on the heretical Goths, who had converted to Arian Christianity, and forced them to accept the orthodox faith. The alliance with the Franks helped Catholicism gain a strong foothold among the barbarian tribes. A general rule of the time was "as the leader goes so goes the tribe." If the king converted, the people would follow his lead. The Magyars became Catholic because of the conversion of their king, St. Stephen; the Bohemians because of the baptism of St. Wenceslaus; the Poles because of the conversion of their leader, Mieszko.

Missionaries of the Era

The conversion to Christianity, though aided by the conversion of the rulers, took many centuries of missionary work and evangelization to accomplish in many places. This work was also hastened by the establishment of monasteries.

A case in point was the legendary work of St. Patrick (389–461), known as the "Apostle to Ireland." Born a Roman citizen in Britain, the son of Christian parents, Patrick was captured by

➤ *St. Patrick*   Irish pirates when he was sixteen and enslaved in Ireland. He learned the customs and a difficult language of the Celtic tribes there. After six years of captivity, he returned to Britain and then entered a monastery in Gaul. Made a bishop in 432, Patrick returned to Ireland where he vigorously traveled throughout the island and converted most of the local Celtic kings while establishing monasteries to continue the work of evangelization and education. Gradually, many Irish converts were attracted to the monastic life either as monks or nuns. Isolated from the wars on the European continent, Irish Christianity thrived and helped to preserve Christianity in the so-called Dark Ages. Many great missionaries like the great St. Columban (543–615) were spawned in Ireland. They in turn went to spread the faith to Scotland, Switzerland, Germany, and northern France.

Conversion of the Anglo Saxons in Britain was due to a combination of the missionary work of St. Augustine of Canterbury (d. 605) and the Benedictines along with the peaceful welcome they received from the Anglo-Saxon king Ethelbert. King Ethelbert converted to Christianity because of the loving witness of the missionaries. However, Ethelbert did not force conversion on his people, a policy that was compatible with Pope Gregory the Great's words of instruction to Augustine:

> Destroy as few pagan temples as possible; only destroy their idols, sprinkle them with holy water, build altars and put relics in the buildings, so that, if the temples have been well built, you are simply changing their purpose. (*Letters*, XI, 56)[4]

It took nearly a century from the time of the first missionaries before all of Britain became Christian. One British monk, St. Boniface (675–755) evangelized on the continent and was made a bishop, setting up monasteries to aid in the work of converting the pagans, and engaging in a wandering ministry of direct contact with his potential converts in Germany. He preached with gentleness and won over the pagans by challenging the tribal gods. A famous story tells of how he chopped down a sacred oak tree dedicated to Thor, a Frankish god. When Boniface was not killed by Thor, many pagans converted. Acting in the spirit of Pope Gregory, Boniface constructed a chapel with the wood from the tree, thus incorporating an important pagan symbol into Christian life.

Boniface developed an effective relationship with the Frankish leaders —first, Charles Martel and then his son, Pepin the Short. As the Pope's representative, he crowned Pepin Frankish king in 751. This helped to cement an alliance between the Franks and the papacy that would bear great fruit under Pepin's son, Charlemagne (see pages 91–92). Boniface ultimately gave up his

451
Council of Chalcedon condemns Monophysitism
and defines the two natures in Christ

position as bishop and went to the Netherlands as a missionary. He was martyred there in 755.

The Influence OF MONASTICISM

As noted, the missionary efforts of the Church among the people of northern Europe were greatly aided by monasticism and its monks who took up the task of evangelization. Monasticism was a spiritual and social movement in which men and women withdrew from the world to live solitary or communal lives to attain personal holiness. Monasticism had roots in the earliest days of the Church when both men and women took up a celibate lifestyle, practiced works of self-denial, prayed daily, and engaged in the works of mercy.

Monasticism, derived from the Greek word *monos*, which means "alone" or "single," is a form of Christian asceticism that took root from the early fourth century. It is characterized by abandoning the ordinary world to pursue Christ more perfectly. Opportunities for martyrdom were less in a political world that was tolerant of Christianity. Monasticism became an opportunity to live discipleship to its extremes.

Monks withdrew to deserted places to directly confront Satan (who was supposed to live in deserts) and their personal demons, which resulted from their own sinful natures. Monasticism was understood as a kind of "bloodless martyrdom," a way of witnessing to the faith and pursuing pure Christian holiness.

WHAT THE CHURCH BELIEVES ABOUT . . .
Spiritual Perfection

The way of perfection passes the way of the Cross. St. Gregory of Nyssa wrote of seeking out spiritual perfection: "He who climbs never stops going from beginning to beginning, through beginnings that have no end." Spiritual progress consists of asceticism, penance, and mortification that gradually lead to the spiritual peace and joy of the Beatitudes. See *Catechism of the Catholic Church*, 2015.

Origins of Monasticism

St. Anthony of Egypt (251–356), a **hermit**, is considered to be the first Christian monk and served as the father of the movement. Around the age of twenty, Anthony withdrew to live an intense life of prayer, meditation, Bible reading,

476
The last Emperor, Romulus Augustulus,
is deposed by Odoacer, a German general

fasting, and penance in a desert cave. Anthony's reputation grew. Younger hermits sought him out to learn from him, living in nearby huts and caves.

St. Pachomius (292–346), a contemporary of St. Anthony, organized the first monasteries in 320. A group of people would follow a simple role of communal sharing, celibacy, and obedience to a superior. Monks gathered for Mass and worked at simple jobs. The communities were self-sustaining. The monastic movement caught on quickly. In the East, Church Father St. Basil the Great (329–379), developed a form of communal living that stressed poverty, simplicity of living, and obedience to the abbot (father) of the monastery. Basil, a bishop, encouraged intellectual study among the monks. The main "work" of his monks was to be in prayerful union with God; however, they were also to engage in works of charity for poor and sick people. His ascetical writings formed the foundation of Byzantine monasticism.

In the West, another Church Father, St. Athanasius (ca. 295–373), spread the ideal of Egyptian monasticism while he was exiled in Trier. His *Life of St. Anthony* was especially popular and greatly promoted the ideal of monasticism to Western Christianity. In France, St. Martin de Tours (316–397) established monasteries from which he and his monks evangelized the barbarians.

Irish monasteries became important centers for learning. Monks copied and illustrated sacred texts and preserved Western learning during the unsettled times of the barbarian invasions. The monastery became the center of Church life in a society lacking cities and organized parishes. Village Christians, as well as those in the countryside, gravitated to the monks for spiritual direction. In Ireland, the monks introduced the practice of frequent devotional confession, using books known as *Penitentials* to guide them in assigning uniform penances. When Irish monks served as missionaries on the Continent, they encouraged the practice of frequent confession, a practice that caught on in the Church. Recall that the Sacrament of Penance was received once a lifetime for the most serious sins. It included the assignment of severe penances that could last for years before the sinner could be readmitted to the community. The Irish practice of frequent recourse to the sacrament caught on for the whole Church.

WHAT THE CHURCH BELIEVES ABOUT . . .
Frequent Confession

One of the precepts or laws of the Church is that "You shall confess your sins at least once a year." Frequent confession allows for adequate preparation for the Eucharist and continues the graces of Baptism for conversion and repentance. See *Catechism of the Catholic Church*, 2042.

496
Baptism of Clovis and conversion of the Franks to Christianity

Rise of Convents

Monasticism was not just a rural phenomenon or a male-only one. Monastic life provided safe haven for women and nourished their spiritual and intellectual growth. Their prayers and charitable works were a force for good in tumultuous times.

Convents are the name for "monasteries for women." St. Brigid of Ireland (452–525) established several convents in the fifth century, including a unique double monastery at Kildare, Ireland—one for men and one for women—a center for learning and missionary activity. St. Jerome (ca. 342–420), a leading Church Father, founded a monastery for men in Bethlehem, as well as several convents for women there. The monks and nuns followed the same basic rule. St. John Cassian (360–433) and his sister established a double monastery in Marseilles around 416. St. Honoratus (350–429) founded a monastery on the island of Lérin in France; it became the training ground for many monk-bishops. His sister Margaret also established a convent there.

The Benedictines

Benedict of Nursia (480–547), the patron saint of Europe, founded the most influential form of monasticism. In 529, he built his famous, self-sustaining monastery on Monte Cassino, south of Rome. Not far from there, Benedict's twin sister, St. Scholastica (480–543) founded a monastery for women. The monks and nuns, who came from ordinary life, were taught to read so they could study the Bible and read their daily prayers. They lived a simple, practical form of monasticism, one marked by prayer and work (*ora et labora*, in Latin).

Benedict is noted for his *Rule* for religious communities that he composed at Monte Cassino. Building on the experience of monks like Pachomius, St. Basil, St. Jerome, and others, the *Rule of St. Benedict* is a practical approach to religious life based in moderation—two meals a day, a little wine, adequate clothing, sufficient sleep. Benedictines took the vows of poverty, chastity, and obedience to the abbot (for men) or abbess (for women), an office held for life. These vows and Benedict's *Rule* became the model for Western monasticism. They characterize religious community life in the Catholic Church to this day.

Benefits and Drawbacks of Monasticism

There were many benefits to monasticism for the Church and society, including the following:

527–565
Justinian, Emperor of the East;
authorizes the Justinian Code

- Economically self-sufficient monasteries provided the rural countryside a good example of land management and helped reestablish agriculture after the barbarian invasions.

- The monks taught respect for the liturgy and the value of prayer in daily life. Monasteries were spiritual beacons. They provided a countercultural response to a Christianity that had grown tepid.

- Monasteries were islands of stability in unsettled times. They gave refuge to travelers. And as centers of learning, they educated many future Church leaders who often administered secular affairs as well.

- As missionary centers, monasteries Christianized Europe. They kept Christianity alive and spread it.

But monasticism did have some negative effects. For example:

- Monastic asceticism sometimes went overboard. For example, some monks engaged in self-mutilation to tame their weak human nature. St. Jerome praised celibacy so much that he ended up teaching that marriage is not a means to holiness, but a necessary evil.

- Monasticism taught a double standard of spirituality. The educated people in the Church were often monks who held the "religious life" as the only true model of holiness. A healthy lay spirituality was neglected for centuries.

✸ SOME PROVISIONS FOR COMMUNITY LIFE FROM THE *RULE OF ST. BENEDICT* ON VARIOUS TOPICS

Laughter: Guard your lips from harmful or deceptive speech and speak no foolish chatter, nothing just to provoke laughter; do not love immoderate or boisterous laughter.

Obedience: Obey the orders of the abbot unreservedly, even if his own conduct—which God forbid—be at odds with what he says. Remember the teaching of the Lord: Do "what they say, not what they do" (Matt 23:3).

Prayer: On hearing the signal for an hour of the divine office, the monk will immediately set aside what he has in hand and go with utmost speed, yet with gravity and

529
St. Benedict of Nursia establishes his monastic order

without giving occasion for frivolity. Indeed, nothing is to be preferred to the Work of God.

Respect: Wherever brothers meet, the junior asks his senior for a blessing. When an older monk comes by, the younger rises and offers him a seat, and does not presume to sit down unless the older bids him. In this way, they do what the words of Scripture say, "They should each try to be the first to show respect to the other" (Rom 12:10).

Temperance: We read that monks should not drink wine at all, but since the monks of our day cannot be convinced of this, let us at least agree to drink moderately, and not to the point of excess, for, "wine makes even wise men go astray" (Sir 19:2).

Work: Idleness is the enemy of the soul. Therefore, the brothers should have specified periods for manual labor as well as for prayerful reading.[5]

The Fathers OF THE CHURCH

The fourth and fifth centuries were the pinnacle years of the "Age of the Fathers" of the Church. Their great intellects and holiness of life were major influences on their times and future directions for the Church. Their writings helped combat heresy, explain the collapse of the Roman Empire to their contemporaries, and formulate doctrine for all time. Many of these Fathers have been mentioned in passing in this chapter, but here special mention must be made of four: the Greek Father, St. John Chrysostom, and the three Latin Fathers: St. Ambrose, St. Jerome, and St. Augustine.

St. John Chrysostom (ca. 344–407)

Born and raised in Antioch, John Chrysostom was nicknamed "Golden Mouth" because of his skills as a preacher. Ordained a priest in 386, he began a preaching ministry in Antioch that won him high acclaim, leading to his consecration as bishop of Constantinople in 398. There, his fiery rhetoric against moral laxity in high places earned him the enmity of the Empress Eudoxia; the hatred of the local clergy whom he tried to reform; and the displeasure of other influential people, including the patriarch of Alexandria who was jealous of

553
Second Council of Constantinople

590–604
St. Gregory the Great's pontificate; model for medieval papacy

him. John was driven into exile, reinstated to his post as bishop, and exiled a second time, eventually resulting in his death.

St. Ambrose (ca. 340–397)

Ambrose, a Roman noble and governor of Milan, became bishop in an unusual way. When a riot broke out in the city over who was to succeed the late Arian bishop, Ambrose led his military guard to the cathedral to peacefully settle the affair. In the meantime, the people shouted for Ambrose to be made bishop. He tried to dissuade the crowd from this appointment, claiming that he was not even baptized. But after fleeing and hiding from the populace, and on the advice of the emperor, he finally gave in and accepted the lofty office of bishop. In rapid order, Ambrose received the sacraments of initiation (Baptism, Confirmation, and the Eucharist), was ordained a priest, and consecrated a bishop. He immediately gave away his wealth to the Church and the poor of the city.

Ambrose proved to be a quick study, learning Scripture and theology from the most learned priest of his day—Simplician. He was known for his administrative and legal skills. He argued effectively against the Arians, who had great influence at the imperial court. As advisor to the Emperor Gratian, he convinced him to outlaw all heresy in the Western Empire. He melted down and sold Church treasures to pay ransom for captives taken by the invading Goths. He lectured the rich to share their wealth with the poor. He refused Arian Empress Justina's demands that he surrender his basilica to the Arians, lecturing her against civil interference into Church affairs. He excommunicated the Emperor Theodosius until he repented for his barbaric act of slaughtering thousands of innocent civilians to avenge the death of one of his generals.

St. Jerome (342–420)

Born in northeast Italy, Jerome was sent to Rome as a young man to study the Latin and Greek literature of ancient Rome. His early education in the classics inspired him to lifelong study and helped make Jerome perhaps the most learned of all the Church Fathers. At the age of eighteen, he accepted Baptism. After further travels and study, he entered a strict monastic community near his home at Aquileia where he continued his studies, including the difficult Hebrew language. Later, in Antioch, Jerome had a vision which criticized him for his devotion to secular learning, for being "a follower of Cicero and not of Christ."

Ordained a priest in Antioch, Jerome then traveled to Constantinople and studied under the Church Father, Gregory of Nazianzus in 380. He eventually made it back to Rome to serve as Pope Damasus's secretary. Jerome was a fierce polemicist with an explosive temper, often using his sharp pen to write fierce letters to his opponents. The Pope saw beneath Jerome's sometimes-irascible personality, however, and discovered in Jerome a man of unique holiness, learning, and integrity. As a result, the Pope commissioned Jerome to translate the Bible into Latin, a task that eventually took him to Bethlehem. There he founded a monastery for men and several convents for the noblewomen who were his Scripture students in Rome.

Laboring relentlessly in a cave, Jerome, with the help of his disciples, completed his translation and commentary of the Bible into Latin, a task that took twenty-three years. Known as the Latin Vulgate translation (382–405), it became the authorized Bible used in the Catholic Church up to modern times.

In his later years, Jerome also wrote against Pelagianism and Origenism and corresponded with St. Augustine. As an old man worn down with a number of infirmities, he died peacefully. He is recognized as one of the Church's greatest minds and defenders of orthodox faith. St. Augustine said of him, "What Jerome is ignorant of, no man has ever known."[6]

MEMBER OF THE CHURCH

St. Augustine: THE MAN AND HIS WORK

The greatest of the Church Fathers was St. Augustine, the most influential theologian following St. Paul. He was born in Africa in 354 and raised a Christian, though not baptized one (see pages 67–68). A brilliant student, Augustine studied the Latin classics and mastered law and rhetoric in Carthage where he ended up teaching.

During his youth, Augustine abandoned Christianity and lived with a mistress for fifteen years. When he was eighteen years old, he fathered a son by the name Adeodatus. After some years, Augustine began to grow intellectually restless. He joined the Manicheans, a heretical group that rejected the Old Testament and lived an austere life of self-discipline. For a time, this soothed his guilty feelings over his sexual morality.

622
The Hegira, the beginning of the Muslim faith

638
Jerusalem falls to the Arabs

Conversion and New Life

Augustine eventually made his way to Rome where he opened a school for boys. Within a year he secured a teaching job in Milan. There he came under the influence of Ambrose, Milan's eloquent bishop. Ambrose's sermons clarified Augustine's problems with the Old Testament and helped put in his heart a burning desire to change his life. In his spiritual autobiography, *The Confessions*, Augustine tells how he converted to Jesus Christ, accepting baptism in 387:

> I was . . . weeping . . . when all at once I heard the sing-song voice of a child in a nearby house. . . . "Take and read, take and read." At this I looked up, thinking hard whether there was any kind of game in which children used to chant words like these, but I could not remember ever hearing them before. I stemmed my flood of tears and stood up, telling myself that this could only be a divine command to open my book of scripture and read the first passage on which my eyes should fall. . . .

> So I hurried back to the place where Alypius was sitting, for when I stood up to move away I had put down the book containing Paul's epistles. I seized it and opened it, and in silence I read the first passage on which my eyes fell: "Not in carousing and drunkenness, not in sexual excess and lust, not in quarrelling and jealousy. Rather, put on the Lord Jesus Christ, and make no provision for the desires of the flesh (Romans 13:13–14)." I had no wish to read more and no need to do so. For in an instant, as I came to the end of the sentence, it was as though the light of confidence flooded into my heart and all the darkness of doubt was dispelled.[7]

His New Life

After his conversion, Augustine went back to Africa. His mother, St. Monica, died as they were returning home. When he arrived in Africa, his beloved son also died. Augustine founded a monastery and became so popular with the people that he was named bishop of Hippo in 396. From that post, this remarkable man became an eminent preacher and a sensitive pastor who lived simply in the midst of his people. He organized works of charity, administered the sacraments, and served as judge in the bishop's

681
Third Council of Constantinople condemns Monothelitism
and defines doctrine of two wills in Christ

court. Furthermore, he tirelessly defended the Catholic faith against heresies like Donatism, Pelagianism, and Manicheism. In addition, Augustine authored some of Christianity's most influential theological works.

Augustine's final years saw the dissolution of the Roman Empire. He lived to see the Vandals' invasion of North Africa and grieved to see the destruction of many churches and the persecution of many Christians. He opened Hippo to refugees and comforted them in their sorrow. Augustine died on August 28, 430, before he could see his own beloved diocese sacked by the Vandals.

The Writings of St. Augustine

Among St. Augustine's most famous writings are his *Confessions* and *On the Trinity*, a brilliant theological treatise on the Blessed Trinity still studied today. Another famous work is *The City of God*, which he wrote in the wake of the Visigoth Alaric's sack of Rome in 410. *The City of God* is a sweeping view of human history. It divides history into a massive struggle between the sinful inhabitants of the City of Man, exemplified by the dying Roman Empire, and the pilgrims or believers in God who live in the City of God. Citizenship in these cities depends on one's values. Augustine points out, however, that the Church is not automatically the City of God. Because the Church includes sinners, it must always cooperate with God's grace and work diligently to be a sign of God's active love in the world.

The Rise OF ISLAM

"There is no God but Allah, and Mohammed is his prophet." In 610, an Arabian merchant, Mohammed (570–632), had a conversion experience. Mohammed claimed that the angel Gabriel visited him and gave him a series of revelations which his followers recorded in the Koran (Qur'an). Mohammed lived in Mecca for ten years after his conversion, teaching and developing his faith, but in 622, he and his followers met persecution. Their flight—called the **Hegira**—is the event that marks the first year of the Muslim era. Mohammed raised an army there and returned to Mecca as a triumphant warrior. Their new faith, called Islam ("submission" in Arabic), spread like wildfire across the Arabian deserts.

After Mohammed's death in 632, his early successors spread the Islamic faith through previous Christian areas like Damascus (635) and Antioch (637) in Syria, Jerusalem (638) in Palestine, Alexandria (642), and Carthage (695)

711–712
Arabs conquer Spain, destroy the Visigoth Kingdom

719
St. Boniface begins conversion of the Germans

in Northern Africa, Persia (ca. 650), Cyprus, southern Italy, and even parts of Spain (711). A war-weary, collapsing Empire was virtually defenseless against the onslaughts of Islam. Although Muslims in general did not force their vanquished peoples to convert, they did impose taxes on the "infidels" (non-believers). This was incentive enough for many Christians to embrace Islam, especially in the East.

Fortunately for Christian survival, divisions within Islam over leadership helped weaken its forward thrust. The emperor Leo the Isaurian checked Eastern expansion in 717. And in the West, the Franks under Charles Martel ("the Hammer") finally stopped the Muslim advance at the Battle of Tours (or Poitiers) in 732.

Consequences for Christianity

The Islamic invasion had enormous consequences for Christianity. The three ancient patriarchates of Jerusalem, Antioch, and Alexandria fell; as a result, their influence in the Church ceased. The Eastern Empire was continually occupied with fending off the advancing Muslims. Before the founding of Islam, Christianity had embraced the Mediterranean Basin, running from West to East. Now in the West, the axis shifted from the south in Rome led by the papacy to the northern kingdom of the Frankish dynasty—the Carolingians—who was the Pope's strongest ally in these perilous times.

Because the Muslims controlled the Mediterranean Basin, Europe became economically, socially, and culturally isolated. The disorder and strife of the age helped create the feudal system in which feudal lords made their own law and often declared war on their neighbors. However, the cooperation between the Franks and the Church helped create the Christian Middle Ages and spread Christianity throughout Europe.

Muslims became the adversaries of Christians for the next seven centuries. It took several centuries for Christians to pull out of the Dark Ages. Eventually, Christianity launched a series of holy wars, the Crusades, to win back the Holy Land. Though the Muslim invasions were a major setback for Christianity, Muslim scholarship helped preserve ancient Greek learning. Scholars like Avicenna (Ibn Sina, 980–1037) and Averroës (Ibn Rushd, 1126–1198) helped introduce the philosophy of Aristotle to the West. During the High Middle Ages, theologians like St. Albert the Great and St. Thomas Aquinas would use Aristotelean philosophy to advance Catholic philosophical and theological thought.

732
Charles Martel stops Muslim invasion in Gaul

✳ FIVE PILLARS OF ISLAM

The "Five Pillars of Islam" include the religious obligations of Muslims:
1. **Faith**: "There is no God but Allah and Mohammed is his prophet."
2. **Prayer**: five times a day while bowing in the direction of Mecca.
3. **Fasting**: a total fast from sunrise to sundown during the holy month of Ramadan.
4. **Almsgiving**: charitable giving to the poor, travelers, those engaged in a holy war, etc.
5. **Pilgrimage**: Once a lifetime, if possible, every Muslim must go to the holy shrine of the Ka'bah in Mecca.

The Holy ROMAN EMPIRE

With the aggressive nature of Islam, and the expansionist activities of the Lombards who captured Ravenna, the Byzantine emperor was becoming less able to help protect the West. This forced the Pope to look to the Franks for protection. At first he turned to Charles Martel, who saw no personal benefit to enter into an alliance with the papacy against Lombard aggression. But not so with his successor, Pepin, who saw it much to his advantage to ally himself with the Pope.

Under Pepin's way of thinking, aligning himself with the Pope would gain him status as the legitimate Christian ruler of the Franks. Pepin had recently usurped the Frankish throne from Clovis's descendants, the Merovingians, and he petitioned Pope Zachary to declare him the legitimate ruler because he (Pepin) held de facto power. Pope Zachary consented by having St. Boniface crown Pepin king in 751. The next Pope, Stephen III (752–757), recognized Pepin as king and his sons' right to succeed him. Subsequently, when the Church appealed to Pepin for protection against the Lombards, Pepin's forces not only defeated them but also returned to the Pope several previously captured territories.

Pepin recognized the Pope as ruler of a large part of Italy, granting him control of a wide strip of land in the middle of the Italian peninsula. This controversial grant of land to the papacy and the right to rule it—called the Donation of Pepin (756)—was enormously important for the Pope's secular power and provided a major source of revenue for the papacy.

751
Carolingian Dynasty begins in France

The Crowning of Charlemagne

Pepin's son, Charlemagne ("Charles the Great"), was a devoted family man, devout Christian, visionary ruler, and ideal knight. Charlemagne's goal was the Christianization of Europe.

After the death of his brother in 771, Charlemagne emerged as a powerful king who ruled for forty-three years until his death in 814. He was relentless in combating the Lombards. After Charlemagne defeated the Lombards in 774, the Pope gave him the title "Protector of the Papacy." In gratitude to Charlemagne, the Pope submitted to his directives on how to rule the Papal States. A vigorous military leader, Charlemagne believed in the forceful conversion of conquered peoples, like the Saxons. Among his many military campaigns, Charlemagne did suffer military setbacks. A notable one was a near disaster as part of a campaign against Spanish Moors. As part of that campaign, a battle fought in 778 at Roncevalles, in the Basque-controlled Pyrenees, was the inspiration for the famous medieval classic, *The Song of Roland*. Eventually, Charlemagne did capture Barcelona, and made it the capital of the Spanish March. By the year 800, Charlemagne had created the most powerful empire in the West since the Roman Empire.

Pope Leo III recognized Charlemagne's importance to Western Christianity by crowning him Holy Roman Emperor at the Christmas Mass in Rome in 800. The Holy Roman Empire included a territory that in name included present-day Europe, but was now centered in Aachen (Germany). The creation of the Holy Roman Empire alienated the Byzantine Empire. It clearly indicated the Church's break from the East. For the next four hundred years, the Pope would crown the Holy Roman Emperor, stressing that the Catholic faith was the principle of unity holding together the various, often warring, groups in the West.

For his part, Charlemagne had a genuine love of the Church evidenced by his establishment of monasteries and schools for the training of clerics and others. He arranged for the copying of manuscripts. He appointed educated bishops and directed them to reform the clergy throughout the realm. He donated property and money to the Church and insisted on tithing to support the Church's work. He also adopted the *Roman Sacramentary* for use in the liturgy, hoping that the common use of Latin would be a unifying force throughout the Empire.

When Charlemagne died in 814, the Holy Roman Empire resembled what would become modern Europe. Unfortunately, the Empire would soon divide into East and West. Viking invasions from the north and the lack of strong

787
Second Council of Nicea: allows veneration of sacred images

imperial leaders led to feudalism with its system of patrons and vassals. For both Europe and the Church, feudalism became the dominant political, social, and economic system during the coming difficult centuries. Chapter 4 will look more closely at feudalism. It will also report the story of much needed papal reform. The revitalization of the papacy would be a major factor in the full blossoming of Christendom in the Middle Ages of the twelfth and thirteenth centuries.

800
Pope Leo III crowns Charlemagne head of the Holy Roman Empire

Summary

- With Constantine's Edict of Milan (313), Christianity became a tolerated religion. Constantine saw in Christianity a unifying force in the Empire. One of his motives for convoking the First Ecumenical Council at Nicea (325) was to confront the heresy of Arianism which was tearing Christianity apart. In 380, under the Emperor Theodosius, Christianity became the official religion of the Roman Empire. Legalization of Christianity helped the efforts of evangelization. The Church also benefited from Roman methods of administration and the Justinian Code of law. On the down side, the state got too involved in the affairs of the Church. And since everyone had to be Christian, the quality of religious commitment declined.

- A series of Church councils helped settle doctrinal debates that had generated various heresies, especially during the fifth and sixth centuries. The Council of Nicea condemned Arianism, proclaimed the divinity of Jesus Christ, and issued a creed of major Christian beliefs. It was reaffirmed at the Council of Constantinople (381). This council also condemned Macedonianism, which erroneously taught that the Son created the Holy Spirit. St. Cyril of Alexandria and the Council of Ephesus (431) taught that Jesus is one divine person and that Mary is truly the Mother of God (*Theotokos*). The Council of Chalcedon (451) adopted the position of Pope St. Leo the Great's *Tome*. Jesus, one divine person, possesses both a human and a divine nature. The Second Council of Constantinople (681) reaffirmed Chalcedon. It further defined that Jesus had a human will as well as a divine will. St. Augustine of Hippo successfully argued against the heresy of Pelagianism which denied Original Sin and the need for grace to obtain salvation.

- After the collapse of Rome in 476, the Pope and bishops were looked to more and more as civic as well as religious leaders. Pope Gregory the Great (590–604) was especially effective in stabilizing central Italy and serving the people of Rome.

- Monasticism was a strong force for Christianity's growth. St. Anthony of Egypt was the first Christian monk; St. Pachomius founded the first monasteries; and St. Benedict's *Rule* was the model for future monasteries. Monasteries became centers of learning and evangelization, islands of stability in unsettled times, and spiritual beacons for tepid Christians.

- The fourth and fifth centuries were the pinnacle years for Fathers of the Church. St. John Chrysostom was a fiery preacher; St. Ambrose, an adept administrator; and St. Jerome, a fierce polemicist. Jerome's translation of the Bible into Latin—the Vulgate—was a monumental achievement. The greatest Church Father, however, was St. Augustine of Hippo. He authored some of theology's greatest Christian works including his *Confessions*, *On the Trinity*, and the *City of God*.

- The Western Church allied itself with the Franks after their king Clovis converted to orthodox Christianity. The ties to the Franks were further tightened under Pepin who donated the Papal Estates to the papacy in exchange for approval of his dynasty. When Pepin's son Charlemagne was crowned Holy Roman Emperor in 800 by Pope Leo III, the Church and state were united in an alliance that would prove decisive in the Middle Ages.

- The Muslim invasion resulted in the loss to Christianity of Syria, Palestine, Egypt, Africa, and Spain. It isolated the Western Church from the Eastern Church and contained the spread of Christianity for five centuries.

- The last strong Eastern emperor was Justinian, whose legal Code became the basis of European law. The Patriarch of Constantinople also became subservient to the emperor. In an alliance known as caesaropapism, both emperor and patriarch were reluctant to take direction from the Bishop of Rome. This helped lead to the tragic Great Schism in 1054.

Prayer REFLECTION

This prayer of great faith is attributed to St. Patrick.

Celtic Benediction
May the strength of God pilot us.
May the power of God preserve us.
May the wisdom of God instruct us.
May the hand of God protect us.
May the way of God direct us.
May the shield of God defend us.
May the host of God guard us
   —Against the snares of the evil ones,
   —Against temptations of the world.

May Christ be with us!
Christ above us!
Christ in us,
Christ before us.

May thy salvation, Lord,
Always be ours,
This day, O Lord, and evermore.[8]

Review and DISCUSSION QUESTIONS

1. Discuss the consequences for Christianity in the aftermath of the conversion of Constantine.

2. How did the Church deal with doctrinal heresies that surfaced in the fifth through seventh centuries? Discuss the teachings of three of these heresies.

3. List three doctrinal truths about Jesus Christ that emerged from the early Ecumenical Councils of the Church.

4. How did the Western Church cope with the barbarian invasions?

5. Discuss the contributions of Pope Leo the Great and Pope Gregory the Great to the growing prestige of the papacy.

6. What was the significance of the conversion of Clovis?

7. What were some of the long-term effects of the conversion of Ireland and Britain for European Christianity?

8. What was the appeal of monasticism? How did it contribute to the growth of the Church?

9. Discuss the contributions of any three Fathers of the Church who lived in the fourth or fifth centuries.

10. How did Islam initially impact Christianity?

11. Name and discuss some steps that led to the creation of the Holy Roman Empire.

12. Identify:

Events

Edict of Milan	Fall of Rome
Battle of Tours	Conversion of Clovis
Council of Nicea	Council of Ephesus
Council of Chalcedon	Charlemagne's coronation
First Council of Constantinople	Third Council of Constantinople

People

Arius	Charlemagne
Charles Martel	Justinian
Mohammed	Pepin

Saints

Ambrose	Anthony of Egypt
Athanasius	Augustine of Canterbury
Augustine of Hippo	Benedict
Boniface	Brigid of Ireland
Cappadocian Fathers	Cyril of Alexandria
Gregory the Great	Jerome
John Chrysostom	Leo the Great
Monica	Pachomius
Patrick	

Terms

Arianism	caesaropapism
Donation of Pepin	Hegira
hypostatic union	Justinian Code
Koran	Macedonianism
monasticism	Monophysitism
Pelagianism	Theotokos
Vulgate	

Scriptural CONNECTION

Read the qualifications of a good bishop according to one of the Pastoral Epistles written toward the end of the first century or beginning of the second: **1 Timothy 3:1–7**.

Learn BY DOING

1. Report on one of the heresies or Church councils mentioned in this chapter.

2. Report on one of the saints mentioned in this chapter. Some websites on the lives of the saints include these:

   - for scholarly sources: The Internet Medieval Sourcebook: www.fordham.edu/halsall/sbook3.html#earlymed
   - Patron Saints: www.catholic-forum.com/saints/indexsnt.htm
   - American Catholic.org—Saints: www.americancatholic.org/Features/Saints/byname.asp
   - Saints and Angels: www.catholic.org/saints

3. Research and report on one of the following:

   - the influence of Roman law on the Christian Church
   - places of worship in the early Church
   - Christianity's use of pagan customs

4. Prepare a report on the reasons for the fall of the Roman Empire.

5. Visit a monastery in person and report on the lifestyle of the monks who live there. If this is not possible, visit the website of the Monastery of Christ in the Desert and report on the work of the monks there: www.christdesert.org. Follow their links to discover other monasteries.

6. Read and briefly summarize the Edict of Milan: www.fordham.edu/halsall/source/edict-milan.html

7. Read and report on any three chapters from Einhard's *Life of Charlemagne*: www.fordham.edu/halsall/basis/einhard.html

8. Read about and report on the early history of Byzantium at the Metropolitan Museum of Art: www.metmuseum.org/explore/Byzantium/byz_1.html. Be sure to check out the bust of Constantine.

4
The Church
IN THE MIDDLE AGES

The Dictates of Pope Gregory VII (1073–1085)

- That the Roman Church was founded by God alone.
- That the Roman pontiff alone can with right be called universal.
- That he alone can depose or reinstate bishops.
- That of the Pope alone all princes shall kiss the feet.
- That it may be permitted to him to depose emperors.
- That he may be permitted to transfer bishops if need be.
- That no synod shall be called a general one without his order.
- That he himself may be judged by no one.
- That the Roman Church has never erred; nor will it err to all eternity, the Scripture bearing witness.
- That he who is not at peace with the Roman Church shall not be considered Catholic.
- That he may absolve subjects from their fealty to wicked men.[1]

St. Francis and CHURCH RENEWAL

The Middle Ages formed the "middle" period in a classical division of European history into three ages from the time of the Roman Empire to modern times. The Middle Ages—also known as the medieval period—are commonly dated from the fifth century division of the Roman Empire and barbarian invasions to the Protestant Reformation of the sixteenth century. This chapter covers a portion of the Middle Ages from the ninth to the thirteenth centuries.

Though a period in the Church marked with controversy, division, and ultimately one of healing and new strength, the person who best defines the era is St. Francis of Assisi. He remains a Catholic saint beloved by all Christians. This is both ironic and appropriate as this era was marked by a schism in the Church before recommitment to orthodox teaching and practice. The son of a wealthy Italian cloth merchant, and a bon vivant as a young man, Francis gave his life to Christ at the age of twenty. Influenced by Jesus' words to the rich young man who was asked to give up everything (Mt 10:7–10), Francis distributed all his earthly possessions to the poor, wandered the countryside to preach the Gospel, and begged from the rich to give to the poor.

Before long, Francis's life of absolute poverty and unselfish devotion began to attract other men of his hometown of Assisi. They too sold their possessions and joined Francis in his life of service. These new partners and structure required that Francis write a rule for his brothers which he did in 1209. He also decided to seek formal approval for his rule in Rome.

Francis's local bishop put him in contact with Cardinal Ugolino, the nephew of the great Pope of the Middle Ages, Innocent III. The cardinal was apprehensive about the new rule since it lacked the prescriptions for communal life that were the norm in other religious orders. Further, Francis's radical poverty might have suggested that Francis was influenced by the Albigensians, a heretical group that preached the inherent evil of material possessions.

➤ *St. Francis of Assisi*

However, the cardinal saw much good in Francis and arranged for him to meet the Pope in the splendid Lateran Palace. Pope Innocent III looked askance at the disheveled, tunic-clad beggar and considered him to be a swineherd. He dismissed Francis and his rule and instructed him to go find his pigs and preach to them.

Francis was not to be deterred. He found the nearest pig sty, smeared mud on himself, and then returned to the Pope. Innocent was impressed with this strange man. He sent him away to get cleaned up and consented to see him again. After Francis explained his rule, Innocent acknowledged Francis's sincerity, but questioned whether his followers would be able to live it. Francis replied that the Lord Jesus would provide for him and his disciples.

Pope Innocent took the matter up with a consistory of his cardinals, most of whom did not favor Francis's

843
Treaty of Verdun divides Charlemagne's
Empire into three parts

858–867
Pontificate of Nicholas I

lifestyle of absolute poverty. However, one cardinal observed that these men only wanted to live the Gospel, arguing that it would insult Christ to forbid them since he commended his followers to do so. A decision was delayed until Francis could explain himself once again.

God's will cannot be thwarted. The night before the meeting with Francis, the Pope had a strange, fearful dream in which he saw the Lateran church shaking and the church walls ready to cave in. Suddenly, a small ordinary-looking man clad in peasant garb, barefoot, with a rope securing his tunic, rushed to the tottering building. He placed his shoulder against its wall and pushed until the church straightened once again.

The Pope was convinced that Francis of Assisi was meant to build up the whole Church. At the meeting the next day, he gave verbal approval for Francis's rule. Thus, approval was granted to this itinerant preacher. Through the centuries, he became the spiritual father of more than thirty communities of male religious orders and three hundred provinces of female religious.

This meeting of the Pope and poor preacher represents a marriage between the stature and influence the Church achieved during the Middle Ages and her core roots of discipleship and dependence on God's providence. On the one hand, Pope Innocent III typifies the heights of the medieval papacy and the splendor the Church achieved in the age of Christendom, the ideal of a unified society guided by Christian beliefs, piety, and values. On the other hand, St. Francis of Assisi represents the Gospel lived in all of its radical beauty and stark simplicity. Francis is one of history's true originals—a lover of nature, which he saw as a reflection of the Beauty of the Creator. Unlike the monks of his day, Francis did not withdraw from the world. Rather, he engaged the world by ministering directly to the poor in the growing cities of medieval society. His witness to the Gospel is timeless. And words attributed to him speak to the hearts of Christians as much today as they did centuries ago: "Preach the Gospel always, and if necessary, use words."

Chapter 4 will examine the era of Pope Innocent III and St. Francis—the High Middle Ages—by highlighting these topics:

- the Dark Ages and Feudalism
- the Rise of the Medieval Papacy
- the Eastern Schism
- Hallmarks of Christendom:
  - Crusades

863
Missionaries Cyril and Methodius, brothers, become Apostles to the Slavs and fathers of Slavonic literature

- Mendicant Orders
- Cathedrals
- Universities
- Scholastic philosophy
• Decline of Papal Influence.

WHAT THE CHURCH BELIEVES ABOUT . . .
Identifying with the Poor

Detaching oneself from riches is necessary for securing entrance into the Kingdom of Heaven. Jesus calls on everyone to prefer him to everything and everyone. "Everyone of you who does not renounce all his possessions cannot be a disciple," Jesus said (Lk 14:33).
See *Catechism of the Catholic Church*, 2544.

The Dark Ages AND FEUDALISM

Christianity had a strong influence on the medieval world for two reasons: a sense of unity in the area known as the Holy Roman Empire and a strong papacy that provided vision and leadership.

The ideal of a holy, Christian empire never came to full fruition when Charlemagne died. His sons and grandsons fought for control of the Empire. Their disunity led to the Treaty of Verdun (843) which fragmented the Empire into three main regions: France, central Europe (as far south as Italy), and eastern Europe. With this political breakup of the Holy Roman Empire, disorder and civil wars followed. Weak leaders caused even more fragmentation. With the lack of central authority, anarchy was just around the corner. Europe was open to a new wave of invaders. Ordinary people had no recourse but to turn to the only available group able to protect them—the armed nobility. A system of vassaldom emerged, and a feudal society gained prominence. Sadly, this state of affairs also affected the papacy which suffered a serious decline in the coming centuries.

Political and Religious Instability

Civil war brought political instability, which in turn led to the economic and social system of feudalism which rested on strict division among social classes:

869–870
Fourth Council of Constantinople; Photius condemned

nobility, clergy, and serfs who farmed the land of the nobility. Land fell into the hands of warriors who defended it. They in turn pledged themselves as vassals to stronger lords. The more powerful lords, including kings, granted fiefdoms to their vassals in exchange for loyalty in times of war.

Because the Church was a landholder, she too got caught up in the web of economic and political relationships which was feudalism. Some bishops and abbots became powerful barons involved in vassal relationships and endless warfare. Their spiritual responsibilities often fell by the wayside. Other bishops became vassals of strong lords and even kings. This made them subservient to secular leaders and led to the practice of **lay investiture** by which secular lay leaders (like the Emperor of Germany, Otto I) selected the bishops throughout their domains.

Lay investiture and Church involvement in feudalism led to many abuses. One of these was **simony**, the buying and selling of Church offices, usually to a lay person, for financial gain. The feudal system handsomely rewarded the holder of Church offices. Men who aspired to Church positions were often greedy and unspiritual. To secure power, they willingly took orders from the barons and kings.

Another abuse was the decline of the morals of the clergy. For example, although various Popes and councils had called for clerical celibacy, worldly bishops did little to enforce it or to educate their clergy. Many priests married. Others took mistresses. Still others tried to pass on Church lands and benefits to their children or relatives (called **nepotism**). Barons protested nepotism because it kept them from economic gain; they wanted to take up the lands of the bishops when they died and then resell them to the highest bidder.

WHAT THE CHURCH BELIEVES ABOUT . . .
Simony

Simony is defined as the buying or selling of spiritual things. The term comes from an incident in the Acts of the Apostles when Simon the Magician offered money to the disciples when he saw that the Spirit was conferred by the laying on of hands (see Acts 8:18–25). It is impossible to receive spiritual blessings in exchange for money. All spiritual blessings come from God alone without payment.
See *Catechism of the Catholic Church*, 2121.

909
The reform monastery of Cluny is founded

The Popes Under Feudalism

Pope Nicholas I (858–867) stands out as the rare strong Pope in the era of feudalism. He successfully influenced secular rulers. Nicholas also involved himself in a controversy with the Eastern Church. Ignatius, the patriarch of Constantinople, had been deposed by the emperor and replaced by Photius. Nicholas sided with Ignatius, excommunicated Photius, and thereby began the so-called Photian Schism.

In general, though, the papacy of the ninth through the first half of the eleventh centuries was filled with corruption. For example, because the Pope ruled the Papal States, his office became desirable for the dominant noble families who wanted to rule these lands. For example, the Theophylact, Crescentii, and Tusculani families vied for control of the Roman Church and manipulated papal elections in a scandalous way, at times even putting adolescents, as well as the most incompetent people imaginable, on the throne of St. Peter. The Popes were mere pawns in the hands of these wealthy nobles. The fact that the Church did not veer from the teaching of true doctrine or morals and that she survived this era of papal corruption is proof that Christ is indeed faithful to his promise: "And behold, I am with you always, until the end of the age" (Mt 28:20).

Otto the Great of Germany (b. 912) was the most effective emperor of the tenth century. In 962, he pressured one of history's worst Popes, John XII, to crown him emperor in Rome in 962. In a year's time, Otto deposed John and appointed his own Pope. His two successors followed suit; thus the German nobles controlled the papal states for nearly a century. Not until the eleventh century under more forceful Popes would the papacy gain control of the nobles.

A New Wave of Invasions

As the Frankish kingdom declined, Europe became vulnerable to a new set of invasions. The Norsemen ravaged England and Ireland, demolishing most of the important monasteries that had served as centers of learning and missionary work. Danish Vikings penetrated deep into Europe, cruising up and down rivers and pillaging everything in their path. They destroyed Hamburg and sacked Paris. For fifty years they terrorized Europe. Meanwhile, the Muslim Saracens renewed their attacks, even successfully raiding Rome and destroying several shrines there. From the East came the ancestors of the Hungarians, the Magyars, who raided Germany, central France, and Italy until they were turned back by Otto the Great in 955.

936–973
Reign of Otto I

One of the reasons this era was called the "Dark Ages" was because of the havoc wreaked by these invasions. Many Europeans thought the world would end soon. The Frankish empire collapsed, learning declined, Church discipline weakened, feudalism took a firm grip, and the papacy became corrupt. Was there no hope of emerging from these perilous times?

Light Out of the Darkness

In 910, the layman William of Aquitaine donated land for a new Benedictine monastery, Cluny, in France. From its founding the monastery was to be free of the corrupt control of lords and bishops. It had free elections of abbots and was answerable only to the Pope. Prayer was to be the primary activity, and a strict observance of Benedict's *Rule* was the norm. Serious Christian discipleship, sacrifice, and generosity to the poor became the hallmarks of the Clunaic lifestyle.

As a result, Cluny became a fountainhead of reform activity. It founded many daughter monasteries, answerable only to Cluny. This helped unify Christian communities all over Europe and wrested some control of the Church from the secular authorities. Within two hundred years, more than twelve hundred monasteries adopted Clunaic reforms.

Several able abbots from Cluny, for example, Odo and Odilo, called for a general reform in the Church. Free from the clutches of feudalism, the reforms begun at Cluny eventually influenced some strong-minded reformers. One of these was Hildebrand, a future Pope who would win back for the Church much of the spiritual authority lost in the Dark Ages.

The Rise of the MEDIEVAL PAPACY

Through the reforms of Cluny, a series of forceful Popes sought to free the Church from secular control. A German, Pope St. Leo IX (1049–1054) was the first of these reformer Popes. A relative of Emperor Henry III, he traveled widely to fight against the abuses of clerical incontinence, lay investiture, and simony. A successor, Pope Nicholas II (1058–1061), helped the cause of the papacy by creating the College of Cardinals to elect future Popes. The early efforts at reform were led by St. Peter Damian and Hildebrand, the brilliant monk from Cluny, who became Pope Gregory VII.

Pope St. Gregory VII and the "Investiture Controversy"

Gregory VII's pontificate (1073–1085) was a milestone, the beginning of a reform that gained for the Church unparalleled status and power in Europe over

988
Conversion of Vladimir I of Russia

the next two centuries. Baptized Hildebrand, Gregory gained the nickname "Hellbrand" for his fiery temperament, intellectual brilliance, and unflagging devotion to the Church's independence.

Pope St. Gregory VII

Gregory's reforms included an insistence on clerical celibacy throughout the Church, a move that led to revolts in some areas. He also staunchly moved to eradicate simony and stamp out lay investiture. Gregory firmly held that God founded the Church and commissioned it to welcome all humanity into a single society ruled by divine law. Because the Church was founded by Christ, she is above all other human societies, including the state.

Gregory's foundational beliefs were expressed in his controversial *Dictates of the Pope*, which, in twenty-seven propositions, spelled out the rights of the Pope in relationship to secular rulers. Claiming absolute spiritual and temporal power, Gregory decreed that only the Pope can make new laws, depose emperors, wear imperial insignia, and convoke councils. The Pope also had the power to release vassals from fealty (loyalty) to sinful rulers. The *Dictates* banned lay or imperial election of bishops or the Pope. Gregory was determined to abolish lay investiture, the means used by secular rulers to control the Church. The German emperor Henry IV crossed Gregory on this issue and was excommunicated, a move supported by the German aristocracy and the peasants who were their serfs. Excommunication was a powerful weapon because medieval people believed that to die outside the Church was a sentence to eternal damnation. A politically savvy Henry begged for the Pope's forgiveness by standing barefoot in the snow outside a castle in Canossa, Italy (1077), where Gregory was on his way to a council. Henry received his pardon; however, he was quick to display his true colors when he returned to Germany and reestablished his power there. He marched on Rome with his armies, deposed Gregory, and set up his own puppet Pope. Rescued by some Normans, Gregory died shortly afterwards, proclaiming, "I have loved justice and hated iniquity; therefore, I die in exile."

Though it took several decades to sort out the mess Henry created by appointing an anti-Pope, papal reform was well underway. The *Concordat of Worms* (1122) finally solved the question of lay investiture. It was a compromise

1000
St. Stephen crowned king of Hungary

that distinguished between the spiritual and temporal aspects of conferring power on a bishop. The emperor invested the bishop with the temporal signs of the office (the scepter), but only other churchmen received permission to invest him with the spiritual signs (a ring and a staff).

WHAT THE CHURCH BELIEVES ABOUT . . .
Excommunication

Certain grave sins bring about excommunication from the Church, a penalty which keeps the person from receiving the sacraments and for which absolution cannot be granted except by the Pope, the local bishop, or priests authorized by them. However, if the person is in danger of death, any priest can absolve from any sin and excommunication.
See *Catechism of the Catholic Church*, 1463.

Other Results of the Papal Reforms

Pope Urban II (1088–1099) exemplified the papacy's claim to temporal power when, in 1095, he called the First Crusade to help the beleaguered Eastern Empire and to rescue the Holy Land from the Muslims. During the next century, there were many good and talented Popes. They envisioned Church reform principally in terms of secular rulers surrendering power to the Pope. They made many gains.

For example, Pope Alexander III (1159–1181), blessed with a brilliant legal mind, allied himself with the Lombards and crushingly defeated the German emperor Frederick Barbarossa. Alexander also successfully made King Henry II of England yield to papal authority after Henry had St. Thomas Becket (1118–1170) assassinated for refusing to cooperate with Henry's attempts to gain control of Church courts.

The medieval papacy reached its zenith of worldly influence under Pope Innocent III, a brilliant canon lawyer who believed that Christ granted both spiritual and secular leadership to the Pope. Innocent saw Europe as one large monastery with himself as the abbot. People were to live as brothers and sisters and obey their father, the Pope. If kings or others disagreed, they were disciplined.

Like other reform Popes, Innocent used both spiritual and political weapons to help assert Church power. For example:

1. *Excommunication and interdict*. Innocent placed England under interdict (meaning that the sacraments could not be celebrated) because King John

Lackland would not accept the papal candidate, Stephen Langdon, as Bishop of Canterbury. John submitted by becoming Innocent's vassal and agreeing to pay a feudal tax to the Pope. Innocent also used interdict against King Philip-Augustus of France to keep him from divorcing his Danish wife, Ingeborg.

2. *Political Alliances*. Like Popes before him, Innocent entered into alliances with various kings if it helped his goals. For example, he joined the king of France to help put the papal candidate, Frederick II, on the throne in Germany against a rival, Otto, who was excommunicated for going against a promise made to Innocent not to annex Southern Italy or Sicily.

3. *Crusades*. Innocent called a Crusade that conquered the Eastern capital of Constantinople (1204). He set up a Western hierarchy there, an act that alienated Greek Christians for centuries to come. Innocent also called a Crusade against a dangerous heretical group, the Albigensians, which had cropped up in Southern France. The Albigensians taught that material reality was evil, marriage was bad, and suicide was moral. At first, Innocent tried to reason with the heretics, sending preachers like St. Dominic Guzman to them. However, Dominic met little success. When the heretics killed a papal legate in 1208, Innocent called a Crusade to drive them out of southern France. After six years of brutal bloodshed, the campaign ended. The heresy was temporarily stamped out, though it went underground and caused problems in later years.

The Albigensian heresy led to the creation of the **papal Inquisition** by Pope Gregory IX in 1233 to confront future heretics. In collaboration with secular authorities, papal representatives employed the Inquisition to judge the guilt of suspected heretics with the aim of getting them to repent. Unfortunately, before long, many abuses crept into the process—anonymous accusations, torture to exact confessions, and executions by the state. Most Christians of the Middle Ages, however, believed that the Inquisition was necessary to bring order to society. To them, a false teaching about the faith was an assault on civic order and the unity necessary for a stable Christian society.

4. *Canon Law and Taxation*. Innocent reorganized the Papal Curia (bureaucracy) and issued many laws to regulate all aspects of Church life. He reserved to himself the right to grant indulgences and canonize saints. He levied taxes on his clergy as well as on nations to support the charitable activities of the Church. These taxes also underwrote the Crusades and supported the ever-growing institution with its many lands, courts, and churches.

5. *Ecumenical Council*. Innocent's greatest achievement was the convoking of the Fourth Lateran Council in Rome (1215). Attended by more than 1,200

1056–1106
Reign of German
Emperor Henry IV

1058–1093
St. Margaret of Scotland initiates the religious reforms of Pope Gregory VII during the reign of her husband, King Malcolm III Canmore.

leading churchmen, this council was a call to spiritual reform. Among its many teachings were the following:

- instructions to the faithful were to be in the language of the people;
- reform of clerical life, including enforcement of clerical celibacy and the elimination of simony;
- condemnation of heresies like Albigensianism; non-Christians—like the Jews and Muslims—had to wear distinctive clothing and live in a ghetto in Rome;
- secrecy of the confessional (betraying this would result in the loss of the priestly office and lifelong penance);
- annual confessions and reception of Eucharist during the Easter season;
- fixing the number of sacraments at seven;
- the clear definition of the doctrine of Jesus' real presence in the Eucharist (transubstantiation).

Innocent III became one of history's most influential rulers. In his reign, the Church emerged from the Dark Ages where she was at the mercy of feudalism. The papacy united both spiritual and temporal power to help create a glimmer of Christendom. However, in later centuries, kings increasingly resented Church encroachments into the secular realm and the secular outreach of papal power was not to last.

WHAT THE CHURCH BELIEVES ABOUT . . .
The Body and Blood of Christ at Eucharist

The term "transubstantiation" indicates that through the consecration of the bread and wine by the priest at Eucharist, there occurs a change of the entire substance of the bread into the substance of the Body of Christ and of the entire substance of the wine into the Blood of Christ—even though the appearance of bread and wine remain.
See *Catechism of the Catholic Church*, 1376.

1073–1085
Pontificate of St. Gregory VII, Gregorian Reform underway

MEMBER OF THE CHURCH

St. Bernard Clairvaux:
THE WAY TO HAPPINESS IS LOVE

 St. Bernard, considered the last Father of the Church, was also a crusading reformer, brilliant organizer, eloquent speaker, and spiritual master of his day. In 1112, Bernard joined a new order of religious, the Cistercians, which lived a very strict form of the Benedictine *Rule*. (The regular order of Cistercians, of which Bernard was a part, still exists today.) Such was his magnetic personality that he brought along with him thirty of his friends and relatives, including five of his brothers. In 1115, Bernard began his own monastery at Clairvaux in France.

Bernard's own life was one of strict fasting and penance. He wrote on many spiritual topics, especially on the love of God as the perfect way to happiness. He promoted devotion to the Blessed Mother and helped mediate a schism over the rightful Pope (a crisis that afflicted the Church from 1130–1138) as well as disputes between secular rulers. He was a key figure in obtaining the recognition of the Knights Templars, whose rule he helped compose.

Despite almost constant bad health, caused in part by his own penitential austerities, Bernard traveled far and wide. At the command of Pope Eugene III, he encouraged the disastrous Second Crusade, the failure of which he blamed on the sins of the crusaders. In his final years, sick and worn-out from years of ministry, Bernard even traveled to the Rhineland to defend Jews who were being unjustly attacked there.

Bernard died on August 20, 1153. Here are some of his lofty thoughts from his *Book on the Love of God*:

> Admit that God deserves to be loved very much, yea, boundlessly, because he loved us first, he infinite and we nothing, loved us, miserable sinners, with a love so great and so free. This is why I said at the beginning that the measure of our love to God is to love immeasurably. For since our love is toward God, who is infinite and immeasurable, how can we bound or limit the love we owe

him? Besides, our love is not a gift but a debt. And since it is the Godhead who loves us, himself boundless, eternal, supreme love, of whose greatness there is no end, yea, and his wisdom is infinite, whose peace surpasses all understanding; since it is he who loves us, I say, can we think of repaying him grudgingly? "I will love you, O Lord, my strength. The Lord is my rock and my fortress and my deliverer, my God, my strength, in whom I will trust" (Ps. 18.1f). He is all that I need, all that I long for.[2]

Eastern SCHISM

The Eastern Schism in 1054 was largely a theological struggle between the Western Church, centered in Rome, and the Eastern Church, centered in Constantinople. The definitive break between East and West festered for centuries and had many causes. The split persists to our own day, though there have been several encouraging signs of repairing hurts since the Second Vatican Council.

Political factors helped separate the East from the West, starting from when Diocletian gave the Roman Empire two capitals. The distance between Constantinople and Rome made for difficult communication. The barbarian invasions also isolated the West from the Eastern Empire which increasingly was unable to protect the West. The Western Church looked to the Franks as protectors when the imperial forces from Constantinople became unreliable. The East had its own problems caused by the Muslim invasions which conquered three of the four ancient patriarchies—Antioch, Alexandria, and Jerusalem. The Christians that remained in these territories often held heretical views (like Nestorianism) and were now isolated from Rome and the papacy. The sole remaining Eastern patriarchy was Constantinople. It assumed primacy over the churches in the East. The patriarch of Constantinople, however, was appointed by the emperor and subject to him. In contrast, in the West, the Popes increasingly asserted their rights over the state.

Cultural and theological issues also added to the growing distrust between East and West. For example, Easterners spoke Greek, which had been the universal language of the Church through the third century. Westerners spoke Latin, which after the fourth century became the liturgical language in the West. The lack of a common language caused suspicion between the two, especially in an age of many heresies that often were caused by the precise definition of terms. Theologically, Easterners were more speculative, with the laity taking an active and learned role in religious questions. Western theology

1099
Jerusalem falls to the crusaders

was more practical, and there was a wider gap between the educated clergy and the typical uneducated faithful. The Eastern Church also allowed for a married clergy, while in the West clerical celibacy was becoming the practice insisted on by the Pope.

The major problem revolved around how the two churches viewed authority. In the East, the emperor, who saw himself as Christ's vicar on earth, had a major role in naming the patriarch of Constantinople. In doctrinal matters, the Eastern Church looked to councils aided by emperors to settle disputes. In the West, however, the Pope claimed primacy over the Church as well as both secular and spiritual authority. Only a Pope could call a council.

Conflicts with Church Authority

A series of four conflicts—all involving a differing view of Church authority—built up to the schism of 1054. The first conflict resulted from Pope Leo the Great's condemnation of canon 28 from the Council of Chalcedon. This canon gave the Church of Constantinople jurisdiction over all the territories of the Byzantine Empire on the grounds that Constantinople was the "New Rome." Pope Leo could not accept this surrendering of Church authority to Constantinople because the Pope, as the successor to Peter, was the legitimate source of ultimate authority. A coldness began to set in between the Eastern and Western Churches over this authority issue. It intensified because the Byzantine Church became more tightly bound to the Byzantine Empire. This was in contrast to the Western Church's increasingly dependence on French and German rulers for protection.

A second dispute involved the Byzantine Emperor Leo III's condemnation of the veneration of sacred images, known as *iconoclasm* ("image breaking"). Because he believed that venerating images was equivalent to idolatry, in 726, he ordered their destruction and then attempted to impose his policy on the worldwide Church. The Pope would not sanction Leo's condemnation, holding the popular position that the veneration of icons was an important means of educating the largely illiterate laity in the sacred mysteries of the faith. The emperor was so outraged at the Pope that he sent a fleet to attack Rome, but it sank in a huge storm. Eventually the Second Council of Nicea (787) supported the Pope's view of this emotion-laden issue by permitting the use of icons. The Council bolstered the role of the Pope as the prime teacher of the faith to the whole Church.

· ....

1115
St. Bernard founds the monastery at Clairvaux

The third conflict was the ninth-century Photian schism. The Pope supported Ignatius's claims to the office over Photius. In retaliation, Photius reacted violently against the Latin Church by condemning Western theology and practice. For example, he condemned the Western practice of fasting on Saturday, the use of dairy products in Lent, and the papal demands for clerical celibacy. His strongest weapon was a condemnation of the Western Church's addition of the phrase *filioque* ("and from the Son") to the Nicene Creed. The phrase was added to the statement approved at the Council that the Holy Spirit proceeds only from "the Father." The East objected because the filioque was added without the approval of a Church council. The Eastern Church wanted to say that the Holy Spirit descended *through* the Son, not *from* the Son. Photius condemned the Western Church, accusing it of heresy, a serious charge that went way beyond previous political issues of liturgical practices or disciplines. In response, the Pope condemned Photius's views. A permanent East-West split would have happened at that time, but the Pope died and Photius softened his harsh views.

The definitive split took place in the eleventh century when the Popes finally emerged from under control of the German emperor and they began to assert their authority over the whole Church. Also, a fiercely anti-Latin attitude of the patriarch of Constantinople—Michael Cerularius—and the slowness of the papal legates to understand the Byzantine viewpoints on the issues sped up the division. What precipitated the crisis was Cerularius' closing of all Latin churches in the city and his excommunication of all priests who insisted on saying Mass in Latin. He also violently opposed the Western practice of clerical celibacy, the use of unleavened bread for the Eucharist, and the use of the *filioque* clause in the Nicene Creed.

Pope Leo IX sent legates to Constantinople to investigate Cerularius and to demand his submission to the Pope. The patriarch refused to do so. In the meantime, the Pope died and the legates, led by an uncompromising Cardinal Humbert, excommunicated Cerularius. In turn, the patriarch convoked a council and excommunicated the Pope. Most Eastern churches sided with the patriarch and refused to recognize the primacy of the Pope. They eventually took the name Orthodox (meaning "correct or right teaching") and accepted only the teachings of the first eight Ecumenical Councils.

At the time of the break, most Eastern and Western Christians probably did not notice the schism, thinking it just another in a line of troubles between East and West. But a split had taken place nonetheless. Relations deteriorated further in 1204. Crusaders were sent to help the Byzantines defend against the Muslims. However, they ended up sacking and pillaging Constantinople,

1122
Concordat of Worms ends investiture controversy

proclaimed the Western emperor king of Constantinople, and installed a Latin bishop to take charge of the ancient Eastern patriarchy. Eastern Christians were infuriated and would not soon forget these Western affronts to their traditions. There were efforts to heal this breach, for example, at the Second Council of Lyons (1274) and the Council of Florence (1439), but political turmoil inevitably prevented reconciliation from taking place. When Constantinople fell to the Turks in 1453, the hope for Christian unity was set back for centuries.

The Second Vatican Council (1962–1965), and the Popes who followed it, made Christian unity a top priority in the contemporary Church. High-level ecumenical commissions have met in the prayerful hope that true reunion will take place. In 1965, Pope Paul VI and the Patriarch Athenagoras I lifted the mutual excommunications imposed in 1054. In an effort to promote Christian unity, in 2004, Pope John Paul II returned to Istanbul the relics of Sts. John Chrysostom and Gregory Nazianzen. Crusaders took the relics of St. John as war booty in 1204; Byzantine monks brought St. Gregory's bones to Rome in the eighth century during the iconoclast controversy. In 2001, Pope John Paul II apologized for the Catholic involvement in the siege of Constantinople. Today, both Catholics and Orthodox believers are praying for unity and continuing their ecumenical efforts.

WHAT THE CHURCH BELIEVES ABOUT . . .
Church Unity

Christ always gives his Church the gift of unity, but the faithful must always pray and work to maintain and reinforce the unity Christ intends. There are several ways to promote unity, for example through: a renewal of the Church's vocation, a conversion of heart of the faithful, common prayer with other Christians, fraternal knowledge of each other, ecumenical formation of the faithful (especially the priests), dialogue among theologians, and collaboration in various human-related services. See *Catechism of the Catholic Church*, 820.

◉ LOOKING FOR PEACE

Even though many of the bishops of the Middle Ages operated like feudal lords who engaged in battle with neighboring knights, the Church did make efforts to limit warfare. One such effort was the **Peace of God** movement which spared women, clergy, children, and peasants from attack. Although some nobles took an oath to respect innocent non-combatants, many did not.

1123
First Lateran Council

1139
Second Lateran Council

More effective was the **Truce of God**, first proposed by Pope John XV in 958 and eventually put into practice in 1027. In its final form, it outlawed fighting from Wednesday evening to Monday morning as well as all religious holidays, leaving only eighty days each year for fighting. By 1123, anyone violating the Truce was excommunicated. The Truce of God helped to end many of the small wars fought among neighboring knights. However, by the thirteenth century, both the Peace of God and the Truce of God became ineffective in curbing war though both demonstrated the deep influence the Church had on all of society in the Middle Ages, especially that of taming the tendency to war and savagery.

Just-War Theory

Today, the Roman Catholic Church promotes the "just-war" theory as a way to limit violence in a world prone to it. The principles of a just-war were first articulated by St. Augustine in the fifth century and elaborated on by St. Thomas Aquinas in the thirteenth century. The criteria were further developed in subsequent centuries so that today they include very strict conditions for a war to be just. The strict conditions for legitimate defense by military force and for governments to participate in a just war of defense must meet the following conditions:

1. The damage inflicted by the aggression is lasting, grave, and certain;

2. The war is truly a last resort after all other means to resolve the conflict have first been exhausted;

3. There must be serious prospects of success;

4. The use of arms will not produce evil graver than the evil to be eliminated. (See *CCC*, 2309.)

Once a just war is engaged, civilian non-combatants must be immune from attack; only the minimum force necessary to achieve military objectives must be used; and the war must be fought to achieve peace with justice, thus curbing vengeful and violent acts.

Hallmarks OF CHRISTENDOM

The two hundred years spanning from about 1150 to 1350 are generally considered the High Middle Ages, a time of great achievement for the Church known as *Christendom* when the Catholic Church and Western society were one. Politi-

CA. 1150
Universities of Paris and Oxford are founded

cally, the previous section explained how the papacy had wrested control from the emperor to the point where Pope Innocent III was a major power in the affairs of Germany, England, and France. To the common citizen, the Catholic Church and Europe were synonymous, not only politically, but socially and culturally as well. Christian faith permeated every facet of life.

The age of Christendom was marked by chivalry and military battles, but also rich vitality. It calls to mind images of Ivanhoe, Robin Hood, chivalry, and Richard the Lionhearted. The Crusades took place during this period. New religious orders like the Dominicans and Franciscans arose to witness to Gospel simplicity and to serve people in cities during a changing economic and social climate. Christendom also spawned a revival of learning in the West with the founding of many universities. This was the classic age of canon law and scholastic theology, which, under brilliant thinkers like St. Thomas Aquinas, put human reason at the service of divine revelation. Finally, there was an outpouring of faith expressed in the devotional life of the laity (a prime example was the popularization of the rosary) and the erecting of magnificent cathedrals to leave a lasting legacy of faith. These elements of Christendom are treated in more detail in the subsections that follow.

Crusades

Various Popes and reformers called the crusaders organized expeditions to free the Holy Land, especially Jerusalem from the Seljuk Turks who conquered Palestine in 1073. Previously, Christian pilgrims were allowed by the Muslim authorities to visit the Holy Land, but the Turks began to persecute Christians and prevented them from making pilgrimages to the holy sites. A second religious motivation for the Crusades was defense of the faith, for example, against heretics like the Albigensians. In exchange for their participation, crusaders were promised special graces, for example, the remission of suffering in Purgatory. Economic and political factors were also involved in the crusading spirit as landless peasants and lords hoped to gain territory from the Muslims. A chronology of the eight Crusades provides a lens to understand both their positive and negative impact.

The goal of the First Crusade was to gain control of Jerusalem and it was a military success. Called by Pope Urban II in 1095, the First Crusade set out from Constantinople. The crusaders captured Nicaea followed by Antioch in successive Junes of 1097 and 1098. Jerusalem fell on July 18, 1099. A massacre of Muslims and Jews ensued. When the battle ended, many knights went

1152–1190
Reign of Frederick Barbarossa

1159–1181
Pontificate of Alexander III

home but others remained and ruled the Crusade States of Jerusalem and the surrounding areas until 1187.

The Second Crusade (1147–1149), an effort to retake Edesa, was a disaster. It was led by King Louis VII and Emperor Conrad III of Germany. Conrad's forces were destroyed by the Turks. Louis led his crusaders to Damascus, only to be forced to withdraw. The defeat damaged the spirit of the crusaders.

The Third Crusade (1189–1192) was a response to the fall of the Kingdom of Jerusalem. Led by Richard the Lionhearted of England, Philip II of France, and the German emperor Frederick Barbarossa, it failed to recapture the holy city which the brilliant Muslim leader, Saladin, had reconquered. However, Christian pilgrims did gain the right to visit the holy city.

Even while the Third Crusade was being fought, Pope Innocent III was rounding up crusaders for another effort. The Pope's intentions were for the Crusades to address the Muslim influence in the Holy Land. However, the crusaders were offered money to overthrow Constantinople on behalf of opponents of the Byzantine emperor. The city was taken on April 13, 1204, and the Latin Empire of Constantinople was founded. The Latin (Roman) rite was forced on the Byzantine population. The crusaders' behavior disgusted the Pope who now realized that many Catholic princes were more interested in their own power and enrichment than in winning non-believers over to the faith. The Catholic faithful also began to see that the Muslims were strongly committed to their faith and possessed military might.

The other crusades likewise were military failures. The so-called Children's Crusade (1212) was the most notable of the misguided efforts. The call to children to march to Jerusalem and reclaim the city in God's name was answered by many children. In 1212, they set out and were soon destroyed by disease, starvation, and the climate. The children who survived were sold into slavery to the Turks. The other Crusades also did not achieve their intended goals. The last Christian stronghold in Muslim territory, Acre, fell in 1291, thus ending Christian control of the Holy Land.

Overall, the Crusades had mixed results. On the negative side, many sincere, zealous Christians died in what eventually became a military and religious failure. In addition, the violence of some of these Crusades was often misdirected. As crusaders assembled to go East, they killed innocent Jews in many cities. The misguided takeover of Constantinople in the Fourth Crusade ended hope for reconciliation between Eastern and Western Christianity.

The positive effects of the Crusades were mainly economic. The Crusades stimulated trade and helped to weaken the feudal system and thus aid the

1170
St. Thomas Becket martyred

growth of cities and a new merchant class. They reopened Europe to the ideas, culture, and art of the East and brought back the advances made by Muslim science, astronomy, mathematics, and architecture. The crusaders acquired Arabic commentaries on Aristotle, which significantly contributed to the revival of Catholic philosophy and theology. In addition, the Crusades saw the rise of some notable semi-religious orders of knights like the Knights Templars, loosely based on the Rule of St. Benedict. These orders promoted religious observance like Mass attendance and prayer among its members and provided guards to protect Christian pilgrims. The Crusades also strengthened the idea of chivalry. Finally, the Crusades opened up the Holy Land to pilgrims. Like the Crusades themselves, pilgrimages were important for bringing people together and reinforcing the idea of a universal Church.

Mendicant Orders

With the end of the Crusades came an increase of commerce, the growth of cities, and the birth of a new social class, the *bourgeoisie* ("city people") who in turn developed trades. These changes helped hasten the end of feudalism. To respond to the ever-growing migration to cities, the new form of religious life developed in the Church to serve the needs of the city people—the mendicant or "begging" orders. They served God's people by witnessing to simple Gospel values. Among the new religious orders founded at this time were the Carmelites and Augustinians. However, the two most important new orders were the Dominicans and the Franciscans. Unlike members of earlier orders who lived in monasteries, the early Dominican and Franciscan friars kept on the move. They lived a simple life of poverty, preaching in towns and begging for their food and shelter. In time, because of the hundreds of friars who joined these orders, they had to settle for communal living arrangements and the ownership of property to help support their large numbers.

St. Dominic Guzman (1170–1221), a Spanish priest, founded his Order of Preachers (the Dominicans) to combat heresies, most notably the Albigensian heresy in southern France. The Dominicans modeled their rule on that of St. Augustine's and prized learning as an effective means to defend the faith. Dominicans took the vow of poverty and became leaders in the emerging universities. In later years, they also assumed a prominent role on the court of the Inquisition, a special Church tribunal to curb the spread of heresies. Pope Honorius III called the Dominicans "invincible athletes of Christ" whose main mission was to preach the Gospel. They are also known as the Black Friars

1179
Third Lateran Council

1198–1216
Pontificate of Innocent III

because their religious habit was a white robe covered with a black cloak. St. Thomas Aquinas (1224–1274), the greatest theologian of the Middle Ages, was a Dominican.

St. Francis of Assisi (1183–1226) founded the Order of Friar Minors, popularly known as the Franciscans. Like the Dominicans, the Franciscans took the vows of poverty, chastity, and obedience and lived simply among the people, bringing Christ to the marketplace.

Francis never planned to found a religious order. By following Christ in a literal way, preaching and living a Gospel of simplicity, Francis attracted followers. By 1208, when the number grew to twelve, he traveled to Rome to ask approval of his rule (see pages 99–101). Early Franciscans lived in Umbria, but members preached throughout Italy and were known for their life of poverty. Francis himself ministered to the sick and preached peace, even joining the Fifth Crusade (1219).

St. Clare (1194–1253), a friend of Francis, left her affluent family to found an order of religious women known as the Poor Clares. Inspired by Francis's ideals, the Poor Clares lived a contemplative life, relying on the generosity of others to take care of their material needs. Francis referred to the feminine counterpart of his friars as his Second Order. Third Orders of lay people committed to the ideals of the Franciscans and Dominicans also began to flourish at this time.

The mendicant orders helped the Church at a critical time. Radical reforming groups, for example, the Waldensians (founded by Peter Waldo) had begun to emerge as a response to a Church grown rich and powerful. These heretical reformers attacked the hierarchical nature of the Church and her sacramental and priestly system. They preached that the only true Christian was one who vowed total poverty. In contrast, the mendicants showed that Christians could reconcile the Gospel within the Church without destroying the office of apostolic authority with which Christ endowed his Church through bishops and priests.

Cathedrals

The magnificent cathedrals and abbey churches built between 1000 and 1400 symbolize the spirit and grandeur of the medieval Church. They testify to the influx of people to cities. In turn, they attracted people to towns and served as a source of civic and religious pride for the faithful. Each cathedral contained the bishop's cathedra (chair), symbolizing his teaching authority and power.

1204
Knights of the Fourth Crusade sack Constantinople

Thus, the bishop's church was the center of worship and a symbol of unity for the people in a given diocese. The very design of the cathedral shows the development in Eucharistic worship from the small intimate meals of New Testament times. The people would stand in the nave, the main body of the

church, and witness the spectacle that was going on in front of them. The choir area (chancel) contained the high altar, the bishop's chair, and stalls for the priests who would chant the daily prayers of the Divine Office. The typical cathedral also had a high pulpit from which Sunday sermons

▶ *The Cathedral of Florence, Italy*

would be preached to the faithful, a baptismal font, and along the nave many side altars where priests would celebrate private or small-group Masses. These small altars indicated a focus at Eucharist on the priestly act of worship for the particular intentions of the faithful.

The construction of a cathedral required a tremendous investment of time, energy, and resources. As the largest building in town, it also served as a meeting place for social activity and even trade. Pilgrims would sleep on their floor. Cathedrals also became a source of rivalry among towns; each trying to outdo the other in trying to construct bigger and better cathedrals. One attempt to build the most impressive cathedral of the time resulted in the roof of the Beauvais Cathedral in France collapsing several times as successive bishops engaged in poor planning with their architects.

The older Romanesque style of cathedrals had very thick walls and small openings for light. Romanesque cathedrals' similarity to fortresses stood for the strength of the Church against the forces of darkness in a turbulent society. The Gothic style, appearing first in northern France in the twelfth century had high thin walls, ribbed vaulting, and flying buttresses to distribute the weight of the ceilings. This style lent itself to the use of many stained-glass windows which allowed streams of colored light to filter in to the worshipers below. The cathedrals stand as a living memorial to the countless anonymous ancestors in the faith of today's Christians. Their hard work was part of an unprecedented institutional effort to praise God in stone.

1209
Francis of Assisi founds Order of Friars Minor

> ## WHAT THE CHURCH BELIEVES ABOUT . . .
> ### Divine Office
> The Liturgy of the Hours, or Divine Office, is the daily, public prayer of the Church which makes the whole course of the day and night holy. The Divine Office is prayed by priests as they remain diligent in prayer and service and by religious according to the charism of their vocation. The Divine Office is also intended for all the faithful as much as possible, praying from the book of Psalms at certain points from morning to night.
> See *Catechism of the Catholic Church*, 1174–1178.

Universities

Another achievement of the Middle Ages was the rise of the university. This institution helped the Church in many ways, but especially by producing eminent theologians and canon lawyers. Universities grew out of the cathedral schools which were established by bishops to train priests. Over eighty of them came into existence before 1300. Imitating the guilds of craftsmen, universities resulted when students and teachers grouped together for mutual protection, forming a *universitas*, a kind of corporation. As in guilds, the masters (teachers) had to earn a license while students earned degrees to mark off the progress of their studies. Students (males only) entered the university at age fourteen or fifteen and took six years to study the liberal arts—arithmetic, geometry, astronomy, music theory, grammar, logic, and rhetoric—before earning a bachelor's degree. If students wanted to advance in their studies, they would take up to twelve more years to earn a master's and doctoral degree in one of three fields: medicine, law, or theology.

There were two major types of universities in the Middle Ages. The southern type, modeled on the University of Bologna in Italy, stressed law and medicine. Students controlled the corporation by hiring or firing teachers and determining the curriculum. If a teacher announced a series of classes, and students did not come, the teacher could not collect a fee and would lose his job. The northern universities like Oxford (ca. 1200), Cambridge (1209), and especially the University of Paris (late twelfth century) stressed theology, canon law, and the liberal arts. Professors had more authority in these institutions. For example, they made rules to govern student swearing and gambling. They also fined students for breaking curfews or displaying bad table manners. The professor's salaries came from the Church, not from students.

1209–1229
Crusade against the Albigensian heresy

Learning at the university consisted mainly of listening to lectures in Latin (since students came from many nations). Books, which were hand-transcribed, were expensive and limited, and notes were rarely taken. Students relied on their memories to learn and then proved their mastery of the subject by passing oral exams in which they gave reasons for or against the various propositions taught by the teachers.

Scholasticism and Thomas Aquinas

The medieval universities gradually developed a way to advance learning known as scholasticism. Peter Abelard's influential work titled *Sic et Non (Yes and No)* helped develop the scholastic method of teaching whereby various authorities and their contradictory positions were cited, analyzed, debated, disputed, and then reconciled. The scholastic method encouraged two or more masters (professors), and sometimes students, to question, postulate, examine, and logically arrange details into a meaningful whole. Logic, in fact, was the driving force behind the method.

Scholasticism tried to reconcile the newly rediscovered philosophy of Aristotle with the truths of the Church. Aristotle, a brilliant Greek philosopher of antiquity, had studied most fields of human knowledge. His detailed observations and conclusions cogently explained many phenomena of the world. However, from a Christian point of view, Aristotle could not explain everything. He did not have the benefit of Divine Revelation to aid him in his quest for knowledge. The scholastics attempted to bridge this gap. Their goal was to synthesize the knowledge of philosophy and theology and create one integral system of thought.

This was a monumental task, but one of history's true geniuses, St. Thomas Aquinas, met it admirably. His work is the summit of the intellectual achievements of the Middle Ages. Born around 1225 into a family related to the emperor, Thomas defied his parents by joining the Dominicans. They had two of his brothers kidnap and imprison him in the tower of their castle hoping he'd change vocational plans. But Thomas persisted, and eventually returned to the order.

Thomas went to Cologne where he became the student of St. Albert the Great, a brilliant scholastic thinker and teacher. Thomas's classmates called him "The Dumb Ox" because of his weight, seriousness, and slow movement. However, Albert defended his prize pupil by prophesying, "This dumb ox will fill the world with his bellowing." And Aquinas did just that. He lectured

1215
Fourth Lateran Council;
St. Dominic founds the Dominican Order

1245
First Council of Lyons

in many of the leading universities in Europe, including the top school of the day, the University of Paris. He also wrote prolifically, producing his masterpiece of theological thought, a twenty-one-volume work known as the *Summa Theologica*.

In the *Summa*, Thomas showed the reasonableness of faith. He also defended human intelligence as a prelude to faith. Thomas argued that human reason is supreme in its own domain, but it can't master everything, especially the mysteries of faith. However, Thomas showed that these revealed truths are not beyond rational explanation. With the gift of faith, believers can make some sense out of the mysteries of our Christian religion, for example, the Incarnation, the Resurrection, and the Trinity.

➤ *St. Thomas Aquinas*

Thomas's masterful thought did not gain easy acceptance in his own lifetime. The Archbishop of Paris believed Aquinas's teachings were heretical. Other philosophers, like St. Bonaventure (1221–1274), distrusted Thomas's well-developed and ordered theological system. Bonaventure and his allies emphasized the mystical approach to God through prayer, contemplation, and meditation. They stressed the will and downplayed the role of human reason. Toward the end of his life, Thomas had a direct experience of God. Commenting on it later, he said that all he had written was chaff compared to what he had experienced. He stopped writing, and three months later he died (1274).

Although Thomism (the philosophy of Aquinas) had its opponents even after Thomas's death, the Church finally endorsed his thought. In his encyclical *Aeterni Patris* (1879), Pope Leo XIII gave special theological prominence to Thomas's thought. Thus, Thomas's writings—especially the *Summa*—have powerfully influenced Church teaching. Aquinas's clarity of thought, insistence on truth, respect for human reason, and defense of Christian revelation have helped the Church explain and defend its teaching up to our own day.

> "Three things are necessary for the salvation of man: to know what he ought to believe; to know what he ought to desire; and to know what he ought to do." (St. Thomas Aquinas, *Two Precepts of Charity*)

1266–1273
St. Thomas Aquinas writes *Summa Theologica*

1274
Second Council of Lyons

Decline of CHRISTENDOM

The unity of Christendom achieved under Pope Innocent III was based on a strong papacy that was able to control the secular powers of Europe. But with the breakup of feudalism, the corruption of the kings, and the decline in the prestige of the papacy beginning with Pope Boniface VIII, any vestige of Christendom was nearing the end. However, by the time of his pontificate, nationalism was on the rise. Strong leaders opposed him at every turn. Two of his notable opponents were the politically astute Kings Edward I of England and Philip the Fair (Philip IV) of France, both of whom wanted to reassert control of the Church in their territories. One way they did it was to tax the clergy.

Boniface met the threat to his authority by issuing a papal bull, *Clericis Laicos*. (A papal bull was an official document sealed with a red wax seal known as *bulla*.) The document forbade taxation of the clergy and threatened excommunication for anyone who tried to collect or pay tax without papal permission. Edward retaliated by removing the clergy from police protection and issued economic and other penalties on the Church. Philip refused to recognize one of Boniface's candidates for bishop. Outraged at the direct challenge to his authority, Boniface issued yet another bull, *Unam Sanctam* (1302). It asserted that Popes were supreme over kings in both spiritual and temporal affairs. His claim to papal supremacy was the strongest of any medieval Pope: "We declare, we proclaim, we define that it is absolutely necessary for salvation that every human creature be subject to the Roman Pontiff."[3]

Philip insulted the Pope and had him arrested while treating him roughly at Anagni, an Italian diocese near Rome. Boniface died shortly thereafter, a broken old man of eighty-six. Philip's action was a warning: Strong kings would no longer take directions from a foreign Pope. After the brief pontificate of Boniface's successor, Philip manipulated the next papal election to secure the papal throne for a French cardinal, who took the name Clement V. At Philip's insistence, Clement withdrew the decrees of Boniface VIII and moved his residence to Avignon in southern France. Thus began a sixty-eight year exile of the Popes from Rome. This, in turn, led to the Western Schism—a period during which there were at times two and even three Popes. Chapter 5 addresses how the Western Schism and other factors contributed to the Protestant revolt and Catholic Reformation.

1294–1303
Pontificate of Boniface VIII

1302
St. Gertrude the Great, a mystic devoted to the Sacred Heart, dies in Saxony.

Summary

- The Dark Ages of European history were ushered in by the breakup of Charlemagne's Holy Roman Empire, a new wave of invasions by Norsemen and Vikings, and the rise of feudalism.

- Feudalism was instrumental in strengthening secular control over the Church through abuses like lay investiture, simony, and nepotism.

- Pope St. Nicholas I (858–867) and the abbots at the reform monastery of Cluny—who were free from the clutches of secular rulers—helped lay the groundwork for Church reform and the rise of the medieval papacy.

- The High Middle Ages were known as the Age of Christendom—a time when the Catholic Church and Western society were culturally, politically, and religiously united.

- Notable Popes of this era included Nicholas II who created the College of Cardinals to help free the papacy from secular control. Pope St. Gregory VII stamped out various abuses, most notably by winning a victory over the German emperor on the issue of lay investiture. Gregory insisted on clerical celibacy and issued his famous *Dictates of the Pope*, a document that spelled out papal rights over secular rulers. Pope Urban II called for the First Crusade, while Pope Alexander III won political victories over Frederick Barbarossa and King Henry II of England.

- Pope Innocent III is known as the most influential Pope of his era. Pope Innocent used tools like excommunication and interdict, political alliances, and reforms in canon law and taxation to further the cause of the Church. He called the Fourth Crusade against the Muslims, which ended in the tragic sacking of Constantinople, and another Crusade against the intransigent Albigensian heretics. He also convoked the Fourth Lateran Council (1215).

- The Fourth Lateran Council called for spiritual reform in the Church and clearly defined traditional points of Catholic doctrine, including the real presence of Christ in the Eucharist (transubstantiation).

- The Eastern Schism was the result of centuries of differences in language, culture, theology, and politics between the Eastern and Western

Churches. The fight over the acceptability of icons, the Photian Controversy which heated up over the inclusion of the *filioque* clause of the Nicene Creed, and unfortunate personality conflicts involving the patriarch of Constantinople—Michael Cerularius—and papal legates led to mutual excommunications and the definitive split in 1054.

- The Peace of God and the Truce of God were two means the Church used to help moderate violence in the Middle Ages.

- The Crusades were holy wars fought initially to open up the Holy Land to Christian pilgrims. The Crusades had mixed results including violence directed against innocent people and the sacking of Constantinople. On the positive side, the Crusades stimulated trade and opened the West to new ideas, which in turn helped bring the end of feudalism.

- Christendom also saw the rise of mendicant ("begging") orders that helped call the Church back to Gospel simplicity, the erection of impressive cathedrals, and the advent of universities. A major fruit of the universities was scholastic theology, which tried to reconcile revelation and human reason. It produced a method of learning based on logical analysis, debate, and synthesis.

- The greatest thinker produced at this time was St. Thomas Aquinas whose *Summa Theologica* is used to this day as a sure guide in the teaching of Catholic theology.

- The Golden Age of Catholic influence over European culture began to decline under the pontificate of Pope Gregory VIII whose bull *Unam Sanctam* asserted the Pope's absolute sovereignty over kings. Strong kings of the day, however, refused to obey him. The French King Philip IV abused Boniface and was able to appoint a Frenchman to the holy office shortly after the brief reign of Boniface's successor.

Prayer REFLECTION

Pray this simple prayer of St. Thomas Aquinas (1225–1274), one of the most complex yet brilliant theologians in history.

Grant me, O Lord my God,
a mind to know you,
a heart to seek you,
wisdom to find you,
conduct pleasing to you,

faithful perseverance in waiting for you,
and a hope of finally embracing you.
Amen.[4]

Review and DISCUSSION QUESTIONS

1. Discuss some of the factors that contributed to the breakdown of Charlemagne's Empire, the rise of feudalism, and the advent of the Dark Ages.

2. Discuss some of the abuses associated with feudalism that helped weaken Church authority in the Dark Ages.

3. How did the reform movement at the monastery of Cluny lay the groundwork for the Church's emergence from the Dark Ages?

4. Discuss some of the reforms during the eleventh century, many inspired by Hildebrand—Pope St. Gregory VII, that helped wrest the Church from secular control.

5. Discuss several ways Pope Innocent III used spiritual and political means to assert Church power and help the papacy reach its most prestigious place of honor in the High Middle Ages.

6. Why was the papal Inquisition created?

7. What were some of the key teachings of the Fourth Lateran Council?

8. What were some factors that led to the Eastern Schism (1054)?

9. Which was the most successful of the Crusades? Evaluate the pluses and minuses of the Crusades in total.

10. Describe the mendicant orders. Identify several of them.

11. Why were the teachings of the Albigensians and the Waldensians considered heretical?

12. Explain how the cathedrals symbolize the ideals of the Middle Ages. Distinguish between Romanesque and Gothic cathedrals.

13. How did the method of learning advocated by scholastic philosophy and theology work? What did scholasticism try to achieve?

14. Tell how the papacy was exiled to Avignon.

15. Identify:

Events:

Concordat of Worms

Dictates of the Pope

Donation of Constantine

Eastern Schism

Fourth Lateran Council

investiture controversy

Treaty of Verdun

People

Albigensians

Emperor Henry IV of Germany

Michael Cerularius

Otto I

Philip IV of France

Photius

Waldensians

Popes

St. Nicholas I (858–867)

St. Leo IX (1049–1054)

Nicholas II (1058–1061)

St. Gregory VII (1073–1085)

Urban II (1088–1099)

Alexander III (1159–1181)

Innocent III (1198–1216)

Boniface VIII (1294–1303)

Saints

Bernard of Clairvaux

Clare of Assisi

Dominic Guzman

Francis of Assisi

Terms

Christendom

Dark Ages

feudalism

filioque

interdict

lay investiture

mendicant

nepotism

papal Inquisition

Peace of God

scholasticism

simony

transubstantiation

Truce of God

Unam Sanctam

Scripture CONNECTION

Read and write your reaction to the following Gospel passage that convinced Francis of Assisi to give his all to Christ: **Matthew 10:7–10**.

Learn BY DOING

1. Visit an Eastern Orthodox or Byzantine Rite church. Tour the church building and note the icons and other religious decorations. Report on differences and similarities to your own parish church—its liturgy and religious art. *Optional*: Attend a liturgical celebration at the church.

2. Locate and report on St. Thomas Aquinas's five proofs for the existence of God from his *Summa Theologica*. You can find them online at:
   - www.newadvent.org/summa/100203.htm.
   - www.nd.edu/Departments/Maritain.

3. Interview either a male or female member of one of the mendicant religious orders mentioned in this chapter (Franciscans, Dominicans, Carmelites, Augustinians). Report on the current ministries of the order and how they reflect the intention of the founders of the particular religious community.

4. Report in detail on one of the Crusades.

5. Report in detail on the purpose, procedure, and results of the Papal Inquisition.

6. After checking out some of these websites to learn background information of medieval cathedrals, design a cathedral floor plan:
   - www.bbc.co.uk/history/british/architecture_cathedral_02.shtml.
   - www.newyorkcarver.com/cathedrallinks2.htm.
   - www.elore.com/gothic.htm.

7. Discover the Internet Medieval Sourcebook online: www.fordham.edu/halsall/sbook.html.
   - Peruse the section on saints' lives, discovering the rich documentation available.
   - In the period of the High Middle Ages, look at the references for St. Dominic. Read and report on his nine ways of prayer.

8. Locate a copy of St. Francis of Assisi's "Canticle of Brother Sun." Create a PowerPoint® presentation to illustrate it. Or write your own version of this famous prayer.

9. Prepare a one-page biographical sketch of one of the Popes or secular leaders mentioned in this chapter.

10. Prepare a report on feudalism.

5
Schism, Reform,
AND RENEWAL

Patience is necessary in this life because so much of life is fraught with adversity. No matter how hard we try, our lives will never be without strife or grief. Thus, we should not strive for a peace that is without temptation, or for a life that never feels adversity. Peace is not found by escaping temptations, but by being tried by them. We will have discovered peace when we have been tried and come through the trial of temptation.[1]   —THOMAS À KEMPIS (1380–1471)
THE IMITATION OF CHRIST

"Our lives will never be without strife or grief."

"Peace is not found by escaping temptations."

These words and the passage that opens this chapter come from *The Imitation of Christ,* which has been among the most widely read spiritual books by Christians through the ages (second, in fact, only to the Bible). Written at a time when the Church faced many internal challenges, its advice helped people of its day weather the trials assaulting the Church. It also prepared them for life after death in a world tormented by constant wars, plague, and terminal illness. This particular passage encourages individual believers to endure the tough times. It could have applied equally to a Church of the fourteenth to sixteenth centuries as it faced its most serious challenges since the days of Roman persecution—the Protestant Revolt, also known as the Protestant Reformation.

This chapter will examine these topics:

• The Babylonian Captivity of the Church

• Twilight of Christendom: Fourteenth and Fifteenth Centuries: Black Death, Great Schism, new heresies, and the Renaissance

- Christianity in the East
- Causes of the Protestant Revolt
- The Protestant founders: Luther, Zwingli, Calvin, Knox, Henry VIII, Anabaptists
- The Catholic Reformation: Spanish reformers, Jesuits, the Council of Trent
- Assessment of Trent.

"Babylonian Captivity" OF THE CHURCH

Forces were at work in the fourteenth and fifteenth centuries that would usher in the Protestant Revolt of the sixteenth century. One of these initial forces included the Avignon papacy, also known as the "Babylon Captivity" of the Church. The term *Babylonian Captivity* refers back to the sad chapter of Jewish history in biblical times when the Chosen People were carried off to exile in Babylon.

Recall that the French king Philip IV, buoyed by a growing sense of nationalism, had refused to obey Pope Boniface VIII and had Boniface arrested and beaten before his death. Philip then manipulated the election of a Frenchman, Pope Clement V, after the brief reign of Boniface's successor. The French king now controlled the papacy. The next seven Popes were all French, as were nearly 90 percent of the cardinals. The Avignon Popes lived an opulent lifestyle, exemplified by their building a magnificent palace for their residence and by engaging in an expensive program of centralizing Church government. This ambitious program of centralization added to the costs of running the papacy. As a result, to the large outcry of most Europeans, the French Popes imposed new and heavy taxes throughout the Christian world. They also returned to the old abuse of simony whereby they put friends and relatives on the Church payroll.

The Avignon papacy (1309–1377) scandalized the Church's opponents, including the Englishman William of Ockham whose writings called for a democratic form of Church government. In *Defender of the Peace* (1324), Italian Marsilius of Padua claimed that the Pope had no special power. He believed that the Church was subject to the state, a teaching that was attractive to the secular kings of the day.

The Babylonian Captivity weakened the papacy in the eyes of most Europeans, especially those engaged in combat. For example, England and France

1309
Babylonian Captivity of the Church begins with Popes moving to Avignon in France

were waging the Hundred Years War (1337–1453), begun when the French king tried to confiscate English territories located in southwestern France. This infamous conflict—which consisted of raids, sieges, and naval battles that were broken up by periods of uneasy peace— tilted on the side of the English until the fa- mous Battle of Orleans (1428–1429). It was during this battle that the young girl St. Joan of Arc, the Maid of Orleans, led a force that defeated the English, thus turning the tide of the war in France's favor and resulting in England withdrawing from most French territory (except Calais). In the early years of this war, the English were especially in- censed at the Avignon papacy, asserting that the Pope was just another political arm of the French government. The Germans and Italians were unhappy with the state of af- fairs as well.

➤ *Joan of Arc entering Orleans*

Pious Christians were scandalized by the corrupt lifestyle of the Avignon court and concerned that the Pope was not living in Rome, the proper dio- cese of residence for the successor of Peter. The last of the Avignon Popes, Gregory XI, had been considering returning to Rome, but was reluctant to fol- low through. However, the pleadings of two remarkable women, St. Bridget of Sweden (1303–1373) and St. Catherine of Siena, were instrumental in his overcoming indecision. St. Bridget did not live long enough to see her dream of the Pope residing in Rome realized. A strong voice for reform, she wrote to Pope Gregory XI, "In your curia arrogant pride rules, insatiable cupidity and execrable luxury."[2]

Catherine was more successful. In 1376, she went to Avignon and pleaded with Gregory to return to Rome. She argued that from the see of Peter, he could better help Christians in the aftermath of the horrific Black Death (the plague), a scourge of illness that cost many lives. She also pointed out that he could be a more impartial broker for peace between warring England and France and the continuously fighting Italian city-states if he lived in Rome. Historians debate how much the thirty-one-year-old saint influenced Gregory's decision, but shortly after hearing Catherine's pleas, he did return to Rome. Unfortunately, he lived only a short time. With the election of a new Pope—the Italian Urban VI

1311–1312
Council of Vienne

1321
Dante Aligheri completes
The Divine Comedy

—the Church faced one of the gravest crises in her history, one that would lead to a schism, which would prove to be the fatal blow to Christendom.

MEMBER OF THE CHURCH

St. Catherine of Siena:
COUNSELOR TO POPES

 Catherine of Siena was born in 1347 in an Italian city that had been ravaged by the Black Death (the plague). As a child, she had a deep devotion to Mary and Jesus, and experienced many mystical visions. She refused her parents' wishes to marry and instead, at age sixteen, she became a lay member of the Third Order of St. Dominic. She devoted herself to performing many charitable activities, including caring for the sick, as well as the victims of the many vendettas that plagued Italian families of her day.

Catherine also engaged in many penances of self-denial like eating little or no food, and her personal holiness attracted both male and female followers. Church leaders sought her out to settle disputes. Her forceful personality showed itself in the many letters she dictated to her secretaries to send to leaders around Europe to encourage them to reform. Her single-hearted devotion to peace exerted a profound influence on Church politics. She continuously badgered the Pope's legates and Pope Gregory XI himself to return to Rome. She pulled no punches in condemning the immorality, greed, and pride of the papal court. St. Catherine minced no words in her letters to the Popes. An excerpt from a letter she wrote to Pope Gregory XI exhorting him to come back to Rome typifies her writings:

> . . . For I reflect, sweet my father, that the wolf is carrying away your sheep, and there is no one found to succor them. So I hasten to you, our father and our shepherd, begging you on behalf of Christ crucified to learn from Him, who with such fire of love gave Himself to the shameful death of the most holy cross, how to rescue that lost sheep, the human race, from the hands of the demons; because through man's rebellion against God they were holding him for their own possession. . . .

1347–1353
Black Death

1377
Pope Gregory XI returns to Rome from Avignon

Come, come, and resist no more the will of God that calls you; the hungry sheep await your coming to hold and possess the place of your predecessor and Champion, Apostle Peter. For you, as the Vicar of Christ, should abide in your own place. Come, then, come, and delay no more; and comfort you, and fear not anything that might happen, since God will be with you. I ask humbly your benediction for me and all my sons; and I beg you to pardon my presumption. I say no more. Remain in the holy and sweet grace of God-Sweet Jesus, Jesus Love.[3]

She deeply respected the papacy, but wanted the man filling the office to live up to its responsibilities. She took the unprecedented measure of visiting the Pope and demanding his return to Rome. And soon after Gregory XI did return the papacy to Rome.

Catherine is a model of how a determined person of peace and good will can help the institution change for the better. Upon her death in 1380 she left behind four hundred letters, her work on mysticism, including the famous *Dialogue*, and many prayers. Hers are among the most brilliant writings composed by any Catholic saint, a fact recognized by Pope Paul VI in 1970, when he named her a Doctor of the Church.

The Twilight OF CHRISTENDOM

During the reign of Pope Clement VI in Avignon, a period of political intrigue and an ever-weakening papacy, the bubonic plague spread like wildfire over Europe. A Genoese ship returning from the Crimea, infested with flea-infected rats, carried this highly contagious disease to Europe. For those infected, it caused glandular swelling, fever, and death within a matter of hours. At the height of the plague (1347–1350), some cities were devastated. For example, Venice and Florence each lost one hundred thousand people; in Siena, four-fifths of the population died. Scholars estimate that from one-third to one-half of Europe's population perished. Not one country was spared. The clergy suffered huge losses, especially mendicants like the Franciscans who ministered directly to the suffering masses. Whole monasteries were wiped out. The plague returned several times during the following decades.

Unfortunately, just when the Church needed good servants to counteract the negative effects of a decadent papacy, it was forced to ordain inadequately-prepared priests. Many Christians, despairing of salvation, took up bizarre

1378–1417
The Western Schism of the Church

spiritual practices. Some roamed the streets and performed severe penances hoping to ward off the death which was all around them. Superstition abounded. Panic, despair, and lawlessness were rife. Worry over one's death became the central preoccupation.

Added to the horror of the Black Death was the ongoing One Hundred Years' War being waged by England and France. Because of the diminished population, economic disorder affected all members of society, but especially the poorest members. Periodic outbursts of pent-up peasant rage led to violence directed against the nobility and wealthy Churchmen. These were brutally put down by hired mercenaries.

Though it looked like society was disintegrating, all was not lost. During these despairing times, anonymous holy men and women ministered to the sick, endangering their own lives in the

> *Fourteenth-century migration of bubonic plague*

process. Even at the opulent papal court in Avignon, the Pope organized aid for plague victims and offered sanctuary to Jews who were being scapegoated for causing the plague. And visionary and practical spiritual writers emerged to give the Church hope. For example, works like *The Imitation of Christ* promoted a timeless path to personal holiness—following Christ—as an effective way to face problems regardless of the vicissitudes confronting a Christian in the external world.

The Western Schism (1378–1417)

One reason the French Popes wanted to remain in Avignon was the unruly mobs and belligerent families of Rome, both of whom tried to control papal elections. This is exactly what happened when Gregory died in 1378. Mob pressure helped elect the Italian Urban VI. His abrasive and obnoxious personality grated on the French cardinals who elected him. After a short time,

1382
John Wyclif condemned

these French cardinals claimed that they were pressured into electing an Italian Pope. They left Rome, announced to the world that they made a mistake, deposed Urban, and elected a Frenchman as the new Pope. He took the name Clement VII. He and his retinue of French cardinals returned to Avignon.

Neither Pope gave up his claim to the papal office. Upon their death, they were succeeded by other claimants to Peter's throne, each declaring his rivals illegitimate. Thus, the **Great Western Schism** resulted, a split that confused Christians who did not know who was the true Vicar of Christ. Western Europe was divided between two rival Popes. The French and Scots backed Clement VII; the English and Germans backed the Roman Pope.

The papal schism gave rise to the *conciliar movement*, which was based on the theory that Church reform could best take place by calling a council rather than relying on direct papal rule. A current philosophy of this time known as **Nominalism** helped give the intellectual underpinning to this movement. It held that the People of God as a whole—and their bishops gathered in a council—had final governing authority in the Church. The first council to meet to solve the crisis took place at Pisa in Italy 1409. More than five hundred delegates attended, the majority of them priests or nobles. The major topic of discussion was conciliarism itself, the belief that an Ecumenical Council has supreme authority over the Pope. But this council only worsened matters. It deposed both rival Popes and named a third Pope, Alexander V, as a compromise candidate. Neither papal rival acknowledged the authority of the council. The result was that the papal scene was like a comic opera, except no one was laughing.

Eventually, King Sigismund of Bohemia convoked the Council of Constance (1414–1418) to resolve the scandal. At first, the decrees of the council were hostile to papal authority, claiming that councils were superior to Popes who were bound to obey their decrees. After the council was in session for several months, Pope Gregory XII (recognized by the Church as the legitimate Pope) sent legates to Constance to convoke the council formally and thus make it legitimate. He then abdicated the papal throne of his own free will. The council deposed the other two Popes. Eventually the cardinals and representatives from five different nations elected Pope Martin V, effectively ending the scandal.

While the Council of Constance ended the schism other questions remained. For one, Martin V never signed the council's decree that gave councils supreme governing authority. This created fertile ground for a future clash between the backers of conciliar superiority and the supporters of papal primacy.

1415
John Hus burned at the stake

According to the agreements made at Constance, councils were to meet frequently to work on reforming the Church. However, during the reign of Pope Eugene IV (1431–1449), a crisis took place at the Council of Basel (convoked by Martin V shortly before his death). Eugene dissolved the council, but many of the participants refused to leave. After more discussion, often involving the question of a council's authority in relationship to the Pope, Pope Eugene eventually moved the council to Florence to discuss reunion with Greek Christians. The rebellious holdouts, who refused to assemble at the Pope's new location, deposed him and elected the last so-called anti-Pope, Felix V. But by now very few people or secular leaders supported these schismatics. The Council of Basel lingered on until 1449, when the anti-Pope resigned. Papal primacy was re-established once and for all, triumphing over conciliarism. Pope Pius II formally condemned the "deadly poison" of conciliarism in 1460, and threatened to excommunicate anyone who would appeal to a general council over the Pope.

More Heresies

Rising nationalism and the decline of papal prestige gave rise to new heresies. The atmosphere was suitable for attacks on the Church from a new generation of heretics. England's John Wyclif (1324–1384), for example, severely criticized the financial policies of the Avignon papacy and attacked papal authority. He also dismissed the validity of the hierarchy, the sacraments, and the priesthood. Disgusted with ecclesiastical abuses, he taught that the Church must return to strict poverty. Local English councils condemned Wyclif's ideas, but a group of his followers, the Lollards, spread his ideas, especially the right to read the Bible in the vernacular language.

John Hus (1369–1415) taught Wyclif's teachings in Bohemia. He stressed the authority of the Bible and the important role of preaching. He denied the ultimate authority of the Pope in doctrinal matters. On a promise that he would not be harmed, Hus attended the Council of Constance to defend his ideas. However, before Hus could adequately explain his views, the Council burnt him at the stake as a dangerous heretic. This shameful betrayal backfired. Rising nationalism in Bohemia made Hus a martyr-hero. A bitter twenty-year civil war followed, hurting the cause of the Church in Bohemia for decades.

Heretics like Wyclif and Hus prepared the way for the revolution that would soon take place. The Middle Ages were dying. Commerce was growing. Some merchant families, like the Medicis of Florence, became fab-

1417
The Council of Constance ends the Western
Schism. High point for Conciliarism

ulously wealthy. They dominated local governments, became patrons of the arts, and tried to influence the Church. (The Medici family, for example, produced several Popes.) The Black Death helped contribute to a major decline in monasticism. And although the papacy was restored, a new round of Popes were more interested in becoming Renaissance princes while engaging in nepotism, financial intrigue, and sexual debauchery. The Church was ready for reform. Unfortunately the reform was accompanied by a fragmentation of Christianity.

The Renaissance

The **Renaissance**, a cultural rebirth begun in the late Middle Ages, rediscovered the ancient civilizations of Rome, Greece, and Egypt. Writers, architects, painters and artists applied ancient learning to the emerging Western Civilization. The results of the Renaissance had a profound effect on religious life that still impact the Church today. The Renaissance stressed the natural and the human. It emphasized the pleasures of life, glorified the human body, and celebrated education.

Since human beings in all their natural glory were at the center of the Renaissance, the new outlook was given the name **humanism**. Most humanists were Christian. Eminent scholars like Erasmus of Rotterdam were interested in preserving and learning from classical texts and producing accurate translations of the Bible. They also encouraged the Church to return to her ancient roots and practice the simplicity of the Gospel. Artists celebrated the goodness of God's creatures; works by masters like Michelangelo, Raphael, and Leonardo da Vinci are among the most beautiful creations ever made by humans. Dante's *Divine Comedy*, is a pre-Renaissance classic which details the Christian journey in an entertaining and educational allegory. At the same time, it highlights the corruption of clergy who were not taking appropriate care of God's flock.

The Renaissance, in short, stressed the human more than the divine. Where the medieval world looked heavenward, the Renaissance highlighted human creativity. Although it brought about great advances in learning and unsurpassed achievements in art, the spirit of the Renaissance changed the way people thought about their world and the Church. During the Renaissance, the Church was no longer thought of as the *only* source of beauty, wisdom, and guidance.

1417–1431
Papacy of Pope Martin V

1431
St. Joan of Arc burned at the stake

The effects of the Renaissance created an atmosphere in Northern Europe that would lead to the Protestant Revolt. The ten Popes of this period, for example, heavily supported the lavish building projects, patronage of the arts, and military expeditions. Perhaps the most infamous Pope in history reigned during this time—Pope Alexander VI (1492–1503) from the influential and infamous Borgia family. He used nepotism and simony as ways to enrich his family.

The Renaissance Popes were always in need of money to support their lavish lifestyles, building projects, patronage of the arts, and military expeditions. One of the ways the Church financed these projects was through the selling of indulgences, which were for the remission of time in Purgatory for sins that were already forgiven. The selling of indulgences was an abuse by certain churchmen, and not an action of the Church herself. This would be one of the issues named by German monk Martin Luther at the time of the Protestant Revolt. Pope Leo X (1513–1521) reportedly commented to his brother, "Let us enjoy the papacy because God has given it to us."[4] This casual attitude reveals how Church leadership was not totally aware of the coming revolt.

WHAT THE CHURCH BELIEVES ABOUT . . .
Indulgences

The doctrine and practice of indulgences in the Church are linked to the Sacrament of Penance. An indulgence is the remission before God of the temporal punishment still due to forgiven sins. This means that every sin, even though forgiven, brings with it an unhealthy attachment to things of this earth and must be still purified, whether on earth or after death in the state called Purgatory. Catholics obtain indulgence of punishment from the Church's treasury of Christ's merits and the merits of the saints. As members of the Church, the souls in Purgatory also benefit from the indulgences we gain for them by prayer and devotion to penance and charity. Christians should accept the temporal punishment of sins as grace.

The Church in the East

There was a desire of the Popes and various Greek patriarchs of this era to work toward ending the Eastern Schism. A worthy objective of the Council of Ferrara-Florence (1438–1445) was to reunite the Eastern and Western churches. Present at this council were the emperor of the East, the patriarch of

1439
Council of Florence unites Greeks with Catholic Church

Constantinople, and hundreds of representatives from various Eastern churches. (Part of their reason for attending was to seek aid from the West to combat the Turkish Muslims.) An accord was reached in a bull of reunion and the reunion of the Western and Eastern churches was approved in December of 1452.

But the apparent end of the Eastern Schism was short-lived. The Byzantine Empire was extremely weak when it resumed power in 1261. (This was after Western rule following the sacking of Constantinople at the time of the Fourth Crusade.) The Muslim Turks had been chipping away at Byzantine territories for decades until all that was left of the Eastern Empire was Constantinople itself. The Byzantine emperor successfully petitioned the Pope to call a crusade to help repel the Turks. At first, the crusaders were a help, but they were eventually defeated by the Turks near the Black Sea. Shortly thereafter, in May of 1453, the Turkish sultan Mahomet II assaulted Constantinople, looted the city, and killed or enslaved the inhabitants. The last Byzantine emperor was killed in battle, thus signaling the death of the Eastern Christian Empire. The "second Rome" was no more. The city was now known by its Turkish name, *Istanbul.*

With the end of the Byzantine Empire, the hope for unity of the Eastern and Western churches in these turbulent times was dashed. Christianity was now clearly divided into the Roman Catholic Church in the West and the Eastern Orthodox Churches in Asia Minor, Greece, Russia, and Bulgaria. This split remains to the present day.

The Causes of the
PROTESTANT REFORMATION

The Renaissance and several issues of Church belief and practice spurred the coming of the Protestant Revolt or Protestant Reformation. Reformers like John Wyclif and John Hus preached a return to Gospel simplicity. However, their zeal, and that of their followers, led them down the path of heresy. Girolamo Savonarola, a Dominican monk, attempted moral reform of the citizens of Florence but his overbearing personality turned him into an intolerable dictator and imprudent critic of the Pope, which led his supporters to turn on him and burn him at the stake in 1498.

More peaceful reformers were on the scene as well, most notably the humanist scholar Erasmus of Rotterdam (d. 1536). Erasmus widely traveled throughout Europe and kept up a voluminous correspondence with leaders, bishops, and other humanists. He also published works by ancient Christian writers and produced a scholarly version of the Greek New Testament. His

·· ▶

1453
Constantinople falls to Turks; Eastern Christian Empire ends

famous work *In Praise of Folly* (1511) poked fun at superstitions and corrupt Church leaders. Erasmus hoped to reform society, apply the Gospel to the political system of his day, and prod the Church into self-renewal. Unfortunately, his ideas did not catch on before the Protestant Reformation.

The following sections briefly summarize factors that brought about the Protestant Revolt.

The Renaissance at the Expense of Religion

The Renaissance helped to usher in the modern world. As noted, one of its outcomes was a focus on human achievements over God and religion. Critical thinking, questioning, and doubting were hallmarks of the revival of education. With the invention of the printing press, new ideas could spread like wildfire. Reformers like Luther were encouraged by the free flow of ideas and the new technology.

In general, the Renaissance Popes were among the worst of any Church era. They embraced secular issues and interests more often than they did the Gospel. For example, Pope Julius II (1503–1513) focused more heavily on his military exploits and massive building projects than on his spiritual responsibilities. Also, memories of the Babylonian Captivity of the Church where Popes were at the beck and call of French monarchs, the scandal of the Western Schism, and papal abuses like nepotism and simony were all fresh in recent history. A good number of Catholics, clergy and laity, hoped for reform.

The Black Death brought a morbid fear of death and gave rise to a religion of emotion and superstition. Images of the Last Judgment filled the faithful with dread and terror. Painting and statues of a suffering Christ fired people's imaginations. People turned to relics of saints, bizarre penances, and magical practices to guarantee safety and salvation. Intellectuals began to abandon scholasticism and its clarity of thought. Teachings espoused by the philosophy of Nominalism were attractive to many people, including the belief that the faithful could have direct contact with God through personal reading of the Bible. It largely rejected the Church's sacramental system and any need to follow the teaching authority of the Popes on Christian moral living.

Princes and kings in the newly formed rising nations resented the control the Pope exerted over their territory. They especially disliked papal taxation. They increasingly fought with the Popes, who often were interested in increasing papal power in Italy.

1456
Johannes Gutenberg produces the first bible printed on a movable press

1483
The Spanish Inquisition begins

The Reformers

Another factor in the Protestant Reformation was that some of the instigators had strong and forceful personalities. Through their charismatic preaching and intelligent leadership, they were able to influence many people. When the Church was too slow in addressing their objections, the reformers took matters into their own hands. While Martin Luther, an Augustinian monk, is the best known, other protestors like Ulrich Zwingli and John Calvin, not to mention King Henry VIII, also had a lasting impact. As you read more about these men, recall that the root of Protestant is "protest." What they had in common was their protest against the Catholic Church and some of her teachings and practices. Their protest led to a division in the unity of Christians that never has been completely healed.

Martin Luther was born in 1483, the son of strict, merchant-class parents. Luther began his adult life as a law student; however, when he narrowly escaped a frightful lightening storm, he vowed to enter a monastery. The brooding, hard-working, and intelligent Martin joined the Augustinian monastery in Erfurt, Germany, where he lived a strict monastic life, became a priest, and earned a doctorate in theology. The Augustinians sent him to teach moral theology and scripture at the University of Wittenberg.

➤ *Martin Luther*

During these teaching years, Luther's reputation as a careful thinker and brilliant preacher spread. However, his academic successes did not relieve him of many religious scruples. He had an overwhelming sense of unworthiness, a dread of sin, and fear of death and judgment. He pictured God as a stern judge. No matter what penances he would perform, he could not get a sense of God's love and salvation. Then one day, while studying a passage from the letter to the Romans (3:27–28), Luther concluded that only faith in God's mercy justifies sinners. Luther's insight brought him joy and peace. He sensed the power of this truth and did his best to teach and preach it to others.

The issue of the selling of indulgences gave Luther the opportunity to contrast his views with an almost superstitious piety that had arisen in the Church. Indulgences, the remission of temporal punishment in Purgatory due to sins already forgiven, were a spiritual benefit that some churchmen abused in Luther's day. The Church teaches that it can dispense indulgences from the

1492
Columbus travels to the New World

richness of graces won by Jesus' sacrifice on the cross to remove temporal punishment for sin. However, the scandal was that in Luther's day, the Church was selling these spiritual benefits to finance building projects (like St. Peter's in Rome) and to pay off debts incurred by absentee bishops.

When the Dominican Johann Tetzel came to Germany to sell indulgences while using phrases like, "Another soul to Heaven springs when in the box a shilling rings," Luther acted. The gross materialism and lack of spirituality among many clergymen disgusted him. Superstitious appeals to the faithful that gave the impression that Heaven could be bought went against Luther's own experience of faith in God's gift of salvation. On October 31, 1517, Luther posted his famous *Ninety-Five Theses* on the church in Wittenberg to protest Tetzel's preaching and challenge other theologians to debate his ideas. This dramatic event marked the beginning of the Protestant Reformation. Luther had no intention of leading a revolution or break with the Church. The call to reform had begun, however, and there was no going back.

The Church was slow to respond to Luther's challenge, at first thinking it was a minor quarrel among monks. When called to Rome, Luther refused to go. What Luther really wished to do was to discuss his ideas at a Church council. In 1520–1521, he wrote three works that openly taught the primacy of Scripture over Sacred Tradition, the "priesthood of the belivers [laity]" being essentially equal to the priesthood of the orained, and the doctrine of justification by faith alone. He also taught there were only two valid sacraments, Baptism and the Eucharist. Luther burned the bull of excommunication along with a book of canon law and other materials he had received from the Church. When summoned to the Diet of Worms (1521) to appear before the new Emperor Charles V and some papal representatives, Luther thought he would be involved in a discussion. Instead, he discovered that they simply wanted him to recant his theses. Luther declared, "Here I stand. I cannot do otherwise. God help me. Amen."

The emperor concluded that Luther was dangerous to the Catholic faith. The Pope excommunicated him. Luther had rejected the Pope's primacy and, in an earlier day, would probably have been burnt as a heretic. However, Luther had powerful allies among the German princes, especially Frederick of Saxony who guaranteed him safe passage from the meeting at Worms and agreed to hide him. Nationalism, the movement for a united, independent German nation, helped to explain the strong support Luther received. The Germans grew tired of a corrupt Italian papacy extracting money from their country.

1512
Michelangelo completes his painting of the Sistine Chapel

While in exile, Luther translated the Bible into German and wrote many pamphlets explaining his ideas. The recently invented printing press helped to reach more people than ever before. Eventually, Luther came out of exile, married, fathered children, preached widely, wrote catechisms, and composed many beautiful and moving hymns. His disciple, Philip Melanchthon, drafted the basic creed of the new religion, Lutheranism, under the title *Augsburg Confession* (1530).

As Lutheran influence grew, especially in northern Germany, German leaders agreed to a compromise at the **Peace of Augsburg** (1555). This established the principle of *cuius regio, eius religio* (Latin for "whose region, his religion"). This meant, simply, that subjects had to adopt the faith of the ruler in whose lands they lived. The intention of this compromise was good—to keep down petty religious quarrels between Lutherans and Catholics. Unfortunately, this less-than-adequate solution sowed the seeds for the bitter Thirty Years' War that would erupt in coming decades.

WHAT THE CHURCH BELIEVES ABOUT . . .
Merit

Merit is the reward a person receives from God for cooperating with his grace. There is no strict right to any merit on the part of anyone. "Between God and us there is an immeasurable inequality, for we have received everything from him, our Creator" (CCC, 2007). The love of Christ for us is the source of all our merits before God. We have been given the freedom to respond or not to the grace God has given us; merit is the result of God's grace and our cooperation with his grace.
See *Catechism of the Catholic Church*, 2006–2011.

Around Luther's time, several reformers came on the scene in Switzerland and Germany. Many of them were priests. Ulrich Zwingli set up a reform Protestantism in Zurich, Switzerland, where he encouraged a democratic rule for the Church. More anti-clerical and anti-institutional than Luther, Zwingli removed images from churches, banned Church music, and abolished fast days. He taught that the Eucharist only symbolizes Jesus' presence. Zwingli's reform has influenced the religious practice of all of Switzerland even to our own day.

John Calvin (1509–1564) was a Frenchman who gained a master's degree in theology and a doctorate in law. He left Paris for Switzerland where he wrote his famous *Institutes of the Christian Religion* (1536), the most important theoretical work of the Reformation. Calvin taught the primacy of Scripture

1517
Martin Luther posts his *Ninety-Five Theses*

and the absolute sovereignty of God. He denied the Catholic idea of sacraments and condemned the papacy, monasticism, and clerical celibacy.

Calvin's best-known doctrine is **predestination**. According to this teaching, God determines people for salvation or damnation before they are born. No human effort can merit salvation or entrance into the elect. Grace is God's free gift, independent of one's behavior.

WHAT THE CHURCH BELIEVES ABOUT . . .
Predestination

In a heretical sense, predestination is a belief that one's actions are not only pre-known by God, they are also predetermined. It implies that God can will sin and who goes to Heaven or hell, and thus denies God's gift of free will. Catholic belief is different. God does have knowledge of who will be saved and who will be lost, yet it is God's desire that all will be saved. To this end, he provides graces and helps which we are free to accept or reject. This means that while God knows certain people will be lost, this is not the choice of God, but the choice of those individuals. See *Catechism of the Catholic Church*, 600.

Calvin himself was strict and harsh. His personality affected the type of church that he set up in Geneva, Switzerland. He created a *theocracy*, a civil government controlled by the church. He and his followers regulated all aspects of people's lives, even punishing children for laughing while playing. His council outlawed dancing, card playing, and many other forms of entertainment.

Calvin's influence throughout Europe grew because of his university at Geneva. Especially attractive was Calvin's brand of church governing which included pastors, doctors (teachers), elders, and deacons. Calvin's brand of Protestantism spread much further than Lutheranism, which was mostly limited to Germany and the Scandinavian countries. Holland adopted his reforms as did parts of France and Hungary. Eventually, Calvin's reforms made their way to England. John Knox (1505–1572), a former Catholic priest, brought Presbyterianism, an offshoot of Calvinism, to Scotland. Knox stressed the equality of all believers, teaching that everyone is a priest (presbyter), thus requiring no separate clergy. Reformed, Congregationalist, and Presbyterian churches today look to John Calvin as their spiritual father. Calvin's emphasis on clean living, a harsh and judgmental God, thrift in business dealings, and strictness in religious observance came to America with the Puritans.

1520
Martin Luther excommunicated

1523
Ulrich Zwingli leads the Swiss reformation in Zurich

King Henry VIII cannot be technically called a "reformer" because the Protestant Revolt came to England not over a doctrinal dispute but because the Pope would not allow Henry VIII (king from 1509–1547) to divorce his wife Catherine of Aragon. Catherine had not borne him a male heir, so Henry VIII wished to marry Anne Boleyn.

Henry's solution to the conflict was to make himself head of the Church in England. For the most part, Henry accepted Catholic doctrine. In fact, he had won the title "Defender of the Faith" for his eloquent rebuttal of Luther's teaching that Jesus only intended two sacraments. He also issued his *Six Articles* (1539) which insisted on Catholic teachings and imposed penalties on anyone who denied the Eucharist, confession, or clerical celibacy.

His most controversial action, however, was the Act of Supremacy which required an oath of allegiance to himself as head of the English church. A few brave Catholics refused to take this oath, most notably, Cardinal John Fisher and Sir Thomas More. Thomas was Henry's close friend and the Lord High Chancellor of England. Nevertheless, More refused to violate his conscience which forbade him to deny the primacy of the Pope. Henry had both Fisher and More beheaded in 1535.

Henry confiscated the monasteries, claiming for himself vast Church holdings and sapping the strength of the Catholic Church in England. This prepared the way for Calvinists. After Henry died, Archbishop Cranmer exerted considerable influence through his *Book of Common Prayer* (1549) and the *Forty-Two Articles of Religion*. Half of these articles contained Catholic doctrine while the other half espoused Calvinist and Lutheran teachings. Cranmer was able to control the Church of England.

Mary Tudor (1553–1558), daughter of Henry and Catherine of Aragon, tried to restore Catholicism during her reign, but she did it through violent means. She executed almost three hundred people, earning the name "Bloody Mary" from her Protestant opponents. Her attempts at a Catholic restoration failed. When she died, the Catholic restoration in England ended. The long reign of Elizabeth I (daughter of Henry VIII and Anne Boleyn) from 1558–1603 established the Anglican religion in England. Elizabeth synthesized Calvinist, Lutheran, and Catholic elements into what became known as the Anglican faith. Anglicanism upheld traditional forms like the episcopate and elaborate liturgical worship, but it also fostered doctrines that were Calvinist at heart. Like her father, Elizabeth required the Oath of Supremacy and persecuted Catholics and radical Protestants who refused to take it. Priests were executed if they were caught celebrating the Catholic Mass.

1530
Philipp Melanchthon releases his *Augsburg Confession*

Anglicanism, also known as the Episcopal Church, became the official religion of England. More than twenty thousand Puritans, a branch of Calvinism, left England in the 1620s and 1630s and sailed to the New World because of persecution. They were the Pilgrims of the new nation who came to set up holy commonwealths. However, they mirrored the religious prejudice of their day and passed laws against other religious groups, for example, Catholics and Quakers. Some Catholics also left England for America in the 1630s, as much for financial opportunity as for religious freedom. They largely settled in Maryland, which was founded by a Catholic family, the Calverts. Maryland was the first colony to allow freedom of worship.

WHAT THE CHURCH BELIEVES ABOUT . . .
Divorce and Remarriage

The remarriage of King Henry VIII to Anne Boleyn would still be invalid if it occurred today. Henry's marriage to Catherine of Aragon was a valid sacramental marriage. Christian marriage is a lifelong commitment. The Church teaches that a sacramental marriage between Christians in which there has been valid matrimonial consent and consummation is absolutely indissoluble except by the death of one of the spouses. Though civil authority may dissolve the legal aspects of marriage, the state has no authority to dissolve a true Catholic marriage. Legally separated Catholics (divorced under civil law) may not remarry while their spouses are alive. This teaching comes from the words of Jesus: "Everyone who divorces his wife and marries another commits adultery" (Lk 16:18).

Comparing Protestant Groups

The word *protest* means both "to object to, especially formally" and "to promote or affirm." The word *Protestant* was first used to describe German "princes and free cities who declared their dissent from the decision of the Diet of Speyer (1529) denouncing the Reformation." German Lutherans took up the name, although the Swiss and French preferred the word *Reformed*. *Protestant* soon became the word used for reformers in Germany and any Christian in the West outside the Roman Catholic Church.[5]

Today, Protestantism refers to a large movement that encompasses hundreds of different religions. It does not specify any particular group. The accompanying chart presents some of the major teachings of the three main groups that arose in the sixteenth century.

•···

1534
Henry VIII's Act of Supremacy makes him head of the Church of England

Lutheran	Calvinist	Anglican
Key event: publication of *Ninety-Five Theses* in 1517	*Key event*: publication of *Institutes of Christian Religion* in 1536	*Key event*: King Henry VIII declares himself head of Church in England in 1534 (*Act of Supremacy*)
1. Human beings have a fallen nature. Only faith brings salvation.	1. Human nature is utterly depraved.	1. Accepts most Catholic teachings about faith and good works. Does not recognize papal primacy.
2. Primacy of the Bible. Encourages individual interpretation of Scripture.	2. The doctrine of predestination. Christ died only for the elect. The elect cannot resist God's grace. Nor can they backslide.	2. The monarch is head of the church in England. The monarch establishes what is allowable religious practice in the realm.
3. Accepts only the sacraments of Baptism and the Eucharist. Believes in *consubstantiation*—body and blood of Christ coexist with the bread and wine which do not change.	3. Accepts only Baptism and Eucharist. Believes only in Christ's spiritual presence in the Eucharist. Encourages Bible reading, sobriety, thrift, capitalism, and a strict Sabbath observance. Stresses the priesthood of all believers and democracy in the church.	3. Believes in the Seven Sacraments. Liturgy very similar to Catholic liturgy. Bishops head dioceses and priests serve in parishes. Priests can marry.
4. *Rejects*: holy days, fast days, honoring saints, indulgences, the rosary, monasticism, the other five sacraments.	4. *Rejects*: whatever is not in the Bible—for example, vestments, images, organs, hymns.	4. *Accepts*: *The Book of Common Prayer* and most Roman Catholic beliefs and practices.

1535
Execution of St. Thomas More by King Henry VIII of England

Lutherans, Reformed Protestants (the descendants of Calvin), and English Protestantism (Anglicans, Puritans, and later Methodists) represent the three major streams of the Protestant Reformation in the sixteenth century. However, other branches broke off from Roman Catholicism, many of them going by the name of *Radical Protestants*. A major stream was the Anabaptists.

The Anabaptists were the source of many of these radical reforming sects, for example, the Baptists, Mennonites, Amish, and Quakers. Anabaptism (literally, "baptism again") taught that infant Baptism was invalid. They believed that the Church was an adult community of like-minded believers. Only adults should be baptized. Many Anabaptists tried to create tight-knit communities based on Gospel simplicity. Common ownership of goods, strict biblical morality, and life in the Spirit were the hallmarks of these communities.

Because Anabaptists and other radical groups seriously challenged the traditional patterns of authority in society, they were persecuted by both Protestants and Catholics as dangerous heretics. Like the Puritans, many of these groups emigrated to America in the seventeenth and eighteenth centuries so they could freely practice their religion. For example, the Quakers under the Englishman William Penn founded Pennsylvania as a haven for religious tolerance. It became a model for the new country that was to be born in the American Revolution of 1776. The Constitution of the United States of America guarantees the freedom of religion to all.

Catholic REFORMATION

The Catholic Church did not stand idly by while the Protestant Reform swept through Europe. The Fifth Lateran Council (1512–1517), convoked by Pope Julius II and concluded by Pope Leo X, reiterated a bull against the role of simony in papal elections and passed other reforms that called for Church renewal. Some far-sighted clergy also took part in some initial reforms. For example, the Capuchins, an offshoot of the Franciscans, revived the spirit of poverty and service that Francis intended for his brothers. New religious orders like the Theatines (1524) were founded, based on the idea that raising the spiritual level of the clergy was the key to reform. This order lived in community and took the three traditional vows of poverty, chastity, and obedience, but also served among the poor. From their ranks would come more than two hundred bishops. The Ursuline nuns, founded in 1535 by St. Angela Merici, dedicated their lives to teaching girls and working among the sick and the poor.

●··

1539
First missionaries—Franciscans—come to the Americas

Spain's Role in the Catholic Reformation

Spain played an important role in the reform of the Catholic Church. King Ferdinand and Queen Isabella were intent on making Catholicism the state religion of Spain. One of the tools they used to unify Spain under the banner of the Catholic faith was the Spanish Inquisition, established with permission from Rome in 1478. Under the notorious First Grand Inquisitor of Spain, Tomás de Torquemada, the Inquisition rooted out heretics. Negatively, the Spanish Inquisition used torture to exact confessions, a method criticized by Pope Sixtus IV.

Cardinal Jiménez de Cisneros (1436–1517), the archbishop of Toledo, was a visionary who worked for Church renewal. Cardinal de Cisneros was a confessor to Queen Isabella. He lived an austere life above reproach and founded the University of Alcala, a center for theological and biblical studies. The university would produce theologians of great achievement who would play an important role at the Council of Trent.

Because of the discipline and rigor found in the Spanish Church, it remained firmly Catholic during the period of Protestant Revolt. Distinct Baroque architecture and

➤ *Cardinal Jimenez de Cisneros*

concert-style Masses indicated the confidence of the Spanish Church. It also produced two of the most influential reformers to help the Church answer the Protestant movement—St. Ignatius of Loyola, who founded the Society of Jesus, and St. Teresa of Avila, who helped reform the Carmelite Order.

The Jesuits

The most important religious order established to help the Catholic Reform was the Society of Jesus—popularly known as the Jesuits. Its founder, St. Ignatius of Loyola (1491–1556), was a Basque from the Pyrenees in Spain. A leg wound ended his life as a knight. During his lengthy recovery, Ignatius read about the lives of Jesus and the saints and decided to serve the Kingdom of God as his life's new work. Ignatius spent a year in prayer and meditation. From his own experiences in the spiritual life, he composed the *Spiritual Exercises* (1523), now a classical work on spiritual life for both Jesuits and lay people.

During a ten-year period of schooling, largely spent at the University of Paris, Ignatius gathered around him six companions, including Blessed Peter Faber and Saint Francis Xavier, who took the traditional vows of poverty,

1540
The Society of Jesus is approved by the Vatican

chastity, and obedience. This company of zealous Apostles also took a fourth vow—obedience to the Pope as a sign of their commitment to fight against the Protestants. This vow distinguished the Jesuits from all other religious orders, making them "shock troops" in the service of the Pope. Pope Paul III approved the Society in 1540, and, until his death in 1556, Ignatius served as general of the order. From his offices in Rome, he wrote more than seven thousand letters, directing the many important ministries around the world.

The Jesuits engaged in preaching, teaching, writing, and the founding of schools and colleges. They directed retreats, advised leaders, and served as confessors. They were also a vigorous missionary order that brought the faith to the New World and to the East. The greatest of all Jesuit missionaries was St. Francis Xavier (1506–1552) who preached the Gospel in India, Indonesia, and Japan.

Jesuit accomplishments in the history of the Church are many. By the time of Ignatius's death, the Society of Jesus had over one thousand members. Vigorous men like St. Peter Canisius (1521–1597) helped the Jesuits win back many Germans, Hungarians, and Bohemians and all of Poland to Catholicism. The Jesuits founded more than eight- hundred schools by 1749. These schools swayed many to return to Catholicism and exerted a strong influence on the learned and the rich. This made the Jesuits a significant force in the politics of the day. However, in a later century (1773), their success would lead to the Bourbon kings of Spain and France conniving to get them dissolved by the Pope. The order was restored in 1814, and is today the largest religious order of men in the Catholic Church, numbering close to twenty thousand companions worldwide.

MEMBER OF THE CHURCH

St. Teresa of Avila: *INTERIOR CASTLE*

At the age of twenty, Teresa de Cepeda entered the Carmelite Incarnation convent in Avila, Spain. At that time convents were like finishing schools for young ladies. They permitted visiting, dancing, entertaining, wearing jewelry, and eating fine foods. Teresa joined in the casual routine of her fellow nuns.

However, Teresa also prayed regularly and performed penances. Gradually, over the course of years, she deepened her spiritual life and received spiritual ecstasies: a trance of joy and delight in the Lord. Teresa developed an intimate friendship with the Lord. Later, she would teach

---

1541–1564
Calvin creates a theocracy in Geneva

1542–1552
Missionary career of St. Francis Xavier in India and Japan

that an excellent way to pray is to imagine talking to Jesus as to a close friend. Her familiarity with Jesus even allowed her to scold him. An oft-quoted example recounts how one day her cart turned over on the road while she was engaging in a good deed. Exasperated, she said to the Lord: "No wonder you have so few friends! Look how you treat them!"

Teresa became a reformer of the Carmelites. She left her original convent and set up a reformed convent of thirteen nuns who wanted a simple, austere life. Eventually, her experiment was so successful that she traveled throughout Spain and set up scores of convents which adopted her strict rule. Her Discalced (shoeless) Carmelites lived an austere life of poverty, withdrew from the world, and a engaged in intense prayer. Her example encouraged a Carmelite priest, St. John of the Cross (1542–1591), to carry through similar reforms in his own order for men.

Teresa's reform efforts met many opponents, including some in her own Carmelite order. On occasion, Teresa even had to defend herself before the Inquisition. But she did so with courage leavened with a marvelous sense of humor. Eventually, her reform resulted in a separate order.

Teresa's profound writings on the spiritual life significantly helped the Church renew itself after the Protestant Revolt. Teresa's *Interior Castle* is an important spiritual classic which outlines the various steps involved in contemplative prayer. The Church honors St. Teresa of Avila as one of the three female Doctors of the Church.

Timeless Advice from St. Teresa of Avila

St. Teresa offers perspective on the following life issues:

On Self-criticism:
"Be kind to others, but severe on yourself."

On Flexibility:
"Never be obstinate, especially in unimportant matters."

On Prayer:
"There are more tears shed over answered prayers than over unanswered prayers."

On Life's Perspective:
Let nothing disturb thee;
Let nothing dismay thee;

1554
St. Philip Neri founds the Congregation of Oratory,
a community of priests and lay people, which
ministered around Rome.

> All things pass:
> God never changes.
> Patience attains
> All that it strives for.
> He who has God
> Lacks for nothing:
> God alone suffices.

The Council OF TRENT (1545–1563)

The various political intrigues of the day stalled Catholic efforts at reform. The thought of calling a Church-wide council brought up fears of conciliarism which might have threatened the papacy altogether. Also, continuous warfare between the emperor and the king of France made finding a suitable place for a council to meet, free from the political control of mon-

➤ *The Council of Trent*

archs and other secular leaders, almost impossible. Eventually, Pope Paul III (1534–1549) convoked the nineteenth General Council of the Church at Trent in the heart of the Alps. The Council had more than twenty-five meetings in three sessions (1545–1547, 1551–1552, and 1561–1563) that were interrupted by various wars. In the beginning, as few as thirty-four bishops participated, but in the later meetings more than 230 attended.

The Council set out to explain clearly what Catholics believed and to reform many of the abuses that the Protestants challenged. The Council of Trent was one of the most important of all Church councils. It shaped and influenced Catholic teaching explicitly until the Second Vatican Council and really to this day. It helped the Church emerge from the Reformation purified, reformed, and strengthened. Some of the major *doctrinal* teachings of Trent include the following.

- Papal supremacy is reaffirmed.

- Both Scripture *and* Tradition are fonts of revelation. Against those who taught the validity of private interpretation of the Bible, only the Magisterium can rightly teach the correct meaning of the Bible.

1545–1563

Council of Trent rejects Luther's theology of *sola scriptura* ("the Bible alone"), *sola gratia* ("grace alone"), and *sola fide* ("faith alone"). The Council agreed with Luther that a person cannot be justified without faith. However, the Council pointed out that Baptism, not personal faith, is the first step toward Salvation.

- Salvation is God's free gift; we respond to this grace God has given us.

- The doctrine of transubstantiation is reaffirmed, expressing that at the consecration of the Mass the reality (substance) of the bread and wine change into the reality of Jesus—his risen, glorified Body and Blood. The Lord is present whole and entire for as long as the Eucharistic species subsist.

- The Mass is a true sacrifice, an extension of Calvary through which Christ's sacrifice is made present. Jesus empowered the Apostles to offer this new sacrifice; the Sacrament of Holy Orders passes this power to priests.

- The Sacrament of Penance is the only ordinary means used to forgive mortal sins committed after Baptism. Although confession of venial sin is not necessary, it is a good way to grow in virtue.

- There are Seven Sacraments. Matrimony, for example, is a true sacrament and marriage is indissoluble. Marriages must be performed before a priest and two witnesses.

- Purgatory exists, and the souls in Purgatory benefit from our prayers, especially the Mass. True indulgences have spiritual value as does veneration of the saints. However, the council condemned superstitious abuses concerning relics, statues, and indulgences.

The Council of Trent also addressed matters of *discipline* in the Church. For example:

- Clerical abuses were corrected. Priestly celibacy was reaffirmed. Bishops were ordered to live in their own dioceses. Priests were to reside in their own parishes, monks in their monasteries, and nuns in their convents.

- Priestly training was given top priority. Because the quality of the priests had been dreadfully low, the Council mandated the establishment of seminaries. St. Charles Borromeo created a model seminary in Milan, Italy. Later, Pope Gregory XIII would create many colleges for priests. (The most famous of these, still operating today, is the Gregorian University in Rome.)

- Church laws that affected the daily life of Catholics were authored. For example, the Council clarified laws about the Lenten fast, fasting

1555
Peace of Augsburg; local rulers
choose religion for their subjects

1566–1572
Pontificate of St. Pius V

before receiving Communion, and abstaining from eating meat on Fridays. It also legislated marriage laws.

- The Council created an *Index of Forbidden Books* to keep Catholics from reading radical and heretical ideas. Unfortunately, the *Index* did include some important intellectual works, including René Descartes, John Milton, Jean-Jacques Rousseau, Immanuel Kant, Victor Hugo, and Gustave Flaubert.

Assessment of the Catholic Reform

In general, the Council of Trent and subsequent Catholic Reformation were successful in correcting abuses and putting the Church on the right course. A series of good Popes who ascended the papal throne after the Council adjourned aided these efforts.

Pope St. Pius V (1566–1572) was a noteworthy leader. Strict in his remedies, Pius, for example, imposed severe sanctions for swearing and violating Sundays and holy days. He also outlawed begging and had public whippings for adulterers. Pius helped promote a Holy League, chiefly made up of Spanish and Venetian forces, to support the fight against the Ottomans at the famous naval Battle of Lepanto (1571). In this historic victory, the Christian fleets inflicted a massive defeat to the Turkish navy, freeing the Mediterranean from Ottoman control. (Miguel de Cervantes, the famous author of *Don Quixote*, was wounded in this battle.) The Pope believed the Christians were victorious because of the intervention of the Blessed Mother and his call for Catholics to recite the rosary to her before the battle began. As a result of the victory, he established the Feast of Our Lady of Victory on October 7, the day of the battle. Pope Gregory XIII later moved this feast to the first Sunday of October, designating it the Feast of Our Lady of the Rosary.

The *Roman Catechism*, a clear summary of Catholic beliefs that served the Church's catechetical efforts well until modern times, was published under Pius's direction and he reformed the Catholic Mass through the *Roman Missal*, which set up a uniform liturgy through the Catholic world. The rituals and prayers of this *Missal*, revised by Popes Clement VIII (1604) and Urban VIII (1634), were the unchanging standard of Catholic worship until the reforms of the Second Vatican Council. Pius's most significant contribution, though, was eliminating corruption from the Roman Curia. He abolished the opulent papal court, and insisted that cardinals live in Rome and live a simple and exemplary life.

1572
The St. Bartholomew's Day Massacre

Pope Gregory XIII (1572–1585) established the papal diplomatic office and reorganized the calendar, which is still known today as the Gregorian calendar. His successor, Pope Sixtus V (1585–1590), appointed reforming cardinals, fixing their number at seventy. Sixtus centralized Church government into fifteen Roman congregations, ministerial offices that helped govern the Church. Pope Paul V (1605–1621) published the *Roman Ritual,* which set up rules for the proper celebration of the sacraments.

Had the post-Reformation Popes not been good men intent on enforcing Trent's decrees, the efforts at reformation would have been futile. Fortunately, many reforming bishops assisted the Popes. The most notable example was St. Charles Borromeo (1538–1584), the zealous reforming bishop of Milan. St. Robert Bellarmine (1542–1621), a Jesuit and Doctor of the Church, produced many scholarly writings that effectively countered the protests of heretics, including material on the relationship between science and faith, even defending Galileo against those who wished to sanction him more severely. Bellarmine also argued democratic theory, showing how authority comes from God and is invested in the people who entrust it to rulers. This principle, greatly admired today, troubled the monarchs of both England and France. Finally, his catechisms for teachers and children were instrumental in handing on the faith to future generations.

1571
Battle of Lepanto

1598
Edict of Nantes gives civil and religious rights to the Huguenots

Summary

- The Protestant Revolt of the sixteenth century had many causes, including the decreased prestige of the papacy brought on by the Babylonian Captivity of the Church.

- Not long after the last Avignon Pope returned to Rome, partly as the result of the pleadings of St. Catherine of Siena, the Church was hit by another crisis: the Great Western Schism. During this crisis lasting from 1378–1417, two and sometimes three claimants were vying for the papal throne. Pious Christians were confused as to the identity of the true Vicar of Christ. Eventually, the Council of Constance (1414–1418) resolved the scandal.

- The Black Death devastated Europe in the mid-fourteenth century, wiping out a third or more of Europe's population.

- Popes of the Renaissance were typically driven by a humanist spirit that focused more on earthly glories than heavenly ones. They became great patrons of the arts but often at the cost of using scandalous practices, like the selling of indulgences by some churchmen, to raise money for their various projects.

- The selling of indulgences, in fact, was the catalyst that moved Martin Luther to post his *Ninety-Five Theses*, the precipitating event of the Protestant Revolt. He argued for the primacy of Scripture over Church Tradition, the priesthood of the laity, and the doctrine of justification by faith alone. Luther was successful in his protest because the papacy was slow to react to the threat he posed. He also benefited from the spirit of nationalism that protected him from papal reprisals. More radical reformers quickly followed Luther including Ulrich Zwingli and John Calvin. Calvin's *Institutes of Christian Religion* was the most significant theoretical work of the Reformation, influencing subsequent reformers like John Knox. King Henry VIII broke from Rome over the issue of his desire to divorce. He insisted on an oath of loyalty that made him the head of the church in the land. His daughter, Queen Elizabeth I, created the Anglican Church in England by synthesizing Calvinist, Lutheran, and Catholic elements.

- The Catholic Reformation was helped by new religious orders like the Theatines. Spain was spared the trauma of the Protestant Revolt because its monarchs instituted the Spanish Inquisition to root out heretics and because it was blessed with good, reform-minded bishops like the humanist Cardinal Jiménez de Cisneros. Spain also gave the Church St. Ignatius of Loyola. His Society of Jesus was in the vanguard of stemming the spread of Protestantism and brought intellectual vigor to the Catholic Reformation. Another Spaniard, St. Teresa of Avila, reformed the lax convents of the Carmelite Order.

- The Church was slow to convoke a council to address Protestantism because of a number of factors: a failure to grasp the seriousness of the threat, constant warfare, and the fear of conciliarism. Finally, Pope Paul III convoked the Council of Trent which met in three sessions from 1545–1563. Though Trent did not bring about the hoped-for reunion between Catholics and Protestants, it clearly restated important points of Catholic doctrine under attack. It also promulgated a number of disciplinary reforms that helped purify the Church of many long-standing abuses.

- A notable reform-minded Pope who implemented the laws of Trent was Pope St. Pius V. His *Roman Catechism* and *Roman Missal* provided the standards for Catholic catechetics and worship until modern times. Trent's reform efforts were also helped by strong bishops like St. Charles Borromeo and scholars like St. Robert Bellarmine.

- Efforts at reunion with the Eastern Church were raised at the Council of Ferrara-Florence (1438–1445) but eventually fell apart when the Byzantine Empire was toppled by the Sultan Mahomet II in 1453. Moscow became the "Third Rome" after the fall of Constantinople.

Prayer REFLECTION

St. Ignatius of Loyola, the founder of the Jesuits, authored this Prayer for Generosity.

Lord Jesus, teach me to be generous;
teach me to serve you as you deserve,
to give and not to count the cost,
to fight and not to heed the wounds,
to toil and not to seek for rest,
to labor and not to seek reward,
except that of knowing that I do your will. Amen.

Review and DISCUSSION QUESTIONS

1. How did the Babylonian Captivity of the Church contribute to the decline of the papacy in the fourteenth century?

2. What caused the Great Western Schism? How was it resolved?

3. Explain how the Renaissance contributed to the Protestant Reformation.

4. Discuss three other causes of the Protestant Reformation.

5. What factors prevented the end of the Eastern Schism during this era of Church history?

6. Discuss the event that gave birth to the Protestant Reformation. Explain the reaction of the Church to Luther's teaching.

7. What does the doctrine of "justification by faith alone" mean? What is the Catholic position on faith, good works, and justification?

8. Discuss some differences between the reforms and beliefs of Lutheranism, Calvinism, and the Anglicanism.

9. What led to King Henry VIII's break from the Roman Church? What role did Queen Elizabeth I have in making Anglicanism the state religion?

10. Discuss how Spain avoided the Protestant Reformation.

11. How were the Jesuits at the vanguard of the Church's response to the Protestant Reformation?

12. Name three doctrinal teachings that emerged from the Council of Trent.

13. Discuss several disciplinary reforms that resulted from the Council of Trent.

14. Discuss some of the means the Popes used to put the decrees of the Council of Trent into effect.

15. Identify and discuss the significance of the following:

Events and People

Augsburg Confession   Babylonian Captivity of the Church
Battle of Lepanto   Black Death

➤ *Jewish Temple in Jerusalem*

➤ *Interior of St. Peter's Basilica*

➤ *Baptism of Constantine the Great by Jacopo Vignali*

➤ *Mont St. Michel, Manche, Normandy, France*

➤ *Pope John Paul I*

➤ *Pope Benedict XVI*

➤ *Pope Paul VI*

➤ *From left to right: Archbishop of Canterbury, Archbishop of Thyteira and Great Britain, Pope John Paul II and the Dalai Lama pray together for world peace*

➤ *Statue of John Carroll near Healy Hall on the campus of Georgetown University*

➤ *Second Vatican Council*

➤ *The coronation of Emperor Napoleon I Bonaparte*

➤ *Mission Santa Barbara, California*

➤ *Pieter Brueghel's depiction of the bubonic plague or "Black Death"*

➤ *Martin Luther before the Reichstag in Worms*

Cardinal Jiménez de Cisneros

Council of Trent

Great Western Schism

Institutes of the Christian Religion

Ninety-Five Theses

Peasants' Revolt

Savaronola

Council of Constance

Erasmus of Rotterdam

Index of Forbidden Books

Johan Tetzel

Peace of Augsburg

Protestant Reformation

Spiritual Exercises

Popes

Alexander VI

Gregory XI

Reformers

Anabaptists

John Hus

John Knox

Marsilius of Padua

Philip Melanchthon

Ulrich Zwingli

John Wyclif

John Calvin

King Henry VIII of England

Martin Luther

Queen Elizabeth I of England

William of Ockham

Saints

Bridget of Sweden

Charles Borromeo

Joan of Arc

Pope Pius V

Teresa of Avila

Catherine of Siena

Ignatius of Loyola

Philip Neri

Robert Bellarmine

Thomas More

Terms

conciliarism

humanism

Nominalism

theocracy

cuius regio, eius religio

indulgence

Renaissance

Scripture CONNECTION

Read Chapter 3 of St. Paul's letter to the Romans, a pivotal New Testament text used by Martin Luther to develop his theology.

Learn BY DOING

1. Obtain a copy of *The Imitation of Christ*. Plan a time for devotional reading using its text.

2. Attend the religious service of a Protestant church (however, not in lieu of your obligation to attend and participate in Sunday Mass). Report on how it differs from a Catholic liturgy.

3. Interview a Protestant who is knowledgeable about his or her faith. Report on the religion's beliefs about the following:

   • the sacraments

   • worship

   • morality

   • Church authority

4. Read the Second Vatican Council's *Lumen Gentium*, nos. 14–15
   (see: www.vatican.va/archive/hist_councils/ii_vatican_council).

   These sections of the document teach about membership in the Catholic Church and the Church's relationship to other Christian bodies. Note the following information:

   • Who is a Catholic?

   • Discuss four beliefs Catholics have in common with other Christians.

   • What unites all Christians to Christ?

5. Prepare a two-page short biography on one of the following:

   a. A founder of one of the radical reforming groups (e.g., George Fox of the Society of Friends [Quakers]).

   b. One of the saints mentioned in this chapter (e.g., Thomas More, Bridget of Sweden—check the references given for saints' biographies at the end of Chapter 3).

c. One of the Popes from this era (e.g., Alexander VII or Pope St. Pius V—check the Catholic Encyclopedia online at: www.newadvent.org/cathen).

d. Another leading Renaissance figure (e.g., Erasmus of Rotterdam, Leonardo da Vinci).

6. Report on the effects of the Black Death. You might begin your research at this website: www.themiddleages.net/plague.html.

7. Read chapters 1–8 from the "Decree of the Most Holy Eucharist" from the thirteenth session of the Council of Trent. You can find it online at: http://history.hanover.edu/texts/trent/ct13.html. Summarize five important teachings from this decree.

8. Take a virtual tour of the Renaissance at the Learner.org website: www.learner.org/exhibits/renaissance.

   Discover answers to these questions:

   a. What was new about humanism versus previous ways of thinking in Europe?

   b. What impact did the Renaissance have on the Catholic Church?

9. Tour the Vatican museums online: http://mv.vatican.va/3_EN/pages/MV_Home.html. Report on one of the great Renaissance artworks represented on the tour.

6
The Church in an
ERA OF CHANGE

We teach and define that it is a divinely revealed dogma that the Roman Pontiff, when he speaks "ex cathedra," i.e., when exercising his office as pastor and teacher of all Christians he defines, by his supreme apostolic authority, a doctrine of faith or morals which must be held by the universal Church, enjoys, through the divine assistance, that infallibility promised to him in blessed Peter and with which the divine Redeemer wanted His Church to be endowed in defining doctrine of faith and morals; and therefore that the definitions of the same Roman Pontiff are irreformable of themselves and not from the consent of the Church.

—FIRST VATICAN COUNCIL
PASTOR AETERNUS, CHAPTER 4[1]

Saint for Peace IN VIOLENT TIMES

The seventeenth century was a violent one born of religious hatred and intolerance. Various groups of Christians constantly fought among themselves for political and religious domination. Thankfully, though, as in every era of Church history, there are examples of gentleness and kindness, of Christians who believed more in the power of love to attract than the games of rivalry and hate that lead to meaningless death. One such Christian was St. Francis de Sales (1567–1622), who was bishop of Geneva, Switzerland, a Calvinist stronghold that had been captured by the Catholic Duke of Savoy. His story is shared below.

The son of an aristocrat, Francis was a gifted student who eventually achieved a doctorate in law. But from his earliest years, Francis was attracted to serving the Church, despite his father's insistent desire for him to live the life of a married nobleman, serving in the senate of Savoy. It took patience and time for Francis to win his father's approval to the idea of his vocation.

As a young man Francis suffered a religious crisis over Calvin's notion of predestination, despairing for his own salvation. But he fervently prayed before a statue of the Blessed Mother asking for deliverance from his despair. One day his temptation fell away from him "like the scales of leprosy." He came away completely convinced of God's unconditional love for everyone, a theme that would be at the heart of his apostolic work. His own spiritual struggles made him a sympathetic counselor to the hundreds of people who would come to him for advice.

After his ordination to the priesthood in 1593, Francis embarked on a mission of preaching to reconquer Calvinists by love and thus restore peace to the Christian family. His preaching was charismatic, yet simple, and supported by the philosophy that one who preaches with love, preaches effectively. One of Francis's famous sayings is widely quoted even today: "A teaspoon of honey attracts more flies than a barrel of vinegar."

➤ *St. Francis de Sales*

At first, Francis's travel in Calvinist territory was fraught with danger and almost insurmountable difficulties. One time, wolves attacked Francis; on other occasions, crowds beat him and assassins tried to take his life. Undaunted, Francis did not give up. He began to produce small pamphlets to explain points of Catholic doctrine. These gentle tracts began to attract Protestants who would then come to hear Francis preach. They listened not to some fiery condemner of Calvinist views but a loving father concerned for his children. In time, Francis's sermons—characterized by love, understanding, and patience—led to forty thousand Calvinists returning to the Church.

After becoming Bishop of Geneva in 1602, Francis put into action the decrees of Trent and became an exemplary bishop. He administered the sacraments and taught catechism. His voluminous writings instructed, edified, and reformed the Christian community. Because of his writings, Francis de Sales, Doctor of the Church, is the patron saint of journalists.

Francis also was an exemplary spiritual director. He believed that every Christian had a vocation to holiness. He counseled many lay people and wrote for them the classic *Introduction to the Devout Life* and the treatise *On the Love of God*. The most famous person Francis served as spiritual director for was a widow, St. Jane Frances de Chantal (1572–1641). With her he founded

1609–1610
Rheims-Douay Bible, First Catholic English translation

the Order of Visitation, a community of sisters who became "daughters of prayer." Their motto is "Live Jesus!"

Had more Catholics and Protestants followed his wise counsel found in the following quote, seventeenth-century Europe could have avoided the violence and intolerance that became its legacy:

> The person who possesses Christian meekness is affectionate and tender towards everyone: He is disposed to forgive and excuse the frailties of others; the goodness of his heart appears in a sweet affability that influences his words and actions, presents every object to his view in the most charitable and pleasing light.[2]

This chapter will discuss the following topics in this era of great change:

- Fallout from the Reformation: Europe in the Seventeenth Century
- Age of Saints
- Missionary Effort
- Eighteenth Century: Age of Revolution
- Nineteenth Century: Liberalism, Reaction, and Pope Pius IX.

Unity in the European Church
IS THREATENED

One of the marks of the Church is her unity. The Church is one because she is in union with the Lord. Unity manifests itself in three ways—oneness in belief, worship, and fidelity to Christ's authority. The members of the Church believe the same doctrines (creed), celebrate the same sacraments, and submit to the Lord's teaching authority through the Magisterium.

Unity is a paradox, however, because each age brings with it forces that seek to destroy Church unity. Some of these threats were present in the era from 1600–1900.

Germany after the Reformation

Nowhere was the hatred spawned by unwavering religious conviction more in evidence than in Germany of the seventeenth century. After the reforms of Trent were put into practice, Catholics were successful in winning back to the Church many areas of central Europe. St. Francis de Sales converted parts of

1611
Publication of the Authorized or
King James Version of the Bible

1618–1648
Thirty Years' War

Switzerland, and similar gains were made in Bavaria and Austria, as well as in Bohemia and Poland. Supporting these gains was the House of the Habsburgs, a royal family that controlled Germany and which had the support of the emperor of Austria and the king of Spain.

But the Habsburgs had many political enemies, especially France. These foreign enemies joined forces with various Protestant groups who feared a Catholic takeover of Germany. They engaged in a series of wars that lasted between 1618–1648, the infamous Thirty Years' War. These conflicts also involved elements of civil war, with various German princes at times supporting the Habsburgs, and at other times trying to overthrow them. The politically and religiously complex Thirty Years' War devastated Germany, with half its population perishing. Historians rate the Thirty Years' War as the most barbaric in Europe's history up to that time: a war tragically fueled by religious intolerance of Lutherans, Calvinists, and Catholics.

At one point in the conflict, the Catholic rulers seemed on the point of victory until France came to the aid of the Protestant princes. Ironically, two famous cardinals were in charge of French policy at the time—Cardinal Richelieu (1585–1642) and Cardinal Mazarin (1602–1661). In this battle, the cardinals put the national interests of the mother country over the Catholic identity of Europe.

The ultimate outcome of the war was devastating for Germany. Survivors in Germany were reduced to severe poverty. The Habsburg Empire was devastated and Spain was no longer Europe's most powerful nation. France emerged as the strongest nation on the continent.

Religiously, the Peace of Westphalia (1648), which ended the Thirty Years' War, legalized Calvinism in Germany and gave Protestantism equal status with Catholicism. The treaty reaffirmed the principle of citizens following the religion of the prince (*cuius regio, eius religio*). It drove the last nail in the coffin of the ideal of a united Christendom in Europe.

England and the Reformation

For reasons discussed in Chapter 5, Spain had remained solidly Catholic throughout the Protestant Reformation. But as a European power, its influence was in serious decline due to a number of defeats it suffered versus England. (However, Spain remained a force in the New World with its many colonies.)

England under Elizabeth I neutralized Spain with the decisive defeat of the Spanish Armada in 1588. When Elizabeth died, she was succeeded by her

1633
Trial of Galileo

1640
Beginning of the Jansenist heresy

cousin, James I, King of Scotland, and then by his son, Charles I. These Stuart kings were suspect to many in England not only because they were Scottish but also because they had ties by marriage to French Catholic monarchs. During James I's reign (1603–1625), the famous Gunpowder Plot (1605) took place, a plan of a few Catholic nobles to blow up Parliament and the king. The plot fizzled when the authorities were warned ahead of time. Connected to this plot, some Catholics were executed, while others fled the country. More restrictive laws were passed, including those that prohibited Catholics from practicing law or medicine.

King Charles I (1625–1649) was married to a French Catholic and opposed Calvinists. Though himself a High Church Anglican, he adopted religious policies that made the Anglican religion resemble Catholicism (especially in the liturgy) even more than it had under Elizabeth. In addition, he was lax in enforcing laws passed against Catholics.

Charles also adopted political policies that led to a severe clash with Parliament, which had been taken over by the Puritans, that is, Calvinists who wished to "purify" the Church of England of its "popish superstition." Eventually, King Charles I found himself in a civil war against the Parliament's forces. He was defeated and executed by the Puritan's leader, Oliver Cromwell (1599–1658). Cromwell ruled as Lord Protector of England from 1653–1658, trying to turn England into a theocracy modeled on Calvin's Geneva. His dreary rule, unpopular laws, divisions among Puritan groups, and the general disgust of the English with the violence Puritans directed against Catholics and Anglicans alike led to the restoration of the monarchy under Charles II.

Charles II (1660–1685) desired to be a Catholic, and was married to a woman who was Catholic, but thought if he said so publicly, he, like his father, would be deposed and executed. He did convert to Catholicism on his deathbed.

Charles's brother James II, a Catholic convert, came to power at a time when Anglican persecution of Catholicism was still severe. James II (ruling from 1685–1688) gave Protestants reason to believe that he was on the verge of restoring Catholicism. He lifted persecution against Catholics and elevated four Catholic bishops as equals to their Anglican counterparts. Moreover, he had a male heir which drove fear into the members of Parliament that England would be destined to be ruled by Catholic monarchs for years to come. As a result, the Parliament deposed James II and elevated his Protestant daughter, Mary, to the throne, marrying her off to William of Orange, a Protestant prince from Holland. This was known as the "Glorious Revolution" of 1688.

1642–1649
The Martyrs of North America

Note how in England the Parliament deposed two kings in forty years. English representative government, and a monarchy whose power was restricted by written constitution, contrasted sharply with the divine right of kings and absolute monarchy that held sway in France. It was in France where its rulers transformed the Catholic Church into a nationalized Church.

France after the Reformation

The effects of the Protestant Reformation also touched France, and led to a series of civil wars (the French Wars of Religion) in the sixteenth century, including the infamous St. Bartholomew's Day Massacre of Protestants on August 24, 1572. Toward the end of the century, the Protestant Henry of Navarre emerged as the leading candidate to become king. Realizing that most people in France would not accept a Protestant king, he converted to Catholicism, ensuring the Catholic nature of the country. However, by signing the Edict of Nantes (1598), French Protestants, known as Huguenots, were free to practice their religion in certain areas of France.

Henry Navarre, who ruled as Henry IV, was a popular monarch who engaged in many works to better the lives of the French people. Nevertheless, he met an untimely death at the hands of a fanatic assassin in 1610. His son, Louis XIII, age nine, succeeded him. Louis's mother, aided by the brilliant Cardinal Richelieu, ruled as regent until he reached the age of sixteen. Through Louis's long reign (1610–1643), Cardinal Richelieu was the real power behind the throne.

Richelieu's policies led to France replacing Spain as the leading European power in the seventeenth century. The policies included centralizing the power of the French king and controlling the influence of the nobles. As indicated in the discussion on the Thirty Years' War, Richelieu's foreign policy was geared to curbing the power of the Habsburg Dynasty in Germany, even if this meant allying himself with Protestant monarchs.

When Cardinal Richelieu died (1642), Cardinal Jules Mazarin took his place. And after King Louis XIII's death a few months later (1643), Mazarin effectively ruled France for King Louis XIV who was five years old at the time he became king. Cardinal Mazarin continued Richelieu's policies of consolidating power in an absolute monarch, extending French power in Europe at the expense of the Habsburgs, and adding territory to France. When Cardinal Mazarin died, one of the seventeenth century's great personalities—King Louis XIV—came into power.

1648
Treaty of Westphalia

Louis XIV—the "Sun King"—ruled seventy-two years, from 1643–1715, living by the motto, "I am the state." He believed in the absolute power of the monarchy. Under this theory of governing, the king (or queen) ruled the country freely, unbounded by any outside legal authority limiting regal power. Louis also extended his theory of governance to religion where he believed there should be one king, one law, one faith. The one faith, of course, was to be Catholicism, but a Catholicism controlled by the state, not by Rome. To promote unity in France, Louis XIV rescinded the Edict of Nantes in 1685, which gave toleration to the Huguenots. He began to persecute them, attacking both their religious

> *Louis XIV, King of France*

and civil freedoms. Many Protestants fled to French Canada and England at this time, just as many Catholics were fleeing England to attain freedom of worship.

Louis XIV sought to dominate the French Church, claiming to be God's representative in his country and desiring to limit any papal control of the national Church. Louis XIV's claim to French independence from the Roman pontiff is known as **Gallicanism** (from the Latin name for France).

In 1682, Louis XIV forced the French clergy to adapt and teach in their seminaries the famous **Four Articles**. These articles made some outrageous claims: first, that the Pope had no power in temporal matters; second, general councils were superior to the Pope in spiritual matters; third, the papacy must adapt its rulings to the French Church; fourth, the decrees of the Pope are only binding on the faithful when a general council agrees to them.

The Pope fought back by refusing to appoint any bishops in France. Eventually, in 1693, Louis gave in. He quietly withdrew the Four Articles, although they continued to have a strong influence in France throughout the next century. Many French churchmen adopted Louis's nationalistic attitudes. They were suspicious of fellow clerics, especially the Jesuits, who were strong supporters of papal primacy. The papal supporters were known as the **Ultramontanes**, a word meaning "beyond the mountains." Ultramontanes looked beyond the Alps to the Pope in Rome for spiritual leadership.

1660–1689
The Stuart Restoration in England and Ireland

In the eighteenth century, rulers throughout Europe imitated Louis's intervention in Church affairs and hostility to papal authority over the national church. The Jesuits especially came under attack and, through many political machinations, found their order suppressed by Pope Clement XIV (1773). A prime example of state control over the Church in another Catholic country was **Josephinism** in Austria. The Emperor Joseph II (1765–1790) believed the Church should simply be another arm of the government with the state controlling Church laws and practices. To this end, he required bishops in his realm to swear an oath to the state, took control of the financial affairs of religious institutions, and even passed laws that micro-managed details of liturgical worship.

Papal political influence was at a low ebb during the seventeenth century. Gallicanism was simply one example of a growing trend that had started after the Thirty Years' War. For example, when the Pope vigorously protested certain clauses of the Treaty of Westphalia, his objections were ignored by both Catholic and Protestant rulers. Historians mark 1648 as a pivotal date when the Pope's influence in the political sphere was greatly diminished.

France also figured in two of the seventeenth-century's misguided efforts at spiritual renewal. The first of these, **Jansenism**, caused great turmoil in France. Inspired by Cornelius Jansen (1585–1638), a bishop of Ypres in France, Jansenism bordered on Calvinism. Jansen and his followers taught the utter depravity of human nature and that God's grace extends to only a few. Like Calvin, Jansenists held that God predetermined some people to Heaven and most others to hell. They believed that most Catholics were not worthy to receive Holy Communion. They looked down on most Christians as spiritually inferior to them. They also had a strict, negative view of the human body, especially sexuality.

The Jansenists especially disliked the Jesuits whom they thought were too lenient in the spiritual advice they gave to penitents. Headquartered at a French convent in Port-Royal near Paris, Jansenist leaders, including the famous philosopher Blaise Pascal (1623–1662), attacked the Jesuits for moral laxity and called their fellow Catholics to the austere practices of early Christianity.

Although condemned by the Pope and most French bishops, Jansenism hung on to influence much of the French Church. Jansenism's negative, fear-inducing approach to religion stressed God's justice over his mercy, suffering over the joy of the Gospel, and the evils of our fallen nature over the goodness of creation. It influenced spiritual writers of the day, including missionaries who imported some of the Jansenistic teachings to future generations of Catholics in the New World.

●···

1682
Gallicanism: the Four Organic Articles

In contrast to Jansenism was another heresy known as **Quietism**. It was inspired by a Spanish priest, Michael Molinos (1628–1696), but became popular in France, especially among some aristocratic women. Quietism also took a dim view of human nature, holding that humans are powerless and should not try to resist temptations since they are God's will. We should not try to live the virtues or concern ourselves with Heaven and hell. As humans possess a fallen nature, this meant that most of those who embraced Quietism fell into immorality and stopped practicing their faith.

The papacy condemned both of these unrealistic views of Christian holiness, Jansenism and Quietism. Catholicism teaches that the life of holiness is not just for the few. Spiritual effort is worthwhile. God gives his grace to every Christian. Prayer, frequent reception of the Sacraments of Penance and the Eucharist, and works of self-denial and charity towards others are ways all Christians can grow close to the Lord. Contrary to Quietism, the Church teaches that growth in holiness does take effort. And against Jansenism, the Church teaches that God is a God of justice, but also a God of infinite mercy and forgiving love who provides his children with many opportunities to grow in holiness and to live the Christian life.

WHAT THE CHURCH BELIEVES ABOUT . . .
Asceticism

Asceticism is the name for the virtue-filled form of Christian self-discipline that is important for the development of an authentic Christian lifestyle. Asceticism calls a person to take the Gospel and baptismal vows seriously in a personal journey toward perfection. This way of perfection passes by the way of the Cross. There is no achievement of holiness without renouncing sin and engaging in a dedicated spiritual battle.

See *Catechism of the Catholic Church*, 2015.

Age OF SAINTS

Jansenism and Quietism were two attempts to define holiness in the Church of seventeenth-century France. Jansenism was too strict in its view of human nature and thought it almost impossible for any human to live a holy life. Quietism was so lax that it totally downplayed any effort of trying to attain holiness.

Fortunately, the Holy Spirit has always provided exemplars of true Christian holiness in every age. Accordingly, some historians have called the seventeenth

1685
Edict of Nantes revoked

century the Age of Saints. It seems that there were many heroic men and women of Christian virtue who came on the scene during this time of post-Reformation adjustment. These included many famous missionaries who preached the Gospel in hostile lands and suffered martyrdom for their efforts.

For example, men like St. Isaac Jogues (1607–1646), and the seven other North American martyrs, willingly put themselves in harm's way to preach Christ's love and salvation to the Native Americans, even knowing that martyrdom was a distinct possibility. Isaac Jogues and his companions were French Jesuits.

WHAT THE CHURCH BELIEVES ABOUT . . .
The Call to Holiness

Holiness is a share in God's own life. It is living a fully human life of conversion and a renunciation of sin. It is a life's commitment to live in faith, hope, and love and service of one's brothers and sisters. Holiness is allowing Jesus to live in us. Holiness is unleashing the power of the Holy Spirit to transform us into people of peace, mercy, kindness, patience, humility and gentleness.

> Thus it is evident to everyone, that all the faithful of Christ of whatever rank or status, are called to the fullness of the Christian life and to the perfection of charity; by this holiness as such a more human manner of living is promoted in this earthly society. In order that the faithful may reach this perfection, they must use their strength accordingly as they have received it, as a gift from Christ. They must follow in His footsteps and conform themselves to His image seeking the will of the Father in all things. They must devote themselves with all their being to the glory of God and the service of their neighbor. In this way, the holiness of the People of God will grow into an abundant harvest of good, as is admirably shown by the life of so many saints in Church history (*Lumen Gentium*, 40).[3]

See *Catechism of the Catholic Church*, 2013–2014.

Saints Who Countered Heresy

France produced a number of admirable saints during this period. One of the most famous Visitation nuns was St. Margaret Mary Alacoque (1647–1690). An invalid as a child, she was cured after she received a vision from the

1688
Glorious Revolution in England

Blessed Mother and committed herself to a life as a cloistered nun. Considered slow intellectually by her religious sisters, Margaret had a rich, contemplative prayer life that did not always fit in with the expectations or experiences of the other nuns. Three years after her final vows, she was praying in front of the Blessed Sacrament when she had a vision of our Lord. In many subsequent visions, he asked her to promote devotion to him as the Sacred Heart. At first, theologians who investigated her thought her delusional. But in time, her confessor, St. Claude de la Colombière (1641–1682), a Jesuit, believed her and helped her to promote what would become one of Catholicism's most popular devotions to the Sacred Heart of Jesus. Its emphasis on Christ's humanity, intimacy with fellow people, and his boundless love counteracted the strictness of Jansenism and the laxity of Quietism. It fostered love and reparation for sin through the reception of Holy Communion on the first Fridays of the month and a holy hour of prayer.

Companion Saints

When it comes to saints, it seems that the old saying, "Birds of a feather flock together," has much truth to it. Recall the lives and partnerships of Francis of Assisi and Clare of Assisi, Francis de Sales and Jane de Chantal, Margaret Mary Alacoque and Claude de Colombière who ministered in close proximity to one another in other eras. The seventeenth century offers another example of saints who worked in tandem. When St. Francis de Sales died, St. Vincent de Paul (1580–1660) became the spiritual director of St. Jane de Chantal.

Vincent de Paul may be the greatest organizer of charity in history. His life was packed with intrigue and adventure from the very beginning. As a young man he was sold into slavery by the Barbary pirates. He eventually converted his master and found his way back home. He then went to Rome where he began to climb the clerical ladder. However, Vincent left the easy life in Rome to begin pastoral work in a rural area where the poverty of the people greatly moved him. He began to organize disciplined teams of charity workers who provided services of food and clothing for the poor.

Vincent's superiors recalled him to Paris where a chance meeting with Francis de Sales affirmed that Vincent's new life of serving the poor was God's will. Vincent founded an order of priests, the Congregation of the Mission, who preached "missions" to bring people back to the faith. He began charity teams, gave retreats to priests, founded a seminary, and created nursing

1738
Methodist Church founded by John Wesley;
Pope Clement XII condemns Freemasonry

homes for the elderly. He also gave advice to the French queen, ransomed slaves, and performed many other charitable works.

One of Vincent's chief helpers was St. Louise de Marillac (1591–1660), a young widow and loving mother. Together with this thoroughly devoted woman, Vincent founded the Daughters of Charity, an order devoted to serving the sick, poor, elderly, and orphans. This order thrived and did incredible good work among God's people. It was a new type of religious order where the sisters took annual vows instead of permanent vows like other nuns. Unlike typical sisters of the day who were required by Church law to live in cloisters, the Daughters of Charity could mingle among the poor people and freely set up hospitals, orphanages, and schools. The Daughters served as a model for new congregations of women that would be founded in subsequent centuries.

St. Vincent's idea of lay involvement in charity was adopted later by Blessed Frederick Ozanam in the 1830s. He founded the St. Vincent de Paul Society, a famous charitable organization that is active even today. Its threefold purpose is to witness to Christ, promote community among its members, and offer direct, person-to-person assistance to those who are suffering and in need of help.

WHAT THE CHURCH BELIEVES ABOUT . . .
Love for the Poor

God blesses those who help the poor and rebukes those who do not. Jesus said: "Give to him who begs from you, do not refuse him who would borrow from you" (Mt 5:42). Christ will recognize his chosen ones based on what they have done for the poor while on earth.
See *Catechism of the Catholic Church*, 2443–2445.

A Saint for Education

Toward the end of the century of saints, St. John Baptist de La Salle (1651–1719), an ordained priest committed to the poor, founded an order of teaching brothers known as the Brothers of the Christian Schools, commonly known as the Christian Brothers.

St. John believed in education for the poor, that classes should be in the vernacular language, not Latin, as was the custom, and that physical discipline methods should not be used. Also, he instituted group instruction, with classes organized according to the mental maturity of the students with

1756–1763
The Seven Years' War

classrooms arranged with desks in rows. (The typical method of instruction has been one-on-one tutoring for wealthy nobility.) His school curriculum consisted of a variety of courses (including ethics, literature, physics, philosophy, and mathematics) taught in an orderly sequence on a fixed schedule. He also outlawed physical discipline. All these innovations were revolutionary for his day.

St. John's schools for the poor were initially attacked by tutors because they feared the new schools would threaten their livelihood. Others who disapproved of the schools were the Jansenists and class-conscious individuals who were against scholarly pursuits for the "lower orders." However, the schools were so successful that over time the persecutions diminished. Part of St. John's legacy was the deep religious atmosphere created in his schools, an atmosphere that is the hallmark of Catholic education today.

WHAT THE CHURCH BELIEVES ABOUT
Catholic Schools

While Catholic schools are "no less zealous than other schools in the promotion of culture and in the human formation of young people" it is the "special function of the Catholic school to develop in the school community an atmosphere animated by a spirit of liberty and charity based on the Gospel" (*Gravissimum Educationis*, 8). Parents have the right to choose a school for their children which corresponds to their own religious convictions.

See *Catechism of the Catholic Church*, 2229.

❋ QUOTATIONS FROM SEVENTEEN CENTURY SAINTS

We should strive to keep our hearts open to the sufferings and wretchedness of other people, and pray continually that God may grant us that spirit of compassion which is truly the spirit of God.

—St. Vincent de Paul[4]

As for your conduct toward the poor, may you never take the attitude of merely getting the task done. You must show them affection; serving them from the heart—inquiring of them what they need; speaking to them gently and compassionately; procuring necessary help for them without being too bothersome or too eager.

—St. Louise de Marillac[5]

1773
Society of Jesus suppressed

It is chiefly by asking questions and in provoking explanations that the master must open the mind of the pupil, make him work, and use his thinking powers, form his judgment, and make him find out for himself the answer.

—St. John Baptist de La Salle[6]

The Gospel Is PREACHED IN NEW LANDS

Today, there are three major branches of Christianity: Catholic, Orthodox, and Protestant. The Catholic Church bears the name that means "universal." Recall that St. Ignatius of Antioch was the first to describe the Church this way: "Where Jesus Christ is, there is the Catholic Church." The Church is universal because she spreads throughout the world. Universal also carries a second meaning: The Church is universal because she is *orthodox*, that is, true to the teachings of Jesus Christ.

The Church is for all people, in all places, at all times. The Catholic Church shows in its Seven Sacraments, doctrines, and organizational structure the fullness of the Christian faith and practice intended by Jesus Christ. The Church continues to teach the same Gospel Jesus taught. It carries out his command to baptize in his name, and administers the Seven Sacraments as signs of grace.

The mark of catholicity implies that the Church must move out to the rest of the world. Catholic missionaries to the New World from the sixteenth century onward rivaled the early Church for spreading the Gospel to the known world. The discovery of new lands opened many opportunities for evangelization.

Missionaries in the New World

Wherever explorers went in the New World, missionaries followed. The motto was "cross and crown." In 1493, Pope Alexander, to avoid conflict between nations, sent Portuguese missionaries to Brazil and Spanish missionaries to the rest of the New World. In what would become the United States, Spanish missionaries were the first to arrive in California, the Southwest, and the Southeast.

The saga of missionary activity includes the stories of many brave Franciscans, Jesuits, Dominicans, and others who risked their lives to bring Christ to the indigenous peoples. Many of the missionaries were saintly and good

1776
American Revolution begins with signing of the Declaration of Independence

to the Indians, learning their languages, teaching them the faith, instructing them in new trades.

Unfortunately, the story of these missionary efforts also has a dark side because they were so closely wedded to the practice of military conquest at any cost. The conquistadors who accompanied missionaries had a thirst for gold that seemed to override any other motive, for example when they conquered the Aztecs in Mexico and the Incas in Peru. The colonizers often thought of the native populations as inferior. Some missionaries had a crusading attitude toward their work. The missionaries often served as government officials who looked after birth and death records and the collection of taxes. The natives saw them more as tools for Spain or Portugal and not as Christians entrusted with the care of souls. Forced conversions, extermination of thousands of natives, exploitation of the populace, refusal to ordain native men as priests for fear of the power of a native clergy to challenge colonial rule—all these were attempts to use the Gospel to further political goals.

Many good missionaries fought these abuses. For example, Dominican bishop Bartolomé de Las Casas (1474–1566) worked vigorously for rights for native people. He was instrumental in getting the so-called New Laws passed that forbade slavery and the enforced labor of native populations and extended them other rights as well. St. Peter Claver (1581–1654) ministered to the slaves in Colombia and the West Indies. St. Martin de Porres (1579–1639) earned the nickname "The Wonder Worker of Peru" for his ceaseless devotion to lessen the evils of slavery. Jesuits also set up model communities in Paraguay and Brazil which tried to preserve native culture while providing education and the benefits of civilization. Unfortunately, complex political realities forced the Jesuits to abandon these missions.

French efforts at evangelization in the New World came later than the Spanish. Their activities were concentrated in North America and, in general, were less successful than Spanish efforts. Some of the French missionaries, like Fr. Jacques Marquette (1637–1675), were great explorers. He not only established missions in places like Michigan, but also was among the first Europeans to explore the Mississippi River. As indicated before, other French missionaries suffered martyrdom.

Missionaries in the Far East

Missionary activity in the Far East differed from that in the West. Many missionaries followed the example of St. Francis Xavier who founded missions

1789
John Carroll of Baltimore becomes first American bishop

in India, Indonesia, and Japan. Many missionaries, exemplified by the Italian Jesuits Matteo Ricci (1552–1610) in China and Robert di Nobili (1577–1656) in India, tried to adapt Christianity to the culture of these Eastern civilizations. Ricci, for example, won the Chinese over because of his knowledge of astronomy. He spoke their language, adopted their dress, and respected their traditions. He gradually began to share his religion, trying to show how Christianity could enhance the Chinese experience.

MEMBER OF THE CHURCH

St. Francis Xavier:
APOSTLE OF THE INDIES

 The greatest missionary to the East was St. Francis Xavier (1506–1552). In 1542, he arrived in Goa on the west coast of India, a Portuguese colony and the trade center in Asia. Known as "the Apostle of the Indies," Francis had a remarkable career founding missions in India and then moving on to Ceylon (today's Sri Lanka), a large island off India's southern coast. He had a magnetic personality, a holiness that was transparent to all, a gentle way of instruction, and a reputation as a miracle-worker that attracted thousands of converts. After converting a Japanese man who had been a murderer, Francis made his way to Japan where later missionaries converted many Japanese to the Catholic faith. Francis wished to go to China, but died on a lonely island before gaining admittance into that country.

At first, the Office of the Propagation of the Faith encouraged toleration of other cultures. (Pope Gregory XV created this office in 1622 to coordinate and centralize missionary activity in Rome.) A later Pope, however, required that the Masses be celebrated only in Latin. Rome did not want the missionaries to accommodate the Gospel to non-Christian cultures. This meant that the Chinese, Japanese, and others would have to adopt Western culture if they were to convert to Christianity. However, the leaders of these countries simply did not want to abandon their traditions and customs to adopt a new religion.

A second barrier to conversion was the fear that the missionaries were the agents of foreign powers. For example, in 1614, the Japanese leaders expelled

1789–1799
French Revolution; persecution of French Church

the missionaries and began to persecute Christian converts. In a twenty-year period, more than forty thousand Christians were martyred. By 1697, only a few of the three hundred thousand Japanese Christians remained. Much of the work of missionaries like St. Francis Xavier was undone. Remarkably, though, when missionaries were allowed back into Japan in the mid-nineteenth century, they found thousands of Christians living near Nagasaki. Over the course of two centuries, led by lay elders, they had secretly learned and practiced their faith underground.

A third handicap to missionary success was fierce rivalry among the religious orders. An example here was how the Jesuits tended to adapt Christianity as much as possible to the people being evangelized while other religious orders tried to get the natives to reject certain customs and their native language in worship. There were also conflicts between priests of different nationalities and later between Protestant and Catholic missionaries. This, of course, scandalized the natives who were trying to discern how best to respond to an invitation to accept Jesus, the loving Savior.

Finally, there was a failure to develop a native clergy. Many missionaries looked on the natives as children who required their care. Even in the most successful Asian mission of the Philippines, it took many years before native Filipinos were allowed to serve their own people.

As the years went on, the Church had more success evangelizing in the Far East. During the seventeenth century, the Jesuits sent missionaries to Vietnam. Spanish and French missionaries had positive results in Africa, though the slave trade and political instability thwarted any major gains. With the ferment caused by the Enlightenment and the French Revolution, missionary activity declined in the eighteenth century. During the papacy of Gregory XVI (1831–1846), new missionary orders brought a burst of missionary activity.

Some of the important orders founded in the nineteenth century were the Oblates of Mary Immaculate (1816), the Marists (1817), the Salesians (1859), and the White Fathers (1868). With the older orders, they evangelized successfully in Sri Lanka, Thailand, Burma, Malaysia, India, Hong Kong, and mainland China. Africa was ripe missionary territory, and the missionaries met considerable success in countries like Uganda.

By the beginning of the nineteenth century, Jesus' command to preach his message around the world had been achieved in a geographical sense; Catholic missionaries had reached every continent. Ideally, the mark of catholicity includes rather than excludes. It stresses *both/and* rather than *either/or*. However, though the Church is universal and for all people, during these

1792–1794
French monarchy abolished; King Louis XVI executed; Reign of Terror begins

missionary centuries the Church did align herself too closely with Western European culture. In later eras, the Church understood more clearly that the Gospel is truly universal and not solely the possession of any one culture or era.

The Age OF REASON

The Protestant Revolt, the Catholic Reformation, the religious wars that followed, the rise of nationalism, and the era of absolute monarchies helped to give birth to thinkers and philosophies that proved to be hostile to both religion and the theory of the divine right of kings. Thus was born the period in history known as the Age of Reason or Enlightenment.

A revolution in thinking, away from religion, in turn gave rise to political revolutions. The American Revolution established a democratic government that granted freedoms to citizens, including, in a pluralistic society, the right to worship as one sees fit. Another revolution, in France, was more repressive. It committed crimes in the name of "liberty, equality, and fraternity" that were much worse than those of the monarchies it meant to replace. The Church was affected adversely due to these revolutions.

A Revolution of Ideas

The term *enlightenment* itself suggests that religious, medieval people were in the dark. Most Enlightenment philosophers taught that only human reason, separated from religious belief, can bring people into the light. Their philosophy, known as rationalism, stressed the power of human reason to explain reality apart from divine revelation and religious authority. Early leading rationalist philosophers included René Descartes (d. 1650), Benedict Spinoza (d. 1677), and Gottfried Leibniz (d. 1716). They rejected anything that is not absolutely clear to human reason. Though Descartes was a believing Catholic and did not apply his method to religious faith, a rationalist like Spinoza rejected supernatural events recorded in the Bible and equated them with legends and superstition.

Other philosophers went even further in their critique. John Locke (d. 1704) and David Hume (d. 1776), known as empiricists, taught that the only reality is what we can perceive with our five senses. Empiricists encouraged doubt about accepted beliefs and ridiculed religion, religious authority, and traditional Christian doctrines.

Many of these revolutionary rationalist and empiricist philosophers created their own natural religion, known as **Deism**. Deism does not deny God's existence, but it does marginalize God's involvement in creation. The typical

1799
Pope Pius VI dies a prisoner in France

deist images God as a watchmaker. Just as the watchmaker has nothing to do with his watch after he makes it, a deist believes that God allows the laws of creation to govern without any involvement on his part. In Deism, reason, not revelation, governs human lives. An offshoot of Deism was the secret society known as Freemasonry, founded in England. It attacked Christianity and was in turn condemned by Pope Clement XII in 1738.

Enlightenment thinkers had less influence in the Catholic countries of Spain and Italy. In contrast, their impact in France was enormous since many of its leading thinkers were aristocratic Frenchmen whose writings profoundly affected the leaders of the French Revolution. Voltaire (1694–1778) was perhaps the most popular Enlightenment writer. Known for his famous motto, "Crush the infamous [Catholic Church]," his satirical writings popularized rationalist thought. He ridiculed Christianity and Church dogmas. Jean Jacques Rousseau (1712–1778) was another influential rationalist whose thought prepared the way for the French Revolution. Perhaps the most outstanding work of the Enlightenment was the famous *Encyclopédie*, edited by Denis Diderot (1713–1784). It promoted freedom of thought, the value of science, and religious tolerance. It typically praised Protestant thinkers and attacked Catholic teaching.

In sum, Enlightenment thinking influenced many people to begin to regard religion as only a small part of their lives. It also created in people a skeptical outlook about everything and a stance toward religion as a private affair with little to offer public life. This attitude, known as **secularism**, is a dominant belief system in today's world.

WHAT THE CHURCH BELIEVES ABOUT . . .
Secularism

Secularism, defined as religious skepticism or indifference, especially when combined with atheism, is a very real danger as claims are made that hope and satisfaction can be achieved in this world without looking to the next. Pope Benedict XVI spoke out against secularism. He wrote: "Secularism is being transformed into an ideology which is imposed through politics and which does not give public space to the Catholic or Christian vision, which runs the risk of becoming something purely private and thus disfigured."

1801
Concordat between the Holy See and France

A Scientific REVOLUTION

The Age of Reason was compatible with a revolution in science that had stressed independent knowledge derived from observable data. Copernicus (d. 1543) and Galileo Galilei (d. 1642) both taught that the earth travels around the sun, and therefore was not the center of the universe.

In trying to protect the traditional view of God's creation of the world, the Church condemned Galileo's views as heretical. The trouble with the seeming opposition between faith and science in the seventeenth and eighteenth centuries was how it alienated some of Europe's best minds. Because so many people saw science as undermining belief in God, the Church typically allied herself with conservative elements in society and was slow to adapt herself to the new age. On the other hand, the Church had always taught that faith and science are not opposed and, interestingly, a good many of the scientists of the time were Catholic priests. Some of the slowness of the Church's adaptation to science was due to the rationalistic or anti-faith tendencies of some scientists and scientific endeavors of the time.

In 1992, 350 years after Galileo's death, Pope John Paul II expressed regret over the misunderstanding that held that faith and science are irreconcilable and the Church's condemnation of Galileo.

Questions of CHURCH AND STATE

Seventeenth-century Catholic philosopher Blaise Pascal once argued that the Catholic Church's claim to divine origin has to be true because the Church had established herself in a hostile world and spread throughout the world despite persecution. The Church survived schism, corrupt Popes, ignorant clergy, superstitious lay people, and a host of heretics. Attacks from within and without have been unable to destroy the Church, not because Catholics have been perfect, but because the Church is what she claims to be—of divine origin with the Holy Spirit animating the Church, which has Jesus as her head.

➤ *Blaise Pascal*

Pascal's reasoning makes sense. How else can one explain the Church's survival through the ages? Never was this truer than during the onslaught of the French Revolution, which tried to blot out the Catholic Church and

---

1814–1815
Congress of Vienna and the Holy Alliance

1830
The Virgin Mary appears three times to St. Catherine Laboure. On November 27, Mary showed Catherine the medal of the Immaculate Conception (now known as the "Miraculous Medal") and commissioned her to have it made and spread its devotion.

Christianity itself. Not even this assault on Christ's body could destroy what Jesus Christ founded as his own.

The French Revolution

Enlightenment ideas gave birth to political revolutions. People believed that human reason would enable them to rule themselves. Fed up with autocratic rule of monarchs, the eighteenth century ended with successful revolutions against autocracy in both America (see pages 246–247) and France.

Most of the Founding Fathers of the new republic in America were Deists. Men like Thomas Jefferson and Benjamin Franklin strongly feared any close alliance of church and state, but they were not hostile to religion. The American Constitution they crafted favored separation of church and state and extended religious toleration to all.

The French Revolution (begun in 1789), in contrast, was a time of unimaginable persecution for the Church. It began when King Louis XVI called the commoners (the Third Estate) to come to Versailles to help settle a financial crisis. Once there, they pressed for sweeping reforms of the absolute monarchy, the economic policies that oppressed the poor and the middle class, and the privileges that nobles thought were their right by birth. At first, the king seemed to compromise with the Third Estate, but in the meantime he commissioned mercenary soldiers to protect his absolute power. His power play was met with Parisians storming the infamous prison known as the Bastille and setting up their own army, the National Guard. The Revolution was on and there was no turning back.

Before long, the Revolution turned bloody and the Catholic Church was one of its major victims. The Church had been associated with the monarchy and the clergy were deeply involved in many activities of civic life. As a result, when the fiercely anti-clerical and anti-religious elements got control of the Revolution, the Church suffered many losses. Church property was confiscated, and monks and nuns were forced to leave their monasteries and convents. Church land was sold with the proceeds underwriting the costs of the Revolution. Universities, shrines, and charitable institutions were destroyed.

When the dictator Maximilien Robespierre (1758–1794) came to power, clergy were forced to take an oath in support of the Revolution's anti-Christian and anti-Catholic manifesto. The oath required them to obey the revolutionary government rather than take direction from the Pope. The Pope at the time, Pius VI (1775–1799), condemned the manifesto. He forbade the clergy to take

1833–1845
Oxford Movement;
conversion of John Newman (1845)

the oath, under pain of excommunication. Most of the clergy did refuse to take it. Many also fled the country. A horrific reign of terror began. It resulted in the beheading of the king and queen and the execution of thousands of nobles, priests, nuns, and brothers.

There was also an effort to wipe out Christianity itself by substituting a state religion, one that enthroned a dancer as "the Goddess of Reason" in the Notre Dame Cathedral in November 1793. The Christian calendar was replaced, churches were destroyed or turned into secular buildings, and sacrilegious ceremonies that mocked Catholic rituals were enacted.

Before long, the radical leaders turned on themselves and ended up killing each other. Dechristianization was reversed in 1795, and the churches were reopened. But another set of revolutionary leaders struck at the heart of the Church herself when the French armies under General Napoleon occupied Rome. They captured Pope Pius VI and transported him to France where he died imprisoned.

Napoleon and Pope Pius VII

In 1799, Napoleon Bonaparte assumed power in a *coup d'état*. Napoleon was smart enough to realize how important the Catholic faith was to the French people. In turn, the new Pope, Pius VII, wanted a semblance of order returned to the Church in France. They settled on a concordat that, among other provisions, allowed the Pope to install new bishops in return for not pressing claims to Church property that had been stolen during the Revolution. The bishops would now look to Rome for leadership, though Napoleon craftily attached seventy-seven articles to the concordat that made it difficult for the French bishops to communicate with the Pope.

But Pope Pius VII was not Bonaparte's puppet. Pius VII refused to grant Napoleon an annulment from his marriage to Josephine or to join in his schemes against England. When Napoleon seized the Papal States, the Pope bravely excommunicated him. To retaliate, Napoleon took Pius captive, first at Savona, Italy, then at Fontainebleau near Paris, and kept him isolated from the outside world for six years.

Eventually, when Napoleon was threatened by the other European powers, including England, Austria, and Prussia, he allowed Pius VII to return to Rome where he was welcomed as a hero. One of Pius VII's first acts was to restore the Jesuit order so they could help revive the Church, which had suffered under

1846–1878
Pontificate of Pope Pius IX, the longest reigning Pope

Napoleon's policies and the wars that had inflamed Europe for years. Pius VII's brave stands against Napoleon greatly enhanced the prestige of the papacy.

Aftermath of Revolution

With Napoleon's defeat at Waterloo, the Congress of Vienna (1814–1815) brought peace to Europe. It turned its back on the Revolution and restored the Bourbon monarchs to the throne in France. Ultimately though, the forces of history could not be reversed. Europe was changed forever because the revolutionary spirit had infected all countries. A secular and anti-clerical mentality infected France. In Germany, princely bishops lost their privileges. Many Catholics were put under Protestant rulers, and the Church was reduced to a state agency, with schools and clergy supported by the state. Spanish colonies in the New World underwent a number of revolutions that threw off Spanish colonial rule. Unfortunately, some of the new governments were openly hostile to the Church, which they saw as too aligned with the old order. In Mexico, for example, Church property was confiscated and priests were killed.

During the nineteenth century, the Church naturally viewed revolutions negatively because they inevitably attacked the Church, a symbol of order and tradition. Socialist-inspired revolutions in 1848 and 1870 led to persecutions and legal restrictions on the Church. Mazzini's taking of Rome in 1848, which resulted in a short-lived republican government, led to Pope Pius IX fleeing the city. France chased out the republicans in 1849, but in 1861, Italy was united under a king and by 1870, Italy achieved national unity under Garibaldi. The papacy lost all secular rule in Italy with the exception of Vatican City in Rome. From that location, Pope Pius IX would call himself the "prisoner of the Vatican." Until 1929, he and his successors would remain there without venturing out onto Italian soil.

The political revolutions spawned by Enlightenment ideals effectively ended the Church as a political power in Europe. Yet, looked at in another way, these revolutions purified the Church. The Church finds power not in political or territorial control but from the Gospel of Jesus Christ who desires the unity of all people to be based on love and justice, not on political power. Blaise Pascal would not have been surprised to see the Church weather the storms of the revolutionary era since he, like all true believers, held that the Church exists because the Lord remains with her. Holy women and men kept the faith during times of persecution and continued to witness to the strength

1848
Revolution of 1848; Marx's *Communist Manifesto* published

of the Gospel. And, though the secular power of the papacy weakened, Catholics continued to rely on the Pope for spiritual leadership.

Response to the Revolution
IN THE NINETEENTH CENTURY

The Church in the nineteenth century found herself in a rapidly changing world. The Industrial Revolution brought new technological inventions and new social problems. As people moved from rural areas to the cities, they often had to work sixteen-hour days and live in crowded, impoverished housing. Industrialists often exploited the new class of urban workers.

Liberalism and the Church

Much of the social ferment in nineteenth-century Europe resulted from a set of ideas inspired by the Enlightenment, known as Liberalism. In general, nineteenth-century liberals opposed rule by aristocrats. They called for constitutional government, the right to vote, complete religious liberty, freedom of speech and the press, and the equality of all citizens. They tried to abolish established churches and clerical privileges and supported the separation of Church and state. Liberals also wanted the state to secularize functions previously handled by the Church, including marriage, charitable efforts, and education.

Our modern world and the Catholic Church embrace many of these liberal ideas. In fact, in recent decades, the Catholic Church has been the most outspoken defender of human rights and human freedom. For example, historians credit Pope John Paul II as a leading figure in the toppling of the former Soviet Union, one of history's most repressive totalitarian regimes.

However, in the nineteenth century many of Liberalism's ideas were revolutionary and often violently anti-religious. Liberal thought was human-centered and often atheistic, holding that humans and societies are not bound by any divine law. It held that power and authority come from the people, not from God. Liberals saw the Church as part of the old order that was passing. They did not distinguish between true religion (Christianity) and other ideologies that did not always promote true human freedom. Socialist reformers like Karl Marx (1818–1883) went so far as to teach that religion was the "opiate of the people," a drug that kept them content with their station in life.

1858
Apparition of Mary in Lourdes, France

Marx and his cohort Friedrich Engels (1820–1895) wished to abolish religion altogether.

Nationalism teamed up with Liberalism to create the modern states of Germany and Italy. Otto von Bismarck (1815–1898) helped create Germany by uniting many smaller German states into an empire under the king of Prussia. Part of his strategy for unification was the *Kulturkampf*, a vigorous campaign to celebrate German identity. Unfortunately, Bismarck saw the Church as an alien and intruding force in the new country. He wished to end papal influence in Germany and set up a national church. To this end, in the 1870s, he enacted laws that expelled the Jesuits, Redemptorists, and others; put the clergy and schools under state control; and fined, imprisoned, deposed, and exiled bishops and priests. Most Catholics remained loyal to their bishops and tried as best they could to ignore the hostile legislation. By the end of the decade, with the growth of socialism in his country, Bismarck discovered that the Catholic Church was a force for stability. With the election of Pope Leo XIII in 1878, the anti-Catholic laws were gradually moderated until the Pope could claim that the *Kulturkampf* was ended in 1887.

As noted above, the Italian Church experienced similar trials. For centuries, Italy was divided into small duchies (territories controlled by dukes) under the control of rival families. A major barrier to a unified Italy was the Papal States, given to the Church by Pepin in 755. Popes through the ages felt that they needed the income from these lands to help pay for the administrative costs of running the Church. But nineteenth-century nationalists saw the Church as a major stumbling block to Italian unity.

An Italian revolution in the 1820s was suppressed by Austrian troops. Another attempt took place in 1848, this one more successful. Pope Pius IX had to flee Rome when Garibaldi declared an Italian republic. The Pope hated the excesses of Liberalism and its declared war on religion. He worked against Italian unity because he feared the Church would become prisoner to the Italian government. Spain, France, and Austria rescued the Pope and suppressed the 1848 rebellion. However, the days of the Papal States were numbered. In 1870, Italy achieved union once and for all. Caught up in the Franco-Prussian War, France abandoned Rome, which it had occupied with troops to protect the Holy Father. In that fateful year, the Church lost the Papal States and thus surrendered its earthly power.

In general, the official Church was out of step with the liberal movements of the nineteenth century. The Church greatly feared the violence,

1864

Syllabus of Errors

social upheaval, and suppression of religion that so many of the revolutions ushered in with them.

However, within the Church, there were thinkers like the Frenchman Félicité de Lammenais who tried to synthesize Catholic and liberal ideas. He and his friends, including the brilliant preacher Lacordaire, thought the Church should accept the fact that monarchies were dying and that the Church should back the democratic wave of the future. His theory was that the Church should "Catholicize" Liberalism. Believing in a strong papacy (he was originally an Ultramontane—one who looked beyond the mountains to the Pope in Rome for leadership), he appealed to Pope Gregory XVI. But the Pope thought any such compromise would be insane. Had not the liberals associated with the various revolutions tried to destroy the Church?

In his encyclical *Mirari vos* (1832), Pope Gregory XVI rejected any accommodation with Liberalism, saying that it leads to an indifferentism (the belief that all religions are equal) that "gives rise to that absurd and erroneous proposition which claims that liberty of conscience must be maintained for everyone."[7]

With the publication of the encyclical, Lammenais left the priesthood and the Church. However, his chief collaborators remained faithful to the Church and worked for a less radical Liberalism, fighting for reforms like the freedom of education from exclusive state control.

A Long-Reigning Pope

While liberal thought was firing up revolutions, inspiring nations to unify, and assaulting monarchies and the clergy who supported them, a Pope of tremendous personal magnetism and strong beliefs came to power on Peter's throne: Pope Pius IX. He was the longest reigning Pope in history, with a pontificate that lasted thirty-two years (1846–1878), serving as a point of focus in a world transforming from one dominated by monarchies to one built on the ideals of Liberalism.

In the first few months of his pontificate, many thought Pope Pius IX would himself be a strong advocate of liberal reform. He granted political amnesty in the Papal States and improved civic administration in these domains. He also permitted constitutional government with a prime minister. All of these reforms were very popular at

➤ *Pope Pius IX*

1869–1870
First Vatican Council; papal infallibility defined

the time. However, Pius IX's thinking was deeply affected by the violence that emerged from efforts to unify Italy, including his traumatic experience of fleeing Rome when Mazzini proclaimed the Roman republic. He greatly opposed the dismantling of the Papal States, which took place gradually but relentlessly between 1850 and 1870. He saw the Papal States as part of a thousand-year legacy granted to the Church to maintain papal independence from foreign rulers and as a source of income to provide for the governance of the Church.

In a strongly worded encyclical, *Quanta Cura* (8 December 1864), to which was attached a famous appendix, the *Syllabus of Errors*, Pius IX clearly stated the Catholic position on the liberal principles circulating in his day. In a scathing attack on eighty propositions held by the liberals, the *Syllabus* condemned rationalism, socialism, liberal capitalism, pantheism, materialism, the defense of divorce, attacks on the traditional family, and accommodation to the modern world. While the last proposition condemned made traditional Catholics happy, it outraged Pius IX's liberal critics: "The Roman Pontiff can, and ought to, reconcile himself, and come to terms with progress, liberalism and modern civilization."[8]

The Pope's intentions were good—he wanted to preserve the rights of the Church against the forces of irreligion. But in attacking the good points of the liberals, he made the Church appear to be against progress and the modern world.

Vatican Council

Against this background of controversies, Pope Pius IX convoked the first Vatican Council (1869–1870). As his political influence waned, Pope Pius IX wanted to reaffirm papal authority in spiritual matters. He also wished to clarify certain Church teachings in light of attacks by Enlightenment thinkers.

The worldwide council, attended by 714 bishops (including forty-six from the United States), reaffirmed the international flavor of Catholicism. This was important in a revolutionary age that often stressed blind nationalism and hatred of anything foreign. The Church in every age must be a sign of Jesus and his Gospel, both of which are for all people everywhere. The Council first approved the document *Dei Filius*, which addressed the official name of the Church ("Holy Roman Catholic Church") and the necessity of Revelation combined with reason in order for a person to know God.

1870
Rome captured; end of Papal estates

The major accomplishment of the council was the declaration of papal infallibility, which holds that the Pope is preserved from error when teaching dogmatically or *ex cathedra* ("from the chair") on matters of faith and morals. This doctrine confirmed what most Catholics always believed. Unfortunately the Italian revolution of 1870 aborted the council before discussion of other important issues, like the role of the bishops in relationship to the Pope.

A second positive benefit of the council was its emphasis on the spiritual authority of the Church. By 1870, the papacy lost all secular power, which emphasized that the Pope is not meant to be a political ruler. Jesus endowed Peter and his successors with the power to proclaim and teach the Gospel authentically, promising that he would remain with his Church and her leaders to guide them in truth. However, Jesus never promised political power to the Church in the community of nations. The doctrine of papal infallibility supports the Church's claim to be truly apostolic. It remained for the Second Vatican Council (1962–1965) to take up the unfinished business of Pope Pius IX's council. Vatican II updated the Church, teaching that the Church does not need to fear the world and that she can learn from it. Vatican II also showed many ways the Church of the Apostles can reach out to contemporary people without sacrificing the authentic Gospel. The Second Vatican Council will be examined in more depth in Chapter 7.

Religious Renewal

Though the reign of Pope Pius IX resulted in loss of the Papal States, it was a time of great religious renewal in the Church. Traditional religious orders grew and engaged in vigorous missionary activity. New orders, like the Salesians of St. John Bosco (1815–1888), came into existence. Vocations to the priesthood and religious life increased. The diocesan clergy generally improved, inspired by humble and saintly priests like the Curé d'Ars, St. John Vianney (1786–1859).

Catholic intellectual life was given a major boost when towering figures like John Henry Newman (1801–1890) converted to the Catholic faith from Anglicanism. Made a cardinal, Newman's writings showed how the pursuit of a liberal arts education and a rigorous intellectual life were a fundamental part of the Catholic tradition. His series of lectures delivered in Dublin, Ireland, entitled *The Idea of a University*, has profoundly influenced the development of Catholic liberal arts colleges since its publication in 1852.

Two other significant religious events during Pius IX's pontificate were the dogmatic definition of the Immaculate Conception of Mary in 1854 and the

1871–1879
Kulturkampf in Germany

appearances of the Blessed Mother to St. Bernadette Soubirous (1844–1879) at Lourdes, France, in 1858. From a spiritual point of view, Pius IX's pontificate was a positive one. Developments in transportation made it possible for pilgrims to come to Rome to visit him. He popularized huge papal audiences, which endeared him to Catholics from around the world, many of whom kept lithographs of him in their homes. The telegraph made communications to the world outside the Vatican easier. The Pope did not seem as distant.

Sympathy for the plight of the Holy Father emotionally and spiritually bonded Pius IX to Catholics in many countries, themselves the victims of prejudice or oppression. At a time when his political power waned, his spiritual authority grew. Catholics fed up with repression in their own countries were ultramontane. They looked to the Pope as a beloved father and a symbol of faith in an era of rapid and troubling change that often ridiculed traditional ideas. Pope Pius IX was beatified by Pope John Paul II in 2000.

At the time of his death, the Church was politically defensive and in retreat. At the same time, she was spiritually strong and vibrant. With the coming pontificate of Pope Leo XIII, the Church would take an increasingly active role in speaking out for human rights in the face of the evils of *laissez-faire* capitalism and the class warfare called on by Marxist communism. Chapter 7 will examine how the Church confronted the various "isms" of the late nineteenth and twentieth centuries and analyze the achievements of the Second Vatican Council.

1878–1903
Pontificate of Pope Leo XIII

1897
St. Thérèse of Lisieux dies at age twenty-four. Known as the "Little Flower," she is canonized only twenty-eight years later.

Summary

- The seventeenth through nineteenth centuries was a period of unprecedented change for both European society and for the Church. The Thirty Years' War (1618–1648) devastated Germany in the seventeenth century. The Peace of Westphalia solidified the principle of *cuius regio, eius religio* and ended any hope for a united European Christendom. During this same century, England saw the reign of the Stuart kings, who were suspected of being Catholic sympathizers, and the Puritan takeover of the government by Oliver Cromwell who persecuted Catholics and Anglicans alike. The restoration of the monarch under Charles II and James II brought renewed fear that England might return to Catholicism. Parliament prevented this by inviting the Protestant William of Orange to assume the throne in a Glorious Revolution.

- France moved gradually to the concept of the divine right of kings. Cardinals Richelieu and Mazarin were instrumental in centralizing authority in the king and fostering a foreign policy that helped France replace Spain as the leading European power. This was fully realized under King Louis XIV whose religious policies rescinded the Edict of Nantes (which had tolerated French Protestants, the Huguenots) and imposed various laws that declared French independence from the Roman pontiff, known as Gallicanism. In the next century, the Emperor Joseph in Austria also tried to take state control of the Church in a set of restrictive policies known as Josephinism.

- France was also a country of spiritual richness as well as spiritual turmoil. It produced great saints like the beloved bishop and spiritual writer, Francis de Sales; his collaborator and founder of the Visitation order of nuns, Jane de Chantal; the missionary-martyr, Isaac Jogues; the visionary, Margaret Mary Alacoque; the dispensers of charity, Vincent de Paul and Louise de Marillac; and the revolutionary educator, John Baptist de La Salle. At the same time, there were misguided efforts at spiritual renewal. Jansenism taught a theology close to predestination, while Quietism held that human efforts to grow in holiness are worthless.

- The post-Reformation Church saw an explosion of missionary activity in the New World and in the East. Far-sighted missionaries like Bartolomé de Las Casas argued against slavery and for the human rights of native populations. St. Francis Xavier, "the Apostle of the Indies," was the great missionary of the East. Fellow Jesuits Matteo Ricci and Robert di Nobili tried to adopt Christianity to Eastern cultures, but their efforts did not meet with official papal approval. A blow to missionary efforts took place when the Jesuits were suppressed and the French Revolution disrupted Church life in Europe. These efforts revived with new vigor in the nineteenth century with the founding of new missionary orders like the Marists and Salesians.

- The eighteenth century was the age of revolution. In philosophy the Enlightenment produced rationalism, which claimed humans could achieve truth apart from Divine Revelation. Empiricists accepted only sense knowledge. Rationalist and empiricist thinkers promoted Deist notions, that is, a creator-God who is uninvolved in the world. An offshoot of Deism was the secret society known as Freemasonry, which was condemned by Pope Clement XII. Voltaire was the most famous of the Enlightenment thinkers who sought to destroy the Catholic Church. Rationalist thought was presented most effectively by the famous *Encyclopédie*, edited by Denis Diderot.

- Enlightenment ideas helped spawn political revolutions in the eighteenth century, most notably in America, which produced a Constitution that was not hostile to religion, and in France, which led to a Reign of Terror that attempted to stamp out Catholicism in that country. Church property was confiscated, clerics were forced to take an oath supporting the revolutionary government, and a state religion was created that mocked traditional Catholic beliefs and practices. When Napoleon Bonaparte assumed power, the worst excesses of the revolution were in the past. He made an attempt to accommodate the new government to the Church, but still tried to control it, even at one point arresting and imprisoning Pope Pius VII in France. With Napoleon's defeat, the monarchy was restored, but the forces of rationalistic and revolutionary change had transformed Europe forever and ultimately ended the Catholic Church as a political power in Europe.

- The nineteenth century continued to be a period of great social ferment caused by a set of ideas known as Liberalism. Today we take for granted many of these ideas, like the right to vote, democratic institutions, and the equality of all citizens. But in the nineteenth century, many of those promoting liberal ideas were also violently anti-religious and wished to destroy the Church. Nationalism also played a part and was suspicious of any religion like Catholicism that looked to an authority other than the state. Otto von Bismarck, for example, wished to curtail Church presence and influence in Germany in his effort of unification known as the *Kulturkampf*. Italy also achieved national unification in this century, but at the cost of the loss of the Papal States, a major blow to the institutional Church, which, for over one thousand years, enmeshed Popes in political intrigues.

- The towering Pope of the nineteenth century was Pius IX, the longest reigning Pope in history (thirty-two years). He resisted Liberalism because of the violence and anti-religious mentality often associated with it. His most famous condemnation of it came in his *Syllabus of Errors*. He reaffirmed papal authority in spiritual matters when he convoked the First Vatican Council (1869–1870), which defined the dogma of papal infallibility. Another notable achievement of his reign was the definition of the doctrine of the Immaculate Conception of Mary in 1854.

- The loss of the Papal States ultimately did not harm the Church. Papal prestige increased under Pius IX who was now seen as a brave spiritual leader, "a prisoner of the Vatican." By the end of the nineteenth century, the Church was in some ways more free to herald the Gospel and serve the needs of God's people. With the papacy of Leo XIII, the Church would confront some of the pressing social-justice issues that were facing workers and families around the world.

Prayer REFLECTION

In his *Introduction to the Devout Life*, St. Francis de Sales outlined a helpful way to pray involving four steps: preparation (putting yourself in God's presence), consideration (e.g., reading and meditating on a Scripture scene), affections and resolutions (e.g., feelings leading to resolutions to improve your life), and conclusion (prayer of thankfulness). Consider this process for your own life as you pray the following words of St. Francis de Sales:

Prayer on Love
O love eternal,
my soul needs and chooses you eternally!
Ah, come Holy Spirit,
and inflame our hearts with your love!
To love—or to die!
To die—and to love!
To die to all other love

in order to live in Jesus' love,
so that we may not die eternally.
But that we may live in your eternal love,
O Savior of our souls,
we eternally sing,
"Live, Jesus!
Jesus, I love!
Live, Jesus, whom I love!
Jesus, I love,
Jesus who lives and reigns
forever and ever. Amen."[9]

Review and DISCUSSION QUESTIONS

1. What effect did the Thirty Years' War have for the population and religious divisions in Germany?

2. Explain why England settled for the Glorious Revolution of 1688.

3. Discuss how the policies of Cardinals Richelieu and Mazarin and the Gallicanism of King Louis XIV affected the Church in seventeenth-century France.

4. Compare and contrast Jansenism and Quietism with authentic Catholic spirituality.

5. Discuss the contributions of three saints in the period of Church history discussed in this chapter.

6. What were some of the abuses in missionary and colonial practice that Bartolomé de Las Casas fought against?

7. Describe Matteo Ricci and Robert di Nobili's method of doing missionary work. Discuss its advantages and disadvantages.

8. Discuss three factors that helped to work against missionary efforts in the East in seventeenth and eighteenth centuries.

9. Describe the main beliefs of rationalistic thought and how they affected the Church during the period of the Enlightenment.

10. How did the French Revolution attempt to stamp out the Catholic Church?

11. What were some of the positive as well as negative aspects of liberal thought in the nineteenth century? Why was the Church against so much of it?

12. Evaluate the papacy of Pope Pius IX.

13. Identify and discuss the significance of the following:

Events and Terms

Deism	Empiricism
Enlightenment	Four Articles
Freemasonry	Gallicanism
Glorious Revolution (1688)	Jansenism
Josephinism	*Kulturkampf*
Liberalism	Office of the Propagation of the Faith
Peace of Westphalia	Quietism
Rationalism	Reign of Terror
Syllabus of Errors	Ultramontanes

People

Bartolomé de Las Casas	Cardinal Mazarin
Cardinal Richelieu	Cardinal John Henry Newman
Denis Diderot	Félicité Lammenais
Giuseppe Mazzini	Henry of Navarre (Henry II of France)
Matteo Ricci	Napoleon Bonaparte
Oliver Cromwell	Otto von Bismarck
Robert di Nobili	Robespierre
Stuart kings of England	Voltaire
William of Orange	

Popes

Pius VI	Pius VII
Gregory XVI	Pius IX

Saints

Bernadette Soubirous	Francis de Sales
Francis Xavier	Isaac Jogues

Jane de Chantal

John Bosco

Louise de Marillac

Martin de Porres

Vincent de Paul

John Baptist de La Salle

John Vianney

Margaret Mary Alacoque

Peter Claver

Scriptural CONNECTION

The doctrine of papal infallibility, defined at the First Vatican Council, has biblical roots. Read and explain these roots from them in these pivotal passages:

- Matthew 16:17–19
- John 21:15–17
- Luke 22:32

Learn BY DOING

1. Read this article on the doctrine of papal infallibility at Catholic Answers:
www.catholic.com/library/Papal_Infallibility.asp

2. Report on one of the following:

- One of the major missionary efforts during this period of Church history.
- The pontificate of Pope Pius IX.
- The Galileo controversy.
- The life of one of the saints mentioned in this chapter. (Check the websites referenced at the end of Chapter 3.)

3. Read and report on the *Syllabus of Errors* online at:
www.ewtn.com/library/PAPALDOC/P9SYLL.HTM

4. Read more about the Thirty Years' War at:
www.pipeline.com/~cwa/TYWHome.htm

5. Report on a brief overview of Liberalism from Encarta online:
http://encarta.msn.com

7
The Catholic Church
IN MODERN TIMES

This Vatican Synod declares that the human person has a right to religious freedom. This freedom means that all men are to be immune from coercion on the part of individuals or of social groups and of any human power, in such wise that in matters religious no one is to be forced to act in a manner contrary to his own beliefs. Nor is anyone to be restrained from acting in accordance with his own beliefs, whether privately or publicly, whether alone or in association with others, within due limits.

The Synod further declares that the right to religious freedom has its foundation in the very dignity of the human person, as this dignity is known through the revealed Word of God and by reason itself. This right of the human person to religious freedom is to be recognized in the constitutional law whereby society is governed. Thus it is to become a civil right.

—THE SECOND VATICAN COUNCIL
DECLARATION ON RELIGIOUS FREEDOM, 2

Christian Witness TO COURAGE

The twentieth century was the most violent in human history with major attacks by world powers to stamp out Christians and Jews. Revolutionary governments in Mexico in the 1920s and 1930s outlawed the Catholic Church, seized Church property, destroyed churches, and executed priests. Behind the Iron Curtain that descended in Eastern Europe after the Second World War, every atheistic communist regime unleashed systematic persecutions of the Catholic Church. They abolished human rights, imprisoned and killed thousands of the faithful, and sought to obliterate religion altogether. And, of course, there was the Holocaust perpetrated on the Jewish people by Germany's Third Reich. It was one of history's most shameful acts of barbarity.

To chronicle the history of the inhuman, atheistic, and anti-God violence committed in the twentieth century is most depressing. Yet, in the midst of the horrific violence are the stories of many brave men and women. Their love for God and their fellow humans is inspiring and life-affirming. One such story is that of St. Maximilian Kolbe.

Raymond Kolbe was born into a devout Catholic family in 1894 in Russia-occupied Poland. He entered the Franciscans in 1910, and took the name Maximilian. While studying in Rome, he, along with six friends, co-founded the *Immaculata Movement*, which was devoted to the conversion of sinners and to the Blessed Mother as a guide on the way to Christ, her son. He also contracted tuberculosis while in Rome. It left him in frail health for the rest of his life.

After Maximilian's ordination in 1919, he returned to Poland and taught history to seminarians, and helped build a friary near Warsaw. The friary became famous as a publishing center. In time, it produced eleven periodicals (with a circulation of more than a million) and a widely-read daily newspaper. Fr. Kolbe went to Asia in 1930, where he established friaries in Nagasaki, Japan, and in India. In 1936, ill health forced him to return to his original friary in Poland where he set up a radio station. Before long, the monastery housed eight hundred men, the largest religious community of its day. But with Hitler's invasion of Poland in 1939, Fr. Kolbe's and Poland's world would change forever. At first, he and other friars were briefly arrested by the Nazis but eventually released to return to their work. Once back in the friary, they organized a shelter for three thousand Polish refugees, among whom were two thousand Jews.

The Nazis kept a close eye on the intellectual publisher, judging him to be a potential problem for their plans. On the charge of anti-Nazi writing, in 1941, Fr. Kolbe's monastery was shut down. He was arrested and, with four companions, sent to the notorious death camp at Auschwitz. There he was enlisted to carry heavy stone blocks that were used to build a crematorium.

All of the prisoners at Auschwitz lived in barbaric conditions, hardly getting enough rations to sustain life. Fr. Maximilian, though suffering from bad health, would at times share his meager portions with other prisoners. At night, he would go from bunk to bunk to ask the prisoners if he—a Catholic priest—could do anything for them. Prisoners testified to his superhuman kindness in hearing their confessions, in forgiving his tormentors after their beating him, and in his gentle instruction for them to overcome evil with good.

1891
Publication of *Rerum Novarum*, revolutionary
document promoting social justice

Near the end of July 1941, a prisoner tried to escape from the death camp. In retaliation for any attempted escapes, and to keep the prisoners in line, the Nazi

punishment was to starve to death ten randomly chosen prisoners. One man chosen was Francis Gajowniczek, who had fought in the Polish Resistance. When told of his fate, Francis couldn't help but cry out, "My wife, my children, I shall never see them again!"

With a heart full of love, Fr. Kolbe stepped out of line and offered to take Francis's place, identifying himself as a Catholic priest and begging compassion for the family man. The storm trooper in charge, known as "Butcher" Fritsch, consented to the substitution.

Fr. Maximilian prayed for and consoled the other nine prisoners as they slowly starved to death. After two weeks, only he and three others were alive. To hasten their death, on August 14, 1941, the camp executioner injected a lethal dose of carbolic acid into their left arms. Fr. Kolbe was the last to die, offering his arm to his executioner with a prayer on his lips.

➤ *St. Maximilian Kolbe*

Thus, in the midst of the inhumanity of one of history's most barbaric death camps, did a "martyr to charity" give up his life for another. This unprecedented act of self-sacrifice at Auschwitz was a beacon of hope for the remaining prisoners and a lasting legacy for future generations of a Christ-inspired life.

In this chapter, the following topics will be discussed:

- The emergence of Catholic social teaching under Pope Leo XIII

- Pope Pius X and Modernism

- World Wars and Totalitarianism: the Pontificates of Benedict XV, Pius XI, and Pius XII

- Pope John XXIII Convokes an Ecumenical Council

- The Second Vatican Council

- After the Council: Positive Developments

- After the Council: Some Difficult Times

- 1978: the year of three Popes.

1897
Death of St. Teresa of the Child Jesus

The Emergence of
CATHOLIC SOCIAL TEACHING

The nineteenth century was an era of unprecedented change in human history, bringing with it the explosive social changes of the Industrial Revolution. With it came railroads that sped travel, telegraphs that revolutionized communications, and a host of machines that increasingly eased the burdens of manual labor. The twentieth century witnessed even more incredible advances. For example, jet travel and television transformed the world into a global village. Computers combined with the creation of the World Wide Web have enabled knowledge to expand at a breathtaking pace. And the advances of medical technology have added years to human life spans while finding cures and treatment for many diseases.

Industrialization, however, has been a mixed blessing. Despite the technological advances that have eased many aspects of human life, industrialization brought with it many economic problems. Most Western nations that built an industrial economy did so because of capitalism. Capitalism requires the accumulation of money—often in the hands of a few. It also thrives on investment, competition, and free enterprise.

Social Darwinism

The late nineteenth and early twentieth-century capitalists were more interested in profit than in the quality of their workers' lives. Many capitalists used the ideas of **Social Darwinism**. In the world of science, Charles Darwin's *On the Origin of Species* (1859) raised the issue of biological evolution from lower life-forms. For many people, his revolutionary ideas called into question God's existence and time-honored beliefs about the creation of humans. Darwin's theories on natural selection were applied by some thinkers to the social realm, hence the term Social Darwinism. This theory held that the concept of "the survival of the fittest" works in economics, too, resulting in an image of the economic jungle and so-called *laissez-faire* ("hands-off") or "liberal" capitalism.

Liberal capitalists believed that governments should stay out of the marketplace. These ideas resulted in human suffering, the type that Charles Dickens describes so eloquently in his novels: sixteen-hour work days, six-year-old chimney-sweeps, factory towns that enslaved workers, dangerous working

1903–1914
Pontificate of Pope Pius X, most recent Pope to be canonized

conditions, and the lack of social security. Furthermore, basic rights of workers were nonexistent, for example, the right to collective bargaining.

WHAT THE CHURCH BELIEVES ABOUT . . .
Creation

The first verse of Genesis—"In the beginning, when God created the Heavens and the earth . . ."— reveals much about creation: that God began everything that exists beyond himself, that he alone is the Creator, and that everything that exists in the world depends on him because he gave it its existence.
See *Catechism of the Catholic Church*, 290–292.

Karl Marx and Communism

As a reaction to the abuses of unbridled capitalism, many workers turned to socialism and communism. In his *Communist Manifesto* (1848) and *Das Kapital* (1867), Karl Marx analyzed economics as a class struggle. The protagonists were the capitalists, who controlled the means of production, and the workers (or proletariat) whom the rich exploited. Marx believed that revolution between the capitalists and the proletariat was inevitable and that the workers would eventually triumph and create a classless society. Marx was both an atheist and a materialist, holding that the only reality is what can be sensed. His brand of atheism was especially hostile to organized religion. He saw the Church as a negative force in society which taught people to be content with their lot in life.

Marx predicted that industrial nations like Britain, Germany, and America would have violent revolutions. He did not live long enough to see that these nations would gradually curb the excesses of capitalism through law. Although the rich selfishly guarded their wealth, they began to see the wisdom of governments intervening to protect workers. Twentieth-century nations like the U.S.S.R. and China, however, adopted Marx's philosophy and underwent communist revolutions. In these countries, atheism became the official religion. Leaders like Russia's Joseph Stalin tried to eradicate religion. Rule by the few—members of the communist party—became the official form of government. Marx's utopian dream of a classless society not only failed, but it wreaked havoc in the twentieth century.

1914–1918
World War I

Seeking Middle Ground Between Socialism and Capitalism

The excesses of the nineteenth-century liberal reformers resulted in many attacks on the Church and formal religion. Consequently, the Church was slow to adapt to the modern era, fearing rapid change and any social movement that might result in revolution. This slow response resulted in many French-Catholics leaving the Church by 1880. Most Church leaders did not see much good in socialism either, an economic and political system that put direct control of some key industries in the hands of the government.

Some Catholic leaders, though, understood the forces of economic change and were able to chart a middle course between socialism and unbridled capitalism. One such example was the bishop of Mainz, Germany, William Ketteler who, as early as 1848, insisted that workers could form their own associations. He also called for reasonable working hours, rest days, profit sharing, factory inspection, and regulation of child labor. England's Cardinal Henry Edward Manning fought for workers' rights, while America's Cardinal James Gibbons, in 1887, successfully defended the Knights of Labor, the most important labor union of the time.

In other countries, Christian trade unions were formed to protect worker rights. An example of such a union was Belgium's Young Christian Workers, founded by Fr. Joseph Cardijn (1882–1967). This union typified the Christian trade movement of the twentieth century. It stressed a spirit of collaboration in achieving worker rights and championed the decentralization of industries in contrast to the socialist ideal of government control. Furthermore, as a Christian union, it underscored the value of the individual.

Cardijn, later named a cardinal, was one of the Church's most profound social thinkers. Besides founding and supporting the Young Christian Workers, an organization that numbered millions in more than sixty countries, Fr. Cardijn inspired the famous social encyclical of Pope John XXIII, *Mater et Magistra* (1961). He also exerted a strong influence on key Second Vatican Council documents on the laity and the Church's role in the modern world. His famous quote, "Observe, judge, act," became a practical method for many Catholic Action groups in the twentieth century.

1914–1922
Pontificate of Benedict XV

WHAT THE CHURCH BELIEVES ABOUT . . .
Economic Life

Economic activity must be subordinate to the moral order. The development of the economy is meant to provide for the needs of human beings. Economic life is not intended only to multiply goods and increase profit or power. Rather, it is first ordered to the services of individuals and of society as a whole.
See *Catechism of the Catholic Church*, 2426–2436.

A Body of Official Catholic Social Teaching

Proclaiming social justice became a major theme of many pontificates since the reign of Pope Leo XIII. In a remarkable series of forward-looking encyclicals, various Popes have spelled out and defended human rights in all areas of life, including, in a special way, worker rights. These encyclicals make up the official body of Catholic social teaching to this day.

The charter document was *Rerum Novarum* ("On the Condition of Workers") issued by Pope Leo XIII in 1891. It steered a balanced course between communism and liberal capitalism. On the one hand, *Rerum Novarum* affirms the right to private property and defends the right of workers to a living wage and to unionize. On the other hand, it teaches that the state can sometimes intervene in the economic sphere to defend workers. Moreover, *Rerum Novarum* underscores the family as society's primary unit and reaffirms the vital role religion has in building a just society. Finally, it condemns a major tenet of communism: inevitable, violent revolution and class warfare.

Every Pope since Leo XIII has strongly advocated human rights, especially those involving economic, social, and political issues. For example, in 1931, Pope Pius XI issued *Quadragesimo Anno* ("On the Reconstruction of the Social Order") to commemorate the fortieth anniversary of Pope Leo's pioneer encyclical. In the height of the Depression, as totalitarian regimes were on the rise, *Quadragesimo Anno* reaffirmed the right to private property while condemning its selfish and arbitrary use. It also introduced the *principle of subsidiarity*, the teaching that social issues should be handled on the lowest possible level. Finally, it taught that justice and charity should dominate the social order. In other encyclicals toward the end of his reign, Pius XI strongly condemned Nazism and communism. Of the latter, he wrote, "Communism, moreover, strips

1917
Marian apparitions at Fatima, Portugal

man of his liberty, robs human personality of all its dignity, and removes all the moral restraints that check the eruptions of blind impulse."[1]

Although he wrote no social encyclicals, Pope Pius XII delivered many addresses where he stressed the importance of natural law as a foundation of national and international justice. He also spoke to many professionals, like medical and business groups, about their obligation to work for the common good of all.

On the seventieth anniversary (1961) of *Rerum Novarum*, Pope John XXIII issued *Mater et Magistra* ("Mother and Teacher"). Pope John taught that the state must sometimes intervene in matters of health care, education, and housing. He especially stressed the need to work toward authentic community among people as a way to promote human dignity. His *Pacem in Terris* (*Peace on Earth*), issued in 1963, was the first Church document addressed to "all men of good will"[2] and was favorably received by Christians and non-Christians alike. One of its major contributions was to list basic human rights and the responsibilities that go along with them. *Pacem in Terris* also explained the necessary conditions for peace in the world.

The Second Vatican Council document *Gaudium et Spes* (*The Church in the Modern World*) and Pope Paul VI's *Populorum Progressio* (*On the Development of People*) and *Octagesima Adveniens* (*A Call to Action*, 1971) eloquently describe basic human and economic rights as does *Justice in the World*, the Second Bishops' Synod (1971) document that teaches that justice is an essential ingredient in the Church's preaching of the Gospel. Christian faith must spill over into creating a just society.

Pope John Paul II strongly advocated social justice in such encyclicals as *Laborem Exercens* (*On Human Work*, 1981), issued ninety years after *Rerum Novarum*. It shows how work can dehumanize but can also be an important way for humans to participate in God's ongoing creation. His *Sollicitudo Rei Socialis* (*On Social Concerns*, 1987) commemorated the twentieth anniversary of *Populorum Progressio*. It treats authentic human development and criticizes both communism and the excesses of capitalism. It also warns that economic development by itself is not enough to free people and may even enslave them more in a consumer society. True development goes beyond what humans possess. Rather, it is rooted in human dignity and is the fruit of solidarity.

In his landmark encyclical *Centesimus Annus* (*On the Hundredth Anniversary of "Rerum Novarum,"* 1991), Pope John Paul II reaffirmed the essential insights of *Rerum Novarum* for the latter part of the twentieth century and beyond. Written after the collapse of communism in Eastern Europe and the Soviet

1922–1938
Pontificate of Pius XI

Union, it points out the fatal flaws in Marxist communism and the weaknesses of modern market capitalism and consumerism. It also stresses the need for Christians to back up their social message with actions, especially by demonstrating a primacy of love for the most needy, that is, a "preferential option for the poor."[3]

In his earlier encyclical, *On Social Concerns,* Pope John Paul II reminded Catholics and other people of good will about the obligations of human solidarity. He also cautioned against the twin dangers in any economic system: the all-consuming desire for profit and the thirst for power. Summing up the Church's modern advocacy for the oppressed, John Paul II wrote that the Church's social doctrine must have an international outlook and be characterized by

> the option or love of preference for the poor. This is an option, or a special form of primacy in the exercise of Christian. . . . It affects the life of each Christian inasmuch as he or she seeks to imitate the life of Christ, but it applies equally to our social responsibilities and hence to our manner of living, and to the logical decisions to be made concerning the ownership and use of goods.
>
> . . . It is necessary to state once more the characteristic principle of Christian social doctrine: the goods of this world are originally meant for all.[4]

WHAT THE CHURCH BELIEVES ABOUT . . .
Covetous Desires

The Tenth Commandment explicitly forbids greed and the desire to acquire goods without limit. The Commandment begins with the words "you shall not covet" which reminds us that our human desires often lead us to covet what is not ours and what belongs to another person or is due to others.

The Church Responds TO MODERNISM

In contrast to his predecessor Pope Pius IX, Pope Leo XIII (1878–1903) saw that the Church had to come to terms with a new age. His encyclical *Rerum Novarum* on social justice was forward-looking and prophetic. He encouraged Catholic scholars by setting up a biblical commission and opening up the Vatican Library for historical research. He worked diligently to defeat Germany's

1929
Lateran Treaty signed

anti-Catholic *Kulturkampf* policies, as well as those in Switzerland. He was also able to restore diplomatic relations with Brazil, Columbia, and Russia and was successful in getting anti-clerical legislation removed in Chile, Mexico, and Spain. With his diplomatic skills, the Church became less defensive and more willing to dialogue with the modern age.

However, Pope Pius X (1903–1914), Leo's successor, looked more critically at the developments of his age. His main interest was in restoring "all things in Christ." His major contributions involved Church life. For example, he reformed liturgical music, restoring the Gregorian Chant to the Mass. Pope Pius X also encouraged frequent reception of Holy Communion and permitted children to receive the Eucharist at the age of reason (around the age of seven) rather than make their First Communion around the age of twelve. He issued a new catechism and undertook a reform of canon law, a task only completed and published after his death. In addition, he promoted a lay movement known as Catholic Action, which was dedicated to works of charity among

➤ *Pope Pius X*

poor people, to combating anti-Christian elements in society, and to defending and supporting the rights of the Church and God wherever possible.

Pope Pius X and Traditional Church Teaching

Pope Pius X lived a holy, pious, and warmly inspiring life that led to his canonization in 1954. During his pontificate he engaged with certain progressive theologians of his day, known as Modernists. Influenced by liberal Protestants, Modernists employed critical and historical methods of research in their attempt to conform to the new philosophies of the day. They began to reject the scholastic thought patterns of traditional Catholic theology, including Thomism (named for St. Thomas Aquinas). Unfortunately, some Modernists uncritically accepted the thinking of evolutionists, historical skeptics, and scientific approaches that excluded all supernatural considerations. Some questioned and even denied traditional Church teaching while others did not see much value in Church authority, especially in scholarly matters.

1931
Quadragesimo Anno of Pius XI published

Pius X was greatly concerned about theologians who deviated from Church doctrine and questioned traditional ways of teaching, and he challenged the need for scholars to follow the teachings of the hierarchy. He termed Modernism "the synthesis of all heresies."   In response to its challenge, in 1907 Pius X issued both a decree (*Lamentabili*) and an encyclical (*Pascendi*), which condemned the approaches and conclusions of the Modernists. He also required teachers in Church institutions and priests to take an anti-Modernist oath.   Finally, a secret network of informers (*Sodalitium Pianum*, League of St. Pius V) advised the Pope on questionable seminary professors in dioceses around the world. These decisive actions did, in fact, contain the Modernist crisis.

Modernism was problematic because some Modernists did, in fact, teach heretical views. For example, the French Bible expert, Alfred Loisy, used the techniques of rational criticism to study the Bible. He treated books of the Bible simply as historical texts, not as inspired documents. He also ignored Church teaching on how to interpret the Bible in light of Divine Revelation. Ultimately, he ended up denying the Resurrection and the divinity of Jesus Christ.

Most scholars identified as Modernists were good and sincere men who attempted to update Church scholarship, especially in the area of Biblical studies. One side effect of the secret informing committees is that sometimes the careers of innocent men suffered. (When he became Pope, Blessed Pope John XXIII learned, to his surprise, that he himself was suspected of Modernism by one of the anti-Modernist watchdog groups.) On the plus side, anti-Modernist efforts preserved the Church from dangerous heretical ideas that undermined and even destroyed traditional dogmatic teaching. However, on the negative side, Catholic intellectual inquiry cooled for decades, especially in areas like Biblical scholarship.

World Wars and the
RISE OF TOTALITARIANISM

An important date in world history is August 4, 1914, the start of World War I, and exactly two weeks prior to the death of St. Pope Pius X. Historians acknowledge that *supernationalism*—"my country right or wrong"—as a major cause of the war, summing up the belligerent attitude of combatants on both sides. The war—termed the "war to end all wars"—was a novelty in human history. It was a total war, involving conflict on land, on the sea, and in the air.

1943
Pius XII encourages modern biblical scholarship in *Divino Afflante Spiritu*

It involved deadly weapons, including poison gas, that enabled combatants to kill their enemies from a distance, without ever meeting face-to-face. And it was truly a world war that involved not only all of Europe but countries in the Western hemisphere like the United States and Canada. Like many European wars of the past, World War I confronted the Church with the dilemma of how it should respond, especially when Catholics fought on both sides of the conflict, each claiming theirs was the moral cause.

Pope Benedict XV Responds

After the death of Pope Pius X, Giacomo della Chiesa, archbishop of Bologna, was the surprise choice as his successor. Pope Benedict XV's election was unexpected. An aristocrat, he was myopic, physically frail, and possessed a congenital condition that caused him to stoop. But he was a moral giant during the conflict, the soul of generosity, who used all his diplomatic skills to foster peace both inside and outside the Church. In internal Church affairs, for example, he toned down the harsh methods used to root out Modernists.

Benedict deplored the war. He refused to take sides and condemned it as unjust. During the war he engaged in significant humanitarian efforts like organizing army chaplains and arranging for prisoner exchanges. In 1917, he offered visionary peace proposals and volunteered to mediate the conflict. However, Benedict's proposals met with criticism from the political powers and fell on deaf ears. Interestingly, though, many of Benedict's proposals were part of President Woodrow Wilson's famous Fourteen Points which eventually helped to bring resolution to World War I though not lasting peace. Benedict offered a Christian solution to the war: peace won through compromise.

The warring nations, however, settled for nothing less than unconditional surrender. Pope Benedict was not invited to help negotiate the terms of peace after the war ended in 1918. This was unfortunate because the Treaty of Versailles of 1919 did not result in a lasting peace. Some of its misguided provisions resulted from revengeful motives and were responsible for crippling Germany's economy in the 1920s. With the devastation of the Great Depression, Germans would turn to the Nazis and one of humanity's truly evil men—Adolf Hitler—to help restore their pride as a nation.

History has judged Benedict more favorably than did his contemporaries. His work for reconciliation was admirable. For example, Benedict worked to smooth relations between the Church and the Italian state, relations strained

1939–1945
World War II

by the confiscation of the Papal States in 1870. He encouraged Catholic politicians to serve in the Italian government. This eventually prepared the way for an amicable solution to the role of the Church in Italian affairs under his successor, Pope Pius XI. Benedict also organized relief efforts for the starving and homeless after the war. His charity knew no bounds as he emptied the Church's coffers to help those in need. His work for peace also inspired Cardinal Joseph Ratzinger to choose the name Benedict XVI at the time of his election as Pope as the world again faced war on a global basis.

WHAT THE CHURCH BELIEVES ABOUT . . .
Modern Warfare

The danger of modern warfare is that nations and militant groups that possess modern scientific weapons like atomic, biological, or chemical weapons, are capable of indiscriminate destruction of whole areas or vast cities filled with innocent people, non-combatants. This type of warfare is firmly and unequivocally condemned by the Church.
See *Catechism of the Catholic Church*, 2314.

Between the World Wars

World War I devastated Europe, physically, psychologically, economically, and spiritually. It is estimated that eight and half million people died. Another twenty-one million were wounded. Vast areas of northeastern Europe were in rubble. France, on whose soil many of the battles were fought, was left with an unrepaired infrastructure. To add to the misery, in mid-1918, the devastating Spanish Flu hit the world, with an estimated twenty-five million deaths resulting in Europe alone. In America, an estimated 675,000 people died of influenza, ten times as many Americans who died in the World War.

The 1917 Russian Revolution resulted in the Marxist state—the Union of Soviet Socialist Republics under Vladimir Lenin. Inspired by an atheistic, materialistic, and anti-Christian philosophy, Lenin, and his successor, Joseph Stalin, ruled their country as totalitarian dictators. They ruthlessly eliminated dissidents and did everything possible to suppress Christianity, both Russian Orthodoxy and Roman Catholicism. Within seventeen years, the Communist Party destroyed 5,300 Catholic churches and chapels. Clergy were dismissed, churchgoers harassed, and Catholics forbidden to join the Communist Party. Two hundred thousand Catholics, including every Catholic bishop, simply disappeared in the first eight years of the so-called Bolshevik Russia.

1939–1958
Pontificate of Pope Pius XII

In light of all the wartime death and destruction, people worldwide became disillusioned and cynical. Some turned to the new science of psychology to make sense of their world. The ideas of Sigmund Freud were influential, though they were hostile to religion, claiming that it was a control mechanism society used to keep people in line. Freud taught that religious belief was childish and God was simply a wish projected by the unconscious mind. Others turned to a morally lax and hedonistic lifestyle that became popular during the "Roaring Twenties" or sought refuge in accumulating wealth as a hedge against hard times. Foolhardy capitalistic ventures abounded leading to speculative markets that eventually crashed during the Great Depression. The worldwide Depression of the 1930s led to mass poverty, social dislocation, and an environment that would cause people to turn to messiahs disguised as dictators who promised relief from the social dislocation of the day.

The Rise of Fascism

Fascism was a new form of totalitarianism that resulted from World War I's revenge-filled peace treaties, political turmoil, fear of communists, and economic turbulence. Like communism, fascism controlled all aspects of people's lives—personal, political, and economic—in trying to create the perfect state. Founded by Benito Mussolini of Italy in 1919, the word fascism comes from *fascia* meaning "bundle (political) group." It was marked by oppressive, dictatorial control. Mussolini, Hitler in Germany, and Francisco Franco in Spain were dictators who mobilized dedicated followers who began to eliminate anyone who opposed their strong-arm tactics. Propaganda, secret police, control of the mass media, lies, the arrest and execution of dissidents were the methods used by dictators to gain and maintain power.

The pontificate of Pope Pius XI (1922–1939) coincided with the growing power of the fascist dictators as well as the communist leader Joseph Stalin in Russia. A former librarian and mountain-climber, Pius XI was a hard-working, disciplined, stern man born in Desio, near Milan. By lending some initial support to Mussolini who, like the Church, hated communism, Pius XI hoped to reconcile the Vatican to the Italian state. His strategy paid dividends in the Lateran Concordat and Treaty (1929). This treaty finally settled the "Roman Question," that is, the long-standing problems between the Church and Italy caused by the confiscation of the Papal States in the nineteenth century. Mussolini gave the Pope a large sum of money for the Papal States in exchange for the Church's surrendering all claims to land in Italy. The Italian

1950
Dogma of Mary's Assumption into Heaven declared

government also recognized Vatican City as a sovereign state and gave the Church privileged status in Italy.

This concordat typified the way Pius XI dealt with dictators. His policy was to make formal agreements with the dictatorial governments to guarantee certain rights for the Church. These rights included the prerogative of the Pope to appoint bishops and freedom for Catholic laity to participate in Catholic Action movements of which Pius XI was a strong supporter. In 1931, Pius XI harshly condemned Mussolini for his attempt to disband Catholic organizations, especially Catholic Action groups. He issued an anti-fascist encyclical, *Non Abbiamo Bisogno*, that insisted on the right of Catholics to organize and condemned fascism's "pagan worship of the state." Mussolini, needing Catholic support to remain in power, backed down. Thus, in Italy, it is accurate to report that the Church helped curb Mussolini's totalitarian power.

The Church's concordat with Germany looked good on the surface, but Hitler—a lapsed Catholic who embraced a weird mixture of Aryan racial superiority, astrology, and the anti-Christian philosophy of Friedrich Nietzsche— couched it in devious language. The Nazis turned on the Church and began to persecute the clergy and dissolve Catholic organizations. In a bold move in 1937, Pius XI smuggled into Germany a hard-hitting encyclical entitled *Mit Brennender Sorge* (*With Burning Concern*). It condemned various Nazi crimes. Pastors read it from every Catholic pulpit in Germany, thus enraging Hitler. The Nazi dictator retaliated by closing the presses that printed the letter. He also imprisoned laity and arrested, falsely accused, and tried priests for sexual immorality.

Pius XI feared communism even more than fascism. He saw its avowedly atheistic claims and program of violent worldwide revolutions as more dangerous than fascism. Many Catholics agreed with the Pope's assessment. Communism, a worldwide movement, was a threat to universal peace. On the other hand, many believed fascism to be dangerous only in the countries which had adopted it. Pius issued another encyclical in 1937, *Divini Redemptoris* (*On Atheistic Communism*), a few days after his anti-Nazi letter. In it, he unequivocally condemned communism:

> Communism is intrinsically wrong, and no one who would save Christian civilization may collaborate with it in any undertaking whatsoever. Those who permit themselves to be deceived into lending their aid towards the triumph of communism in their own country, will be the first to fall victims of their error. And the greater the antiquity and grandeur of the Christian civilization in the regions where

1958–1963
Pontificate of Pope John XXIII

Communism successfully penetrates, so much more devastating will be the hatred displayed by the godless.[5]

Pius XI died in February 1939 while preparing a speech extremely critical of fascism. A few short months later World War II broke out.

World War II

As Pius XI's Secretary of State, Cardinal Eugenio Pacelli was the natural successor to the late Pope. He took the name Pius XII and was Pope from 1939–1958. Pius XII was a master diplomat who helped draft the Concordat with Germany. With the onslaught of World War II, Pius XII tried to be impartial since Catholics once again fought on both sides of the conflict. The new Pope hated and feared both communism and Nazism. He did love the German people, though, because of his association with them as a papal diplomat in Germany. During his lifetime, he was praised for the way he handled the policy of neutrality that he adopted during the War. Fearing Nazi reprisals, Pius XII used the language of diplomacy and decided to work behind the scenes to bring about peace.

➤ *Pope Pius XII*

In recent decades, some critics have accused Pius XII of timidity for failing to condemn more strongly Hitler's crimes. The Holocaust or *Shoa* (the term used by Jews), the unspeakable attempt by the Nazis to eradicate the Jewish people and other minorities, was the great crime of the twentieth century. Why did the Pope decide to work behind the scenes?

First, Hitler systematically targeted Catholics for extermination by the Nazis. Most notably, three million Polish Catholics and twenty percent of Poland's Catholic clergy perished at the Auschwitz concentration camp.

Second, Pius XII believed that if he spoke out, Hitler would be even more cruel than he already was. This actually happened in Holland when, in 1942, the Dutch bishops, at the Pope's urging, publicly deplored the Nazi deportation of the Jews. In retaliation, the Nazis sped up their roundup of Jews, including seizing all Jewish converts to Catholicism and deported them to Auschwitz. Among the imprisoned who perished there was the brilliant convert Edith Stein, the Carmelite Sister Teresa Benedicta of the Holy Cross, canonized a saint in 1998.

1962–1965
Second Vatican Council, Twenty-first ecumenical

Third, he believed that he could do more for the Jews in a clandestine way without arousing the suspicion of the Nazis. There was a basis for this reasoning because he did, in fact, help many Jews escape persecution, providing them with shelter and giving them homes. In 1967, Pinchas Lapide, an Israeli diplomat, reported that Pius XII was instrumental in saving as many as 860,000 Jews, a number estimated to be a full 30 percent of the world's Jews who survived Hitler's "final solution."[6] He was so moved by the sterling character of Pius XII and by his devotion to religious brotherhood that the chief rabbi of Rome, Rabbi Israel Zolli, a devout and strict Jew, converted to Roman Catholicism in 1945 and took as his baptismal name Eugenio.

WHAT THE CHURCH BELIEVES ABOUT . . .
Jewish People

Christians and Jews share a common spiritual heritage. The Second Vatican Council particularly addressed the "spiritual ties which link the people of the New Covenant to the stock of Abraham." In addition, the Council and subsequent Church statements have strongly taught that responsibility for the trial and condemnation of Jesus cannot be laid on the Jews in Jerusalem as a whole, nor especially on Jews of any other age. Rather, the Church "reproves every form of persecution against whomsoever it may be directed. Remembering, then, her common heritage with the Jews and not moved by any political considerations, but solely by the religious motivation of Christian charity, she deplores all hatreds, persecutions, displays of anti-Semitism leveled at any time or from any source against the Jews" (*Nostra Aetate*).

See *Nostra Aetate* and the *Catechism of the Catholic Church*, 601.

Pope Pius XII and Post–World War II

After the war, Pius XII continued to speak for Christian values against the godless forces of the modern age. For example, he helped to mobilize world opinion against atheistic communism which oppressed the Catholic Church and other Christian churches in the countries the Soviets controlled.

When the Soviet Union set up communist governments in countries like Hungary, Yugoslavia, Poland, East Germany, Bulgaria, and Romania, Catholics were systematically persecuted. Priests were exiled, imprisoned, or forced to work in labor camps. Church schools and properties were confiscated. Free and open worship was outlawed. The Church went underground in many Eastern European nations, only to emerge triumphant with the collapse of the

1963–1978
Pontificate of Pope Paul VI

Soviet Union in 1989–1990. The brave witness of Cardinal Stefan Wyszynski in Poland and Cardinal Josef Mindszenty of Hungary are two examples of those whose fidelity in the midst of communist persecution (including their own persecutions) served as beacons of hope to the Catholics in communist-dominated countries.

With the ascent of power by Mao Zedong in China in 1949, the People's Republic of China also became a communist nation. It imprisoned or exiled foreign missionaries, killed professing Catholics, and forced the others to go underground. Today, there are between an estimated twelve to fifteen million Catholics in China, a very small part of a population of 1.3 billion people. Officially, they are allowed to worship openly, but must be part of a registered nationalized Catholic Church. In 2006, the Chinese national church ordained new bishops without the Vatican's approval, risking excommunications.

Pope Pius XII helped the Church move into the modern world and planted many seeds of renewal that would find fruition in the Second Vatican Council. In his encyclical *Divino Afflante Spiritu* (*On the Promotion of Biblical Studies*), he supported the modern historical and scientific study of the Bible. The promotion of biblical studies sent Catholic scholars back to the historical roots of Christianity. Another encyclical, *Mystici Corporis Christi* (*On the Mystical Body of Christ*), taught the value of each member in the Mystical Body of Christ, including the laity, and the universal call to holiness. Pius XII also laid the theological groundwork for the liturgical renewal that would come with the publication of his encyclical *Mediator Dei* (*On the Sacred Liturgy*) in 1947.

The scholarly Pius XII also wrote on important topics like medical ethics and addressed the world frequently on peace issues. He declared 1950 a holy year and defined the dogma of the Assumption of Mary into Heaven. Millions of Catholics made a pilgrimage to Rome to celebrate this momentous occasion.

Pope Pius XII died in 1958. His successor was an aging, compromise candidate, Angelo Roncalli, who took the name John XXIII. This rotund, peasant-like priest became one of the twentieth century's most admired men. His greatest achievement was convoking the Second Vatican Council. Because of John's optimistic, joyful vision, the Church at the Second Vatican Council embraced the modern world.

1964
Patriarch Athenagoras I and Pope Paul VI meet in Jerusalem

> ### WHAT THE CHURCH BELIEVES ABOUT . . .
> ### Sacred Scripture Study
>
> The Second Vatican Council confirmed that "access to the Sacred Scriptures should be opened wide to the Christian faithful" and that the study of the 'sacred page' should be the very soul of sacred theology" (*Dei Verbum*, 22, 24). All Christians are called to frequent reading of the divine Scriptures in order to learn "surpassing knowledge of Jesus Christ." As St. Jerome taught, "Ignorance of the Scriptures is ignorance of Christ." See *Catechism of the Catholic Church*, 133.

Pope John XXIII and the
CALL FOR A COUNCIL

Pope John XXIII was born Angelo Roncalli, the fourth in a family of fourteen children. His parents were sharecroppers. In 1904, he was ordained a priest and then served as secretary to the Bishop of Bergamo, Italy. During this period, he wrote a five-volume biography of St. Charles Borromeo. During World War I he served as a medic and a chaplain; after the war he worked in Rome as the Italian head of the Society for the Propagation of the Faith. Many years of his priestly life were then spent serving as a papal diplomat, most notably to Bulgaria, Turkey, Greece, and France. In 1953, he was named the patriarch of Venice and elevated to cardinal.

➤ *Pope John XXIII*

His election after the death of Pope Pius XII was unexpected. Because of his advanced age (a month shy of seventy-seven), most observers thought of him as an interim Pope who would not serve long or accomplish much. However, Pope John's warmth, sense of humor, and kind heart quickly won over the entire world, contrasting sharply with the aristocratic bearing of his predecessor. One of his first official acts was to visit prisoners in Rome telling them, "You could not come to me, so I came to you." One of his famous jokes involved his response to a question from a reporter, "Holy Father, how many people work in Vatican City?" The Pope responded, "About half of them."

1968
Humanae Vitae of Paul VI published

What surprised most people was John's assertion that the idea for calling the first Ecumenical Council in ninety years came to him like a ray of blinding light, an inspiration from the Holy Spirit. When he announced the council to a gathering of eighteen cardinals in January of 1959, they were dumbfounded. Days later, they voiced their reservations, but John insisted that the Church lived in a new age. The Catholic Church was no longer just a European community, but a worldwide Church embracing many people. Moreover, the Church needed to dialog with the fast-changing world of politics, economics, science, technology, and so forth. This council would be unlike previous councils that were called in times of crisis and heresy. It would be a pastoral council, one of mercy and hope, one that would reach out to the modern world and invite people around the world to consider the joyfulness of the Gospel. Pope John famously gave this as his reason for the council: "I want to throw open the windows of the Church so that we can see out and the people can see in."

Early Signs of Renewal

Though many people were surprised at the convocation of the council, the changes that came with the Second Vatican Council were not totally unexpected. For decades, movements began to transform the Church and prepare the way for the Council. These signs of renewal were very much active in the Church in the three previous decades. They included:

- **Papal social justice teaching.** The prophetic papal encyclicals and other documents asked Catholics and the world to apply Gospel values to the political, social, and economic spheres.

- **Catholic Action.** Pioneering leaders like Cardinal Cardijn with support from Pope Pius X and Pope Pius XI were strong advocates of lay participation in bringing the Gospel to the marketplace.

- **Liturgical movement.** Some scholars turned their attention to renewing the liturgy, stressing that a sacrament should be a sign that people can understand. Their efforts prepared the way for the use of the vernacular language in the liturgy and the renewal of all the sacraments after the Council.

- **Biblical movement.** Pope Pius XII's encyclical *Divino Afflante Spiritu* (1943) gave life to Catholic biblical scholarship. The critical use of modern methods of scholarship stimulated interest in the Bible by

1975
Pope Paul's apostolic exhortation *Evangelii Nuntiandi* stressed the importance for all Catholics—ordained and lay—in evangelizing the world.

Catholics and would eventually lead to Catholics discovering the rich treasures to be found in Scripture.

- **Missionary work.** In the twentieth century, the Church recognized the dangers of blending missionary work to colonialism. Pope Benedict XV told his bishops to look out first and foremost for the welfare of the people in the mission lands, rather than the colonial interests that wanted to exploit those territories. He also urged his bishops to promote priestly vocations among native populations.

- **Ecumenical movement.** Although the Church was slow to join Protestant efforts in promoting Christian unity, some Catholics did get involved in the ecumenical movement prior to the council. The publication of the council's *Decree on Ecumenism*, the landmark work of theological commissions, and recent Popes have further encouraged Catholics to participate in interfaith sharing.

- **Theological renewal.** Although forward-looking Catholic scholars periodically received criticism for their research and publications, many outstanding and courageous Catholic theologians remained in the Church. The writings of theologians like the Jesuits Karl Rahner, Henri de Lubac, and John Courtney Murray and the Dominican Yves Congar came under suspicion in the 1940s and 1950s. However, they all lived to see the day when their work bore fruit, especially when they were asked to serve as theological consultants to the bishops at the Council. The contributions of outstanding theologians have helped the Church bring an intellectual vigor to the problems of contemporary society.

The Second VATICAN COUNCIL

Pope John XXIII's announcement in 1959 that he was going to convoke an Ecumenical Council at the Holy Spirit's prompting was stunning. Recall that previous councils had met only when the Church was under assault or when heresies were confusing the faithful. Pope John XXIII had two major aims for the council: (1) dialogue with the modern world with the goal of Church renewal; (2) vigorous efforts for Christian unity. Some cardinals in the Curia, fearing too much change, tried to control the agenda of the council. However, their efforts eventually failed. As Pope John said, the Holy Spirit had blown open the windows of the Church to let in some fresh air. There was no going back.

The council met from 1962–1965 in four separate sessions. In his opening address, Pope John set the tone, asking the bishops to trust the Holy Spirit, to be hopeful, and to not look for the worst in the modern world. He talked about reading the "signs of the times," trying to find God's presence in ordinary life. He said the council was meeting not to suppress false teaching, but to find new and better ways to present Church doctrine

> *White-clad Council Fathers walk into St. Peter's Basilica at the beginning of the world's Twenty-First Ecumenical Council (Second Vatican Council).*

to people of modern times. The Pope pointed out that the Church "desires to show herself to be the loving mother of all, benign, patient, full of mercy and goodness."[7]

The first session of Vatican II met in the autumn of 1962 with more than 2,500 Church fathers present. The council was the first truly worldwide council with bishops from all races and continents represented. Remarkably, observers from other religions, including the Orthodox, Anglican, and Protestant, were also present. The first session considered more than seventy schemata, that is, texts on various topics. With all the discussion on these many topics, the council did not issue any documents until later sessions.

Pope Paul VI Continues the Council

The first session of the council adjourned on December 8, 1962. Pope John XXIII knew he would not live to see the second session reassemble after the nine-month recess because he was already diagnosed with terminal stomach cancer. His death on June 3, 1963, was widely mourned throughout the world. When the cardinals assembled to choose a new Pope, they elected Cardinal Giovanni Battista Montini, the Archbishop of Milan, Italy. He took the name Paul VI. A shy, hard-working, brilliant thinker, Pope Paul resolutely decided to continue the council.

Under Paul VI the council met three more times. In January 1964, Pope Paul made the additional historical gesture of traveling to the Holy Land. This was the first time in centuries that the Pope journeyed outside of Italy. While there, he met the Patriarch of Constantinople. This symbolic move showed that the Church was indeed serious about Christian unity that was being debated at the council. This meeting eventually led to the lifting of the mutual excommunications that hung over both Churches since the Schism in 1054. This historic event took place on December 7, 1965—a day before the council formally closed on the Feast of the Immaculate Conception of Mary.

In all, the Second Vatican Council issued sixteen documents. In one way or another, all the documents treat the Church, her inner workings, and her relationship to the world. The most authoritative documents issued were the four Constitutions, which present Catholic doctrine. These are:

- *Sacrosanctum Concilium* ("The Constitution on the Sacred Liturgy," December 1963). It emphasizes the liturgy as the summit of Church activity, encourages fuller participation in the Eucharist, and introduces vernacular languages into the liturgy.

- *Lumen Gentium* (*Dogmatic Constitution on the Church*, November 1964). Perhaps the most important Vatican II document, it updates the Church's self-image by emphasizing the mystery of the Church as a community, the People of God, a sacrament or sign of God's presence in the world through Christ's Body, his Church. *Lumen Gentium* reminds believers that everyone in the Church—clerics and laity alike—are called to holiness. The document also stresses collegiality between the bishops and the Holy Father.

- *Dei Verbum* (*Constitution on Divine Revelation*, November 1965). This constitution encourages Bible reading; shows the close relationship between Scripture and Tradition and the Church's Magisterium; and emphasizes revelation as God's self-disclosure.

- *Gaudium et Spes* (*Pastoral Constitution on the Church in the Modern World*, December 1965). The literal translation of the title of this document is "joy" and "hope," thus indicating an optimistic view of the role of Catholics who are citizens of a modern world. The document highlights the model of Church as servant of the world, committed to doing social justice in building God's Kingdom. It also calls for the

Church to read the signs of the times in light of the Gospel so Catholics can be effective instruments of the Gospel in their daily lives.

The Second Vatican Council also issued nine decrees, which renewed Catholic life in important areas and applied the theological principles of the Constitutions. *The Decree on Ecumenism*, while reaffirming that the Catholic Church is entrusted with the fullness of the means of salvation, committed the Church to the ecumenical movement and affirmed the many positive qualities in other religions. Other decrees were on these topics: the renewal Eastern Catholic Churches, the Instruments of Social Communication, Bishops' Pastoral Office in the Church, Priestly Formation, Renewal of the Religious Life, Apostolate of the Laity, Ministry and Life of Priests, and the Church's Missionary Activity.

Finally, the Council issued three Declarations that outlined principles, guidelines, and policies on specific topics: *The Declaration on Christian Education, The Declaration on Religious Freedom* (affirms the dignity of each individual and the freedom of conscience in matters of religious belief and practice, regardless of the faith chosen), and *The Declaration of the Relation of the Church to Non-Christian Religions* (the Church accepts what is good and true in other religions, shows special respect to Jews, and strongly condemns religious bigotry).

After the Council: Positive Developments

The Second Vatican Council took place in the 1960s, a historic decade of exciting and often turbulent change in society the world over. The sexual revolution, the Vietnam War, the breakdown of traditional morality including in areas of sexuality, the questioning of authority and tradition—all of these social changes and more took place during and after the Council. Catholics were bound to be affected by them, and they were.

However, on the positive side of the ledger, the Second Vatican Council was a gift of God both to the Church and to the world. It helped bring about *aggiornamento* (an Italian word favored by Pope John XXIII which means "modernization," "updating," or "adaptation"). The pilgrim Church that emerged from the council was more willing to embrace the good in modern society and was willing to learn from its cultural and scientific advances. This attitude of openness led to an initial burst of optimism and enthusiasm after the council. Some of the positive achievements that resulted from the Second Vatican Council included:

- **A renewed embracing of God's word found in the Bible.** The Second Vatican Council helped Catholics rediscover the Bible and its riches both for prayer and spiritual nourishment. It encouraged the reading of sacred Scripture:

  > Through the reading and study of the sacred books, let "the word of the Lord run and be glorified" (2 Thes 3:1) and let the treasure of revelation entrusted to the Church increasingly fill the hearts of men. Just as the life of the Church grows through persistent participation in the Eucharistic mystery, so we may hope for a new surge of spiritual vitality from intensified veneration for God's word, which "lasts forever" (Is 40:8; cf. 1 Pt 1:23–15). (*Lumen Gentium*, 26)

- **Religious freedom and social justice.** The Council reiterated much of the social teaching of the Popes since Leo XIII emphasizing that working for social justice is an essential task of following Christ. Fostering peace, defending human rights, and achieving solidarity with the poor are three major emphases emerging from Vatican II.

  > The Church encompasses with love all those who are afflicted with human weakness. Indeed, she recognizes in the poor and the suffering the likeness of her poor and suffering Founder. She does all she can to relieve their need and in them she strives to serve Christ. (*Lumen Gentium*, 8)

- **More active role of the laity, including ecumenical efforts.** The Council reminded all baptized Catholics that they are responsible for the mission of the Church. Laity and clergy alike have the vocation to strive for holiness. As befits their station in life, everyone must preach the Gospel in both deed and word. One visible fruit of the council is how lay people have assumed a more active role in various Church ministries as catechists, readers and extraordinary ministers of the Eucharist, counselors, and activists promoting social justice. The Council also called Catholics to work for ecumenism, that is, unity among Christian religions. Mutual prayer, joint service projects, sharing one's faith, learning from others, and befriending people of other faiths are some of the ways post–Vatican II Catholics have engaged in works to foster Christian unity.

- **Collegiality**. The Council highlighted the concept of collegiality between the Pope and bishops. Collegiality is the principle that the bishops of the Church with the Pope at their head form a single "college" that succeeds the Twelve Apostles with Peter at their head. This principle holds that the bishops together with the Pope, and never without him, have full authority as they interact and collaborate in governing the Church. One way this has been achieved since the Council is through a permanent Synod of Bishops that meets periodically to advise the Pope on various issues. Pope Paul VI also encouraged the formation of national bishops' conferences. In countries like the United States, the bishops have been leaders in implementing Vatican II reforms. For example, the United States Conference of Catholic Bishops has issued important pastoral letters on many topics of modern concern including peace and war, abortion and bioethics, and the economy.

WHAT THE CHURCH BELIEVES ABOUT . . .
Participation of the Laity in Society

Initiative of lay Christians is necessary especially when discovering or inventing the means for participating in the social, political, and economic life of society. As Pope Pius XII wrote: "Lay believers are in the front line of Church life; for them the Church is the animating principle of human society. Therefore, they in particular ought to have an ever-clearer consciousness not only of belonging to the Church, but of being the Church . . ." (Discourse, 20 February 1946).
See *Catechism of the Catholic Church*, 897–903.

Challenges after the Council

Change in any institution can be difficult. Some people and institutions are able to embrace change with open arms; others are more reluctant to move into new territory. Some don't think change happens quickly enough; others look with nostalgia to the past. Post–Vatican II Catholics reacted similarly to the changes ushered in by the council. Friction between those who resisted change and those who did not think it came quickly enough resulted in some difficult times that persist to today as the Church tries to adapt its timeless message to the modern world.

One of the most visible changes brought by the Council involved how the Mass was celebrated. Formerly, the Mass had been in Latin with the priest facing the altar, back toward the congregation. After the Council, the liturgy of the Eucharist was celebrated in the vernacular. The altar was moved closer to the people, the priest faced them, and the laity were to participate more actively in the service through their responses. Before, the music had a dignified quality about it, with Latin hymns accompanied by an organ. After, many new songs that were introduced were similar to folk music, played with guitars and other instruments. In some parishes, unapproved liturgical innovations were more radical. Some priests, in order to be relevant, began to give homilies that were more inspired by modern pop psychology than by the Gospel of the day.

In response, especially to liturgical changes, some ultraconservative traditionalists, like the retired French archbishop, Marcel Lefebvre, rejected the Second Vatican Council as heretical. Lefebvre founded the international group, the Priestly Fraternity of St. Pius X, which clung to the old order of the Latin Mass, questioned and challenged Second Vatican Council's liturgical reforms, and was critical of the new ecumenical efforts with non-Catholic communities. Soon finding him in open schism with the Catholic Church, in 1976 Pope Paul VI suspended Lefebvre from his functions as a priest and bishop. Pope John Paul II excommunicated him in 1988 for disobeying his order not to ordain his own bishops.

Other tradition-minded Catholics simply stopped going to Mass because they did not like the changes or they used the open spirit of Vatican II as a sign that they had some "wiggle room" in accepting or rejecting Church teaching. Mass attendance fell for other reasons, too, including the adoption of the secular, materialistic, and consumer mindset of modern times. For devout Catholics, the statistics are very discouraging. In the United States, the rate of attendance of Catholics at Mass in the 1960s was two out of three; today, it is one out of three and falling. In Italy, 97 percent of the population describes itself as Catholic, yet only 30 percent go to Mass on Sunday. In France, three-quarters of the population calls itself Catholic, but only 5 percent attend Mass.[8]

On the other side, there were Catholics who fully expected much more rapid change including optional priestly celibacy, the ordination of women, and a change in the Church's teaching on birth control. Disappointed by Pope Paul VI's *On Priestly Celibacy*, which reaffirmed the Church's centuries-old practice of mandatory celibacy, thousands of priests, especially in the more affluent Western and European nations, requested dispensations from their vows. In America alone, ten thousand priests left. Vocations to the priesthood in these countries severely declined as well, partly due to secularization and a declining family culture that promotes vocations. But the vocation crisis was not worldwide. In contrast, in the forty years between 1961 (the year before Vatican II began) and 2001, the numbers of priests in Africa increased by 60 percent, in Latin America by 68 percent, and in Asia by 57 percent.[9]

A major crisis shook the Church when Pope Paul VI published the encyclical, *Humanae Vitae* (*On the Regulation of Birth*), in 1968. This life-affirming encyclical eloquently reminded us that life is a gift from God, that sexuality is sacred, and that human life must not be destroyed by abortion. But it also restated traditional Catholic Church teaching that bans the artificial means of birth control. This teaching should not have been controversial but became so when it was learned that the Pope banned contraception against the recommendation of a papal commission he called to advise him on the issue. Many Catholics and theologians fully expected Paul VI to modify the traditional teaching to allow for artificial means of birth control.

➤ *Participants at a Pro-Life rally.*

In reaction, many European and North American theologians reacted negatively and some national bishops' conferences gave only lukewarm support to the encyclical. Many laity went ahead and simply ignored the teaching. This brought about a major crisis in the Church over the teaching authority of the Pope. Pope Paul VI was shocked by the reaction to his effort to combat a "contraceptive mentality," a mentality that has resulted in increased promiscuity, the legalization of abortions, the increase of pornography, the acceptance of homosexual marriages, and other abuses that contradict the natural law and God's law. Perhaps due to being distraught, the Pope did not publish another encyclical during the rest of his pontificate, which would last another ten years.

Theologians who openly challenged Church teaching in sexual morality (like American Fr. Charles Curran) or on topics like papal infallibility (like Swiss Fr. Hans Küng, a theological consultant at the Council) were not allowed to teach as Catholic theologians. Under the pontificate of Pope John Paul II, other dissenting theologians, for example, those who bought into Marxist forms of liberation theology, were also disciplined. To help Catholic universities maintain their Catholic identity, Pope John Paul II issued an Apostolic Constitution, *Ex Corde Ecclesiae* (*On Catholic Universities*), in 1990. One of its provisions requires that theology instructors have special permission (a *mandatum*) from the proper Church authority which "recognizes the professor's commitment and responsibility to teach authentic Catholic doctrine and to refrain from putting forth as Catholic teaching anything contrary to the Church's Magisterium."[10]

Many who claim that the Second Vatican Council was not necessary for the Church ignore the role of cultural factors like the growing influence of secularism and materialism on the Catholic faithful. The decline of traditional religious practices like regular confession and Mass attendance, the lack of vocations to the priesthood and the aging of religious orders to the point where many face the possibility of extinction, the widespread ignoring of Church teaching in areas of sexual morality by the laity, the rising rate of divorces among Catholics with the fragmented families that result—all of these can be explained more by cultural influences than by disappointments over the rate of change following the Second Vatican Council.

Admittedly, there were mistakes made by many in trying to implement reforms "in the spirit of Vatican II." But compare the turmoil after the Second Vatican Council to the turmoil and open rebellion after the First Council of Nicea in 325 when, in many areas of the Roman Empire, civil war broke out. It took fifty years before one even knew if the council would be accepted or not. This was not the case with Vatican II. With the exception of very few Catholics, like Archbishop Lefebvre, Catholics embraced the Council and are embracing it today. The issue has always been the pace of change, what is permitted and what is not, what is part of the tradition and what subverts it. The Church of today is still struggling with these questions.

WHAT THE CHURCH BELIEVES ABOUT . . .
The Aim of Marital Sex

Sex in marriage is directed to two aims simultaneously: the procreation (and rearing) of children and the mutual love and affection of the couple. Thus sexual relations which are selfishly engaged in by one partner without taking note of the feelings and desires of the other partner are wrong because one of the aims of marriage—mutual love—is destroyed. Likewise any artificial means used to frustrate the natural processes of procreation go against the very nature of marriage.
See *Catechism of the Catholic Church*, 2370, 2399.

The Year of the THREE POPES

Church history will remember 1978 as the year of the three Popes: Pope Paul VI, Pope John Paul I, and Pope John Paul II. Pope Paul VI, of course, was the Pope who saw the Second Vatican Council to its successful completion. Against criticisms from both conservatives and liberals, he saw to the implementation of many of the Council's reforms.

Pope Paul VI (1963–1978)

Although he is perhaps best known for the controversies surrounding his encyclical *Humane Vitae*, Pope Paul VI was a strong advocate for peace and social justice. His encyclical *Populorum Progressio* (*On the Development of Peoples*), issued in 1967, called for the redistribution of wealth to the benefit of poor nations. It also appealed for more just economic policies that would allow the economies of impoverished nations to develop and compete in a global market.

Pope Paul VI was the first Pope to travel outside Italy since Pius VII's imprisonment by Napoleon in France. Paul VI visited all five continents and was the first Pope to visit the Holy Land since St. Peter. He flew around the globe in efforts to end conflict in the Middle East, Northern Ireland, and Vietnam. His famous visit to the United Nations in 1965 to appeal for the end of the Vietnam War resulted in his oft-quoted challenge to the nations of the world: "No more war! Never again war! If you wish to be brothers, drop your weapons." He offered to act as a mediator in a conflict between India and Pakistan and bravely offered himself in exchange for hostages who were held by terrorists, including his friend, Aldo Moro, the former Italian Premier who had been kidnapped and eventually killed by Marxist militants.

Pope Paul VI worked diligently for Christian reunion and reached out to non-Christian religions. In 1964 his meeting with Eastern Orthodox Patriarch Athenagoras I led to the rescinding of the excommunications that took place at the time of the Great Schism of 1054. It is unfortunate that the controversies surrounding his reaffirmation of priestly celibacy and traditional Church teaching on birth control overshadowed the last years of his papacy, which strove so hard to call nations to peace and social justice. He died on August 6, 1978, on the Feast of the Transfiguration, requesting a simple funeral.

•···

1978
The year of three Popes: death of Paul VI, thirty-three-day pontificate of John Paul I, the election of the Polish John Paul II

Pope John Paul I (1978)

On the third ballot at the papal conclave, the cardinals elected as Paul VI's successor, Albino Luciani, Patriarch of Venice. He was the first Pope to take a double name, indicating his desire to continue the work of his two immediate predecessors. Known for his humility, he refused to wear the papal crown, the tiara. John Paul I was a beloved pastor and a gifted speaker and writer with a common touch. His gentleness and human warmth quickly gained him the name "the smiling Pope."

But John Paul I, who could never understand why he was chosen Pope, was not in good health. He died of a heart attack in his sleep after only reigning for thirty-three days. A nasty rumor, clearly debunked by competent researchers, arose that he was assassinated by unnamed curial figures who were afraid of changes the new Pope might make. Had he lived longer, it is likely he would have upheld traditional dogmatic statements, continued the trajectory of Vatican II reforms started by Paul VI, and spoken out on behalf of the poor and dispossessed.

Pope John Paul II (1978–2005)

When the cardinals met in October of 1978 to elect a new Pope, they chose Cardinal Karol Wojtyla, the fifty-eight-year-old Archbishop of Kraków, Poland, the first non-Italian Pope in more than 450 years. As a Pole, he had lived a remarkable life as a survivor of both Nazism in his youth and communist tyranny as an adult. Multi-talented and athletic, Karol was a gifted actor, poet, playwright, and profound philosopher. He was chosen for his youth and his dedication to implementing the principles of Vatican II. The cardinals also thought he would be savvy enough to stabilize a Church that was experiencing problems associated with secularization from without and dissidents from within its ranks.

Karol Wojtyla took the name John Paul II to signal his desire to continue the work of his three predecessors. He was the third-longest reigning Pope in history, behind St. Peter (approximately thirty-five years) and Pope Pius IX (31.6 years). His death on April 2, 2005, ended his twenty-six-year papacy. The massive outpouring of affection for him at the time of his death was unprecedented in history. For many Catholics, he was immediately acclaimed, "John Paul the Great." This is an honorific title used for only three other Popes in history, Pope Gregory I, Pope Leo I, and Pope Nicholas I. Cardinals in New York and Dublin are among high-ranking clergy who have publicly used the title "the Great" for John Paul II. Millions of admirers of Pope John Paul II viewed him as a faithful and holy Apostle to humanity and one of history's great figures, due in no small measure to the role he played in the collapse of the communist regimes in Eastern Europe, thus ending the Cold War. Chapter 9 examines in more detail the highlights of his papacy and the trials of the Church during his exceptional pontificate.

MEMBER OF THE CHURCH

Mother Teresa of Calcutta:
SOMETHING BEAUTIFUL FOR GOD

The winner of the 1979 Nobel Peace Prize was a frail old nun, Mother Teresa of Calcutta. Born Agnes Boyaxhui in Yugoslavia in 1910, she joined the order of the Sisters of Loretto. In 1948 she left the order and began to care for those dying on the streets of Calcutta. She eventually began her own religious order, the Missionaries of Charity. Besides taking the traditional vows of poverty, chastity, and obedience, Mother Teresa's community takes a fourth vow: service to the poorest of the poor.

Mother Teresa's single passion was to assure every person she met of God's love. She shared a message that never got old: "Do something beautiful for God."

Besides the Nobel Peace Prize, Mother Teresa was honored many times over in her lifetime. In 1992 she was asked to come to New York to be presented with $100,000 for her work by a Catholic organization. The occasion was a fancy dinner where filet mignon would be served. Mother Teresa accepted the check. Next she scolded the crowd for its extravagance, telling them before she came to New York it took her three hours to scrape the maggots from a dying man's body. Then she left without eating. A few days later, she received another $100,000, equal to the cost of the banquet.

Mother Teresa died on September 5, 1997. She has since been beatified and is a candidate for sainthood.

Summary

- The nineteenth century's industrialization, along with the excesses of liberal capitalism, brought great misery to the working class. One reaction to the social question was Marxist communism, which believed in violent class struggle to bring justice to the proletariat.

- The Church was slow to adapt to the modern age because of the anti-religious stance of liberal reformers. However, there were Catholic leaders like Bishop Ketteler in Germany, Cardinal Manning in England, and Cardinal Gibbons in America who promoted worker rights.

- In 1891, Pope Leo XIII issued his landmark social-justice encyclical *Rerum Novarum*. On the one hand, it affirmed the right to private property and workers' rights to a fair wage and unionization. On the other hand, it permitted state intervention to defend workers. It also highlighted the vital role of the family and the role of religion in building a just society. Subsequent Popes issued encyclicals to continue this solid teaching and build a remarkable tradition of Catholic social justice teaching.

- Pius XI's *Quadragesimo Anno* introduced the principle of subsidiarity. Pius XII's many addresses highlighted the role of natural law as the foundation for just international institutions. John XXIII's *Pacem in Terris*, addressed to all people of good will, outlined basic human rights and their corresponding responsibilities. The Second Vatican Council's *Gaudium et Spes* and Pope Paul VI *Populorum Progessio* and *Octagesima Adveniens* taught about human and economic rights and the need for the wealthy to share their riches with impoverished peoples. Pope John Paul II's *Laborem Exercens* treated the subjective and objective dimensions of work. His *Sollicitudo Rei Socialis* critiqued both communism and the excesses of capitalism. And his *Centesimus Annus* highlighted the principle of a preferential option for the poor and addressed the worldwide scene after the collapse of communism.

- Pope St. Pius X (1903–1914) renewed Church life. He reformed liturgical music, issued a new catechism, promoted Catholic Action, and encouraged frequent reception of the Eucharist. Theologically a conservative, Pius X discouraged the progressive theologians of his day, known as Modernists, some of whom were clearly heretics. He required an anti-Modernist oath of teachers and clerics and set up watchdog groups in dioceses to look for heretics.

- Pope Benedict XV (1914–1921) called off the spying on suspected Modernists. As the Pope during World War I, he was neutral in the conflict and used the moral authority of his office to plead for an end to the conflict. He also used Church finances to relieve wartime suffering. Many of his suggestions for a peaceful resolution to the War ended up in Woodrow Wilson's peace plan.

- Pope Pius XI (1921–1939) became Pope during the rise of fascist regimes, most notably in Italy and Germany. He signed the Lateran Concordat and Treaty with Mussolini in 1929, which settled the Roman Question once and for all. He deplored fascism and issued important encyclicals against Mussolini's fascist attacks on the Church and Hitler's Nazism. He also condemned atheistic communism, which found a foothold in Russia after the 1917 revolution and brought havoc to that country under the repressive regimes of Lenin and Stalin.

- Pope Pius XII (1939–1958) stood as a brave symbol of Catholicism during World War II, doing more than any other human being to save the Jews from Hitler's "final solution." He coordinated relief efforts during the war and helped save Rome from destruction. After the war, he mobilized world opinion against communism, which was oppressing so many Catholics and Christians in Soviet-controlled regimes. His encyclical *Divino Afflante Spiritu* helped encourage biblical scholarship. Such renewed scholarship would help pave the way for the council called by his successor.

- Pope John XXIII (1958–1963) was the most beloved Pope of the twentieth century. Looking at the signs of the time, he was inspired to convoke the Second Vatican Council to bring *aggiornamento* (updating) to the Church. This council was brewing for decades due to the papal social justice teaching, active lay participation in Catholic Action groups, the liturgical and biblical movements that went back to the roots of Catholicism, missionary approaches that were sympathetic to native populations, the work of a few Catholics in the ecumenical movement, and the writings of some forward-looking Catholic theologians.

- Pope Paul VI (1963–1978) continued the council after the death of Pope John XXIII. He tried to implement its reforms in a balanced way between ultraconservatives like Archbishop Lefebvre, who thought the council was heretical, and dissident radicals, who advocated for faster reforms, including a married clergy. The council issued sixteen documents. The four Constitutions—on the liturgy, the Church, revelation, and the Church in the Modern World—were the most important. The nine decrees (for example, on ecumenism) renewed Catholic life by applying the theological principles of the Constitutions. The three declarations were policy statements on Christian education, religious freedom, and the Church's relation to non-Christians.

- By and large, though, Catholics embraced the reforms of Vatican II which brought the Church into the modern age.

- In 1978, Pope Paul VI died. He was followed by the smiling Pope, John Paul I (1978), who had one of history's shortest pontificates, reigning for only thirty-three days. The third Pope to serve that year was Karol Wojtyla who, as Pope John Paul II (1978–2005), would go on to have one of history's most exceptional and longest pontificates.

Prayer REFLECTION

The bishops assembled at the Second Vatican Council prayed this prayer before every commission meeting. Tradition holds that St. Isidore of Seville composed it in the seventh century. The invocation was used at several regional councils and also at the First Vatican Council.

We are here before you, O Holy Spirit, conscious of our innumerable sins, but united in a special way in your Holy Name. Come and abide with us. Deign to penetrate our hearts.

Be guide of our actions, indicate the path we should take, so that with your help, our work may be in all things pleasing to you.

May you be our only inspiration and the overseer of our intentions, for you alone possess a glorious name together with the Father and the Son.

Thus united in your name, may we in our every action follow the dictates of your mercy and justice, so that today and always our judgments may not be alien to you, and in eternity we may obtain the unending reward of our actions. Amen.

Review and DISCUSSION QUESTIONS

1. Discuss the major differences between unbridled capitalism and communism. How do they both result in human suffering?

2. How did *Rerum Novarum* address the challenges of both communism and liberal capitalism?

3. Identify five twentieth-century papal encyclicals on social justice. Note their authors and a key teaching from each encyclical named.

4. Discuss a major contribution toward Church life of each of the twentieth-century Popes.

5. What was Modernism? What effect did it have on Catholic scholarship in the first half of the twentieth century?

6. How did Pope Benedict XV react to World War I? How was this war unlike any that preceded it?

7. List some factors that led to the rise of totalitarian states and dictators in the 1920s and 1930s.

8. What was the Lateran Concordat? Discuss its long-term effects for the Church.

9. Why did the twentieth-century Popes condemn communism?

10. Discuss the role of Pope Pius XII in helping the Jewish people during World War II.

11. Discuss some of the developments that led up to the Second Vatican Council.

12. What were the aims of the Second Vatican Council?

13. Discuss several of the major achievements of Vatican II.

14. What were some of the challenges the Church faced after the Second Vatican Council?

15. Identify *Humanae Vitae*. How did it cause a crisis in the post–Vatican II Church?

16. Briefly identify the following:

People

Joseph Cardijn   William Ketteler

Marcel Lefebvre

Terms

aggiornamento   Catholic Action

collegiality   ecumenism

Modernism   preferential option for the poor

principle of subsidiarity   Social Darwinism

totalitarianism

Provide the English translation for the following documents. Identify the author of each.

Centesimus Annus   *Dei Verbum*

Divino Afflante Spiritu   *Gaudium et Spes*

Laborem Exercens   *Lumen Gentium*

Mater et Magistra   *Pacem in Terris*

Populorum Progressio   *Quadragesimo Anno*

Rerum Novarum   *Sacrosanctum Concilium*

Sollicitudo Rei Socialis

Scripture CONNECTION

Read Ephesians 4–6, St. Paul's great letter on the Church. These chapters stress unity—a theme of the Second Vatican Council—and harmonious Christian living.

Learn BY DOING

1. Read and report on the life of one of the twentieth-century Popes at the Vatican website: www.vatican.va/holy_father/index.htm.

2. Summarize the teaching of one of the Social Justice documents of the Church. Check this excellent website for starters: *The Busy Christian's Guide to Catholic Social Teaching* (http://salt.claretianpubs.org/cstline/tline.html).

3. Compile a list of ten good quotes on social justice themes that come from Catholic Social Justice documents. Check the Archdiocese of St. Paul and Minneapolis Office for Social Justice website. Look under "Notable Quotations" in the "Social Teaching" Index. Website (www.osjspm.org).

4. Prepare a report defending the actions of Pope Pius XII in regard to the Jewish people during World War II.

5. Interview two Catholics raised in the pre-Vatican II Church. Ask them to note the most significant changes in the Church during their lifetimes. Ask them to evaluate whether the changes were positive or negative and why. Prepare a report on what you learned.

6. Research and report on the life of one of these Catholic heroes of World War II: Franz Jägerstätter, Edith Stein, or Maximilian Kolbe.

7. Read the Vatican II document *Nostra Aetate* (*Declaration on the Relation of the Church to Non-Christian Religions*). Prepare a summary on what the Church says about the Muslim and Jewish faiths.

8
The Church IN AMERICA

As followers of Christ, we are challenged to make a fundamental "option for the poor"—to speak for the voiceless, to defend the defenseless, to assess life styles, policies, and social institutions in terms of their impact on the poor. This "option for the poor" does not mean pitting one group against another, but rather, strengthening the whole community by assisting those who are the most vulnerable. As Christians, we are called to respond to the needs of all our brothers and sisters, but those with the greatest needs require the greatest response.

—UNITED STATES BISHOPS
ECONOMIC JUSTICE FOR ALL, 16 (1986)[1]

The Church Reaches THE NEW WORLD

When Christopher Columbus first traveled to the New World in 1492, a new corner of land became ripe to hear the Gospel message. Spanish missionaries joined explorers on their expeditions and the Catholic Church in America was founded in the Americas.

At the beginning of the American Revolution in 1776, there were approximately twenty-five thousand Catholics in the colonies, constituting about one-tenth of one percent of the population. Today, the Catholic Church in America is the largest religious group in the United States. There are more than 69 million Catholics, in the United States, making up more than 23 percent of the population.[2] Hispanic Catholics make up roughly 39 percent of the total Catholic population, with further growth expected year by year.[3]

The growth in American Catholicism in every era is a remarkable story of its own. American Catholics survived outright persecution in the colonial years, keeping the faith alive despite having few priests and no bishop to serve them. In the nineteenth century, waves of immigrants brought their Catholic faith to America, but they had to weather the storms of prejudice and suspicion as they adapted to American life. In the twentieth century, Catholics became a leading force in all aspects of American life, even electing a Catholic president, John F. Kennedy in 1960. In the twenty-first century, American

Catholics are meeting new challenges. These include surviving the aftermath of revelations of clerical sexual misconduct, learning how best to minister effectively to a growing Hispanic presence in the Church, and adapting to the reality of a diminishing number of priests and religious.

In many ways, the Catholic Church in America embodies the Church's *catholic* (universal) nature in the way she has embraced a host of people of every racial, cultural, and ethnic background. The Church has learned from America's tradition of the separation of church and state. And it has shared with the universal Church the American traditions of representative government, religious pluralism and toleration, and the due process of law.

Over its years of growth, American Catholicism has developed a unique personality. Unlike many national churches in Europe, the Church in America never dominated or became indebted to the government. In the words of historian Charles R. Morris, American Catholicism has been "one defined by its prickly apartness from the broader, secular American culture—*in* America, usually enthusiastically *for* America, but never quite *of* America."[4]

One question that has always been constant with American Catholicism is how much it should "go along to get along." Throughout history, there have always been some who have argued that the Church should assimilate to the American culture. In contrast, other voices, including influential bishops and cardinals of the nineteenth and twentieth centuries, argued that the Church should strive at all costs to maintain Catholic identity against a Protestant or secular culture by building her own institutions to serve its members— schools, hospitals, youth groups, newspapers, and so forth.

The debate continues today. May Catholics vote for Catholic politicians who tolerate abortion . . . or capital punishment? In the face of medical advances, what stance should a Catholic take on stem cell research? How does a Catholic support family values in the midst of the plea of homosexual persons who want the state to recognize "gay marriages"? How does one remain faithful to Jesus Christ *in* America, *for* America, but not *of* America?

This chapter will briefly survey the story of American Catholicism, focusing on these major divisions:

- Colonial Beginnings (1492–1815)

- Growth of the American Church (1815–1900)

- Distinctive American Catholicism (1900–present)

1540
Franciscan missionaries accompany Coronado in his search for the Seven Cities of Gold in America's Southwest

Colonial BEGINNINGS

There is a natural tendency for today's Catholics to look first to the original thirteen British colonies for the beginning of the American Catholic story. However, the real roots of American Catholicism are found in the Spanish and French missionaries who evangelized before the English came to the New World.

Spanish Missionaries and Colonization

Spain was the first colonial power in the New World. When the Spanish explorers came to America, religious priests and brothers joined them. The missionaries tried to convert Native Americans to Christianity while soldiers imposed Spanish rule and extracted gold from New World conquests. After a few generations, only a few Mexicans had converted to Christianity. In 1531 something miraculous happened. Mary, the Mother of God, appeared to a humble Indian, St. Juan Diego, at Guadalupe. Her appearance was the impetus to acceptance of Christianity on a large scale.

Spanish efforts in America also contain the following list of firsts:

- San Juan, Puerto Rico, is the oldest diocese in the present-day territory of the United States (1511).

- Franciscan missionary Fr. Juan de Padilla was the first American martyr. When he tried to preach the Gospel to the Wichita Indians in Kansas, he was martyred sometime in 1542–1543.

- Spanish-founded St. Augustine (Florida) boasts the nation's oldest parish and diocese (1565).

- Santa Fe, New Mexico, founded in 1609, is the oldest capital city in the United States.

Spanish missionaries labored in the Southeast, primarily in Florida. It is estimated that by the mid-1600s, there were around twenty-five thousand Christian Indians in Florida. However, shortly after the start of the eighteenth century, English colonists from the Carolinas wiped out these missionary efforts in this region by killing or enslaving most of the Indians.

Spanish explorations in the Southwest to look for gold came up empty. In their search, explorers discovered Pueblo tribes near Santa Fe, New Mexico, a town that grew prosperous and served as a center for missionary activity and trade. By 1630, there may have been as many as thirty-five thousand Indians

1565
America's oldest mission established at St. Augustine, Florida, America's first city

who had converted to Christianity in the area of New Mexico. However, the Spanish conquerors unwisely raided Indian settlements for slaves, resulting in an Indian uprising in 1680 that burnt down churches and killed Franciscan missionaries. Indians reverted to their native religions and customs. When the Spaniards returned in 1692, the Indians who remained in the area put up no resistance. Some were converted by a new wave of Franciscan missionaries. The Spanish settlers spread into the fertile regions of New Mexico, Colorado, and Utah. The influence of the Spanish Catholicism of these early settlers is in strong evidence today in the southwestern states. Also, today there are many Native American Indians who are Catholic in these regions, though many have become Protestant Christians or follow their ancient religious practices.

The wedding of cross and crown all too often made the missions too dependent on the Spanish government, which encouraged the economic exploitation of the Indians. Some missionaries viewed the Indians as savages and thought it beneath their dignity to learn the native languages. However, other missionaries (for example, Bartholomew de Las Casas) did try to defend the rights of the Indians. They had the support of Pope Paul III who decreed the following (1537):

> [T]he said Indians and all other people who may later be discovered by Christians, are by no means to be deprived of their liberty or the possession of their property, even though they be outside the faith of Jesus Christ; and that they may and should, freely and legitimately, enjoy their liberty and the possession of their property; nor should they be in any way enslaved; should the contrary happen, it shall be null and have no effect.[5]

Holy and persistent missionaries did result in some notable successes in the Southwest and California. For example, the Jesuit Fr. Eusebio Kino set up a string of missions throughout Texas, Arizona, New Mexico, and California. Kino baptized four thousand Indians and drew detailed maps of the Southwest. Franciscan Blessed Junípero Serra carried on extensive missionary work in California. He baptized six thousand Indians and helped to found nine missions in places like San Diego, Santa Clara, San Juan Capistrano, and San Francisco before his death in 1784. In time, Spanish missionaries built twenty-one missions in California.

➤ *Memorial Mural to Fr. Eusebio Kino*

1617
St. Rose of Lima, the first native saint in the Americas, dies in Lima, Peru. She is the patroness of Latin America and the Philippines.

1634
Lord Calvert founds Catholic mission in Maryland

The basic idea behind the missions was to keep the nomadic Indians from wandering, settle them by teaching them farming techniques, and then trying to convert them to the faith. Thus, missionaries set up schools, churches, and marketplaces. They taught women domestic arts like sewing, weaving, and cooking. They trained men to be farmers, carpenters, ranchers, and tanners. Missions, often a day's walk from one another, helped civilize the nomadic Indians. A criticism of the mission system was that in most cases once the Native Americans had converted to Christianity they were not free to leave the missions.

When Spain lost its control of Mexico in 1828, the missions declined. Some friars left for Spain. A secular government took over in Mexico. Greedy politicians looted and ruined missions, exploiting and killing Indians. Religious practice declined. By the time America took over California from Mexico in 1847, there were only thirteen priests in that vast territory.

WHAT THE CHURCH BELIEVES ABOUT . . .
Ministering to Native Americans

The United States Conference of Catholic Bishops ad hoc committee on Native American Catholics made three primary recommendations for ministering to Native Americans and presented those to the entire body of bishops at a recent conference. They are:

- First, get to know who the Native people are in your diocese, and then learn the gifts they have to offer and the needs they have.
- Second, make sure that at least one person in your diocese is well prepared to work with Native people. In addition, everyone who works with Native Catholics should have a basic understanding of Native life and culture.
- Third, work to identify and then prepare Native people to be ministers—clergy, religious, lay—to serve the needs of the Native Catholic population.

Native people were the first to hear the Gospel preached in the Americas. Among some of our Native peoples are families who have been Catholic for more than four hundred years. All they ask is that the Church continue to be present for them.[6]

French Missionaries and Colonization

Brave French missionaries typically left the safety of university life in France and came to the New World to share the Gospel with Native Americans. They

1646
Jesuit missionary Isaac Jogues martyred by Iroquois Indians

followed French traders in beaver pelts who had established trading posts in New France (Canada). Some of the missionaries were outstanding explorers in their own rights. For example, Jesuit Jacques Marquette traveled the Mississippi River with Louis Joliet. Franciscan Louis Hennepin discovered Niagara Falls. The names of many of today's American cities attest to the explorations of the adventurous French: Duluth, New Orleans, and St. Louis.

The French missionaries, in contrast to their Spanish counterparts, made a greater effort to learn the language of the Native Americans. They lived among the Indians and took the time to instruct them in the faith. Conversions came slowly. Many of the tribes were nomadic, and it was difficult to sustain instruction with the constant movement. Jesuits had the most success with conversions, especially among the Huron tribe, which was friendly to the French. However, the Iroquois Indians, fierce enemies of the Hurons, resisted missionary efforts. The Mohawks, an Iroquois tribe, captured, tortured, and enslaved the Jesuit Isaac Jogues. He was rescued and returned to France to recover, missing several fingers. But after a year, he insisted on returning to the missions. Once again he was captured and eventually killed by the Mohawks. Seven of his companions were also martyred between 1646 and 1649.

A famous Indian convert was the "Lily of the Mohawks," Blessed Kateri Tekakwitha, who was born in 1656 near Auriesville, New York, to a non-Christian Mohawk chief and a captured Christian Algonquin mother. She was orphaned when her parents died of smallpox, a disease she also contracted that resulted in severe facial scarring and impaired vision. Nevertheless, her relatives raised her as a Mohawk princess. When she was twenty, a French missionary baptized her, which caused her much suffering and ridicule from her relatives and the other Indians of her village. She escaped from her tormentors and made her way to the Christian Indian village of Caughnawaga near present-day Montreal. There, she devoted her life to prayer, penance, and care of the sick and aged. She died in 1680 when she was twenty-four. She was the first North American Indian to ever be beatified, the step preceding canonization, when Pope John Paul II named her "blessed" in 1980.

French nuns also came to New France once the missions were established. The Ursulines set up convents in Quebec and Montreal, founded schools, and engaged in charitable works. Augustinian sisters set up a clinic in Quebec. Conditions for these pioneering women were harsh. In fact, French missionaries generally had more obstacles than the Spanish missionaries of the Southwest. For example, the Indian population was more nomadic and hostile, and the climate and terrain made missionary life miserable. Also, compared to the

1687
Jesuit Eusebio Kino starts missions in Arizona

Spanish monarchs, the French government did not vigorously support the missions.

The French missions declined in the Midwest when Pope Clement XIV suppressed the Jesuit order. Further, there were not enough French settlers to stem the tide of English expansion in the New World. French-English hostilities from Europe spilled over into the New World in the French and Indian War (1754–1763). This conflict saw the Hurons siding with the French and the Iroquois with the English. When English settlers took over the French colony of Acadia, the French Catholics refused to switch their allegiance to the Protestant English monarch. As a result, they were expelled from their lands in Nova Scotia. Many eventually made their way to the southern area of the Mississippi River, to present-day Louisiana, which remained a French possession until President Jefferson acquired it in 1803 in the famous Louisiana Purchase. The descendants of the Acadians—known as the Cajuns, numbering around a half-million people—reside in Louisiana today and continue to practice the Catholic faith.

The Peace Treaty of 1763 ending the French-Indian War ceded Canada to English rule. But the Quebec Act in 1774 gave French Canadians some freedoms, including the right to participate in the political process and practice their Catholic faith. Today, the Canadian province of Quebec has retained its French and Catholic character, with many "Quebecers" agitating for independent Quebec sovereignty.

WHAT THE CHURCH BELIEVES ABOUT
The Witness of Martyrdom

Establishing the Church in the New World brought another age of martyrdom. Bearing witness to the Gospel even to death is the powerful example of martyrdom. All believers in Christ are witnesses to truth. But martyrs offer supreme witness. The martyr bears witness to Christ who died and rose, and to whom he or she is united in love.
See *Catechism of the Catholic Church*, 2473–2474.

Catholicism in the British Colonies

Four observations about Catholicism in the original thirteen colonies merit mention. First, from the very founding of Jamestown in 1607, Protestants persecuted Catholics. When Protestants came to America, they brought with them their anti-Catholic biases. For example, Catholics could not serve in political offices. Catholics were also required to support Protestant churches and could

1727
Ursuline nuns open convent in New Orleans;
first in what is now the USA

not build their own schools. At times, priests were threatened and in certain colonies Catholics were outlawed. This animosity is hard to understand especially when considering most Protestants themselves came to America to escape religious persecution. Yet, despite persecutions lasting over a century, the mostly English and Irish Catholic immigrants clung to their religious faith.

Second, because there were very few priests, only twenty-five at the time of the Revolution, there was no opportunity for Catholics to receive any kind of formal religious education. Thus, Catholicism in colonial days was rooted in the home. Mothers of families were extremely instrumental in keeping the faith alive and passing on Catholic traditions and prayers. Despite their efforts, some second or third generation Catholic colonists became Protestant.

Third, Catholics were responsible for introducing religious toleration in Maryland under the Roman Catholic proprietors, the Calverts. Founded by George Calvert, Maryland was a haven for Catholics. George's son, Cecil, granted religious freedom to all Catholics and other Christians in the famous Act of Toleration (1649). Unfortunately, the Puritans seized power in 1652, drove Catholics from public office, and repealed the Toleration Act. However, in 1658, Lord Baltimore restored the provincial government and reinstated the Toleration Act. Jesuit priests worked diligently as plantation-owning missionaries to the Catholic population in Maryland during these years. (The first Jesuit to land in Maryland in 1634 was Fr. Andrew White; two companions accompanied him.) Catholic fortunes declined once again, however, after England's Glorious Revolution. By 1691, Maryland became a Crown colony. Anglicanism was declared the official religion and Catholics were taxed to support the Anglican Church and forbidden to practice their religion.

Fourth, Catholics in all the colonies supported the principle of religious freedom. Like the Quakers of Pennsylvania, Catholics wanted toleration for all religions in the New World. William Penn's colony welcomed Catholics and allowed them freedom of worship. As a result, some Irish and many Germans immigrated to Pennsylvania and were able to practice their faith without fear of persecution. For a time, St. Joseph's church in Philadelphia was the only legal Catholic Church in the colonies.

Catholicism and the American Revolution

The religious fortunes of American Catholics began to change during the American Revolution. Although some Catholics fought on the loyalist side of the conflict, many other Catholics gained notoriety as trustworthy American

1769
Franciscan Junipero Serra begins to establish missions in California

patriots. They fought in disproportionately large numbers because they saw that freedom from the tyrannical British government would give them a better chance to practice their religion openly. Further, the principles of the Declaration of Independence and the American Constitution coincided with Catholic thought concerning the natural law, which recognizes human dignity and natural rights.

Charles Carroll (1737–1832), a Catholic from Maryland and perhaps America's richest man, was a leading revolutionary. The Continental Congress sent him on a delicate, but unsuccessful, mission to Canada with Ben Franklin, where they tried to win the Canadians to the American cause. Carroll also signed the Declaration of Independence and supported the cause of liberty in Maryland. He signed his name with great pride, adding "of Carrollton" to help the king know which Carroll was proudly affixing his name to this great document. Daniel Carroll (1730–1796), Charles's cousin, influenced the writing of the Constitution by arguing for the election of the president by the people rather than the Congress. He was also instrumental in choosing the site of the new national Capitol, which stands on the site of the large plantation he once owned along the Potomac River.

Another notable Catholic Revolutionary figure was John Barry, the father of the American Navy. Catholics from Europe also came to help the freedom fighters: the Poles Thaddeus Kosciusko and Casimir Pulaski fought heroically while Frenchman Marquis de Lafayette gained renown as a commander under George Washington.

Protestants admired these patriots and began to soften their prejudices. They also realized America needed the help of Catholic France to win the Revolution. Hence, they began to treat Catholics more favorably. Finally, after the successful rebellion, the Founding Fathers thought it best to write into the Constitution the principle of religious toleration.

America's First Bishop

Yet another prominent member of the Carroll family was Daniel Carroll's younger brother, John Carroll, who became America's first bishop in 1789. He was educated in Europe where he entered the Society of Jesus and taught in Belgium. Carroll eventually decided to return to Maryland, where he served as priest and was appointed superior of the American mission.

America needed a bishop, even if the Protestants distrusted bishops as agents of a foreign Pope. For too long, the American Church had been

1785
Catholics number approximately 25,000 among a population of four million

unable to even celebrate the Sacraments of Confirmation and Holy Orders because both sacraments
are ministered by bishops. With Rome's consent,
the priests in America elected John Carroll bishop
(the vote was 24–2). His work to build an American
Catholic Church was impressive. He supported a
strong Catholic press, Catholic education, and English in the liturgy. In trying to build a well-educated,
American-born clergy, he brought the Sulpician priests
to Baltimore. They founded St. Mary's Seminary, a
training ground for future Church leaders. Carroll was

➤ *Archbishop John Carroll*

instrumental in the foundation of Georgetown University in 1789, America's
first Catholic university. In addition, he encouraged the work of pioneering
nuns like the Poor Clares and the Sisters of Charity of St. Joseph, founded by
St. Elizabeth Ann Seton. Carroll also created four more dioceses in New York,
Philadelphia, Boston, and Bardstown, Kentucky. Carroll was appointed archbishop of the five separate United States dioceses in 1810.

Archbishop Carroll helped to settle another chronic problem of an expanding Church, the problem of **lay trusteeism**. Lay trusteeism refers to the
practice of incorporating Church property in the name of the laity, a practice
that was necessary in the early years of the republic because some states had
laws against the Church holding property in its name. Lay involvement had
its positive features, but it also led to some abuses.

Carroll permitted limited lay trusteeism, but he refused to give the laity
the right to hire or fire priests. Some laity tried to do this when foreign-born
priests came into their parishes. Unfortunately, some of these priests did not
bother to learn the customs or languages of their parishioners, often leading
to needless squabbles and divisions. Eventually the first provincial council of
Baltimore (1829) condemned lay trusteeism. This decision helped to diminish
the voice of lay Catholics in Church affairs up until recent times.

As he grew older, Archbishop Carroll emphasized more the authority of
the bishop as a symbol of unity and uniformity. Carroll was a giant in American
history, held in high esteem by early American leaders like George Washington and Thomas Jefferson. When he died in 1815, the Catholic population had
grown from thirty-five thousand in 1790 to two hundred thousand. This impressive growth was just a small sign of the even greater numbers of Catholics
who would come to America in the nineteenth century.

1789
John Carroll named first American bishop; Georgetown University
is the first Catholic college in the United States

> ## WHAT THE CHURCH BELIEVES ABOUT . . .
> ### The Laity and Church Governance
> Lay people can be called to cooperate with their pastors in the gover-
> nance of their parish or even dioceses. The Church provides opportuni-
> ties for the laity to participate in particular councils, diocesan synods,
> pastoral councils, in the exercise of pastoral care at a parish, collabora-
> tion in finance committees, and the participation in Church tribunals,
> and more.
> See *Catechism of the Catholic Church*, 908–913.

Growth of the AMERICAN CHURCH

A second period of American Church history is the age of the immigrants
and it extends from roughly 1815–1900. Consider the following dramatic facts:

- Largely because of the influx of Irish immigrants, the Catholic population increased from 500,000 (out of a total United States population
  of 12 million) in 1830 to more than 3,100,000 in 1860 (out of a United
  States population of 31.5 million).

- From 1860–1890, the Catholic Church tripled in size while the national
  population only doubled. During this period, German Catholics began to equal the number of Irish immigrants.

- From 1890–1920, mostly Italians and Eastern Europeans came to
  America. More than two million Catholics immigrated in the first decade of the twentieth century.

- In 1890, four out of every five people in greater New York City were
  either immigrants or the children of immigrants.

This rapid growth posed great problems of assimilation into the American
way of life. The Church had her hands full ministering to an increasing population and meeting other challenges of the nineteenth century, including the
problem of anti-Catholicism.

Anti-Catholic Attitudes

Immigrant Catholics had to face the suspicion of their Protestant neighbors.
Their foreign accents and social and religious customs made Catholic immigrants suspect. Furthermore, many immigrants were poor and unskilled

1809
Elizabeth Ann Seton founds the first American
religious congregation for women

laborers willing to compete in the economic marketplace for low wages. Fear, suspicion, and prejudice caused **nativism**, the belief that America should be preserved for "native-born Americans" that America was only for "White, Anglo-Saxon Protestants" (WASPs) who had been in the country for a while.

Outbursts of nativist anti-Catholic violence were especially strong between 1830 and the Civil War. The debate involved feuds over the use of Protestant bibles in the public schools, the burning of convents, riots, and the destruction of Church property. One notorious outbreak of anti-Catholic prejudice took place in 1834 in Charlestown, Massachusetts, near Boston, when a bigoted mob burned down an Ursuline convent. The mob violence also spread into the Irish neighborhood where homes were torched. Venomous anti-Catholic literature also peaked during this period with the publication of Maria Monk's *Awful Discourses*. This infamous fabrication reported the allegedly unspeakable crimes committed by nuns and priests in convents. It was later proven that Monk had never been a nun and that the lies were fabricated by virulent anti-Catholic Protestant ministers who profited monetarily from the large sales the book garnered (three hundred thousand copies before the Civil War).

In the 1850s, the Protestant-sponsored American Party (nicknamed the "Know-Nothings" because, when questioned about the group, members would respond, "I don't know") spewed out hateful literature calling into question the patriotism of Catholics. One of their major charges was that Catholics only gave allegiance to the Pope who, they claimed, was planning to invade the United States. The Know-Nothings incited riots in Louisville, fired shots at a St. Louis cathedral, fixed elections in Baltimore, and harassed convents in Massachusetts. Know-Nothing bigotry was especially bitter during the election of 1856. Abraham Lincoln was quoted as saying,

> When the Know-Nothings get control, it will read "all men are created equal, except Negroes, and foreigners, and Catholics." When it comes to this I should prefer emigrating to some country where they make no pretence of loving liberty—to Russia, for instance, where despotism can be taken pure, and without the base alloy of hypocrisy.[7]

The Catholic press in America was founded to counteract the attacks of anti-Catholic bigots. Bishop John England of Charleston founded the *U.S. Catholic Miscellany* (1822–1861) especially for this purpose. It was the first of many Catholic newspapers established in the nineteenth century.

1822
Bishop John England starts the *U.S. Catholic Miscellany*, the first Catholic newspaper in the USA

Catholics and the Civil War

Concerning slavery of African Americans prior to the Civil War, in general, Catholics reflected the same attitudes as Protestants: Some Catholics were for slavery, others against it. Although Pope Gregory XVI condemned the slave trade in 1839, no American bishop, nor the current reigning Pope, issued an official teaching on slavery itself.

When the Civil War came, Catholics fought on both sides of the conflict. General William Sheridan, a Catholic, was a commander for the Union; General P.G.T. Beauregard, a Catholic, led a Southern army. Church leaders could also be found on both sides of the conflict. Bishop John Hughes of New York traveled to Europe at President Lincoln's request to explain the Union position. Meanwhile, Bishop Patrick Lynch of Charleston went to Rome to defend the Confederate side. Priests also served as chaplains while more than five hundred sisters from more than twenty different orders heroically ministered to the wounded on both sides. President Lincoln singled out the Catholic sisters, praising them for their hospital service during the war. The loyalty and sacrifice of both Union and Confederate Catholic soldiers impressed their fellow citizens. Their heroism and devotion largely put to rest nativist charges that Catholics were unpatriotic.

More Prejudice

Although Catholic participation in the Civil War quieted anti-Catholicism for a time, it emerged again in the 1880s with the founding of the American Protective Association. This largely rural society founded in Iowa was made up of many Irish-Protestants. Its goals were to restrict Catholic immigration, make English a prerequisite for citizenship, and to remove Catholics from teaching in public schools and participating in public offices.

Nativism survived into the twentieth century as well. Because of the increasing number of Catholic immigrants from southern and eastern Europe, anti-Catholics successfully enacted laws to limit immigration in the 1920s. The Ku Klux Klan, a nativist group opposed to African Americans, Catholics, and Jews, was active in this decade, but mostly in rural areas where the Catholic population was sparse. Bigotry also figured in the defeat of Catholic Al Smith in the 1928 presidential election. A widely circulated rumor leveled at Smith was that if he won, the Pope would take up residence in the White House and Protestants would lose their citizenship.

1853
Anti-Catholic "Know-Nothing" Party founded

Despite the fact that the Catholic population was generally part of mainstream America in the 1950s and that he was a popular war hero, John F. Kennedy, the first Catholic president, also had to overcome the concern that his patriotism and religion would conflict. Protestants feared that the Pope would control the presidency. In the 1960 campaign, Kennedy had to directly confront anti-Catholic sentiment. In a famous speech to Southern Baptist leaders, Kennedy reassured them he would be answerable to the American Constitution, not the Pope. He declared, "I am not the Catholic candidate for President [but the candidate] who happens also to be a Catholic. I do not speak for my Church on public matters—and the Church does not speak for me."[8] Kennedy's words reassured many, but his margin of victory was slim, less than a half-percent margin. Surveys conducted after the election revealed that anti-Catholic prejudice contributed to the close race.

WHAT THE CHURCH BELIEVES ABOUT . . .
Prejudice and Discrimination

Through the centuries, the Church has defined that all people—men and women—are created in God's image, have the same nature and origin, and as they are redeemed by Christ, enjoy the same calling and destiny. There is a basic equality of human beings that must be given greater recognition. As the Second Vatican Council defined: ". . . forms of social or cultural discrimination in basic personal rights on the grounds of sex, race, color, social conditions, language, or religion, must be curbed and eradicated as incomprehensible with God's design" (*Gaudium Spes*, 23).

Coping with Assimilation

With the influx of millions of Catholic immigrants in the nineteenth century, the Church was a major player in assimilating them into the American Church and into the larger, sometimes hostile, society. The Church used a variety of means to accomplish this.

Nineteenth-century immigration coincided with the growth of public schools in America. However, Protestants dominated the policies of the emerging public schools. Textbooks were anti-Catholic. For example, history texts ridiculed the Catholic Church and the Pope. Teachers required students to sing Protestant hymns and read the Protestant Bible. When Catholics complained, civil unrest often resulted. As a result, bishops began to turn to **parochial schools** as the answer for providing religious instruction to Catholics.

1875
Father James Healy, first black bishop consecrated in America;
New York's Archbishop John McCloskey named first American cardinal

At the Third Plenary Council of Baltimore (1884), the American bishops ruled that each Catholic parish must have its own school. By 1900, there were nearly four thousand Catholic schools in the country. Many of these parochial schools found their model in those set up by St. Elizabeth Ann Seton and her Sisters of Charity.

However, not all bishops agreed that parochial schools were the answer for providing religious education to Catholic youth. Archbishop John Ireland of the Diocese of St. Paul, for example, argued for a released-time system of cooperation with the public schools. The Vatican allowed Archbishop Ireland to try an experiment, but his idea did not catch on. Many fellow bishops considered this idea too liberal and a dangerous compromise with the state.

Catholic schools were an important instrument for bringing immigrants into the mainstream of American life. They taught English and the principles of American democracy. The Third Plenary Council of Baltimore also was responsible for the writing of the famous question-and-answer *Baltimore Catechism*, approved by Cardinal James Gibbons in 1885. It provided the basis for a coherent, clear, and uniform education in the Catholic faith from the time of its publication until the catechetical reforms that came after the Second Vatican Council.

The immigrant **parish** was an important agency for building Catholic identity in America. Organized geographically, parishes helped cement Catholic identity and supported parishioners in many aspects of their daily living. Church historian Jay Dolan puts it this way:

> As a social organization that brought people together through a network of societies and clubs, it [the parish] helped to establish a sense of community. As an educational organization, it taught both young and old the meaning of America, its language as well as its culture; as a religious organization, it brought the presence of God to the neighborhood, nurturing and sustaining the presence of the holy through worship, devotional services, and neighborhood processions.[9]

The Church responded in many ways to meet the basic human needs of the rapidly growing Catholic population. One of the ways was the sponsorship of **charitable organizations** like orphanages, hospitals, and homes for the aged. Because there was no government social security, the poor depended on private charity. Individual parishes did their part through agencies like the St. Vincent de Paul Society, which collected clothes and furniture and provided meals for the needy. The Knights of Columbus, founded in the 1880s as a lay fraternal service organization, began with the intent to help widows

1884
Third Plenary Council of Baltimore held;
calls for each parish to establish a school

and orphans. Named after the Catholic discoverer of America, the Knights gave Catholic men an opportunity to bond together in charitable works at a time that many unions and other community help organizations excluded Catholics from participation and provided a way for Catholics to pool their resources for life insurance. The Knights of Columbus was also an alternative to Masonic lodges, banned by the Pope because of Freemasonry's anti-Catholicism.

The immigrant Church benefited greatly from the selfless sacrifices of **religious orders**, especially of women. Catholic heroines like Mother Frances Cabrini, the immigrant-founder of the Missionary Sisters of the Sacred Heart, labored among the Italian immigrants. Her community, which came to New York in 1889, worked selflessly in schools, hospitals, and orphanages. The Church canonized Mother Cabrini a saint, the first American citizen so recognized. She and her sisters set up more than fifty charitable organizations in the South and the Southwest. Other outstanding Catholic women of this century were St. Rose Philippine Duchesne of the Sacred Heart Order who established the first free school west of the Mississippi River; and Rose Hawthorne Lathrop, daughter of the famed author

➤ *St. Frances Cabrini*

Nathaniel Hawthorne, who founded a religious order to care for incurable cancer patients.

Catholic immigrants mimicked the prejudice against African Americans of their fellow citizens. They were not eager to allow blacks to move ahead of them on the social and economic ladder. Only one hundred thousand blacks were Catholics in 1883 out of a total population of seven million African-Americans in the United States. However, there were some positive developments in this area. St. Katharine Drexel and her Sisters of the Blessed Sacrament ministered particularly to African and Native Americans. Her work was often opposed, but her gentle and convincing work for the nation's poorest led her to found Xavier University in New Orleans, the only Catholic college dedicated to African Americans.

Immigrants looked to **clerical leadership** in the persons of their parish priests for both spiritual and temporal leadership. Priests were often the most educated Catholics. As such, they served as counselors, dispensers of charity, spiritual guides, employment brokers, defenders of Catholic rights, and

1885
Publication of the *Baltimore Catechism*

advisors. These many clerical leadership roles fostered docility of the laity toward the clergy.

American bishops also emerged as visible spokespersons for the growing Catholic community. Their influence in the public sector was considerable. For example, Cardinal James Gibbons of Baltimore (1834–1921) was at the forefront of the increasingly active role of the official Church in American life of the nineteenth and early twentieth centuries. Appointed to preside over the famous Third Plenary Council of Baltimore in 1884, his skillful executive abilities helped enact important decrees that would set the policy of the American Church for decades. These included the decrees on the necessity for Catholic schools, the preparation of the *Baltimore Catechism*, the determination of the six holy days of obligation to be observed in America, and the establishment of the Catholic University of America in 1887. One of Cardinal Gibbons's most significant contributions was to convince Pope Leo XIII to approve the Knights of Labor. Against severe conservative opposition to the union, Gibbons felt the Church must side with working people. His victory and his sponsorship of other social issues won the hearts of Catholic laborers in America.

Most of the influential Church leaders of this period were Irish. They gained the respect of both Catholics and Protestants. Among the strong personalities of this era was the first archbishop of New York, John Hughes (1797–1864). Earning the name "Dagger John" for his obstinate refusal to buckle under the pressures of anti-Catholic bigots, he founded St. John's College, which would become Fordham University, and began construction of St. Patrick's Cathedral. Other notable Irish prelates were the liberal Archbishop John Ireland (1838–1918) of St. Paul, Minnesota, Archbishop Michael Corrigan (1839–1902) of New York, and Bishop Bernard McQuaid (1823–1909) of Rochester, New York, a strong supporter of Catholic education.

WHAT THE CHURCH BELIEVES ABOUT . . .
Labor Unions and the Right to Strike

A fundamental right of individual workers is the right to form in associations or unions which "truly represent them and are able to cooperate in organizing the economic life properly, and the right to play their part in the activities of such associations without the risk of reprisal" (*Gaudium Spes*, 68). Participating in a worker's strike is also morally acceptable when negotiations have broken down, or when it is necessary to obtain a particular benefit.

See *Catechism of the Catholic Church*, 2435.

1904
National Catholic Education Association founded

Americanism

The nineteenth century produced an important internal controversy in the Church known as **Americanism**, the belief that Catholics should adapt themselves to the best of American culture rather than seal themselves off as a defensive minority group. The Americanists included prominent bishops like Cardinal James Gibbons, Archbishop John Ireland, and Bishop John Keane, the rector of the newly established Catholic University of America (1887). A prominent spokesperson of the movement was a famous convert, Orestes Brownson. Brownson argued that a Catholic could simultaneously be a good American and a good Catholic. Fr. Isaac Hecker (1819–1888), the founder of the Paulist Fathers, provided intellectual leadership.

Americanists supported public schools and the separation of Church and state. They also favored cooperative efforts with Protestants, emphasizing common beliefs rather than stressing issues that divide. Americanism seemed to call for suppression of traditional Catholic virtues in lieu of sociopolitical values of America: for example, democracy and the separation of Church and state. When a biography of Hecker described him as the "patron saint of Americanism" and caused a stir in France, Pope Leo XIII sent a letter to Cardinal Gibbons of Baltimore that condemned Americanism.

This liberal element of the American Church faced conflict at home as well. For example, because they came to America before the Germans, and because they spoke English, Irish prelates rose to dominate the American Church. German Catholics resented being forced to conform to Irish customs. They felt that Irish bishops and Irish Catholics had a disproportionate influence. They wanted their own German parishes with German priests serving them, especially in places like Cincinnati, St. Louis, and Milwaukee, known as the German Triangle. German immigrants were especially strong supporters of a separate Catholic school system, one which helped pass on the Catholic faith and, at the same time, one that would preserve the German language and customs. They feared the concept of Americanism and were supported in this belief by the Jesuits and by two important Irish bishops: Archbishop Michael Corrigan of New York and Bishop Bernard McQuaid of Rochester, New York, both strong supporters of a separate Catholic school system.

At first, it looked like the Vatican would side with the Americanists on the issue of Catholic schools, but after time the Vatican came out in support of separate parochial schools. The Pope also warned Catholics against making too many contacts with Protestants. Certain key Americanists had to resign

•···

1919
Bishops' *Program of Social Reconstruction* published

influential academic positions. Pope Leo XIII's encyclical *Testem Benevolentiae* (1899) never named anyone a heretic, but it did make it clear that the Church cannot change her doctrines to accommodate modern society.

The outcome of the Americanist crisis reflected a conservative shift in the Church throughout the world. This shift made the Church defensive toward the world and cautious about assimilating too many of its values. Rome was suspicious of some of the values of American democracy. It feared that the American Church might decide to go its own way and not heed the teachings of the Pope. Thus, the American Church stifled some new and liberal ideas as it entered the twentieth century. It would take six more decades before the universal Church would look more kindly on important American contributions like the separation of Church and state and the concept of freedom of religion for all.

MEMBERS OF THE CHURCH

Canonized and BEATIFIED AMERICANS

From the time Christianity first came to America, there have been several models of faith who helped to evangelize and minister in the New World who have been held up for emulation. Included among these Christian heroes is a growing list of canonized saints and "blesseds" whose causes for sainthood are being considered. Brief sketches of these important Catholics follow.

American Saints

North American Jesuit Martyrs. Five French missionaries were martyred in Canada; another three in New York. Those who were killed in New York were Saints Isaac Jogues, René Goupil, and Jean Lalande. Their shrine is at Auriesville, New York. Canonized in 1930.

St. Frances Cabrini (1850–1917). Italian immigrant who became a naturalized American citizen in 1909. Founded the Missionary Sisters of the Sacred Heart. Worked tirelessly among the American immigrants. Known as the "Heavenly Patroness of all Emigrants." Her shrine is in New York City. Canonized in 1946.

1928
Catholic Alfred E. Smith of New York defeated for presidency

 **St. Elizabeth Ann Bayley Seton** (1774–1821). First native-born American to be canonized a saint. Daughter of an aristocratic Episcopalian, New York family. Mother of five children. When widowed, she converted to Catholicism (1805) and founded the American Sisters of Charity (1809). Established many Catholic schools that served as the prototype of the American Catholic school system. Her order also founded many hospitals and served heroically during the Civil War. Canonized in 1975.

St. John Nepomucene Neumann (1811–1860). Native of Bohemia who served as a pioneer diocesan priest in Rochester and Buffalo, New York. Joined the Redemptorists and was named the fourth bishop of Philadelphia in 1852. Was a gentle, prayerful, faithful missionary and example to his flock. Canonized in 1977.

St. Rose Philippine Duchesne (1769–1852). Established a branch of the Religious of the Sacred Heart in the United States. Came as a missionary from France to the Louisiana Territory at the age of forty-nine. Established a mission in Missouri with the first free school west of the Mississippi. Devoted her years of service to educate Native Americans, care for their sick, and combat alcoholism in the tribes. Known by the Pottawatomi Indians as the "Woman-Who-Prays-Always." Canonized in 1988.

St. Katharine Drexel (1858–1955). Called the "Millionaire Nun," Katharine Drexel inherited a fortune that she eventually used for missionary endeavors in the community of Sisters of the Blessed Sacrament, which she founded in 1891. She established sixty missions for the education of Native Americans and African Americans and founded Xavier University in New Orleans, the only Catholic university dedicated to serving African Americans. Canonized in 2000.

St. Anne-Thérèse Guérin (1798–1856). French nun who came to Vincennes, Indiana, and later helped establish the Academy of St. Mary-of-the-Woods (1841) at Terre Haute, Indiana, the first Catholic women's liberal-arts college in the United States. Established schools

 1931
Monsignor Fulton J. Sheen begins his famous preaching career, first on radio, then eventually on television in the 1950s

and orphanages and engaged in many charitable works to help the poor and sick. Canonized in 2006.

American Blesseds

Blessed Kateri Tekakwitha (1656–1680). Called the "Lily of the Mohawk." Iroquois Indian born in New York state who was converted by the early Jesuit missionaries. Lived a prayerful life and maintained a cheerful disposition in the midst of much ridicule for her conversion and for her living a life of chastity and devotion. Beatified in 1980.

Blessed Junípero Serra (1713–1784). Born in Spain and came to America as a heroic, hard-working Franciscan missionary in California. Established nine missions there while showing great love for Native Americans. His many travels brought him much physical pain because of ulcerous varicose veins, but he always remained a man of deep prayer. Beatified in 1988.

Blessed Damien DeVeuster (1840–1889). "The Leper Priest" who heroically served outcast lepers on the colony at Molokai in Hawaii. His devotion to them led to his eventually contracting the disease himself. Beatified in 1995.

Blessed Francis Xavier Seelos (1819–1867). Born in Bavaria and ordained a Redemptorist priest in Baltimore. In Pittsburgh, he served as a priest under St. John Neumann, became pastor, and was beloved as a spiritual director. Other assignments included preaching missions in many states, in both German and English. Died of Yellow Fever after caring for its victims in New Orleans. Beatified in 2000.

Blessed Carlos Manuel Rodriguez (1918–1963). First Puerto Rican to be beatified. Suffered much in his life from ulcerative colitis that led to an early death caused by colon cancer. Kept a cheerful disposition and developed a great love of the liturgy. Known as the "lay Apostle of the liturgical movement," his zealous teaching of the faith, joyous demeanor, and exemplary life led many people to seek a religious vocation. Beatified in 2001.

1933
Dorothy Day and Peter Maurin start Catholic Worker Movement
at height of the Great Depression

Blessed Mother Marianne Cope (1838–1918). Called the "Leprosy Nun." A supervisor in a Syracuse hospital when she volunteered to go to Molokai to help Fr. Damien, "the leper priest." She worked nonstop for thirty years serving the lepers and managing homes for children, leaving at her death a legacy of schools, hospitals, and orphanages. Beatified in 2005.

Distinctive AMERICAN CATHOLICISM

At the beginning of the century, Catholics numbered about 16 percent of the total population (76 million) in the United States. Most of the Catholic immigrants had settled in the cities, making Catholicism in the United States largely an urban phenomenon. Catholic population and influence were small in the country areas, in the South, the West, and in farming districts. When Congress restricted immigration in the 1920s, Catholics had a chance to assimilate into American society and begin to reach for their share of the "American dream."

For some ethnic groups, this was easier than for others. The English-speaking Irish Catholics were eager to fit into American culture, to get involved in politics, to engage fully in the life of America. In cities like New York and Boston with large Irish populations, they dominated civic life, even taking high-ranking roles in the public school system by 1930.

Other immigrant groups were slower to adapt to American culture, preferring to keep alive their national identities. Notable examples include Polish Catholics and Italian Catholics. Poles in Chicago, for example, kept alive their national heritage and religion in large Polish parishes, resenting the influence of Irish and also German bishops over their national churches. Italian-Americans also resented the strong Irish influence in the American Church. Italians kept

➤ *Italian Giglio Festival in Brooklyn, New York*

alive in their neighborhoods their old-world traditions of parades and carnivals to celebrate the feast days of patron saints. Over time, and sometimes

1946
St. Frances Xavier Cabrini canonized: the first United States citizen saint

after nasty disagreements, ethnic parishes were absorbed into the regular diocesan structure, though even today, there are ethnic parishes in many large American cities.

Organization of the American Church

Americans have a well-deserved reputation for efficiency that has been carried to the Catholic Church in America. For example, in 1917, the National Catholic War Council mobilized Catholic relief efforts during World War I. Several years later this important agency took on a new name—the National Catholic Welfare Conference. It served to advise bishops and coordinate their efforts in the areas of education, national legislation, youth and lay organizations, immigration, social action, and the like. This model continued

> until 1966 when the National Conference of Catholic Bishops (NCCB) and the United States Catholic Conference (USCC) were established. The NCCB attended to the Church's own affairs in this country, fulfilling the Vatican Council's mandate that bishops "jointly exercise their pastoral office" (Decree on the Bishops' Pastoral Office in the Church, #38). NCCB operated through committees made up exclusively of bishops, many of which had full-time staff organized in secretariats. In USCC the bishops collaborate with other Catholics to address issues that concern the Church as part of the larger society. Its committees included lay people, clergy and religious in addition to the bishops.
>
> On July 1, 2001, the NCCB and the USCC were combined to form the United States Conference of Catholic Bishops (USCCB).[10]

Missionary Work

In 1906, only fourteen American Catholics were in missionary work overseas. The Church in America was considered missionary territory itself until 1908 and supported by foreign mission-aid societies until the early 1920s. By 2003, more than six thousand five hundred priests, sisters, brothers, and lay volunteers were working in the foreign missions.[11] The Maryknoll fathers, brothers, and sisters and the Jesuits make up the largest missionary orders in America.

The American Catholic laity has generously supported the missions. For example, American Catholics give more money than any other national group to support the Society for the Propagation of the Faith.

1960
John F. Kennedy, first Catholic to be elected President of the United States

Mission work needs to be done at home, too. The National Catholic Rural Life Conference (founded in 1922) helps make the Catholic presence felt in farming communities. In 1939, the Glenmary Society began to work in the home missions, especially in the poor Appalachian area.

Racial Justice

The Church's efforts in the area of racial justice unfortunately reflected general American attitudes during most of the twentieth century. Catholic parishes and schools were segregated until the end of the World War II. Leaders like Fr. John LaFarge, S.J., and the Catholic Interracial Council worked tirelessly to help change Catholic attitudes. In the late 1940s, some bishops began to work vigorously for racial justice in their dioceses. Cardinal Joseph Ritter of St. Louis ended segregation in the diocesan schools in 1947, followed by Archbishop Patrick O'Boyle of Washington in 1948. Bishop Vincent Waters desegregated Catholic schools in Raleigh in 1953, a year before the famous Supreme Court case, *Brown v. Board of Education of Topeka*, ruled that "separate educational facilities are inherently unequal."

Political and Social Action

While Irish Catholics, especially, were more and more involved in local and often national politics, the nativist prejudice did not dissipate. As noted, the presidential campaigns of Al Smith in 1928, and even John F. Kennedy in 1960, were affected by prejudice against Catholics.

However, Catholics did attract national prominence in other ways, including at least one unsavory example. In the 1930s, Fr. Charles Coughlin hosted a radio show with a large national audience. At first, Coughlin began as a social reformer, showing concern for the poor. In reality, this priest from Royal Oak, Michigan, was a demagogue who used the infant media to play to peoples' prejudices and fears. Fr. Coughlin uttered anti-Semitic remarks and began to sympathize with the fascist causes in Germany and Italy. He opposed American entry into World War II. Finally, Coughlin's bishop silenced him and ordered him off the radio in the early 1940s.

On the opposite side of the political and social spectrum, Dorothy Day and Peter Maurin founded the Catholic Worker Movement in 1933. This Movement emphasized radical Gospel living through identification with the poor. They opened Houses of Hospitality in cities around the country. These Houses welcomed the homeless and fed the unemployed and hungry. Dorothy Day

1965
Pope Paul VI visits the United Nations in New York; first Pope to visit USA

also published *The Catholic Worker*, a newspaper devoted to peace and the rights of workers. Over the years the Catholic Workers provided an outlet for the idealism of young Catholics. They also raised the consciences of their fellow Catholics during the Vietnam War, calling into question its morality. The Catholic Workers and other lay organizations, like the Christian Family Movement, reminded Catholics that the Christian vocation belongs to everyone, laity and clergy alike.

Controversies Involving Patriotism

Partly because their allegiance to their country was questioned by non-Catholic bigots in past decades, Catholics have often been zealous for American patriotism. Catholics have supported every war effort of the United States, especially by participating in the military in modern wars from World War I to the war on terrorism engaged shortly after the attacks of September 11, 2001.

However, some Catholics have carried their patriotism to an extreme. One notable example was Senator Joseph McCarthy in the 1950s. His brand of superpatriotism targeted communists in the government. Many times, though, he simply used the Cold War fear of communism to attack his political enemies. Unfortunately, many Catholics and other Americans supported his vindictive measures and thus ruined innocent lives. The United States Senate finally censured McCarthy in 1954.

Another controversial stance was taken by Francis Cardinal Spellman of New York, perhaps the most politically powerful cardinal in American history. He approvingly supported American efforts in Vietnam and, during that conflict, warned Catholics not to question governmental judgments in military decisions. Reflecting on many lessons of that war, the American bishops have since spoken most eloquently to their fellow citizens about how the duties of true patriotism can be enacted in war. In their various pastoral letters over the past thirty years, the bishops have been very strong in advocating that the true path to peace is to work for justice. For example, in the pastoral letter, *The Challenge of Peace* (1983), the bishops questioned the arms race and issued cogent guidelines on the morality of the possession and use of nuclear weapons. In this prophetic document, the bishops also clearly stated the right citizens have to protest unjust wars. The bishops also applied the just war principles before America engaged in the war in Iraq in 2003. They seriously challenged the George W. Bush administration's position on preemptive war by stating that all the conditions for a just war were not present.

1966
National Conference of Catholic Bishops and United States Catholic Conference established

In another influential pastoral letter, *Economic Justice for All* (1986), the American bishops taught that good citizenship requires caring in a special way for poor people, by testing economic decisions on what effect they will have on those in poverty. Too often, the wealthy make economic decisions that have a negative effect on poor people. The bishops want American leaders to apply the Gospel principles of justice to the economic marketplace.

The United States Conference of Catholic Bishops has been a strong voice for social justice in this country, speaking out on many issues, including the protection of human life from womb to tomb, the rights of minorities, the treatment of immigrants, and so forth.

Golden Years of American Catholicism

American Catholics achieved economic and social equality with their fellow citizens between the end of World War II and 1960. Many consider the 1950s a special time for American Catholics. The Baby Boom generation helped the Catholic population double between 1940–1960. Catholics built almost two thousand new schools during this decade. The public face of Catholicism during this time was a kindly bishop, Fulton J. Sheen. His *Life Is Worth Living* television series was a smash hit in prime time, drawing both Catholics and countless non-Catholics to his brilliant, entertaining, and thought-provoking lectures. And, some Catholic ethnic groups, most notably the Irish, surpassed their WASP counterparts economically.

However, there were storms brewing amidst these golden years. Interestingly, the public faces of the era were two men named John. President John F. Kennedy's brief time in office coincided with the nearly as brief reign of Pope John XXIII who convoked the Second Vatican Council. Kennedy's election was a source of great pride and exhilaration for American Catholics. His youthful vigor, idealism, and charming ethnic heritage appealed to many Americans. Catholics held their heads high during his brief presidency. In return, most Americans saw that they had nothing to fear from a Catholic president. In the future, being an American Catholic would not present the handicap for achieving political office that it had been. For example, in the 2004 presidential election, Senator John Kerry, a Catholic, was never questioned about whether he would give prime allegiance to the Pope. Rather, the controversy surrounding his candidacy was oppositely whether a Catholic in good conscience could vote for Kerry since, although Kerry said he was "personally opposed to abortion," he supported a woman's "right to choose" to have an abortion.

1970
Publication of the *New American Bible*, first American Catholic translation of the Bible from the original languages

In the late 1950s and early 1960s, everyone loved Pope John XXIII, a warm peasant Pope who accepted people of all faiths. The Council he convoked gave new hope to Catholics and non-Catholics alike. It also allowed American Catholics to make significant contributions to the universal church. For example, John Courtney Murray, S.J., helped draft the important Vatican II document, *Declaration on Religious Freedom*. This enlightened document gave to the universal Church American Catholicism's positive experiences with separation of Church and state and religious liberty and pluralism.

The American Church Since Vatican II

The Second Vatican Council transformed the American Church. In the pre–Vatican II era, the Church was known for her stability. The Church had many long-standing traditions that most Catholics supported without question. The post–Vatican II Church brought with it many new challenges. Changes came; some of these were accepted while others met with challenge from clergy and laity alike.

To compound the issues after the Council, the 1960s was a decade known for its social turmoil and rapid change. In America, leaders like John F. Kennedy, Martin Luther King, Jr., and Robert Kennedy were assassinated at the height of their power and influence. The Civil Rights movement was gathering steam, but was tarred by race riots in cities across America. The Vietnam War was escalating as many people were questioning its morality.

America was also affected by the almost cataclysmic changes the world was experiencing: a sexual revolution where the sanctity of marriage and family was challenged, the widespread and cynical questioning of authority, and a rapidly increasing secularization of society. These changes hit the Catholic Church in America like a tidal wave. America's social, moral, and cultural revolution produced what many observers have termed crisis conditions in American Catholicism. Liberals argued that the American Church should assimilate to American culture even more as a result of the Council. Conservatives thought things had gotten out of control, that to accommodate the Church to America's changing society would be a disaster for the Church. Regardless, drastic change was the order of the day. Consider these comparisons between the Church in 1965 with the Church in America recent times:

- In 1965, about 65 percent of Catholics attended Mass every Sunday; it is estimated that the rate was 33 percent in 2005.[12]

1973
Supreme Court legalizes abortion in its *Roe v. Wade* decision

- In 1965, there were 58,132 priests; in 2004, there were 44,212; in 1965, there were 179,954 religious sisters; in 2004, there were 71,486. Whereas Church membership has grown by 21 percent since 1985, the number of priests has declined by 15 percent. Today there are 1,453 lay persons per priest in America compared to 652 back in 1950, and 778 in 1965. In 2005, the average age at ordination was 37.3, and this was up from 35 in 1998.[13]

- In 1965, there were 15,000 parish elementary schools, with 4.5 million students, about 50 percent of the Catholic school-age population; in 2004, there were 6,853 elementary schools, with 1.89 million students, less than 25 percent of the school-age population.

- In 1965, Catholics gave an estimated 2.2 percent of their income to the Church; in 2002, they gave less than half of that.[14]

The American Church of today faces ongoing transitions in many areas. With the declining number and aging of priests, there are an increasing number of parishes not served by a fulltime pastor. Parishes themselves are closing at an alarming rate. Boston closed sixty-seven parishes in a recent year alone and Pittsburgh closed 30 percent of its parishes between 1990 and 2003.[15] Many of these changes are due to the expense involved in maintaining aging buildings and a declining parish population to support them, especially in urban areas. Others result from a shift of the Catholic population out of the Northeast and Midwest to the warmer climates of places like the Carolinas, Georgia, and the Southwest.

In 2002 a severe crisis in the American Church came to light when the sexual scandal involving child molestation by a few hundred priests over a forty-year period garnered massive media attention. The vast majority of the cases involved teenage boys and were committed years before the media frenzy began. Lawsuits resulted in million-dollar payouts leading to bankruptcy in several dioceses. Bishops were sharply criticized for not recognizing the severity of the problem. Many of them had acted on the advice of psychologists who had treated the deviant priests and had concluded that they were able to resume their priestly ministries. As a result, many bishops reassigned pedophile priests to parishes where they once again had access to youngsters. Some of the reassigned priests, giving in to their sickness and sin, relapsed.

In their summer meeting in 2002 in Dallas, the bishops approved *A Charter for the Protection of Children and Young People*. They also issued some tough norms and policies to be applied to priests, deacons, and other Church personnel

1979
Pope John Paul II visits USA for first time to great acclaim; he would later visit in 1987, 1993, 1995, and 1999

against whom charges of sexual impropriety are made. This Charter and the strict enforcement of the guidelines have helped to assure many of the faithful, but the fallout from this scandal has been a serious crisis of confidence of American Catholics in the leadership of the Church and ongoing financial difficulties for many dioceses.

To any outside observer, the Catholic Church in America has suffered much in recent years. But American Catholics are resilient. Many non-Catholics continue to find Catholicism attractive; more than seventy thousand annually convert to the faith. The influx of Hispanic immigrants in recent years can only enrich the Church through sheer numbers and a new perspective on faith and spirituality. Newcomers from Eastern European and Asian countries have also been a positive influence on the Church in America. The United States Conference of Catholic Bishops has remained a challenging yet compassionate voice on a host of social issues confronting the nation and the world. Since the Second Vatican Council, the laity have participated in more and more parish ministries, including the area of religious education. Women especially are leaders in this area, with more than 80 percent of parish lay ministers being women. In addition, strides have also been made in ecumenical relations with other religions.

Christ's promise to be with the Church until the end of time remains in effect. It is the Lord's abiding presence that continues to attract new members and sustain the baptized.

❀ THE CHURCH IS ALWAYS MYSTERY

The Church's human history must always be examined in light of the teaching that the Church is mystery. What does this mean? The Church is mystery because she is the culmination of salvation history. The Church is the permanent union of the divine and human, the permanent physical presence of God on earth. Because of the Church's divine element, she will survive always to the end of time.

Also, recall that the Church is the Body of Christ which is in history and which also transcends history. Because the Church is human, she is in history and is affected by history, and she must change in response to history. Because the Church is divine, she transcends history; she has aspects which are permanent and which will not change no matter how much the world changes. The aspects which do not change are what make it possible for the Church to be the Body of Christ and to function as the Body of Christ. These permanent aspects of the Church are the basic hierarchical structure and the permanent ethic and permanent

1993
World Youth Day held in Denver

body of dogma, that is, a body of revealed truths around which we must structure our lives.

Challenges for the Church in the United States
OF THE TWENTY-FIRST CENTURY

The influx of new immigrants is but one challenge with great promise for the future of the Church in America. When reflecting on recent trends in the story of American Catholicism in the twenty-first century, it is clear that the Church will have to address the following ten challenges (including immigration), among others, in the coming decades. Consider these issues and questions.

- **Ecumenism**. How can the Church reach out to people of other faiths, including Islam? A related issue is how the Roman Church can help Eastern Catholics establish hierarchical jurisdiction within their own rites and share their rich presence with the Church in the United States.

- **Gospel witness**. How can American Catholics remain true to the vision of Jesus in a pluralistic and increasingly secular society that accepts as "normal" behaviors and lifestyles contrary to the Gospel? How can the Church best remind people of the reality of sin and the need for conversion? How can the Church challenge national leaders to work for peace in just ways in the midst of a world besieged by terrorism? How can the Church best use her material resources (for example, sponsorship of health-care facilities and social services through Catholic Charities) to help the poor and needy?

- **Immigrants**. How can the Church best embrace the fast-growing number of Hispanic-American Catholics? Will an English-speaking Church impose her customs on them? Or will she respect the cultural and linguistic diversity of this important Catholic community? How can the Church help other Catholic immigrants adjust to American society? How should it better embrace the contributions of African-American Catholics?

- **Leadership**. How can the bishops strengthen their credibility among the laity? How can they exercise their authority in a consultative and collegial way? How should they deal with dissenting theologians and

2001
Bishop Wilton Gregory is elected first African-American president of the United States Conference of Catholic Bishops

politicians who undermine their teaching authority? How can they most effectively share the best of America's cultural and societal values with the universal Church?

- **Parish life**. How can the Church reanimate the person in the pew through a better appreciation of the Eucharist? How can the Church better support lay people in their family and work lives? How can she affirm life and family issues more effectively and teach a respect for the beauty of human sexuality?

- **Religious education**. How can the Church most effectively reach out to disaffected Catholics, those who have dropped out, particularly young adults? How can the Church appeal to Catholics who subscribe to the American values of individualism and consumerism in contrast to Christ's call to community and responsibility? How can the Church win over the minds and hearts of those Catholics whose attitudes toward abortion, stem-cell research, cloning, and sexual issues mirror those of their non-Catholic fellow citizens?

- **Schools**. What is the future of Catholic schools on all levels— elementary, secondary, and collegiate? What is their specific *Catholic* identity and mission?

- **Vocation crisis**. How can the Church call and train priest leaders to provide vision for the laity who will assume even greater roles of leadership? How can the Church form priests to lead worship and preach God's word most effectively to an educated and increasingly secularized laity? How can the Church mobilize the laity to support those in religious life and priests in their difficult ministries?

- **Women**. What role should women have in the Church? How best can the Church meet their needs and desire for service to God's people?

- **Self-identity**. How does Catholicism in America remain faithful to the *Roman* Catholic Church as she continues her life and witness in the pluralistic American culture? How can the Church in America be American and yet Catholic? How can the Church in America best be the servant of Jesus Christ? Once and for all, Catholics must answer these questions: In the quest to become acceptable to Americans, has the Church lost its soul? Is the Church too materialistic, too rich, too concerned with numbers and buildings?

2002
Sexual abuse crisis is made public; bishops pass norms to protect children

These questions ask in one way or another how the Church in America can remain true to Jesus. On the one hand, the Church must be a worshiping community centered on the Eucharist; on the other hand, she must be the conscience of America by calling everyone to justice and truth. The Church of the twenty-first century must strive to embody the various models of the Church discussed in Chapter 1. The Catholic Church must be

- a Church that loves with the love of Christ;
- a herald of good news in a country that all too often is titillated by superficialities;
- an institution that coordinates the resources of American Catholics for the good of others;
- a pilgrim in a land of plenty that will always remember its eternal destination;
- a true sacrament, a sign of love in a country that searches for love down many false paths;
- a servant that mobilizes Catholics to "wash the feet" of those who are less fortunate.

Like the universal Church, Catholicism in America must embody Jesus for a society that desperately needs him and his salvation.

2006
Hispanics make up approximately 40 percent of the United States Catholic population

Summary

- Today, Catholics number around 23 percent of the American population, and thereby constitute the largest religious group in the country. The Church's beginnings in this country started with brave missionaries who accompanied Spanish explorers in the New World. Spanish missionaries labored in Florida, where they founded the nation's oldest parish in St. Augustine. They also brought the Gospel to New Mexico where a significant Pueblo uprising, reacting to the enslavement of some of their numbers, burnt down churches and killed Franciscan missionaries in 1680. The efforts of tireless missionaries like the Jesuit Eusebio Kino set up missions in the Southwest. Most notable was the activity of the Franciscan Blessed Junípero Serra who built nine of the twenty-one missions in California.

- French missionaries brought the Gospel to native tribes in states like Maine and New York, the provinces of Ontario and Quebec in Canada, and all along the Great Lakes region. Indians were slow to convert. The eight North American martyrs bravely witnessed to their faith and suffered horrific tortures. The Indian convert, Blessed Kateri Tekakwitha, suffered for her faith but lived a quiet life of service and prayer. Many French Canadian Catholics, the Acadians, chose to emigrate from Canada to Louisiana rather than switch their allegiance to the English monarch after the French and Indian War. Their Catholic descendants, the Cajuns, reside in Louisiana today.

- Catholics were sparse in number in the British colonies. They were often persecuted or outlawed. There were few priests to minister and no bishops. The Catholic Calvert family of Maryland passed the Toleration Act. It granted freedom of worship to all Christians, but when Maryland became a crown colony, Anglicanism became the official religion and Catholics were forbidden to practice their faith. William Penn's colony of Pennsylvania promoted religious freedom. It was the most Catholic-friendly of the British colonies, allowing Irish and German immigrants to practice their Catholic faith openly there.

- Catholics fought bravely in the Revolutionary War, in disproportionately large numbers. Notable Catholic patriots included Charles Carroll who signed the Declaration of Independence, and his cousin, Daniel Carroll, who influenced the writing of the Constitution and helped to select the site of the new Capitol. Daniel's younger brother, John Carroll, became the first bishop of the United States. In that capacity, he founded the first Catholic college—Georgetown; supported the work of the Poor Clares and Sisters of Charity, who founded many elementary schools; established the first seminary to train American-born clergy; and supported a strong Catholic press. One of Archbishop Carroll's most daunting problems was lay trusteeism, a necessity in the American Church because of state laws that prohibited Church ownership of property. The First Provincial Council of Baltimore (1829) condemned this practice.

- American Catholicism grew at an astonishing rate in the nineteenth century, becoming the country's largest religious group. This was due to the millions of Irish, German, Italian, and later Eastern European immigrants. The immigrant influx brought about nativist-inspired riots, discrimination, and venomous anti-Catholic literature. The Catholic press was founded to counteract the attacks of anti-Catholic bigotry. The brave participation of Catholics on both sides of the Civil War helped quell questions about Catholic patriotism, but anti-Catholicism flared up again periodically in the 1880s with the American Protective Association and in the 1920s with the Ku Klux Klan. Anti-Catholicism figured in the presidential campaign of Al Smith in 1928 and John Kennedy in 1960.

- The Catholic school system helped assimilate Catholics into American life; at the same time it helped support Catholic identity and provide a uniform religious education using tools like the *Baltimore Catechism*. Strong parishes helped build Catholic identity in America and charitable institutions like the St. Vincent de Paul Society helped meet the material needs of struggling Catholics. The sacrifices of many religious women, inspired by saintly women like Frances Cabrini, Rose Philippine Duchesne, and Katharine Drexel, helped meet the physical, spiritual, and psychological needs of Catholic immigrants and others. Their work in orphanages, schools, hospitals, and the like helped build the Church in America.

- On the local level, nineteenth-century Catholicism was led by parish priests who were generally the most educated Catholics in the community. In turn, they were directed by some forceful bishops like John Hughes, James Gibbons, and John Ireland who looked out for the rights of Catholics and tried to find ways to accommodate Catholicism to the new republic. One issue that arose at the end of the century was Americanism, which resulted in a liberal-conservative debate on how to adapt the American principles of freedom and individual initiative to the Catholic Church. The debate was settled when Pope Leo XIII issued an encyclical. It held that Church doctrines cannot be watered down to appeal to either converts or the contemplative virtues abandoned in favor of active life. Mixed in the debate was the feeling of German bishops that the Irish prelates were too heavy-handed in running the American Church. The German bishops, in contrast to Archbishop John Ireland, argued strongly for a separate Catholic school system to help maintain a Catholic and ethnic identity.

- Twentieth-century Catholicism was noted for its assimilation into American life and the acceptance of Catholics as full American citizens. American organizational abilities were reflected in the creation of the National Catholic War Council. It would later evolve into today's United States Conference of Catholic Bishops, an organization that enables the bishops to exercise their pastoral office collaboratively and deal with issues that concern the Church as part of American society.

- Once a missionary territory, the Church in America provided personnel and financial resources to help the Church's worldwide efforts at evangelization. Today, served by missionaries like the Maryknollers, an American-founded mission society, American Catholics send more than six thousand five hundred men and women to missions around the world.

- Although Catholics in America reflected the racial attitudes of their fellow citizens, leaders like Fr. John LaFarge helped change Catholic attitudes. Bishops and cardinals like Joseph Ritter, Patrick O'Boyle, and Vincent Waters desegregated the Catholic schools in their dioceses.

- Catholics, especially Irish Catholics in the big cities of the East and Midwest, continued to be involved in local politics in the twentieth century. Fr. Charles Coughlin garnered an immense radio audience in the 1930s but was silenced for his bigoted views. Dorothy Day and Peter Maurin founded the Catholic Worker Movement. It became a significant advocate for the poor and challenged Americans with its pacifist views.

- Catholic participation in the wars of the twentieth century demonstrated to anti-Catholic bigots that Catholics were patriots and helped win acceptance of Catholics as part of mainstream America.

- A significant and popular Catholic of the 1950s was Bishop Fulton Sheen whose prime-time television program enamored him to

Catholics and non-Catholics alike. The Golden Years of American Catholicism took place in the 1960s with the election of John F. Kennedy, the first Catholic president. Pope John XXIII was also immensely
popular with Americans. The Second Vatican Council and its aftermath took place during a period of rapid social change. In general, the
Church in America welcomed the liturgical changes and the new lay
involvement that came with the Council, but it also experienced many
setbacks: the mass exodus of priests; the decline in Mass attendance;
and the closing of schools and parishes.

- The clerical sex-abuse crisis was examined in the media frenzy of
2002. As Church leaders struggle to regain credibility among the faithful, they are faced with the difficult task of calling Catholics back to
an authentic Christian life, a life that is constantly challenged by the
secular and consumer values that infect American society.

Prayer REFLECTION

The Trappist monk Thomas Merton (1915–1968) was a most influential American Catholic of the twentieth century. He was a renowned spiritual writer,
poet, commentator on current events, peace activist, and ecumenist. One of
his most famous prayers stresses trust in a loving God, an appropriate prayer
for a Church in crisis.

The Road Ahead
My Lord God,
I have no idea where I am going.
I do not see the road ahead of me.
I cannot know for certain where it will end.
Nor do I really know myself, and the fact that I am following
    your will does not mean that I am actually doing so.
But I believe that the desire to please you does in fact
    please you.
And I hope I have that desire in all I am doing.
I hope that I will never do anything apart from that desire.
And I know that if I do this, you will lead me by the right
    road though I may know nothing about it.
Therefore will I trust you always though I may seem to be lost and
    in the shadow of death.
I will not fear, for you are ever with me, and you will never
    leave me to face my perils alone.[16]

Review and DISCUSSION QUESTIONS

1. Characterize the efforts of the Spanish and French missionaries in early America.

2. How did the British colonies treat Catholics?

3. Explain the participation of Catholics in the Revolutionary War.

4. What were some of the major contributions of the first American bishop, John Carroll?

5. Discuss three ways the Church helped immigrants assimilate during the nineteenth century.

6. What was nativism and how did the Church cope with it?

7. What was at stake in the Americanist crisis? How was it resolved? Discuss some good aspects of American life that Catholics have to offer the universal Church. Discuss some possible dangers of the American culture that Catholics must guard against.

8. What role did the clergy have in nineteenth-century Catholicism?

9. Discuss several factors that helped Catholics in America gain acceptance in the twentieth century.

10. Discuss the contributions of four important Catholic Americans of the twentieth century.

11. Discuss three major achievements of the American Catholicism during the twentieth century.

12. Argue for or against this proposition: "There is a crisis in American Catholicism."

13. Discuss the three greatest challenges facing the Catholic Church in America today.

14. Identify:

People

Frances Cabrini   George and Cecil Calvert

Charles Carroll	Daniel Carroll
Charles Coughlin	Dorothy Day
James Cardinal Gibbons	Isaac Hecker
Archbishop John Ireland	Juan de Padilla
Eusebio Kino	Isaac Jogues
Thomas Merton	John Courtney Murray
Bishop Fulton J. Sheen	Junípero Serra
Elizabeth Seton	Francis Cardinal Spellman
Kateri Tekakwitha	

Others:

Americanism	*Baltimore Catechism*
Catholic Miscellany	Know Nothings
lay trusteeism	nativism
Testem Benevolentiae	United States Conference of Catholic Bishops

Scripture CONNECTION

The Catholic Worker Movement is based on the norms of the spiritual and corporal works of mercy. Read the following Scripture citations and write how they summarize more about these basic works of Christian charity.

Matthew 25:31–46

Isaiah 58:6–7

Hebrews 13:3

1 John 3:17

Tobit 4:5-11

Matthew 6:2–4

Luke 3:11, 11:41

James 2:15–16[17]

Learn BY DOING

1. Read about and report on the Catholic Worker Movement or Dorothy Day. Check the Catholic Worker website: www.catholicworker.org.

2. Attend Mass at a nationality parish in your diocese. If possible, participate in an ethnic function sponsored by the parish, for example, a fair or bazaar. Talk to several parishioners about how their ethnic background enriches their Catholic faith.

3. Report on the various works of Catholic Charities in your diocese. You can read about Catholic Charities USA® at: www.catholiccharitiesusa.org.

4. Report on the activities of the American-based Catholic mission movement, the Maryknollers at: http://home.maryknoll.org/index.php?module =MKArticles.

5. Visit the United States Conference of Catholic Bishops' website: www.usccb.org. Do one of the following:

   • Report on several articles from the "News" section of the website.

   • Research some facts unique to the Catholic Church in America.

   • Locate the website of your diocese. Report on some interesting things about your home diocese you learned there.

9

Pope John Paul II
Ushers in the Church of the
TWENTY-FIRST CENTURY

It is not wrong to want to live better; what is wrong is a style of life which is presumed to be better when it is directed towards "having" rather than "being," and which wants to have more, not in order to be more but in order to spend life in enjoyment as an end in itself.

—POPE JOHN PAUL II
CENTESIMUS ANNUS, NO. 36[1]

John Paul THE GREAT

On April 8, 2005, the world witnessed a remarkable event in human history. On that day, Cardinal Joseph Ratzinger, the Dean of the College of Cardinals, celebrated the Requiem Mass for Pope John Paul II. It is estimated that two million people came to Rome to be near the late pontiff for his funeral; another two billion people watched the proceedings on television. This means that one out of every three people on earth was focused on the same event.

The people who were in Rome and present at the funeral became themselves part of the story. Almost immediately, thousands in the crowd began proclaiming the sanctity of the late Pope. Many chanted "Magnus, Magnus, Magnus," translated "Great, Great, Great." The public acclamation for "John Paul the Great" calls to mind three other Popes of the first millennium who bore that title—Pope Leo the Great (d. 461), Pope Gregory the Great (d. 604), and Pope Nicholas the Great (d. 867). With Pope John Paul II, the world recognized something very special in the Pope whose almost twenty-seven-year papacy was the third longest in history after that of St. Peter (about thirty-five years) and Pope Pius IX (thirty-one years). For many observers, Karol Wojtyla was the "Man of the Twentieth Century" who also ushered in the twenty-first century. Certainly, Church history will note his influence on an era.

This chapter will highlight some of the achievements of Pope John Paul II's papacy and will look to some of the challenges the Church under Pope Benedict XVI, the former Cardinal Joseph Ratzinger, and those who follow him will face in the coming decades.

The Pontificate of POPE JOHN PAUL II

When Pope John Paul I died after thirty-three days in office, the cardinals turned to a younger (age fifty-eight), vigorous, athletic cardinal, Karol Wojtyla of Kraków, Poland, to serve God's people as the 263rd successor of St. Peter. He was the first Polish Pope ever and the first non-Italian since the Dutch-German Pope Adrian VI (1522–1523).

Karol Wojtyla was born on May 18, 1920, in Wadowice, a town near Kraków. His father was an officer in the Austrian army. Karol, called "Lolek" by his friends, had an unhappy early childhood. When he was eight years old, his mother died of kidney failure and congenital heart disease. His older brother, a medical doctor, died of scarlet fever in 1932 at the young age of twenty-six. (He had an older sister who died a few days after birth.) In the summer of 1938, he and his father moved to Kraków where Lolek enrolled at the Jagiellonian University. He studied languages and literature and became active in an experimental theater group. He had many close friends, including Jews, and went on dates. His studies would help him master foreign languages. As Pope, he was fluent in ten languages in addition to Latin, the official language of the Church. His ability to speak in so many tongues endeared him to God's people around the world.

When the Nazis invaded Poland, the university was closed and Karol was eventually forced to work in a quarry and later in a chemical plant. During this dark period of human history, a friend introduced him to the writings of St. John of the Cross and St. Teresa of Avila. He participated in an underground theater group and helped Jewish friends find refuge from the Nazis. He also began studies for the priesthood in the clandestine seminary run by the cardinal of Kraków. He was ordained after the war in 1946, and then went to Rome for further studies, eventually earning doctoral degrees in both philosophy and theology.

Back in Poland, Karol served as a parish priest and a chaplain for university students. He taught ethics at two universities. He served as mentor to an ever-growing group of young people who met together to pray, discuss, and engage in charitable works. His close friends called him "Uncle," and he

1978
Election of Pope John Paul II

often accompanied them on annual skiing and kayak trips. His experience of sharing his life so intimately with this extended family of friends enriched his experiences which he included in articles he wrote for a Catholic newspaper and the poems and plays he composed.

Pope Pius XII named Fr. Wojtyla a bishop at the young age of thirty-eight. Bishop Wojtyla attended the sessions at the Second Vatican Council. He contributed to two important decrees of the Council: *Declaration on Religious Freedom* and the *Pastoral Constitution on the Church in the Modern World*. His book, *Love and Responsibility*, published in 1960, was a major source for Pope Paul VI's encyclical *Humanae Vitae (On the Regulation of Birth)*, which upheld the Church's ban on contraception.

Named Archbishop of Krakow in 1963 and honored as a cardinal in 1967, he served the Church in Poland during the difficult time of communist control. Considered "tough but flexible," Cardinal Wojtyla patiently and cleverly accommodated the atheistic regime while defending honorably the faith and traditions of his Catholic flock. He was a powerful preacher who championed human rights, demanded of the communist regime the right to construct churches, and defended the right of Catholic youth to organize. He also displayed courage by ordaining priests to serve clandestinely in communist-controlled Czechoslovakia.

His accomplishments as Pope were monumental. He was history's most traveled Pope and an evangelizer to the world, covering well over 700,000 miles in 104 pastoral visits to 130 countries, engaging with all people in a "Dialogue of Salvation." He also took part in 146 visits within Italy. As the Bishop of Rome, he also visited almost all of Rome's 333 parishes. His voluminous writings included fourteen encyclicals, fifteen apostolic exhortations, eleven apostolic constitutions, forty-five apostolic letters, and five books including the best-seller, *Crossing the Threshold of Hope* (1994). He beatified more than 1,300 men and women and canonized 482 saints, both more than any other Pope in history. He also created 232 cardinals, convened six plenary councils of the College of Cardinals, and presided over fifteen synods of bishops.

It is likely that no other human being in history encountered more people face to face than did Pope John Paul II. To note: more than 17,600,000 pilgrims participated in the Wednesday General Audiences, untold millions saw him in his many travels outside of Vatican City, and millions more saw him on pilgrimages to Rome (eight million pilgrims came to Rome alone during the Great Jubilee Year of 2000).[2] Facts like these reveal that, on the human level, John Paul II's impact will be felt and studied for decades, if not centuries.

1981
Assassination attempt on the life of Pope John Paul II

A Saintly Pope

Jesus' command to his disciples to "Go, therefore, and make disciple of all nations, baptizing them in the name of the Father, and of the Son, and of the Holy Spirit, teaching them to observe all that I commanded you" (Mt 28:16) was taken seriously by Pope John Paul II. His unprecedented jet travel and the unforgettable image of him kissing the ground of many continents and countries he visited are memorable images of a man who symbolized Christ's love for his flock. As a former actor who knew well the impact of the media, Pope John Paul II used the world stage to preach the Gospel message and apply it to the events of the time and place. One papal visit in the Philippines in 1980 directly led to the revolt against and toppling of the dictatorship of Ferdinand Marcos. The Pope's highly publicized visit to Cuba in 1998 led to the release of three hundred political prisoners.

Pope John Paul II preached constant themes in light of the Gospel. The main theme of his pontificate was *Totus Tuus*, expressing his consecration to Mary. He visited various shrines to Mary around the world such as Fatima in Portugal, Lourdes in France, Our Lady of Guadalupe in Mexico, and Knock in Ireland. He believed that Our Lady of Fatima intervened to save his life when Mehmet Ali Agca, an assassin from Turkey, shot and critically wounded him in St. Peter's Square on May 13, 1981. (May 13 is also the anniversary of the first of the reported Fatima visions.) The Pope also encouraged frequent praying of the rosary and, at the start of the twenty-fifth year of his papacy, issued an apostolic letter that added five new mysteries, the Mysteries of Light, which focus on the events in Jesus' life from his baptism to the institution of the Eucharist at the Last Supper. Other themes for Pope John Paul included teaching on human dignity and the new evangelization.

Pope John Paul II embodied forgiveness. A famous photo of the Pope shows him forgiving his would-be assassin two days after Christmas in 1983. He not only forgave Mehmet Ali Agca publicly, but kept in contact with him over the years of his imprisonment and even met with his mother and brother. The Pope not only forgave,

➤ *Pope John Paul II talking with his would-be assassin*

1983
Revised Code of Canon Law promulgated

he also *asked* for forgiveness for various sins committed by Christians and Catholics through the ages. Examples include apologies for the persecution and trial of Galileo, the violation of women's rights, and for the crusaders' attacks on Constantinople. Perhaps the most notable apology took place in Jerusalem during the Holy Year of 2000. The Pope told the Jewish people of the Church's sadness for the hatred, persecution, and displays of anti-Semitism committed by Christians through the ages and that the seeds of the Holocaust were fostered in Germany, a Christian country.

For Catholic youth, Pope John Paul II merited their attention as if he were a pop star of music or movies. Actually, the Pope was a spiritual leader and hero to Catholic youth. In 1984, he established World Youth Day with the purpose of assembling Catholic youth from around the world to celebrate their faith. Hundreds of thousands of teenagers and early-twenties Catholics from around the world greeted the Pope every two years in countries like Argentina, Spain, Poland, the United States, the Philippines, France, and Canada. Their popular rhythmic chant went "JPII, we love you." The Pope's message to the youth was constant: strive for holiness in order to live heroic Christian lives in the midst of a secular and materialistic world. Countless young people who attended these gatherings over the years have testified to how their participation helped them commit themselves more intensely to Jesus Christ, following the example of the Pope himself.

The Pope's spiritual authority was rooted in a deep personal prayer life. He cared deeply about the priesthood. In 1979 he began a tradition of issuing letters on Holy Thursday to the world's priests, uplifting their morale. Some who were closest to John Paul believed him to be a mystic. A bishop who witnessed him at prayer said, "His relationship with the Lord is so total and consuming that to be in his presence when he is at prayer enables one to experience the presence of God."[3] One of the many symbols of his life was that the subject of his last encyclical was the Eucharist and that it was written during the "Year of the Eucharist" (2004–2005). The Pope had proclaimed that year in order to remind Catholics that the Eucharist is the gift of Christ to his followers and "the source and summit of the life and mission of the Church."

John Paul's holiness was perhaps most evident in the way he died. If it is true that one's death punctuates the sentence of one's life, John Paul II died with an exclamation point! His last years were wracked with suffering brought on by various infirmities. His health was never the same after the assassination attempt. In the 1990s he had a tumor removed from his colon, suffered a dislocated shoulder and a broken femur, and had his appendix re-

1989–1991
Fall of Communism in Soviet Union and Eastern European countries

moved. He suffered severe arthritis in his knee that made it almost impossible for him to walk. His most serious illness was Parkinson's disease, which made it difficult for him to speak and unable to smile. The Pope serenely accepted his suffering as God's will and showed the world the dignity of an old person in declining health. His last two months involved great suffering from the effects of flu, difficulty in breathing that led to his receiving a tracheotomy, and eventual systemic infection that led to heart failure. The outpouring of love for him in his final hours was exemplified by the thousands of young people who prayed for him beneath his Vatican apartments. When told of their presence, he gave his last message—both to them and to the youth of the world, "I have looked for you. Now you have come to me. And I thank you."

The Pope as World Leader

For many historians, Pope John Paul II played a pivotal role in the downfall of communism in Eastern Europe in the late 1980s. His visits to Poland in 1979 and 1983, as Poland's favorite son returning as Pope, electrified the Polish people. He brought great pride to them as Catholics and emboldened them to resist nonviolently the communist regime by supporting the nation's Solidarity labor movement as the way to fight for human rights. Courageous leaders like Lech Walesa, supported by the Holy Father, helped lead nonviolent freedom movements like Solidarity that ultimately led to the downfall of the communist-controlled governments in Poland and other Eastern European countries. The tearing down of the Berlin Wall, the dissolution of the Soviet Empire, and the creation of democracies in most of the former totalitarian states soon followed.

Pope John Paul II also advocated strongly for world peace. Having lived under the horrors of Nazi occupation during World War II, and the Soviet Union's communism in the decades afterward, he knew firsthand the evils of humans torturing and killing in the name of totalitarian and godless tyrannies. Early on in his papacy, in 1979, he mediated a border conflict between Argentina and Chile. He supported efforts at reconciliation in conflicts in Lebanon and the Balkans. He established a World Day of Peace at Assisi, Italy, in 1986, where he met and prayed with the representatives of many religions. He tried to turn the world away from the Gulf War in 1991.

The Pope taught that the way to achieve world peace in today's world is not through unilateral aggression, which is a violation of international law, but through diplomacy and the intervention of the United Nations. So strongly did he oppose the sending of troops to Iraq in 2003 that he sent a personal rep-

1992
Catechism of the Catholic Church approved

resentative, Cardinal Pio Laghi, to petition President George W. Bush to avert war. His effort at peace through diplomacy failed, but many of his warnings predicting increased violence and instability unfortunately came true.

As a world leader, Pope John Paul II was also a strong advocate for human rights, especially the rights of the poor and defenseless. He left a great legacy in his social justice encyclicals, which will be studied for generations for their strong defense of human rights. For example, *Laborem Exercens* ("On Human Work,"1981) details the rights of workers and the dignity of work, both of which the Pope saw as essential ingredients to social justice in its many forms. His *Sollicitudo Rei Socialis* ("On Social Concern," 1987) calls attention to the widening gap between rich and poor nations. It also teaches that true development involves more than wealth and the accumulation of riches, which both liberal capitalism and Marxian socialism failed to understand. The Pope championed the belief that a "preference for the poor" should be at the center of our response to those who are suffering.

Finally, *Centesimus Annus* (*The Hundredth Year*, 1991) challenges its readers to have a correct view of the human person, a being of incomparable worth created in God's image and redeemed by the Death of Jesus Christ. The pontiff reiterated the human rights (for example, the right to private property) discussed in Pope Leo XIII's *Rerum Novarum*, issued one hundred years previously. However, in the post–Cold War era, John Paul II pointed out the burdensome foreign debt of impoverished nations and appealed to rich nations to defer, lessen, or even forgive these despair-causing loads whenever possible. He addressed the folly of the destruction of the environment while also reminding the world that human beings are God's supreme gift to mankind, the human ecology. The first and fundamental structure for human ecology is the family, rooted in the love of a father and mother, who teach their children how to love. Societies are called to promote family policies like a family wage and ones that enrich the lives of children and the care for elderly persons so they are not isolated.

The Pope as a Promoter of Life

Pope John Paul II challenged a world that increasingly promotes a "culture of death," especially by assaulting innocent human life through acts of genocide, abortion, and euthanasia. In his many talks and writings, the Pope strongly affirmed traditional values that honor life. For example, he consistently upheld the teaching of *Humanae Vitae* which praises married love, promotes the

1994
Pope John Paul II publishes encyclical *Ordinatio Sacerdotalis*, which definitively teaches women cannot be ordained priests

dignity of women, and outlines God's plan for human procreation. His 129 Wednesday talks on the Book of Genesis are known as a series on the Theology of the Body. They teach about the sacrament of marriage and God's original design for human sexuality. In his *Evangelium Vitae* (Gospel of Life, 1995), he defended human dignity from womb to tomb. This defense of life is at the heart of the Gospel and should be of concern to every human being. Perhaps the most readable of all John Paul II's scholarly encyclicals, *Evangelium Vitae* condemns any direct and voluntary killing of innocent human life, especially through abortion and euthanasia. Furthermore, the Pope called on the nations of the world to limit severely, and even abolish the death penalty. Citing the *Catechism of the Catholic Church*, he wrote:

> If bloodless means are sufficient to defend human lives against an aggressor and to protect public order and the safety of persons, public authority must limit itself to such means, because they better correspond to the concrete conditions of the common good and are more in conformity to the dignity of the human person.[4]

Ecumenical Efforts of John Paul II

John Paul II made ecumenical relations a top priority of his pontificate. He met frequently with other religious leaders, for example, with Orthodox Patriarchs of Constantinople and Anglican Archbishops of Canterbury, the Dalai Lama, and various other leaders, including those of the Moslem faith. He visited countries like Romania and the Ukraine with high populations of Orthodox Christians, often expressing the wish for Christian unity. He joined Lutheran bishops in an ecumenical prayer service to mark the sixth centenary of the

> ➤ *From left to right: Archbishop of Canterbury, Archbishop of Thyteira and Great Britain, Pope John Paul II, and the Dalai Lama pray together for world peace.*

canonization of St. Bridget of Sweden. He opened diplomatic relations with the State of Israel, prayed at the Western Wall, apologized for the anti-Semitism of Catholics, and worked tirelessly to heal the past injustices directed against the Jews. In a highly symbolic ceremony during the Jubilee Year (March 12, 2000),

1995
Publication of Pope John Paul's encyclical, *The Gospel of Life*

the Pope presided over a Day of Pardon asking forgiveness for the sins that Catholics committed over the centuries.

In 1995, Pope John Paul II published two major documents promoting ecumenism: the encyclical *Ut Unum Sint* (*That They May Be One*) and the apostolic letter *Orientale Lumen* (*Light of the East*), a plea for union of the Catholic and Orthodox Churches. *Ut Unum Sint* explains how individual and communal reformation, love, prayer, and dialogue should undergird ecumenical efforts. It also reviews the fruits of ecumenical efforts after the Second Vatican Council and outlines areas needed for further study, including the role of the Pope as the "servant of the servants of God." As did his predecessor Pope Paul VI, John Paul II asked for forgiveness for causing any painful recollections in the cause of Christian unity. After the death of Pope John Paul II, Pope Benedict XVI continued his ecumenical efforts and those of the Second Vatican Council, focusing on healing differences with the Church of the East, Oriental Orthodox, Eastern Orthodox, and Protestants.

The Church's Internal Renewal Under Pope John Paul II

Critics of John Paul II's pontificate claim that he slowed down, and perhaps even reversed, some of the reform efforts sparked by the Second Vatican Council. More accurately, the Pope's policy of renewal honestly reflected the intent of the Council Fathers. John Paul II was very interested in the internal renewal of Church life. Some of his work in this area is detailed in this section.

Discipline of dissident theologians. The Pope worked to end public dissent over *Humanae Vitae* and other traditional Church teachings on sexual morality. For example, he disciplined the theologian Fr. Charles Curran, who lost his right to teach as a Catholic theologian at the Catholic University of America. Similarly, the Swiss theologian Fr. Hans Küng lost his license to teach theology in the name of the Church because of his dissenting views on papal infallibility.

Liberation theologians, some of whom applied Marxist analysis of class warfare to the situation of widespread poverty in Latin America, were also disciplined. One notable example was the silencing of the Brazilian Leonardo Boff, who eventually left the Franciscans. The publication of *Ex Corde Ecclesiae* (1990), endorsed by the American bishops in 1999, also helped to bring in line theologians teaching at universities calling themselves Catholic. Theologians at most universities are required to obtain a *mandatum*, an acknowledgment from the local bishop to certify that their teaching is in union with the Church.

1997
Historic apology by the Pope for Catholic anti-Semitism through the ages;
death of Mother Teresa of Calcutta

Centralization of Church governance. John Paul II's moves to re-centralize authority in Rome stressed internal Church unity in an ever-fragmented world. Control of local and national churches fell more and more to the Roman Curia. For example the translation of the liturgy into the vernacular was carefully monitored by Roman Curia.

Reaffirmation of Church doctrines against moral relativism and secularism. Pope John Paul II's *Veritatis Splendor* (*The Splendor of the Truth*, 1993) reaffirmed objective morality in an age of moral relativism and taught that there are moral absolutes that are always valid and that some acts are always intrinsically evil. In another encyclical—*Fides et Ratio* (*Faith and Reason*, 1998)—he called for a renewal of philosophy in a way that it would conform to traditional Western thought to show that it is possible to discover and know the truth. Modern thought patterns have resulted in a severe state of doubt that has led to *nihilism*, "which is at the root of the widespread mentality which claims that a definitive commitment should no longer be made, because everything is fleeting and provisional."[5]

The Pope appointed Cardinal Joseph Ratzinger, a renowned theologian later to be elected Pope Benedict XVI, as the Prefect of the Congregation for the Doctrine of the Faith. Besides publishing important documents on bioethics and liberation theology, the Congregation under Cardinal Ratzinger also condemned same-sex unions.

Another notable achievement of John Paul II was the publication of the *Catechism of the Catholic Church* in 1992, the first universal catechism since the Council of Trent. Its influence remains strong and will provide a lasting resource of Church teaching well into the future. A compendium of Catholic doctrine, the *Catechism* serves as a point of reference for catechesis and will help assure orthodoxy in future catechetical works.

The Pope wrote a papal letter, *Ordinatio Sacerdotalis* ("On Reserving Priestly Ordination to Men Alone," 1994), which reaffirmed the Church's teaching that priestly ordination cannot be conferred on women. The letter instructed Catholics to accept this judgment as definitive and closed to debate.

He also saw to the completion of the revised *Code of Canon Law* (1983), begun under Pope John XXIII. In 1990 he promulgated the Code of Canons for the Eastern Churches. These codes provide discipline and order by establishing the norms and standards for life in the Catholic Church.

Fostering of lay involvement in the Church. The letter *Christifidelis Laici* (1989) encouraged lay people to build the Kingdom of God by re-evangelizing the world through authentic Christian living. The Pope stressed that everyone

2000
Holy Year 2000 celebrated;
Pope visits the Holy Land

has a role to play, even young people, in turning toward the world and being Christ for others. He warned against separating one's Christian life from one's secular life.

John Paul also commended the various lay associations and organizations that have begun, or reorganized, since the Second Vatican Council. Throughout his pontificate, John Paul II has been a strong supporter of certain of these groups, for example, the Focolare Movement, founded by Chiara Lubich in 1943. Its goal is world unity achieved through putting the Gospel love of Jesus Christ into action.

Displaying sensitivity to women's issues. Though he was attacked by some feminists for reaffirming the Church's inability to ordain women, the Pope's many writings demonstrated a profound appreciation for women. His plays and writings celebrate married love. His letter *Mulieris Dignitatem* (*On the Dignity and Vocation of Women*, 1988) and his apostolic letter written before the United Nations' Fourth World Conference on Women (1995), praise mothers, wives, daughters, sisters, and consecrated women. They also bless women who work, apologize for the part the Church played in discriminating against women in the past, and call for equal pay for women in the workplace and just treatment for women who choose to be mothers and wives. He also strongly condemned sexual violence committed against women.

Challenges for THE FUTURE

In many ways, Pope John Paul II humanized the papacy and brought the Catholic faith to a worldwide stage. His many travels, his love of youth, his outreach to people of other faiths, his advocacy for the poor—all of these made him admired by people of all faiths around the globe. However, the Pope had critics, even within the Church. Some saw him as too authoritarian and unbending. His staunch defense of *Humanae Vitae*, ban on women's ordination, the silencing of dissident theologians, and the cutback in the authority of national bishops' conferences were viewed as polarizing by his opponents.

The Pope faced criticism for his staunch views on issues like the ban on condoms as a way to combat the AIDS epidemic in Africa or his slow response to the sexual abuse crisis in the Church. "Liberal" Catholics questioned his support of the sometimes controversial group known as Opus Dei, a secular institute created as a personal prelature to the Pope and with its own bishop independent of the typical diocesan framework. On the other hand, "conservative" Catholics did not like John Paul II's opposition to capital punishment

2001
Islamic terrorists attack World Trade Center in New York;
War on Terror begins

or his pacifist views on the Gulf War and the War in Iraq. And, so-called "traditionalist" Catholics pined for a return to the Latin Mass and pre-Vatican II practices and devotions.

Only time will tell Pope John Paul II's lasting impact on human history. At his death, Pope John Paul II was widely praised as a promoter of human rights and a defender of life. However, many of the Pope's teachings have not yet been embraced by the world at large and some Catholics. The assault on human life continues. Legalized abortion and euthanasia are on the rise. Cloning and embryonic stem cell research are increasingly accepted. Those promoting same-sex unions are on the offensive. Consumerist secular humanism is replacing Christianity in the West. Christianity and Catholicism are on the decline in Europe.

The continued disobedience of Church teaching marks some of the future challenges Pope Benedict XVI will face in the coming years. What will be the history of the Catholic Church in the twenty-first century? Only God knows. But recent history would seem to indicate the following issues are challenges the Catholic Church will be confronting in the coming years.

The Future Church as Sacrament

The Church is the Sacrament of Jesus Christ in the world, a union of the divine and the human, Christ's presence for all people. To continue to be a universal "Sacrament of Salvation," the Church must continue with her fourfold task of message, community, service, and worship. Some of the future challenges in each of these areas include those that follow.

Message. In her role as herald of the Gospel, the Church's evangelization efforts must propose the good news in solidarity with the hearers of the word, not impose on them extraneous elements of a foreign culture. Perhaps the major challenge facing the Church's evangelization efforts in the twenty-first century is to find an authentic way to adapt the Gospel to the profoundly spiritual African peoples, the fastest growing Catholic community in the world. In the past twenty-five years, Catholics have almost tripled in number in Africa.[6] Past experience has taught the Church to use caution in evangelizing native peoples. Imposing European culture in mission territories is not a necessary adjunct to preaching the good news of Jesus. However, the challenge lies in modifying some deeply ingrained African customs like polygamy, which are at odds with traditional Church teaching.

●···

2005
Pope John Paul II, third-longest reigning Pope dies;
Cardinal Joseph Ratzinger elected as Pope Benedict XVI

A second challenge is for the Church to continue to develop new ways to preach the Gospel to a tech-savvy generation. Surveys continue to show that many Catholics lack basic religious literacy. Many are ignorant about fundamental doctrines and what is required for the practice of the faith. Pope John Paul II was effective in using the media to proclaim the Gospel. Now, the Church in each nation must develop effective evangelists who know how to use television, the Internet, and other modern media to preach the Gospel of Jesus Christ. Catholic artists should be encouraged—as Michelangelo was in a previous age—to use their creative energies to produce movies, literary works, musical productions, and so forth to proclaim the Gospel. Think of the influence of the film *The Passion of the Christ* (2004). Though in some respects controversial, its worldwide impact in presenting Christ's sacrificial suffering was perhaps unprecedented in human history.

Community. The Church is the People of God, the Body of Christ. Demographically, the Church of the future will not be Eurocentric. By 2025, 80 percent of the world's Catholics will be African, Asian, and Latin American. This means that future Catholics will be blacker, browner, poorer, and younger than the members of today's Church. Many will also come from countries where there is a severe shortage of priests, for example, Latin America. Thus, the Church will have to continue to develop new ways for Catholics of the future to experience the fullness of the Body of Christ.

Service. All Christians are called to service. One of the Second Vatican Council's positive outcomes was the encouragement to lay people to accept their baptismal call to holiness and service:

> The laity are called in a special way to make the Church present and operative in those places and circumstances where only through them can she become salt of the earth. (*Constitution on the Church*, No. 33)

Tomorrow's Catholics will have the continuing challenge to witness to the Gospel wherever they are and whatever they do. Homemakers, lawyers, teachers, nurses, high tech workers, accountants, truck drivers, and everyone else must witness to the Lord in their every day lives by performing works of mercy—feeding the hungry, educating the ignorant, comforting the elderly, healing the sick, reforming the prisons, caring for the homeless, and finding jobs for the unemployed. In addition, the rich body of the Church's social justice teachings gives the laity a blueprint on how to combat the sinful structures in society that keep people from achieving justice. In a recent assault against

2006
Pope Benedict XVI publishes his first encyclical
on Christian love, *Deus Caritas Est*

religious liberty in the United States, it was youth and young adult Catholics who helped support the Church's efforts at protest.

In many ways, the Church of the Middle Ages expected political power and glory. The Church of the twenty-first century has lost any claims to secular power. She will only win the hearts of people when Catholics are Christ's presence in the world while living in imitation of the Lord.

Worship. The Church must be a worshiping community that assembles around the table of the Lord. The Eucharist is the heart of Catholic life. Recent trends, however, are alarming. Mass attendance in many of the Western nations is at an all-time low. For example, a survey from Georgetown University reported that slightly more than 20 percent of American Catholics born after 1960 reported attending Mass at least once a week or more.[7] Australia's Cardinal George Pell reported that only about 18 percent of Australian Catholics go to Mass weekly. He pointed to the popularity of sports, which has become a religion for many people, as a main culprit in low Mass attendance in Australia.[8] It has been widely reported that Mass attendance in the traditionally Catholic country of France is only six percent on a given Sunday.[9] These figures caused Pope Benedict XVI to lament the weakening of churches in Europe, America, and Australia. He told Italian priests, "There's no longer evidence for a need of God, even less of Christ. The so-called traditional churches look like they are dying."[10]

By any standard of membership and commitment to the Catholic faith, Mass attendance is crucial. For far too many nominal Catholics, their identification has become more a cultural one with Catholicism than one of a deep religious commitment. Contrast this with the seeming vitality of the Islamic faith, the only growing religion in Europe. Religion seems to be the dominant reality in all aspects of the daily lives of Muslims.

The Second Vatican Council renewed all the sacraments so they would communicate more effectively what they signify. The Mass is now in the vernacular, the presider faces the congregation around the Lord's table, and the laity are encouraged to actively participate. Other sacraments have also been renewed. For example, the Sacrament of Penance permits the option of face-to-face confession to underscore the personal forgiveness of the Lord. The Sacrament of Anointing of the Sick is not only for dying persons, but also for the seriously or chronically ill. The Rite of Christian Initiation for Adults has enlivened parish life by promoting active participation of the entire community and highlighting the lifelong nature of the Christian journey.

●···

2007
Pope Benedict XVI publishes his first apostolic exhortation, *Sacramentum Caritatis* ("Sacrament of Charity"). It focuses on the Sacrament of Holy Eucharist

It is both ironic and sad that now that the sacraments are more pastorally sensitive, fewer Catholics are going to Mass on a weekly basis. In a similar vein, the celebration of the Sacrament of Penance has fallen off precipitously. The Church faces a tremendous challenge to continue to battle the forces at work in the secular, materialistic, pleasure-seeking, and consumer world. The Church must find new ways to invite and challenge Catholics to worship as a vital Christian community. Catholics cease to be Catholics without the Eucharist to sustain them and give them life.

The Future Church as Institution

In an age that is disrespectful of authority in other areas, the Church will face challenges in the future to encourage Catholics and others to pay attention to the Magisterium, the living teaching office of the Church. It is the Magisterium's task to give authentic interpretation to the Word of God in both Scripture and Tradition.

The principle of collegiality holds that the bishops worldwide form a college (community) in union with the Pope as head. Decision-making involves cooperation and shared responsibility between the Pope and the bishops. Additionally, consultation and communication should characterize national conferences of bishops, diocesan priests' senates, and parish councils.

With this principle in mind, the Church of the twenty-first century is likely to see synods of bishops and national bishops' conferences strengthened while the Roman Curia plays less of a role in the governing of local churches. There may even be more of a role for the diocesan clergy and lay people in suggesting names for candidates for bishop.

The Church will also have to address the concerns of both so-called conservative and liberal Catholics who are hoping the Magisterium will make a priority of addressing the following questions in the near future:

- Will the Church continue to state firmly and clearly traditional teaching on issues like the sanctity of marriage, natural family planning, and adoption?

- Will the Church find effective ways to combat poverty?

- Will there be openness to greater role for the laity in Church governance?

Also of concern to all Catholics are issues like the following:

2013
On February 28, Pope Benedict XVI becomes the first pope since Pope Gregory XII in 1415 to resign his office, citing advanced age. On March 13, Cardinal Jorge Mario Bergoglio of Buenos Aires, Argentina is elected pope. He is the first pope from the Americas. He is also the first Jesuit pope.

- The loss of faith in the Western world caused by a secular, materialistic, and consumer society turned in on itself.

- The vocations crisis in the Western world. A recent hopeful sign has been the regrowth of seminaries in several dioceses and an increase in religious vocations, especially in traditional communities for women religious.

- The AIDS epidemic in Africa. In many parts of Africa, the Catholic Church is the most effective institution in helping people, for example, in health-care services and education. The Church is also a strong voice against tyranny. The African people are suffering greatly from the AIDS epidemic, yet many are not heeding the Church's call to abstinence as the only foolproof way to stem the growth of the epidemic.

The Future Church as Pilgrim

With the historic travels of Pope John Paul II, the Church has come to understand her role as pilgrim more clearly than ever. Papal visits not only taught the nations of the world about Christ's love, but also served as opportunities for the Church to learn from various cultures. The Second Vatican Council's the *Church in the Modern World* instructs Catholics to be open to all the good the world has to offer while prioritizing the Church's faithfulness to Jesus Christ, her biblical foundations, and her own history as Christ's presence in the world.

Like the rest of the world, the Church will follow very closely the political and economic debates that will take place over the issues of the growing population in poor countries, the dwindling resources of our planet, and ecological crises like global warming. She will pay very close attention to discoveries in the area of bioethics, supporting advances in adult stem cell research that have recently been shown to help advance patient benefits in seventy-three medical conditions. She will be very willing to learn about the scientific and technological advances that will transform how we live in ways that we can only imagine today.

But in the face of all the advances in human knowledge, the Church will not retreat into a fortress. She will surely engage in the great issues confronting humanity. As a pilgrim, the Church also has an important mission to point out to all of God's people the eternal destiny that awaits each human being. Therefore, armed with the Gospel entrusted to her, the Church will continue to challenge everything that threatens human dignity, diminishes the essential equality of human beings, and weakens the solidarity God intends for his children. As a follower of the Prince of Peace, the Church will remain a strong voice for peace and reason, especially in the face of the ever-growing threats of terrorism.

The Church of the future will continue to be openly ecumenical, knowing well that to have peace among the nations there must be peace among religions. Christian unity, especially with Orthodox Christians, has been a strong goal of the post–Vatican II Popes, and it will continue to be in the future. A few steps forward and a few steps back have been the course with other Christian groups, especially Anglicans and Lutherans. Ecumenical efforts will continue among Christians, and joint efforts in areas of social justice will be more evident. Great strides were made in Jewish-Catholic relations under the pontificate of Pope John Paul II. Efforts at reconciliation between Catholics and their Jewish ancestors in faith will continue.

For many observers, though, the real challenge of the future is how the Catholic community will relate to Islam, the fastest growing of the world religions. A special problem is Islamic fundamentalism that has turned violent and is engaging in a battle for world domination. How does the Church approach this faith on an international level, especially when the Muslim faith does not have a central authority figure like the Pope?

Another issue facing the Church is how to establish relations with China, which only permits a state-controlled Church. Evangelization in Eastern Europe, now freed of communist control, will also be a challenge. Orthodox Christianity in these nations does not seem open to Catholic proselytizing. In Latin America, evangelical and pentecostal Christians are converting millions of nominal Catholics. How to appeal to the emotional and spiritual needs of Catholics in this part of the world is a major challenge for the Church.

Finally, the Church, which must remain true to her mission of preaching the whole of Christ's truth, must continue to challenge "cafeteria Catholics" in the United States who only select certain beliefs and practices from the "menu" of Church doctrine and the nominal Catholics in European countries like France, have become increasingly secular and even hostile to traditional Catholic teaching.

Faithful Catholics may look at the future and feel overwhelmed at the problems the Church faces. However, a study of Church history reveals that the Church has always been confronted with problems: persecutions, doctrinal debates that turned violent, corrupt leaders, tepid faith among the faithful, outside political pressures to control the Church, crises brought on by new

2015
Pope Francis releases his second encyclical, *Laudato Si'*, (*On Care for Our Common Home*). In it the pope critiques consumerism, environmental degradation, global warming, and irresponsible development.

discoveries, and so forth. It is a marvel, explainable only with the eyes of faith, how the Church has survived for twenty centuries.

As the Church moved forward in the twenty-first century, she did so under the leadership of the first pope from the Americas, the Jesuit cardinal of Buenos Aires, Argentina, Jorge Mario Bergoglio, who took the name "Francis" when he was elected successor to Pope Benedict XVI on February 28, 2013.

Pope Francis further challenged the pilgrim Church to be a Church which "goes forth;" that is a community of missionary disciples. He expanded in a 2015 message on the Feast of the Ascension: "I dream of a 'missionary option'—that is, a missionary impulse capable of transforming everything, so that the Church's customs, ways of doing things, times and schedules, language and structures can be suitably channeled for the evangelization of today's world rather than for her self-preservation."

The pastoral leadership of Pope Francis was dramatic early in his pontificate. He traveled extensively, welcomed refugees to the Vatican, and surprised poor people and the sick with personal visits. "I prefer a Church which is bruised, hurting, and dirty because it has been out on the streets rather than a Church which is unhealthy from being confined and from clinging to her own security," he explained.

His message recapitulates the final words of Jesus prior to his Ascension:

Go, therefore, and make disciples of all nations, baptizing them in the name of the Father, and of the Son, and of the Holy Spirit, teaching them to observe all that I have commanded you. *And behold, I am with you always, until the end of the age.* (Mt 28:19–20)

Summary

- The first Polish Pope ever, John Paul II (1978–2005) had the third longest reign in papal history. He was also the most traveled Pope, having visited 130 countries. More people encountered him than any other person in human history. Greatly beloved and admired, he was a deeply spiritual man who promoted devotion to the Blessed Virgin. He also was an inspiration to young people with his deep faith, vitality, and youthful spirit exhibited at the World Youth Days, which he inaugurated in 1984.

- Historians rate John Paul II as one of the giants of the twentieth century and a forerunner of the twenty-first century because of his instrumental role in toppling communism in Eastern Europe. He was an avid promoter of human dignity, and his various social-justice encyclicals argued for the rights of workers, the need for a "preferential option for the poor," and a strong defense of human life "womb to tomb." He made ecumenical relations with the Orthodox a priority and strengthened Catholic-Jewish relationships to an unprecedented degree.

- As a post–Vatican II reformer, John Paul II disciplined dissident theologians; gained greater control over national conferences of bishops; combated moral relativism in his encyclical, *The Splendor of Truth*; oversaw the publication of the revised *Code of Canon Law* and the *Catechism of the Catholic Church*, the first universal catechism since the Council of Trent; and fostered lay involvement in the Church. His various writings demonstrated a profound respect for women, calling for society to treat them with justice and respect.

- John Paul II's funeral in April of 2005 drew more television viewers than any other event in human history.

- The Church in the twenty-first century is faced with many challenges, including an increasingly secular and materialistic Western World. But the Church is strong, growing in great numbers in Africa, Latin America, and Asia. By 2025, 80 percent of the world's Catholics will be from these areas. Issues confronting the future Church include ways to encourage lay people to witness to the Gospel in their daily lives and to better use the talents and gifts of Catholic women. Other challenges include addressing the falloff in Mass attendance, the vocation crisis, how to implement collegiality, and Islamic fundamentalism that has led to terrorism.

Prayer REFLECTION

Pope John Paul II composed this prayer to the Blessed Mother for the defense of life. Pray these words as a reminder to "defend the defenseless."

> O Mary, bright dawn of the new world,
> Mother of the living, to you do we entrust the cause of life
> Look down, O Mother, upon the vast numbers
> of babies not allowed to be born,
> of the poor whose lives are made difficult,
> of men and women who are victims of brutal violence,
> of the elderly and the sick killed by indifference or out of misguided mercy.
> Grant that all who believe in your Son
> may proclaim the Gospel of life with honesty and love
> to the people of our time.
> Obtain for them the grace to accept that Gospel as a gift ever new,
> the joy of celebrating it with gratitude throughout their lives
> and the courage to bear witness to it resolutely, in order to build,
> together with all people of good will, the civilization of truth and love,
> to the praise and glory of God, the Creator and lover of life.[11]

Review and DISCUSSION QUESTIONS

1. Rate what you believe are the three most important achievements of Pope John Paul II and his pontificate.

2. Give the English titles for the following writings of Pope John Paul II, their date of publication, and a significant teaching contained in each.

   - *Centesimus Annus*
   - *Christifidelis Laici*
   - *Evangelium Vitae*
   - *Laborem Exercens*
   - *Ordinatio Sacerdotalis*
   - *Sollicitudo Rei Socialis*
   - *Ut Unum Sint*
   - *Veritatis Splendor*

3. Identify each of the following:

Persons

Leonardo Boff   Fr. Charles Curran

Chiara Lubich   Fr. Hans Küng

Cardinal Joseph Ratzinger

Other

Focolare   Opus Dei

4. Discuss what you believe are the three biggest challenges facing the Roman Catholic Church in the twenty-first century. Share reasons for your choice.

Scripture CONNECTION

A timeless blueprint for Christian living is the teaching of Jesus found in the Beatitudes. Read **Matthew 5:1–16** to see how the Lord challenges the Church of the future to be light of the world and salt of the earth.

Learn BY DOING

1. Interview three practicing Catholics of three different generations. Ask them to list what they see are the challenges facing the Church in the twenty-first century.

2. Investigate and report on the different ministries open to lay persons in your parish.

3. Report on some aspect of the pontificate of Pope John Paul II. Check one of these websites:

   • Answers.com: www.answers.com/topic/john-paul-ii

   • *St Anthony Messenger*, "Pope John Paul II: Model of Heroic Faith":www. americancatholic.org/Messenger/May2005/Feature1.asp#F6

   • *Our Sunday Visitor,* special issue on the Pope: www.osv.com/Portals/0/images/pdf/JPII_Tribute_Web.pdf

4. Report on one of these organizations:

   • Community of Sant'Egidio: www.santegidio.org/en

   • Communion and Liberation: www.clonline.org/FirstPage.htm

- Focolare: www.rc.net/focolare
- Neocatechumenal Way: www.christusrex.org/www2/ncw
- Opus Dei: www.opusdei.org

Afterword

The Church is a part of human history, but she also transcends human history. The Church is made up of sinners, but she herself is sinless. The Church is both a human and divine institution.

None of the above statements about the Church are contradictory. It is only in our awareness of the Mystery of the Church that we can at once examine in detail her visible history while at the same time living in awareness of her spiritual reality as a bearer of divine life.

This Pilgrim Church continues on her journey to perfection, which she will reach only in the glory of heaven. "At that time, together with the human race, the universe itself, which is so closely related to man and which attains its destiny through him, will be perfectly reestablished in Christ" (*Lumen Gentium*, 48).

This is the journey to which we participate as sojourners of this earth and baptized members of Christ's Church. We do so in hope and longing for the time when the Lord "will wipe every tear from [our] eyes and there shall be no more death or mourning, wailing or pain, [for] the old order has passed away" (Rev 21:4).

Glossary of SELECTED TERMS

aggiornamento—An Italian word that literally means "bringing up to date." It was a key word used to describe the Second Vatican Council.

apologist—A name used for Christian writers who defended the Church against anti-Christian writings or heresies through the use of reason and intellectual defenses.

apostasy—A term that means total abandonment of the Church or the Catholic faith.

Apostle—One who is sent by Jesus to continue his work.

Apostolic Father—The name for a late first century or early second century writer who personally knew the Apostles or their disciples. St. Clement, St. Ignatius of Antioch, and Polycarp are three Apostolic Fathers of the early Church.

Arianism—A heresy of the fourth century that took its name from Arius, a heretical priest from Alexandria. The heresy denied the divinity of Jesus, claiming that he was like the Father except that he was created.

caesaropapism—The political theory that held that a secular ruler should also have authority over the Church, including in matters of doctrine.

canon (of the Bible)—The official list of the inspired books of the Bible. Catholics list forty-six Old Testament books and twenty-seven New Testament books in the canon.

Catholic Action—Defined by Pope Pius XI as the "participation of Catholic laity in the apostolate of the hierarchy," the movement focused on works of charity among poor people, combating anti-Christian elements in society, and defending and supporting the rights of the Church and God wherever possible.

Christendom—A term to describe a time of great achievement in the Middle Ages with the Church and Western society were one. It a wider sense, the term refers to a larger territory where most people are Christian.

Church—The name given the "People of God" who come together from the ends of the earth. For Christians, the term has three meanings: the People of God gathered from the whole world; the local church (diocese), and the liturgical assembly (primarily at Eucharist).

collegiality—All the bishops of the Church with the Pope as their head. This college together, but never without the Pope, has supreme and full authority over the universal Church.

conciliarism—An idea that was popular in the Middle Ages that a general council of the Church had more authority than the Pope, and could depose him if they so desired. The First Vatican Council condemned conciliarism. The Second Vatican Council affirmed collegiality, but emphasized it was never superior to the powers of the papacy.

cuius regio, eius religio—Latin for "whose region, his religion." This means that whatever is the religion of the king or ruler of a nation would be the religion of the people. This term was used in the Peace of Augsburg signed in 1555.

Dark Ages—A term used to describe the lack of cultural and historical achievements in the early Middle Ages as well as some of the havoc wreaked by invasions of the period.

Deism—A natural religion that developed in the Age of Enlightenment that embraced the belief that while God does exist and did create the world, he refrains from any kind of interference or direct participation in his creation.

diakonia—A Greek term for "service." Christ commissioned his Church to translate words of love into concrete acts of service for all people, especially the poor, the lonely, the imprisoned, the sick and suffering.

Didache—The earliest known writing in Christianity aside from the New Testament. It includes a summary of Christian moral teaching and an explanation of Baptism and Eucharist. It is a Greek word that means "teaching."

Donation of Pepin—The grant of a large strip of land in the middle of the Italian peninsula by Pepin III to the papacy while granting the Pope the right to rule it.

Ecumenical Council—A worldwide, official assembly of the bishops under the direction of the Pope. There have been twenty-one Ecumenical Councils in history, the most recent being the Second Vatican Council (1962–1965).

ecumenism—The movement that seeks Christian unity and eventually the unity of all peoples throughout the world.

efficacious symbol—A description of sacrament; a sign of grace instituted by Christ and entrusted to the Church. A sacrament is an efficacious symbol because it is a concrete, outward, visible sign that is, at the same time, what it represents.

Empiricism—A belief from the Age of Enlightenment that taught that the only reality is what we can perceive with our five senses. Empiricists encouraged doubt about accepted beliefs and ridiculed religion, religious authority, and traditional Christian doctrines.

Enlightenment—A name associated with the Age of Reason following the Protestant Reformation where it was generally held that only human reason, separated from religious belief, can "enlighten" people.

episkopos—The Greek term for bishop or "overseer."

feudalism—The governing system which prevailed in Europe in the Middle Ages in which a superior or lord granted land to a vassal in return for military services of that vassal.

filioque—The Latin term for "and from the Son." The addition of this term to the Creed was one of the central causes of the 1054 schism between the Eastern and Western Churches.

Focolare—A movement, founded by Chiara Lubich in 1943. Its goal is world unity achieved through putting the Gospel love of Jesus Christ into action.

Gallicanism—A religious and political theory of the sixteenth century that asserted the independence of the French Church from the authority of the Pope.

Gnosticism—The name for movements in the second century which claimed secret, revealed knowledge of God which had been transmitted to either the Apostles or the leader of a gnostic sect.

heresy—A false teaching that denies an essential (dogmatic) teaching of the Church.

hermit—A person who separates himself or herself from the world in prayer and penance in order to be devoted to the praise of God and salvation of the world.

hierarchy—The sacred leadership of the Church that is made up of the Pope, bishops, priests, and deacons. The Pope is the symbol of unity in the Church and the successor to St. Peter.

humanism—A cultural and intellectual movement of the Renaissance that emphasized the rediscovery of the literature, art, and civilizations of ancient Greece and Rome.

hypostatic union—The doctrine, formally taught at the Council of Chalcedon, that in Jesus Christ, one divine person subsists in two natures, the divine and the human.

indulgence—The remission before God of the temporal punishment still due to forgiven sins.

interdict—A Church ruling that excludes a person or region from participating in the sacraments.

Jansenism—A heretical belief of Cornelius Jansen (1585–1638), a bishop of Ypres in France, that taught the utter depravity of human nature and that God's grace extends to only a few. It was an offshoot of Calvinism.

Josephinism—Heretical theory launched by Joseph II in the eighteenth century that advocated the control of state in matters of religion, including the control over naming bishops.

Justinian Code—A collection of laws written in Latin that became the basis of European law that were instituted by Byzantine emperor Justin (527–565).

kerygma—A Greek word for the "proclamation" of religious truths about Jesus Christ (e.g., that he is the way, the truth, and the life.).

koinonia—The Greek word for "fellowship." Christians are called to build fellowship with one another so that they can be a sign of Christ to the world.

lay investiture—A practice in the medieval Church whereby secular rulers chose the bishops for their territories thus usurping the right of the Pope to choose bishops.

leitourgia—Latin term for liturgy, which means "work of the public." The liturgy is the work of the Blessed Trinity; the Father is the source of liturgy, Christ pours out the blessings of the Redemption he won for us on the cross through the sacraments, and the Holy Spirit enlightens our faith and encourages our response.

Liberalism—The term that described the efforts of the nineteenth century to attempt to reconcile Church teaching with the liberal ideas that emerged out of the French Revolution.

Macedonianism—A fourth century heresy named for a bishop of Macedonius that claimed that that the Son created the Holy Spirit who was in turn subordinate to the Father and the Son.

Magisterium—The teaching authority of the church. The Lord bestowed the right to teach in his name on the Apostles and their successors, that is, the bishops with the Pope as their leader.

marks of the Church—Traditional signs of the Church: one, holy, catholic, and apostolic.

martyr—Literally a "witness." A martyr is someone who has been killed because of his or her faith.

mendicant—The name comes from the Latin word which means "to beg." Mendicants are distinguished from monks because members of these religious orders traditionally take a vow of poverty and take on a willingness to beg or work for food.

Modernism—A movement that arose in the late nineteenth century that attempted to reconcile Church teaching with modern advances in science, history, and biblical research.

monasticism—Religious life in which men or women leave the world and enter a monastery or convent while devoting themselves to prayer, contemplation, and self-denial in solitude.

Monophysitism—A heresy of the late fifth and early sixth centuries that taught that there is only one nature in the Person of Christ, the divine nature.

mystery—A term to describe God's hidden plan for mankind. The Church is a mystery. St. Augustine defined mystery as "a visible sign of invisible grace."

Office of the Propagation of the Faith—Created in 1622 by Pope Gregory XV, the purpose of the Office was to coordinate and centralize missionary activity in Rome.

Opus Dei—Worldwide association founded in 1928 in Madrid that is composed of both the laity and clergy that is dedicated to incorporating Christian principles at all levels of society.

orthodoxy—The state of adherence to accepted and traditional teachings of the faith.

papal Inquisition—A Church tribunal established in the thirteenth century that was first designed to curb the Albegensian and Cathar heresies. In collaboration with secular authorities, papal representatives employed the Inquisition to judge the guilt of suspected heretics with the aim of getting them to repent. Unfortunately, before long, many abuses crept into the process.

Pax Romana—A Latin term for "Peace of Rome." It was relatively brief period in history around the time of Jesus' birth.

Peace of God—An initiative beginning in the late tenth century which was intended to make roads and cities safer for pilgrims and traveling merchants.

Peace of Westphalia—A treaty that ended the Thirty Years' War in 1648 and solidified the principle of *cuius regio, eius religio* ending any hope for a united European Christendom

Pelagianism—A fifth century heresy that held that humans could save themselves without God's supernatural help.

Pharisee—A Jewish sect at the time of Jesus with whom he had much in common, including belief in Resurrection, the need for virtuous living, and the importance of the Law.

Paschal Mystery—The saving love of God, most fully revealed in the life and especially the Passion, Death, Resurrection, and glorious Ascension of his Son Jesus Christ.

preferential option for the poor—Pope John Paul II's teaching in *Centesimus Annus* that Catholics must develop a primacy of love for the most needy, that is, a "preferential option for the poor."

principle of subsidiarity—The social teaching that social issues should be handled on the lowest possible level; for example, the family or local community should take precedence over the national government.

Quietism—Seventeenth century heresy inspired by a Spanish priest, Michael Molinos, that took a dim view of human nature, holding that humans are powerless and should not try to resist temptations since they are God's will.

Rationalism—A philosophy of the Age of Enlightenment that taught that only human reason, separated from religious belief, can bring people into the light.

Renaissance—A cultural rebirth begun in the late Middle Ages, rediscovered the ancient civilizations of Rome, Greece, and Egypt. The Renaissance stressed the natural and the human. It emphasized the pleasures of life, glorified the human body, and celebrated education.

sacrament—A visible sign of invisible grace. An efficacious symbol, a sacrament is an outward sign instituted by Christ to confer grace.

Sadducee—An aristocratic Jewish sect that controlled Temple worship in Jesus' time.

schism—A break in Christian unity that takes place when a group of Christians separates itself from the Church. This happens historically when the group breaks in union with the Pope, for example, when the Eastern Orthodox Church broke from the Roman Catholic Church in 1054.

scholasticism—A general term that encompasses the theological and philosophical system developed by major Catholic thinkers, notably St. Thomas Aquinas.

simony—A buying and selling of Church offices. The Church condemns this practice.

Social Darwinism—The theories of Charles Darwin applied to the social realm. For example, the concept of "the survival of the fittest" works in economics, too, resulting in an image of the economic jungle and so-called *laissez-faire* ("hands-off") or "liberal" capitalism.

Syllabus of Errors—A list of eighty errors published by Pope Pius IX in 1864 that had previously been highlighted in earlier Church teachings.

theocracy—A civil government controlled by the Church.

Theotokos—In Greek, the supreme title for Mary, "God bearer" or "Mother of God."

totalitarianism—A form of government in which the political authority exercises total authority all aspects of a citizen's life.

transubstantiation—The teaching of the Church that the substance of the bread and wine is changed into the substance of the Body and Blood of Jesus Christ at the consecration of Mass.

Truce of God—First proposed by Pope John XV in 958 and eventually put into practice in 1027, in its final form, it outlawed fighting from Wednesday evening to Monday morning as well as all religious holidays, leaving only eighty days each year for fighting. By 1123, anyone violating the Truce was excommunicated.

Ultramontanes—A word meaning "beyond the mountains," it described supporters of the Pope in opposition of the nationalistic position of other French churchmen in the seventeenth century.

Vulgate—The Latin translation of the Bible completed by St. Jerome. It became the authorized Bible used in the Catholic Church up to modern times.

Zealot—In Jesus' time, a radical Jewish sect that hated Roman rule and was successful in starting a revolution against Rome.

Notes

Chapter 1: The Mystery of the Church in Salvation History

1. Sources for this information include the Center for Applied Research in the Apostolate (CARA) <http://cara.georgetown.edu/bulletin/> and United States Conference of Catholic Bishops, Catholic Information Project: The Catholic Church in America—Meeting Real Needs in Your Neighborhood, August 2006 <http://www.usccb.org/comm/2006CIPFinal.pdf>.

2. *Encyclopaedia Britannica Book of the Year 2006*, quoted at Wholesome Words, "Worldwide Missions" <http://www.wholesomewords.org/missions/greatc.html>.

3. Quoted by Fr. Alphonse de Valk, C.S.B. in his book review of *The Christians: Their First Two Thousand Years*, July/August 2002 <http://catholicinsight.com/online/culture/article_227.shtml>.

4. Maxwell Staniforth, *Early Christian Writings: The Apostolic Fathers* (New York: Penguin Books, 1968), 104–105.

5. St. Ignatius of Antioch, "Letter to the Smyrnaeans" found online at the Apostolate for Eucharistic Life website. Letter made available to the net by Paul Halsall <http://www.eucharisticlife.com/ELimages/Timeline/200/Smyrnaeans.html>.

Chapter 2: Christianity Takes Root

1. Darrell J. Doughty, "Tacitus' Account of Nero's Persecution of Christians: Annals 15.44.2-8" <www.courses.drew.edu/sp2000/BIBST189.001/Tacitus.html>.

2. "Trajan's Epistle to Pliny," taken from *The Works of Josephus*, translated by William Whiston (Hendrickson Publishers, 1987) cited online PBS Frontline, *Jesus to Christ* <http://www.pbs.org/wgbh/pages/frontline/shows/religion/maps/primary/pliny.html>.

3. Quoted in William A. Jurgens, *The Faith of the Early Fathers*, vol. 1 (Collegeville, MN: Liturgical Press, 1970), 51–52.

4. Maxwell Staniforth, *Early Christian Writings: The Apostolic Fathers* (New York: Penguin Books, 1968), 230–231.

Chapter 3: The Spread of Christianity

1. "Dogmatic Definition of the Council of Chalcedon, 451," EWTN Faith: Teachings <http://www.ewtn.com/faith/teachings/incac2.htm>.

2. Rodney Stark, *The Rise of Christianity* quoted by Jon Meacham, "From Jesus to Christ," Newsweek, March 28, 2005, vol. CXLV, no. 13, 48.

3. *The Tome of St. Leo the Great of Rome*, Monachos.net <http://www.monachos.net/patristics/christology/leo_tome.shtml>.

4. Quoted in Jean Comby, *How to Read Church History*, volume 1 (New York: Crossroad, 1985), 123.

5. Taken from "A Topical St. Benedict." Found online at <http://www.geocities.com/art_carroll/Notes/TopicalRB> (06 September 2006).

6. The Catholic Community Forum, Patron Saints, "Jerome" <http://www.catholic-forum.com/saints/saintj06.htm>.

7. *Confessions*, VIII.12. Quoted at the Augustinians' the Province of St. Augustine website, "St. Augustine" <http://www.osa-weSt.org/saintaugustine.html>.

8. F. Forrester Church and Terrence J. Mulry, *The Macmillan Book of Earliest Christian Prayers* (New York: Collier Books, 1988), 113–114.

Chapter 4: The Church in the Middle Ages

1. Translated in Ernest F. Henderson, *Select Historical Documents of the Middle Ages* (London: George Bell and Sons, 1910), 366–367. Accessed online at the Internet Medieval Sourcebook <http://www.fordham.edu/halsall/source/g7-dictpap.html>.

2. From Chapter 6 of St. Bernard of Clairvaux's *On Loving God*, Christian Classics Ethereal Library at Calvin College <http://www.ccel.org/ccel/bernard/loving_god.viii.html>.

3. Papal Encyclicals Online, Pope Boniface VIII, Bull of *Unam Sanctam*, November 18, 1302 <http://www.papalencyclicals.net/Bon08/B8unam.htm>.

4. The Catholic Community Forum, Patron Saints Index: Thomas Aquinas <http://www.catholic-forum.com/saints/saintt03.htm>.

Chapter 5: Schism, Reform, and Renewal

1. Thomas à Kempis, *The Imitation to Christ* cited in *Devotional Classics*, ed. Richard J. Foster and James Bryan Smith (San Francisco: HarperSanFrancisco, 1993), 185–186.

2. Quoted by Fr. Alfred McBride, O. Praem., *The Story of the Church: Peak Moments from Pentecost to the Year 2000* (Cincinnati, OH: St. Anthony Messenger Press, 1996), 105.

3. *Letters of St. Catherine of Siena*, translated by Vida D. Scudder (1906). Cited at EWTN Library's website http://www.ewtn.com/library/MARY/CATSIENA.HTM

4. Cladio Rendina, *The Popes: Histories and Secrets*, translated by Paul D. McCusker (Santa Ana, CA: Seven Locks Press, 2002), 443.

5. *Online Etymology Dictionary*, "protest" and "Protestant" <http://www.etymonline.com/index.php?l=p&p=34>.

Chapter 6: Church in an Era of Change

1. Quoted by the Catholic Information Network <http://www.cin.org/docs/pastorae.html>.

2. Quoted at the Catholic Community Forum Patron Saints website, "Francis de Sales" <http://www.catholic-forum.com/saints/saintf03.htm>.

3. *Lumen Gentium* accessed online at the Vatican website <http://www.vatican.va/archive/hist_councils/ii_vatican_council/documents/vat-ii_const_19641121_lumen-gentium_en.html>.

4. The Catholic Community Forum, Patron Saints, "Vincent de Paul" <http://www.catholic-forum.com/saints/saintv01.htm>.

5. Vincentians Eastern Province, USA, "St. Louise de Marillac" <http://www.cmeaSt.org/pages/marillac.html>.

6. Quoted at the Confraternity of Penitents website <http://www.penitents.org/value.html>.

7. Pope Gregory XVI, *Mirari Vos—On Liberalism and Religious Indifferentism*, 14. Found at Papal Encyclicals Online <http://www.papalencyclicals.net/Greg16/g16mirar.htm>.

8. Pope Pius IX, *Syllabus of Errors*, proposition 80. Cited at the EWTN Library <http://www.ewtn.com/library/PAPALDOC/P9SYLL.HTM>.

9. St. Francis de Sales, *Treatise On the Love of God*, vol. 2, Book 12, Chapter 13. Translated by Rt. Rev. John K. Ryan (Rockford, IL: TAN Books and Publishers, Inc., 1974), 281–282.

Chapter 7: The Catholic Church in Modern Times

1. Pope Pius XI, Encyclical Letter *Divini Redemptoris* (1937), 10 <http://www.vatican.va/holy_father/pius_xi/encyclicals/documents/hf_p-xi_enc_19031937_divini-redemptoris_en.html>.

2. Pope John XXIII, Encyclical Letter *Pacem in Terris* (1963), 1 <http://www.vatican.va/holy_father/john_xxiii/encyclicals/documents/hf_j-xxiii_enc_11041963_pacem_en.html>.

3. Pope John Paul II, Encyclical Letter *Centesimus Annus* (1991), 11 <http://www.vatican.va/holy_father/john_paul_ii/encyclicals/documents/hf_jp-ii_enc_01051991_centesimus-annus_en.html>.

4. Pope John Paul II, Encyclical Letter *Solicitudo Rei Socialis* (1987), 42 <http://www.vatican.va/holy_father/john_paul_ii/encyclicals/documents/hf_jp-ii_enc_30121987_sollicitudo-rei-socialis_en.html>.

5. Pope Pius XI, Encyclical Letter *Divini Redemptoris* (1937), 58 <http://www.vatican.va/holy_father/pius_xi/encyclicals/documents/hf_p-xi_enc_19031937_divini-redemptoris_en.html>.

6. Cited by Peter Gumpel, "Pius XII as He Really Was," *The Tablet Online*, February 13, 1999 <http://www.thetablet.co.uk/cgi-bin/register.cgi/tablet-00257> (27 September 2005) and H. W. Crocker III in his *Triumph: The Power and the Glory of the Catholic Church* (New York: Three Rivers Press, 2001), 403.

7. Pope John XXIII, "Opening Speech to the Council," October 11, 1962 <http://www.christusrex.org/www1/CDHN/v2.html>.

8. Carol Eisenberg, "The Changing Face of Faith," April 17, 2005, Newsday.com <http://www.newsday.com/news/specials/ny-woeuro174221977apr17,0,3904587.story>.

9. Gunther Simmermacher, "No Vocations Crisis," *The Southern Cross*, August 4 to August 10, 2004 <http://www.thesoutherncross.co.za/editorials2004/editorial040804.htm>.

10. United States Conference Catholic Bishops, *"Ex Corde Ecclesiae": An Application to the United States* <http://www.usccb.org/education/excorde.htm>.

Chapter 8: The Church in America

1. United States Conference of Catholic Bishops, *Economic Justice for All: Pastoral Letter on Catholic Social Teaching and the U.S. Economy* (1986). The entire document can be found at the Office for Social Justice website of the Archdiocese of St. Paul and Minneapolis <http://www.osjspm.org/cst/eja.htm>.

2. United States Conference of Catholic Bishops, Catholic Information Project: The Catholic Church in America—Meeting Real Needs

in Your Neighborhood, August 2006, 4 <http://www.usccb.org/comm/2006CIPFinal.pdf>.

3. United States Conference of Catholic Bishops. Committee on Hispanic Affairs, 1999.

4. Charles R. Morris, *American Catholic: The Saints and Sinners Who Built America's Most Powerful Church* (New York: Vintage Books, 1997), p. vii.

5. Pope Paul III, *Sublimus Dei (On the Enslavement and Evangelization of Indians in the New World)*, 1537 <http://www.catholic-forum.com/saints/Pope0220a.htm> (28 September 2005).

6. "Native American Catholics at the Millennium: a presentation of Bishop Donald E. Pelotte, SSS to the United States Conference of Catholic Bishops, 2003.

7. Abraham Lincoln, "Letter to Joshua Speed," August 24, 1855, Abraham Lincoln Online, "Speeches and Writings" <http://showcase.netins.net/web/creative/lincoln/speeches/speed.htm>.

8. John F. Kennedy, "Address to Southern Baptist Leaders," 1960 <http://usinfo.state.gov/usa/infousa/facts/democrac/66.htm>. Original source credited as *New York Times*, September 13, 1960.

9. Jay P. Dolan, *The American Catholic Heritage* (Garden City, NY: Doubleday & Co., Inc., 1985), 204.

10. United States Conference of Catholic Bishops, "About Us" <http://www.usccb.org/whoweare.htm>.

11. *Our Sunday Visitor's Catholic Almanac: 2005*, citing the *U.S. Catholic Mission Handbook 2004 Mission Inventory 2002-2003*, 426.

12. Cathy Lynn Grossman and Anthony DeBarros, "Church Struggles with Change," *USA Today*, November 8, 2004 <http://www.usatoday.com/news/religion/2004-11-07-church-main_x.htm>.

13. Dean R. Hoge, "The Current State of the Priesthood: Sociological Research." A paper presented to Corpus U.S.A., June 15, 2005 <http://www.corpus.org/page.cfm?Web_ID=565>.

14. The sources for the last two statistics came from *Our Sunday Visitor's 2005 Catholic Almanac* (Huntington, IN: Our Sunday Visitor, Inc., 2004), 429, and Peter Steinfels, *A People Adrift: The Crisis of the Roman Catholic Church in America* (New York: Simon & Schuster, 2003), 29–30.

15. Grossman and DeBarros, loc. cit.

16. Thomas Merton, *Thoughts in Solitude* (New York: Farrar, Straus and Giroux, 1958), 83.

17. Citations provided on the Catholic Worker Movement's website <http://www.catholicworker.org/aimsandmeanstext.cfm?Number=28>.

Chapter 9: Pope John Paul II Ushers in the Church of the Twenty-First Century

1. Pope John Paul II, *Centesimus Annus*, 1991, No. 36 <http://www.vatican.va/holy_father/john_paul_ii/encyclicals/documents/hf_jp-ii_enc_01051991_centesimus-annus_en.html>.

2. Holy See Press Office, "His Holiness John Paul II: Short Biography" <http://www.vatican.va/news_services/press/documentazione/documents/santopadre_biografie/giovanni_paolo_ii_biografia_breve_en.html>.

3. Bishop Joseph A. Galante, "Pope John Paul II: 25 Years of Service: Lost in Prayer," *St. Anthony Messenger*, October 2003 <http://www.americancatholic.org/Messenger/Oct2003/Feature2.asp#F5>.

4. Pope John Paul II, *Evangelium Vitae*, 1995, No. 56, quoting No. 2267 of the *Catechism of the Catholic Church* <http://www.vatican.va/holy_father/john_paul_ii/encyclicals/documents/hf_jp-ii_enc_25031995_evangelium-vitae_en.html#$1C>.

5. Pope John Paul II, *Fides et Ratio*, 1998, No. 46 <http://www.vatican.va/holy_father/john_paul_ii/encyclicals/documents/hf_jp-ii_enc_15101998_fides-et-ratio_en.html>.

6. Catholic Online, "Statistics Reveal Africa Is Church's New Hope," May 17, 2005 <http://www.catholic.org/cathcom/international_story.php?id=14581>.

7. Office of Communications, Georgetown University, "U.S. Catholic Mass Attendance Remains Constant," January 12, 2005 <http://www1.georgetown.edu/explore/news/?DocumentID=1634>.

8. Catholic News, "Pell Blames Sunday Sport for Decline in Mass Attendance," December 17, 2003 <http://www.cathnews.com/news/312/99.php>.

9. History News Network, Thomas C. Reeves, "The Temptation of Secularism," August 3, 2005 <http://hnn.us/blogs/entries/13606.html>.

10. Noelle Knox, "Religion Takes a Back Seat in Western Europe," *USA Today*, August 11, 2005 <http://news.yahoo.com/s/usatoday/religiontakesabackseatinwesterneurope>.

11. Pope John Paul II, *Evangelium Vitae*, 1995, No. 105 <http://www.vatican.va/holy_father/john_paul_ii/encyclicals/documents/hf_jp-ii_enc_25031995_evangelium-vitae_en.html>.

Subject INDEX

I

Leo the Great, 71, 74, 77–78, 112, 231, 279

Liberalism, 188–90

Liberation theology, 228, 287

Licinius, 69

Lincoln, Abraham, 250

Liturgy, 223

Liturgy of the Hours. *See* Divine Office

Locke, John, 182

Lollards, 138

Lombards, 76, 90

Lord Baltimore, 246

Louis VII, 117

Louis XIV, 170–72

Louis XVI, 185

Louisiana Purchase, 245

Lourdes, 192

Lubac, Henri de, 221

Lumen Gentium, 223

Luther, Martin, 143–45; on indulgences, 140

Lutheranism, 145, 149

Lynch, Patrick, 251

M

McCarthy, Joseph, 263

Macedonianism, 73

McQuaid, Bernard, 255, 256

Magisterium, 23–24; authority of, 228–29, 292; Council of Trent on, 154

Magyars, 78, 104

Mahomet II, 141

Manning, Henry Edward, 206

Mao Zedong, 218

Marcion, 55

Marillac, Louise de, 176, 177

Marists, 181

Marquette, Jacques, 179, 244

Marriage, 229

Marsilius of Padua, 132

Martel, Charles, 79, 90

Martin V, 137

Scripture INDEX

CCC

Photography CREDITS

© Vittoriano Rastelli / CORBIS: p. 6
© Reuters / CORBIS: p. 6
© Gianni Giansanti / Sygma / Corbis: p. 7
© Alessandra Benedetti / Corbis: p. 8

Catholic Handbook FOR FAITH

A. Beliefs

Apostles' Creed

I believe in God,
the Father almighty,
Creator of heaven and earth,
and in Jesus Christ, his only Son, our Lord,
who was conceived by the Holy Spirit,
born of the Virgin Mary,
suffered under Pontius Pilate,
was crucified, died and was buried;
he descended into hell;
on the third day he rose again from the dead;
he ascended into heaven,
and is seated at the right hand of God the Father almighty;
from there he will come to judge the living and the dead.

I believe in the Holy Spirit,
the holy catholic Church,
the communion of saints,
the forgiveness of sins,
the resurrection of the body,
and life everlasting. Amen.

Nicene Creed

I believe in one God,
the Father almighty,
maker of heaven and earth,
of all things visible and invisible.

I believe in one Lord Jesus Christ,
the Only Begotten Son of God,
born of the Father before all ages.
God from God, Light from Light,
true God from true God,
begotten, not made, consubstantial with the Father;

through him all things were made.
For us men and for our salvation
he came down from heaven,
and by the Holy Spirit was incarnate of the Virgin Mary,
and became man.

For our sake he was crucified under Pontius Pilate,
he suffered death and was buried,
and rose again on the third day
in accordance with the Scriptures.
He ascended into heaven
and is seated at the right hand of the Father.
He will come again in glory
to judge the living and the dead
and his kingdom will have no end.

I believe in the Holy Spirit, the Lord, the giver of life,
who proceeds from the Father and the Son,
who with the Father and the Son is adored and glorified,
who has spoken through the prophets.

I believe in one, holy, catholic, and apostolic Church.
I confess one Baptism for the forgiveness of sins
and I look forward to the resurrection of the dead
and the life of the world to come. Amen.

Gifts of the Holy Spirit

1. Wisdom

2. Understanding

3. Counsel

4. Fortitude

5. Knowledge

6. Piety

7. Fear of the Lord

Fruits of the Holy Spirit

1. Charity

2. Joy

3. Peace

4. Patience

5. Kindness

6. Goodness

7. Generosity

8. Gentleness

9. Faithfulness

10. Modesty

11. Self-control

12. Chastity

The Symbol of Chalcedon

Following therefore the holy Fathers, we unanimously teach to confess one and the same Son, our Lord Jesus Christ, the same perfect in divinity and perfect in humanity, the same truly God and truly man composed of rational soul and body, the same one in being (*homoousios*) with the Father as to the divinity and one in being with us as to the humanity, like unto us in all things but sin (cf. Heb 4:15). The same was begotten from the Father before the ages as to the divinity and in the later days for us and our salvation was born as to his humanity from Mary the Virgin Mother of God.

We confess that one and the same Lord Jesus Christ, the only-begotten Son, must be acknowledged in two natures, without confusion or change, without division or separation. The distinction between the natures was never abolished by their union but rather the character proper to each of the two natures was preserved as they came together in one person (*prosôpon*) and one hypostasis. He is not split or divided into two persons, but he is one and the same only-begotten, God the Word, the Lord Jesus Christ, as formerly the prophets and later Jesus Christ himself have taught us about him and as has been handed down to us by the Symbol of the Fathers.

—From the General Council of Chalcedon (451)

B. God and Jesus Christ

Attributes of God

St. Thomas Aquinas named nine attributes that seem to tell us some things about God's nature. They are:

1. *God is eternal.* He has no beginning and no end. Or, to put it another way, God always was, always is, and always will be.

2. *God is unique.* God is the designer of a one and only world. Even the people he creates are one of a kind.

3. *God is infinite and omnipotent.* This reminds us of a lesson we learned early in life: God sees everything. There are no limits to God. Omnipotence is a word that refers to God's supreme power and authority over all of creation.

4. *God is omnipresent.* God is not limited to space. He is everywhere. You can never be away from God.

5. *God contains all things.* All of creation is under God's care and jurisdiction.

6. *God is immutable.* God does not evolve. God does not change. God is the same God now as he always was and always will be.

7. *God is pure spirit.* Though God has been described with human attributes, God is not a material creation. God's image cannot be made. God is a pure spirit who cannot be divided into parts. God is simple, but complex.

8. *God is alive.* We believe in a living God, a God who acts in the lives of people. Most concretely, he came to this world in the incarnate form of Jesus Christ.

9. *God is holy.* God is pure goodness. God is pure love.

The Holy Trinity

The Trinity is the mystery of one God in three persons—Father, Son, and Holy Spirit. The mystery is impossible for human minds to understand. Some of the Church dogmas, or beliefs, can help:

*   *The Trinity is One.* There are not three Gods, but one God in three persons. Each one of them—Father, Son, and Holy Spirit—is God whole and entire.

- *The three persons are distinct from one another.* For example, the Father is not the Son, nor is the Son the Holy Spirit. Rather, the Father is Creator, the Son is begotten of the Father, and the Holy Spirit proceeds from the Father and Son.
- *The divine persons are related to one another.* Though they are related to one another, the three persons have one nature or substance.

St. John Damascus used two analogies to describe the doctrine of the Blessed Trinity.

Think of the **FATHER** as a root,
of the **SON** as a branch,
and of the **SPIRIT** as a fruit,
for the substance of these is one.

The **FATHER** is a sun
with the **SON** as rays
and the **HOLY SPIRIT** as heat.

Read the *Catechism of the Catholic Church* (232–260) on the Holy Trinity.

Faith in One God

There are several implications for those who love God and believe in him with their entire heart and soul (see *CCC*, 222–227):

- It means knowing God's greatness and majesty.
- It means living in thanksgiving.
- It means knowing the unity and dignity of all people.
- It means making good use of created things.
- It means trust God in every circumstance.

C. Scripture and Tradition

Canon of the Bible

There are seventy-three books in the canon of the Bible, that is, the official list of books the Church accepts as divinely inspired writings: forty-six Old Testament books and twenty-seven New Testament books. "Protestant Bibles" do not include seven Old Testament books from its list (1 and 2 Maccabees, Judith, Tobit, Baruch, Sirach, and the Wisdom of Solomon). Why the difference? Catholics rely on the version of the Bible that the earliest Christians used, the *Septuagint*. This was the first Greek translation of the Hebrew scriptures begun in the third century BC. Protestants, on the other hand, rely on an official list of Hebrew scriptures compiled in the Holy Land by Jewish scholars at the end of the first century AD. Today, most Protestant Bibles print the disputed books in a separate section at the back of the Bible BC, called the *Apocrypha*.

The twenty-seven books of the New Testament are detailed in Chapter 2. The New Testament is central to our knowledge of Jesus Christ. He is the focus of that chapter.

There are forty-six books in the Old Testament canon. The Old Testament is the foundation for God's self-revelation in Christ. Christians honor the Old Testament as God's word. It contains the writings of prophets and other inspired authors who recorded God's teaching to the Chosen People and his interaction in their history. For example, the Old Testament recounts how God delivered the Jews from Egypt (the Exodus), led them to the Promised Land, formed them into a nation under his care, and taught them in knowledge and worship.

The stories, prayers, sacred histories, and other writings of the Old Testament reveal what God is like and tell much about human nature, too. In brief, the Chosen People sinned repeatedly by turning their backs on their loving God; they were weak and easily tempted away from God. Yahweh, on the other hand, *always* remained faithful. He promised to send a Messiah to humanity.

Listed below are the categories and books of the Old Testament:

The Old Testament

The Pentateuch		The Historical Books	
Genesis	Gn	Joshua	Jos
Exodus	Ex	Judges	Jgs
Leviticus	Lv	Ruth	Ru
Numbers	Nm	1 Samuel	1 Sm
Deuteronomy	Dt	2 Samuel	2 Sm

1 Kings	1 Kgs
2 Kings	2 Kgs
1 Chronicles	1 Chr
2 Chronicles	2 Chr
Ezra	Ezr
Nehemiah	Neh
Tobit	Tb
Judith	Jdt
Esther	Est
1 Maccabees	1 Mc
2 Maccabees	2 Mc

The Wisdom Books

Job	Jb
Psalms	Ps(s)
Proverbs	Prv
Ecclesiastes	Eccl
Song of Songs	Sg
Wisdom	Wis
Sirach	Sir

The Prophetic Books

Isaiah	Is
Jeremiah	Jer
Lamentations	Lam
Baruch	Bar
Ezekiel	Ez
Daniel	Dn
Hosea	Hos
Joel	Jl
Amos	Am
Obadiah	Ob
Jonah	Jon
Micah	Mi
Nahum	Na
Habakkuk	Hb
Zephaniah	Zep
Haggai	Hg
Zechariah	Zec
Malachi	Mal

The New Testament

The Gospels

Matthew	Mt
Mark	Mk
Luke	Lk
John	Jn

| Acts of the Apostles | Acts |

The New Testament Letters

Romans	Rom
1 Corinthians	1 Cor
2 Corinthians	2 Cor
Galatians	Gal
Ephesians	Eph
Philippians	Phil
Colossians	Col
1 Thessalonians	1 Thes

2 Thessalonians	2 Thes
1 Timothy	1 Tm
2 Timothy	2 Tm
Titus	Ti
Philemon	Phlm
Hebrews	Heb

The Catholic Letters

James	Jas
1 Peter	1 Pt
2 Peter	2 Pt
1 John	1 Jn
2 John	2 Jn
3 John	3 Jn
Jude	Jude

| Revelation | Rv |

How to Locate a Scripture Passage

Example: 2 Tm 3:16–17

1. Determine the name of the book.

   The abbreviation "2 Tm" stands for the second book of Timothy.

2. Determine whether the book is in the Old Testament or New Testament.

   The second book of Timothy is one of the Catholic letters in the New Testament.

3. Locate the chapter where the passage occurs.

   The first number before the colon—"3"— indicates the chapter. Chapters in the Bible are set off by the larger numbers that divide a book.

4. Locate the verses of the passage.

   The numbers after the colon indicate the verses referred to. In this case, verses 16 and 17 of chapter 3.

5. Read the passage.

   For example: "All scripture is inspired by God and is useful for teaching, for refutation, for correction, and for training in righteousness, so that one who belongs to God may be competent, equipped for every good work."

D. Church

Marks of the Church

1. *The Church is one.* The Church remains one because of its source: the unity in the Trinity of the Father, Son, and Spirit in one God. The Church's unity can never be broken and lost because this foundation is itself unbreakable.

2. *The Church is holy.* The Church is holy because Jesus, the founder of the Church, is holy and he joined the Church to himself as his body and gave the Church the gift of the Holy Spirit. Together, Christ and the Church make up the "whole Christ" (*Christus totus* in Latin).

3. *The Church is catholic.* The Church is catholic ("universal" or "for everyone") in two ways. First, it is catholic because Christ is pres-

ent in the Church in the fullness of his body, with the fullness of the means of salvation, the fullness of faith, sacraments, and the ordained ministry that comes from the Apostles. The Church is also catholic because it takes its message of salvation to all people.

4. *The Church is apostolic.* The Church's apostolic mission comes from Jesus: "Go, therefore, and make disciples of all nations" (Mt 28:19). The Church remains apostolic because it still teaches the same things the Apostles taught. Also, the Church is led by leaders who are successors to the Apostles and who help to guide us until Jesus returns.

The Apostles and Their Emblems

ST. ANDREW
Tradition holds that Andrew was crucified on a bent cross, called a *saltire*.

ST. BARTHOLOMEW
Bartholomew was flayed alive before being crucified. He was then beheaded.

ST. JAMES THE GREATER
James the Greater, the brother of John, was beheaded by Herod Agrippa. It is the only death of an Apostle mentioned in Scripture (Acts 12:2). The shell indicates James' missionary work by sea in Spain. The sword is of martyrdom.

ST. JAMES THE LESS
James the Less is traditionally known as the first bishop of Jerusalem. The saw for his emblem is connected with the tradition of his body being sawed into pieces after he was pushed from the pinnacle of the Temple.

ST. JOHN THE EVANGELIST
John was the first bishop of Ephesus. He is the only Apostle believed to have died a natural death, in spite of many attempts to murder him by his enemies. One attempt included his miraculous survival of drinking a poisoned drink.

ST. JUDE
Some traditions have Jude and St. Peter martyred together. It is thought that he traveled throughout the Roman Empire with Peter.

ST. MATTHEW
Matthew's shield depicts three purses reflecting his original occupation as tax collector.

ST. MATTHIAS
Matthias was the Apostle chosen by lot to replace Judas. Tradition holds that Matthias was stoned to death and then beheaded with an ax.

ST. PETER
Simon Peter was the brother of Andrew. The first bishop of Rome, Peter was crucified under Nero, asking to be hung upside down because he felt unworthy to die as Jesus did. The keys represent Jesus' giving to Peter the keys to the kingdom of heaven.

ST. PHILIP
Philip may have been bound to a cross and stoned to death. The two loaves of bread at the side of the cross refer to Philip's comment to Jesus about the possibility of feeding the multitudes of people (Jn 6:7).

ST. SIMON
The book with fish depicts Simon as a "fisher of men" who preached the Gospel. He was also known as Simon the Zealot.

ST. THOMAS
Thomas is thought to have been a missionary in India, where he is thought to have built a church. Hence, the carpenter's square. He may have died by arrows and stones. It is then thought that he had a lance run through his body.

The Pope

The bishop of Rome has carried the title "pope" since the ninth century. Pope means "papa" or "father." St. Peter was the first bishop of Rome and, hence, the first Pope. He was commissioned directly by Jesus:

> And so I say to you, you are Peter, and upon this rock I will build my church, and the gates of the netherworld shall not prevail against it. I will give you the keys to the kingdom of heaven. Whatever you bind on earth shall be bound in heaven; and whatever you loose on earth shall be loosed in heaven. (Mt 16:18–19)

Because Peter was the first bishop of Rome, the succeeding bishops of Rome have had primacy in the Church. The entire succession of popes since St. Peter can be traced directly to the Apostle.

The Pope is in communion with the bishops of the world as part of the Magisterium, which is the Church's teaching authority. The Pope can also define doctrine in faith or morals for the Church. When he does so, he is infallible and cannot be in error.

The Pope is elected by the College of Cardinals by a two-thirds plus one majority vote in secret balloting. Cardinals under the age of eighty are eligible to vote. If the necessary majority is not achieved the ballots are burned in a small stove inside the counsel chambers along with straw that makes dark smoke. The sign of dark smoke announces to the crowds waiting outside St. Peter's Basilica that a new Pope has not been chosen. When a new Pope has been voted in with the necessary majority, the ballots are burned without the straw producing white smoke, signifying the election of a Pope.

Recent Popes

Since 1900 and through the pontificate of Pope Benedict XVI, there were ten Popes. Pope John Paul II was the first non-Italian Pope since Dutchman Pope Adrian VI (1522–1523). The Popes since the twentieth century through Benedict XVI with their original names, place of origin, and years as Pope:

- Pope Leo XIII (Giocchino Pecci): Carpineto, Italy, February 20 1878–July 20, 1903.

- Pope St. Pius X (Giuseppe Sarto): Riese, Italy, August 4, 1903–1914.

- Pope Benedict XV (Giacomo della Chiesa): Genoa, Italy, September 3, 1914–January 22, 1922.

- Pope Pius XI (Achille Ratti): Desio, Italy, February 6, 1922–February 10, 1939.

- Pope Pius XII (Eugenio Pacelli): Rome, Italy, March 2, 1939–October 9, 1958.

- Pope John XXIII (Angelo Giuseppe Roncalli), Sotto il Monte, Italy, October 28, 1958–June 3, 1963.

- Pope Paul VI (Giovanni Battista Montini): Concessio, Italy, June 21, 1963–August 6, 1978.

- Pope John Paul I (Albino Luciani): Forno di Canale, Italy, August 26, 1978–September 28, 1978.

- Pope John Paul II (Karol Wojtyla): Wadowice, Poland, October 16, 1978–April 2, 2005.

- Pope Benedict XVI (Joseph Ratzinger): Marktl am Inn, Germany, April 19, 2005–present.

Fathers of the Church

Church Fathers, or Fathers of the Church, is a traditional title that was given to theologians of the first eight centuries whose teachings made a lasting mark on the Church. The Church Fathers developed a significant amount of doctrine which has great authority in the Church. The Church Fathers are named as either Latin Fathers (West) or Greek Fathers (East). Among the greatest Fathers of the Church are:

Latin Fathers	Greek Fathers
St. Ambrose	St. John Chrysostom
St. Augustine	St. Basil the Great
St. Jerome	St. Gregory of Nazianzen
St. Gregory the Great	St. Athanasius

Doctors of the Church

The Doctors of the Church are men and women honored by the Church for their writings, preaching, and holiness. Originally the Doctors of the Church were considered to be Church Fathers Augustine, Ambrose, Jerome, and Gregory the Great, but others were added over the centuries. St. Teresa of Avila was the first woman Doctor (1970). St. Catherine of Siena was named a Doctor of the Church the same year. The list of Doctors of the Church:

Name	Life Span	Designation
St. Athanasius	296–373	1568 by Pius V
St. Ephraem the Syrian	306–373	1920 by Benedict XV
St. Hilary of Poitiers	315–367	1851 by Pius IX
St. Cyril of Jerusalem	315–386	1882 by Leo XIII
St. Gregory of Nazianzus	325–389	1568 by Pius V
St. Basil the Great	329–379	1568 by Pius V
St. Ambrose	339–397	1295 by Boniface VIII
St. John Chrysostom	347–407	1568 by Pius V
St. Jerome	347–419	1295 by Boniface XIII
St. Augustine	354–430	1295 by Boniface XIII
St. Cyril of Alexandria	376–444	1882 by Leo XIII
St. Peter Chrysologous	400–450	1729 by Benedict XIII
St. Leo the Great	400–461	1754 by Benedict XIV
St. Gregory the Great	540–604	1295 by Boniface XIII
St. Isidore of Seville	560–636	1722 by Innocent XIII

St. John of Damascus	645–749	1890 by Leo XIII
St. Bede the Venerable	672–735	1899 by Leo XIII
St. Peter Damian	1007–1072	1828 by Leo XII
St. Anselm	1033–1109	1720 by Clement XI
St. Bernard of Clairvaux	1090–1153	1830 by Pius VIII
St. Anthony of Padua	1195–1231	1946 by Pius XII
St. Albert the Great	1206–1280	1931 by Pius XI
St. Bonaventure	1221–1274	1588 by Sixtus V
St. Thomas Aquinas	1226–1274	1567 by Pius V
St. Catherine of Siena	1347–1380	1970 by Paul VI
St. Teresa of Avila	1515–1582	1970 by Paul VI
St. Peter Canisius	1521–1597	1925 by Pius XI
St. John of the Cross	1542–1591	1926 by Pius XI
St. Robert Bellarmine	1542–1621	1931 by Pius XI
St. Lawrence of Brindisi	1559–1619	1959 by John XXIII
St. Francis de Sales	1567–1622	1871 by Pius IX
St. Alphonsus Ligouri	1696–1787	1871 by Pius IX
St. Thérèse of Lisieux	1873–1897	1997 by John Paul II

Ecumenical Councils

An ecumenical council is a worldwide assembly of bishops under direction of the pope. There have been twenty-one ecumenical councils, the most recent being the Second Vatican Council (1962–1965). A complete list of the Church's ecumenical councils with the years each met:

Nicaea I	325
Constantinople I	381
Ephesus	431
Chalcedon	451
Constantinople II	553
Constantinople III	680
Nicaea II	787
Constantinople IV	869–870
Lateran I	1123
Lateran II	1139
Lateran III	1179
Lateran IV	1215
Lyons I	1245
Lyons II	1274
Vienne	1311–1312
Constance	1414–1418

Florence	1431–1445
Lateran V	1512–1517
Trent	1545–1563
Vatican Council I	1869–1870
Vatican Council II	1962–1965

E. Morality

The Ten Commandments

The Ten Commandments are a main source for Christian morality. The Ten Commandments were revealed by God to Moses. Jesus, himself, acknowledged them. He told the rich young man, "If you wish to enter into life, keep the commandments" (Mt 19:17). Since the time of St. Augustine (fourth century) the Ten Commandments have been used as a source for teaching baptismal candidates.

I.   I, the Lord am your God: you shall not have other gods besides me.

II.   You shall not take the name of the Lord, your God, in vain.

III. Remember to keep holy the sabbath day.

IV.   Honor your father and your mother.

V.   You shall not kill.

VI.   You shall not commit adultery.

VII. You shall not steal.

VIII. You shall not bear false witness against your neighbor.

IX.   You shall not covet your neighbor's wife.

X.   You shall not covet your neighbor's goods.

The Beatitudes

The word *beatitude* means "happiness." Jesus preached the Beatitudes in his Sermon on the Mount. They are:

- Blessed are the poor in spirit, for theirs is the kingdom of God.
- Blessed are they who mourn, for they will be comforted.
- Blessed are the meek, for they will inherit the land.
- Blessed are they who hunger and thirst for righteousness, for they will be satisfied.
- Blessed are the merciful, for they will be shown mercy.

- Blessed are the clean of heart, for they will see God.
- Blessed are the peacemakers, for they will be called children of God.
- Blessed are they who are persecuted for the sake of righteousness, for theirs is the kingdom of heaven.

Cardinal Virtues

Virtues—habits that help in leading a moral life—that are acquired by human effort are known as moral or human virtues. Four of these are the cardinal virtues as they form the hinge that connect all the others. They are:

- Prudence
- Justice
- Fortitude
- Temperance

Theological Virtues

The theological virtues are the foundation for moral life. They are related directly to God.

- Faith
- Hope
- Love

Corporal (Bodily) Works of Mercy

1. Feed the hungry.
2. Give drink to the thirsty.
3. Clothe the naked.
4. Visit the imprisoned.
5. Shelter the homeless.
6. Visit the sick.
7. Bury the dead.

Spiritual Works of Mercy

1. Counsel the doubtful.

2. Instruct the ignorant.

3. Admonish sinners.

4. Comfort the afflicted.

5. Forgive offenses.

6. Bear wrongs patiently.

7. Pray for the living and the dead.

Precepts of the Church

1. You shall attend Mass on Sundays and on holy days of obligation and rest from servile labor.

2. You shall confess your sins at least once a year.

3. You shall receive the sacrament of Eucharist at least during the Easter season.

4. You shall observe the days of fasting and abstinence established by the Church.

5. You shall help to provide for the needs of the Church.

Catholic Social Teaching: Major Themes

The 1998 document *Sharing Catholic Social Teaching: Challenges and Directions—Reflections of the U.S. Catholic Bishops* highlighted seven principles of the Church's social teaching. They are:

1. Life and dignity of the human person.

2. Call to family, community, and participation.

3. Rights and responsibilities.

4. Option for the poor and vulnerable.

5. The dignity of work and the rights of workers.

6. Solidarity.

7. God's care for creation.

Sin

Sin is an offense against God.

Mortal sin is the most serious kind of sin. Mortal sin destroys or kills a person's relationship with God. To be a mortal sin, three conditions must exist:

- The moral object must be of grave or serious matter. Grave matter is specified in the Ten Commandments (e.g., do not kill, do not commit adultery, do not steal, etc.).

- The person must have full knowledge of the gravity of the sinful action.

- The person must completely consent to the action. It must be a personal choice.

Venial sin is less serious sin. Examples of venial sins are petty jealousy, disobedience, "borrowing" a small amount of money from a parent without the intention of repaying it. Venial sins, when not repented, can lead a person to commit mortal sins.

Vices are bad habits linked to sins. The seven capital vices are pride, avarice, envy, wrath, lust, gluttony, and sloth.

F. Liturgy and Sacraments

Church Year

The cycle of seasons and feasts that Catholics celebrate is called the Church Year or Liturgical Year. The Church Year is divided into five main parts: Advent, Christmas, Lent, Easter, and Ordinary Time.

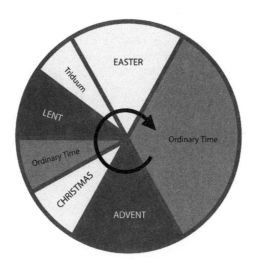

Holy Days of Obligation in the United States

1. Immaculate Conception of Mary   December 8
2. Christmas   December 25
3. Solemnity of Mary, Mother of God   January 1
4. Ascension of the Lord   forty days after Easter
5. Assumption of Mary   August 15
6. All Saints Day   November 1

The Seven Sacraments

1. Baptism
2. Confirmation
3. Eucharist
4. Penance and Reconciliation
5. Anointing of the Sick
6. Matrimony
7. Holy Orders

How to Go to Confession

1. Spend some time examining your conscience. Consider your actions and attitudes in each area of your life (e.g., faith, family, school/work, social life, relationships). Ask yourself, "Is this area of my life pleasing to God? What needs to be reconciled with God? with others? with myself?

2. Sincerely tell God that you are sorry for your sins. Ask God for forgiveness and for the grace you will need to change what needs changing in your life. Promise God that you will try to live according to his will for you.

3. Approach the area for confession. Wait an appropriate distance until it is your turn.

4. Make the Sign of the Cross with the priest. He may say: "May God, who has enlightened every heart, help you to know your sins and trust his mercy." You reply: "Amen."

5. Confess your sins to the priest. Simply and directly talk to him about the areas of sinfulness in your life that need God's healing touch.

6. The priest will ask you to pray an act of contrition. Pray an Act of Contrition you have committed to memory (see page 384). Or, saying something in your own words, like: "Dear God, I am sorry for my sins. I ask for your forgiveness and I promise to do better in the future."

7. The priest will talk to you about your life, encourage you to be more faithful to God in the future, and help you decide what to do to make up for your sins—your penance.

8. The priest will then extend his hands over your head and pray the Church's official prayer of absolution:

    God, the Father of mercies, through the death and resurrection of his Son, has reconciled the world to himself and sent the Holy Spirit among us for the forgiveness of sins; through the ministry of the Church may God give you pardon and peace, and I absolve you from your sins in the name of the Father, and of the Son, and of the Holy Spirit.

    You respond: "Amen."

9. The priest will wish you peace. Thank him and leave.

10. Go to a quiet place in church and pray your prayer of penance. Then spend some time quietly thanking God for the gift of forgiveness.

Order of Mass

There are two main parts of the Mass, the Liturgy of the Word and the Liturgy of the Eucharist. The complete order of Mass:

The Introductory Rites

> The Entrance
> Greeting of the Altar and of the People Gathered
> The Act of Penitence
> The *Kyrie Eleison*
> The *Gloria*
> The Collect (Opening Prayer)

The Liturgy of the Word

> Silence
> The Biblical Readings
> (the reading of the Gospel is the high point of the Liturgy of the Word)

The Responsorial Pslam
The Homily
The Profession of Faith (Creed)
The Prayer of the Faithful

The Liturgy of the Eucharist

The Preparation of the Gifts
The Prayer over the Offerings
The Eucharistic Prayer
The Communion Rite
The Lord's Prayer
The Rite of Peace
The Fraction (Breaking of the Bread)
Communion
Prayer after Communion

The Concluding Rites

Communion Regulations

To receive Holy Communion properly, a person must be in the state of grace (free from mortal sin), have the right intention (only for the purpose of pleasing God), and observe the Communion fast.

The fast means that a person may not eat anything or drink any liquid (other than water) one hour before the reception of Communion. There are exceptions made to this fast only for the sick and aged.

Three Degrees of the Sacrament of Orders

There are three degrees of the sacrament of Holy Orders: the ministries of bishop, priest, and deacon.

The bishop receives the fullness of the sacrament of Orders. He is the successor to the apostles. When he celebrates the sacraments, the bishop is given the grace to act in the person of Christ who is the head of the body of the Church.

Priests are ordained as co-workers of the bishop. They too are configured to Christ so that they may act in his person during the sacraments of Eucharist, Baptism, and the Anointing of the Sick. They may bless marriages in the name of Christ and, under the authority of the bishop, share in Christ's ministry of forgiveness in the sacrament of Penance and Reconciliation.

Deacons are ordained for service and are configured to Christ the servant. Deacons are ordained to help and serve the priests and bishops in their work.

While bishops and priests are configured to Christ to act as the head of Christ's body, deacons are configured to Christ in order to serve as he served. Deacons may baptize, preach the Gospel and homily, and bless marriages.

G. Mary and the Saints

Mother of God

Mary, the mother of Jesus, is the closest human to cooperate with her Son's work of redemption. For this reason, the Church holds her in a special place. Of her many titles, the most significant is that she is the Mother of God.

The Church teaches several truths about Mary.

First, she was conceived immaculately. This means from the very first moment of her existence she was without sin and "full of grace." This belief is called the Immaculate Conception. The feast of the Immaculate Conception is celebrated on December 8.

Second, Mary was ever-virgin. She was a virgin before, in, and after the birth of Jesus. As his mother, she cared for him in infancy and raised him to adulthood with the help of her husband, Joseph. She witnessed Jesus' preaching and ministry, was at the foot of his cross at his crucifixion, and present with the Apostles as they awaited the coming of the Holy Spirit at Pentecost.

Third, at the time of her death, Mary was assumed body and soul into heaven. This dogma was proclaimed as a matter of faith by Pope Pius XII in 1950. The feast of the Assumption is celebrated on August 15.

The Church has always been devoted to the Blessed Virgin. This devotion is different than that given to God—Father, Son, and Holy Spirit. Rather, the Church is devoted to Mary as her first disciple, the Queen of all Saints, and her own Mother. Quoting the fathers of the Second Vatican Council:

> In the meantime the Mother of Jesus, in the glory which she possesses in body and soul in heaven, is the image and the beginning of the Church as it is to be perfected in the world to come. Likewise she shines forth on earth, until the day of the Lord shall come, a sign of certain hope and comfort to the pilgrim People of God. (*Lumen Gentium*, 68)

Marian Feasts Throughout the Year

January 1	Solemnity of Mary, Mother of God
March 25	Annunciation of the Lord
May 31	Visitation
August 15	Assumption

August 22	Queenship of Mary
September 8	Birth of Mary
September 15	Our Lady of Sorrows
October 7	Our Lady of the Rosary
November 21	Presentation of Mary
December 8	Immaculate Conception
December 12	Our Lady of Guadalupe

Canonization of Saints

Saints are those who are in glory with God in heaven. *Canonization* refers to a solemn declaration by the Pope that a person who either died a martyr or who lived an exemplary Christian life is in heaven and may be honored and imitated by all Christians. The canonization process first involves a process of beatification that includes a thorough investigation of the person's life, and certification of miracles that can be attributed to the candidate's intercession.

The first official canonization of the universal Church on record was St. Ulrich of Augsburg by Pope John XV in 993.

Some non-Catholics criticize Catholics for "praying to saints." Catholics *honor* saints for their holy lives but we do not pray to them as if they were God. We ask the saints to pray with us and for us as part of the Church in glory. We can ask them to do this because we know that their lives have been spent in close communion with God. We also ask the saints for their friendship so that we can follow the example they have left for us.

Patron Saints

A patron is a saint who is designated for places (nations, regions, dioceses) or organizations. Many saints have also become patrons of jobs, professional groups, and intercessors for special needs. Listed below are patron saints for several nations and some special patrons:

Patrons of Places

Americas	Our Lady of Guadalupe, St. Rose of Lima
Argentina	Our Lady of Lujan
Australia	Our Lady Help of Christians
Canada	St. Joseph, St. Anne
China	St. Joseph
England	St. George
Finland	St. Henry
France	Our Lady of the Assumption, St. Joan of Arc, St. Thérèse of Lisieux

Germany	St. Boniface
India	Our Lady of the Assumption
Ireland	St. Patrick, St. Brigid, St. Columba
Italy	St. Francis of Assisi, St. Catherine of Siena
Japan	St. Peter
Mexico	Our Lady of Guadalupe
New Zealand	Our Lady of Help Christians
Poland	St. Casmir, St. Stanislaus, Our Lady of Czestochowa
Russia	St. Andrew, St. Nicholas of Myra, St. Thérèse of Lisieux
Scotland	St. Andrew, St. Columba
Spain	St. James, St. Teresa of Ávila
United States	Immaculate Conception

Special Patrons

Accountants	St. Matthew
Actors	St. Genesius
Animals	St. Francis of Assisi
Athletes	St. Sebastian
Beggars	St. Martin of Tours
Boy Scouts	St. George
Dentists	St. Apollonia
Farmers	St. Isidore
Grocers	St. Michael
Journalists	St. Francis de Sales
Maids	St. Zita
Motorcyclists	Our Lady of Grace
Painters	St. Luke
Pawnbrokers	St. Nicholas
Police Officers	St. Michael
Priests	St. John Vianney
Scientists	St. Albert
Tailors	St. Homobonus
Teachers	St. Gregory the Great, St. John Baptist de la Salle
Wine Merchants	St. Amand

H. Devotions

The Mysteries of the Rosary

Joyful Mysteries

1. The Annunciation
2. The Visitation
3. The Nativity
4. The Presentation in the Temple
5. The Finding of Jesus in the Temple

Mysteries of Light

1. Jesus' Baptism in the Jordan River
2. Jesus Self-manifestation at the Wedding of Cana
3. The Proclamation of the Kingdom of God and Jesus' Call to Conversion
4. The Transfiguration
5. The Institution of the Eucharist at the Last Supper

Sorrowful Mysteries

1. The Agony in the Garden
2. The Scourging at the Pillar
3. The Crowning with Thorns
4. The Carrying of the Cross
5. The Crucifixion

Glorious Mysteries

1. The Resurrection
2. The Ascension
3. The Descent of the Holy Spirit
4. The Assumption of Mary
5. The Crowning of Mary as the Queen of Heaven and Earth

How to Pray the Rosary

Opening

1. Begin on the crucifix and pray the Apostles' Creed.

2. On the first bead, pray the Our Father.

3. On the next three beads, pray the Hail Mary. (Some people meditate on the virtues of faith, hope, and charity on these beads.)

4. On the fifth bead, pray the Glory Be.

The Body

Each decade (set of ten beads) is organized as follows:

1. On the larger bead that comes before each set of ten, announce the mystery to be prayed (see above) and pray one Our Father.

2. On each of the ten smaller beads, pray one Hail Mary while meditating on the mystery.

3. Pray one Glory Be at the end of the decade. (There is no bead for the Glory Be.)

Conclusion

Pray the following prayer at the end of the rosary:

Hail, Holy Queen
Hail, holy Queen, Mother of Mercy,
our life, our sweetness, and our hope.
To thee do we cry,
poor banished children of Eve.
To thee do we send up our sighs,
mourning and weeping in the valley of tears.
Turn then, most gracious advocate,
thine eyes of mercy toward us;
and after this our exile,
show unto us the blessed fruit of thy womb, Jesus.
O clement, O loving, O sweet Virgin Mary.
Pray for us, O holy Mother of God,
that we may be made worthy of the promises of Christ.
Amen.

Stations of the Cross

The stations of the cross is a devotion and also a sacramental. (A sacramental is a sacred object, blessing, or devotion.) The stations of the cross are individual pictures or symbols hung on the interior walls of most Catholic churches depicting fourteen steps along Jesus' way of the cross. Praying the stations means meditating on each of the following scenes:

1. Jesus is condemned to death.

2. Jesus takes up his cross.

3. Jesus falls the first time.

4. Jesus meets his mother.

5. Simon of Cyrene helps Jesus carry his cross.

6. Veronica wipes the face of Jesus.

7. Jesus falls the second time.

8. Jesus consoles the women of Jerusalem.

9. Jesus falls the third time.

10. Jesus is stripped of his garments.

11. Jesus is nailed to the cross.

12. Jesus dies on the cross.

13. Jesus is taken down from the cross.

14. Jesus is laid in the tomb.

Some churches also include a fifteenth station, the Resurrection of the Lord.

Novenas

The novena consists of the recitation of certain prayers over a period of nine days. The symbolism of nine days refers to the time Mary and the Apostles spent in prayer between Jesus' Ascension into heaven and Pentecost.

Many novenas are dedicated to Mary or to a saint with the faith and hope that she or he will intercede for the one making the novena. Novenas to St. Jude, St. Anthony, Our Lady of Perpetual Help, and Our Lady of Lourdes remain popular in the Church today.

Liturgy of the Hours

The Liturgy of the Hours is part of the official, public prayer of the Church. Along with the celebration of the sacraments, the recitation of the Liturgy of the Hours, or Divine Office (office means "duty" or "obligation"), allows for constant praise and thanksgiving to God throughout the day and night.

The Liturgy of Hours consists of five major divisions:

1. An hour of readings

2. Morning praises

3. Midday prayers

4. Vespers (evening prayers)

5. Compline (a short night prayer)

Scriptural prayer, especially the psalms, is at the heart of the liturgy of the hours. Each day follows a separate pattern of prayer with themes closely tied in with the liturgical year and feasts of the saints.

The Divine Praises

These praises are traditionally recited after the benediction of the Blessed Sacrament.

Blessed be God.
Blessed be his holy name.
Blessed be Jesus Christ, true God and true man.
Blessed be the name of Jesus.
Blessed be his most Sacred Heart.
Blessed be his most Precious Blood.
Blessed be Jesus in the most holy sacrament of the altar.
Blessed be the Holy Spirit, the Paraclete.
Blessed be the great Mother of God, Mary most holy.
Blessed be her holy and Immaculate Conception.
Blessed be her glorious Assumption.
Blessed be the name of Mary, Virgin and Mother.
Blessed be St. Joseph, her most chaste spouse.
Blessed be God in his angels and his saints.

I. Prayers

Sign of the Cross

In the name of the Father,	*In nomine Patris,*
and of the Son,	*et Filii,*
and of the Holy Spirit.	*et Spiritus Sancti.*
Amen.	*Amen.*

Our Father

Our Father who art in heaven,	*Pater Noster qui es in caelis,*
hallowed be thy name.	*sanctificetur nomen tuum;*
Thy kingdom come;	*Adveniat regnum tuum;*
thy will be done	*fiat voluntas Tua,*
on earth as it is in heaven.	*sicut in caelo, et in terra.*
Give us this day our daily bread	*Panem nostrum auotidianum da*
and forgive us our trespasses	*nobis hodie*
as we forgive those who trespass against us.	*et dimitte nobis debita nostra,*
And lead us not into temptation,	*sicut et nos dimittimus debitoribus*
but deliver us from evil.	*nostris;*
Amen.	*Et ne nos inducas in tentationem,*
	sed libera nos a malo.
	Amen.

Glory Be

Glory be to the Father	*Gloria Patri*
and to the Son	*et Filio*
and to the Holy Spirit.	*et Spiritui Sancto.*
As it was in the beginning,	*Sicut erat in principio,*
is now, and ever shall be,	*et nunc, et semper,*
world without end.	*et in sae cula saeculorum.*
Amen.	*Amen.*

Hail Mary

Hail Mary, full of grace,	*Ave, Maria, gratia plena,*
the Lord is with thee.	*Dominus tecum.*
Blessed art thou among women	*Benedicta tu in mulieribus,*
and blessed is the fruit of thy womb,	*et benedictus fructus ventris tui,*
Jesus.	*Jesus.*
Holy Mary, Mother of God,	*Sancta Maria, Mater Dei,*
pray for us sinners now	*ora pro nobis peccatoribus*
and at the hour of our death.	*nunc et in hora mortis nostrae.*
Amen.	*Amen.*

Memorare

Remember, O most gracious Virgin Mary,
that never was it known
that anyone who fled to your protection,
implored your help,
or sought your intercession was left unaided.
Inspired by this confidence,
I fly unto you,
O virgin of virgins, my mother,
to you I come, before you I stand,
sinful and sorrowful.
O Mother of the word incarnate,
despise not my petitions,
but in your mercy hear and answer me. Amen.

Hail, Holy Queen

Hail, holy Queen, Mother of Mercy,
our life, our sweetness and our hope!
To you do we cry,
poor banished children of Eve;
to you do we send up our sighs,
mourning and weeping in this valley of tears.
Turn then, O most gracious advocate,
your eyes of mercy toward us,
and after this exile,
show us the blessed fruit of your womb, Jesus.
O clement, O loving, O sweet Virgin Mary.
V. Pray for us, O holy mother of God.
R. that we may be made worthy of the promises of Christ. Amen.

The Angelus

V. The angel spoke God's message to Mary.
R. And she conceived by the Holy Spirit.
Hail Mary . . .
V. Behold the handmaid of the Lord.
R. May it be done unto me according to your word.
Hail Mary . . .
V. And the Word was made flesh.
R. And dwelled among us.
Hail Mary . . .

V. Pray for us, O holy mother of God.

R. That we may be made worthy of the promises of Christ.

Let us pray: We beseech you, O Lord, to pour out your grace into our hearts. By the message of an angel we have learned of the incarnation of Christ, your son; lead us by his passion and cross, to the glory of the resurrection. Through the same Christ our Lord. Amen.

Regina Caeli

Queen of heaven, rejoice, alleluia.

The Son you merited to bear, alleluia,

has risen as he said, alleluia.

Pray to God for us, alleluia.

V. Rejoice and be glad, O Virgin Mary, alleluia.

R. For the Lord has truly risen, alleluia.

Let us pray.

God of life, you have given joy to the world by the resurrection of your son, our Lord Jesus Christ. Through the prayers of his mother, the Virgin Mary, bring us to the happiness of eternal life. We ask this through Christ our Lord. Amen.

Grace at Meals

Before Meals

Bless us, O Lord,

and these your gifts,

which we are about to receive from your bounty,

through Christ our Lord. Amen.

After Meals

We give you thanks, almighty God,

for these and all the gifts

which we have received

from your goodness

through Christ our Lord. Amen.

Guardian Angel Prayer

Angel of God, my guardian dear, to whom God's love entrust me here, ever this day be at my side, to light and guard, to rule and guide. Amen.

Prayer for the Faithful Departed

V: Eternal rest grant unto them, O Lord.
R: And let perpetual light shine upon them.
V: May their souls and the souls of all faithful departed,
through the mercy of God, rest in peace.
R: Amen.

Morning Offering

O Jesus, through the immaculate heart of Mary, I offer you my prayers, works, joys, and sufferings of this day in union with the holy sacrifice of the Mass throughout the world. I offer them for all the intentions of your Sacred Heart: the salvation of souls, reparation for sin, the reunion of all Christians. I offer them for the intentions of our bishops and all members of the apostleship of prayer and in particular for those recommended by your Holy Father this month. Amen.

Act of Faith

O God,
I firmly believe all the truths that you have revealed
and that you teach us through your Church,
for you are truth itself
and can neither deceive nor be deceived.
Amen.

Act of Hope

O God,
I hope with complete trust that you will give me,
through the merits of Jesus Christ, all necessary grace in this world
and everlasting life in the world to come,
for this is what you have promised
and you always keep your promises.
Amen.

Act of Love

O my God, I love you above all things, with my whole heart and soul, because you are all good and worthy of all my love. I love my neighbor as myself for the love of you. I forgive all who have injured me, and I ask pardon of all whom I have injured. Amen.

Act of Contrition

O my God, I am heartily sorry for having offended Thee, and I detest all my sins because of thy just punishments, but most of all because they offend Thee, my God, who art all good and deserving of all my love. I firmly resolve with the help of Thy grace to sin no more and to avoid the near occasion of sin. Amen.

Prayer for Peace (St. Francis of Assisi)

Lord, make me an instrument of your peace.
Where there is hatred, let me sow love;
where there is injury, pardon;
where there is doubt, faith;
where there is despair, hope;
where there is darkness, light;
where there is sadness, joy.
O Divine Master,
grant that I may not seek so much to be consoled as to console;
to be understood, as to understand,
to be loved, as to love.
For it is in giving that we receive,
it is in pardoning that we are pardoned,
and it is in dying that we are born to eternal life.